Global Dimensions of Democracy and Human Rights:

Problems and Perspectives

Nika Chitadze
International Black Sea University, Georgia

IGI Global
PUBLISHER of TIMELY KNOWLEDGE

A volume in the Advances in Human Services and Public Health (AHSPH) Book Series

Published in the United States of America by
IGI Global
Information Science Reference (an imprint of IGI Global)
701 E. Chocolate Avenue
Hershey PA, USA 17033
Tel: 717-533-8845
Fax: 717-533-8661
E-mail: cust@igi-global.com
Web site: http://www.igi-global.com

Library of Congress Cataloging-in-Publication Data

Names: Chitadze, Nika, 1969- editor.
Title: Global dimensions of democracy and human rights : problems and perspectives / Nika Chitadze, editor.
Description: Hershey PA : Information Science Reference, [2022] | Includes bibliographical references and index. | Summary: "This book considers the main principles of democracy and human rights, including the analysis of personal, political, economic, social, legal, ethnic, and religious freedoms as well as the importance of democracy enlargement for the establishment of peace and stability in the world"-- Provided by publisher.
Identifiers: LCCN 2022012047 (print) | LCCN 2022012048 (ebook) | ISBN 9781668445433 (hardcover) | ISBN 9781668445440 (paperback) | ISBN 9781668445457 (ebook)
Subjects: LCSH: Democracy--Social aspects. | Democratization. | Human rights. | Economic development.
Classification: LCC JC423 .G588 2022 (print) | LCC JC423 (ebook) | DDC 321.8--dc23/eng/20220422
LC record available at https://lccn.loc.gov/2022012047
LC ebook record available at https://lccn.loc.gov/2022012048

This book is published in the IGI Global book series Advances in Human Services and Public Health (AHSPH) (ISSN: 2475-6571; eISSN: 2475-658X)

British Cataloguing in Publication Data
A Cataloguing in Publication record for this book is available from the British Library.

For electronic access to this publication, please contact: eresources@igi-global.com.

Advances in Human Services and Public Health (AHSPH) Book Series

Jennifer Martin
RMIT University, Australia

ISSN:2475-6571
EISSN:2475-658X

Mission

The well-being of the general public should be a primary concern for any modern civilization. Ongoing research in the field of human services and public healthcare is necessary to evaluate, manage, and respond to the health and social needs of the global population.

The **Advances in Human Services and Public Health (AHSPH)** book series aims to publish high-quality reference publications focused on the latest methodologies, tools, issues, and strategies for managing the health and social welfare of the public. The AHSPH book series will be especially relevant for healthcare professionals, policy makers, government officials, and students seeking the latest research in this field.

Coverage

- Domestic Violence
- Medicare and Medicaid
- Public Welfare
- Health Policy
- Poverty
- Access to Healthcare Services
- Healthcare Reform
- Social Work
- Assistance Programs
- Youth Development

IGI Global is currently accepting manuscripts for publication within this series. To submit a proposal for a volume in this series, please contact our Acquisition Editors at Acquisitions@igi-global.com or visit: http://www.igi-global.com/publish/.

The Advances in Human Services and Public Health (AHSPH) Book Series (ISSN 2475-6571) is published by IGI Global, 701 E. Chocolate Avenue, Hershey, PA 17033-1240, USA, www.igi-global.com. This series is composed of titles available for purchase individually; each title is edited to be contextually exclusive from any other title within the series. For pricing and ordering information please visit http://www.igi-global.com/book-series/advances-human-services-public-health/102256. Postmaster: Send all address changes to above address.

Titles in this Series

For a list of additional titles in this series, please visit: http://www.igi-global.com/book-series/advances-human-services-public-health/102256

Ecological and Evolutionary Perspectives on Infections and Morbidity
P.A. Azeez (Salim Ali Centre for Ornithology and Natural History, Coimbatore, India) P.P. Nikhil Raj (Amrita Vishwa Vidyapeetham University, India) and R. Mohanraj (Bharathidasan University, India)
Medical Information Science Reference • copyright 2022 • 315pp • H/C (ISBN: 9781799894148) • US $325.00 (our price)

Regulating Human Rights, Social Security, and Socio-Economic Structures in a Global Perspective
Emilia Alaverdov (Georgian Technical University, Georgia) and Muhammad Waseem Bari (Government College University, Faisalabad, Pakistan)
Information Science Reference • copyright 2022 • 327pp • H/C (ISBN: 9781668446201) • US $215.00 (our price)

Assessing the Effects of Emerging Plastics on the Environment and Public Health
Sung Hee Joo (University of Seoul, South Korea)
Engineering Science Reference • copyright 2022 • 441pp • H/C (ISBN: 9781799897231) • US $240.00 (our price)

Modern Challenges and Approaches to Humanitarian Engineering
Yiannis Koumpouros (University of West Attica, Greece) Angelos Georgoulas (University of West Attica, Greece) and Georgia Kremmyda (University of Warwick, UK)
Engineering Science Reference • copyright 2022 • 321pp • H/C (ISBN: 9781799891901) • US $240.00 (our price)

Societal Resilience and Response to Contagious Diseases and Pandemics
Amal Adel Abdrabo (Faculty of Education, Alexandria University, Egypt) and Aly Abdel Razek Galaby (Faculty of Arts, Alexandria University, Egypt)
Information Science Reference • copyright 2022 • 344pp • H/C (ISBN: 9781799889731) • US $240.00 (our price)

Tactical Sciences for Biosecurity in Animal and Plant Systems
Kitty F. Cardwell (Oklahoma State University, USA) and Keith L. Bailey (Charles River Laboratories, Inc., USA)
Information Science Reference • copyright 2022 • 454pp • H/C (ISBN: 9781799879350) • US $215.00 (our price)

Handbook of Research on Interdisciplinary Perspectives on the Threats and Impacts of Pandemics
Şahver Omeraki Çekirdekci (Haliç University, Turkey) Özlem İngün Karkış (Doğuş University, Turkey) and Suna Gönültaş (Doğuş University, Turkey)
Information Science Reference • copyright 2022 • 556pp • H/C (ISBN: 9781799886747) • US $270.00 (our price)

IGI Global
PUBLISHER of TIMELY KNOWLEDGE

701 East Chocolate Avenue, Hershey, PA 17033, USA
Tel: 717-533-8845 x100 • Fax: 717-533-8661
E-Mail: cust@igi-global.com • www.igi-global.com

Table of Contents

Detailed Table of Contents

Democracy is a political system based on the method of collective decision-making with the equal influence of participants on the outcome of the processor at its essential stages. Although this method is applicable to any social institution, today its most important application is the state, since it has a lot of power. In this case, the definition of democracy is usually narrowed down to one of the following: 1) The appointment of leaders by the people they govern is through fair and competitive elections. 2) The people are the only legitimate source of power. 3) Society exercises self-government for the common good and the satisfaction of common interests. People's government requires the provision of a number of rights for each member of society. A number of values are associated with modern democracy: legality, political and social equality, freedom, the right to self-determination, human rights, etc.

Human rights are rules that protect the dignity and freedom of each individual. In their totality, fundamental rights form the basis of the legal status of an individual. The specific expression and scope of these rights, both in the positive law of different states and countries and in various international legal treaties, may differ. In public international law, the most famous document that enshrines them is the UN Universal Declaration of Human Rights. In OSCE member states, issues of human rights, fundamental freedoms, democracy, and the rule of law are international in nature and do not belong exclusively to the internal affairs of the state concerned.

Since democracy is accepted as one of the basic human values, some states and societies have accepted democracy as an ideal. However, the content of democracy has a different meaning for every ideology, every society, and every political system. In particular, ideologies tend to see democracy sometimes as an end and sometimes as a tool used to achieve another ideal. The mental worlds of cultures are conveyed by symbols that create simple shortcuts. Political symbolism is an important motif that draws the route of the bridge connecting a country's past to its future. Different perceptions of concepts such as democracy, human rights, freedom, and equality are related to the political culture codes of the relevant society. A liberal dimension of symbolism was examined in the example of the USA and its social dimension in the Soviet Union. France, as the father of nationalism, is also discussed with its experience of democracy. As one of the young nations, Turkey has been examined in terms of symbolism and democracy.

The theory of democratic peace was first invented by the German philosopher Immanuel Kant in his 1795 article "Permanent Peace." In this paper, Kant argues that states with governments of constitutional republics are less likely to go to war because doing so requires the consent of the people who would be at war. While monarch kings and queens can unilaterally declare war, given the security of their subjects, a government elected by the people takes the decision more seriously. The United States first promoted the concepts of democratic peace theory in 1832 by adopting the Monroe Doctrine. In this historic part of international politics, the US has affirmed that it will not tolerate the attempts of European monarchies to colonize any democratic nation in North or South America.

Political regime (fr. régime from lat. regimen – management, command, leadership) is a set of means and methods by which political power is exercised in the state. The political regime characterizes the models of appointing persons to managerial positions, exercising and transferring power, the role of violence in the political process, as well as the activities of political subjects: the level of political competition, the degree of closeness of political elites, the degree of participation of citizens in governance, institutional restrictions imposed on actors. Sometimes the concept of a political regime also includes the degree of political freedom in society and the observance of human rights. In the case of democracy, the following issues represent the main characteristics of a democratic political regime: 1) The appointment of leaders by the people they govern takes place through fair and competitive elections. 2) The people are the only legitimate source of power. 3) The society exercises self-government for the common good and satisfaction of common interests.

UN Convention on the Rights of the Child, the topic must be included in the pre-service study syllabus, more clearly added to the curriculum, and implemented in teacher practice.

This chapter provides a conceptual understanding of the impact of advanced digital technologies on democracy with a special focus on artificial intelligence (AI). The explanation of the impact of the internet and allied technologies is themed into 1) power at the hands of the state or 2) diffuses from the state. In the current global politics, almost all the major powers of the world are vying for an upper hand in developing advanced digital technologies, especially AI. Among these, AI is the major technological development that brings the dichotomy in state's behaviour pitching surveillance against freedom. Anchored to AI, this chapter provides a good understanding of technology impact on the sustenance of democracy. The chapter concludes by providing a co-protectionist approach in formulating a new conceptual framework for digital democracy.

Political participation is an important component of democracy. The aim of this study is to reveal the tendency of citizens' offline and online political participation. As a result of factor analysis, active participation, civic participation, and passive participation are determined as the dimensions of offline political participation. Political participation on social media is determined as two dimensions which are slacktivism and following up. Cluster analysis was used to identify political participation typologies based on the dimensions of offline and online political participation. Four clusters were identified, namely politicized citizens, politically mindful citizens, politically concerned followers, and apolitical citizens. Politicized citizens explicitly express their political tendencies without any hesitation. Politically mindful citizens are aware of the manipulative power of social media so that they do not actively participate politics on social media. Politically concerned citizens only follow political issues passively, and finally, apolitical citizens do not have an interest in politics.

Constitution (from lat. constitutio – "device, establishment, addition") is the basic law of the state, a special normative legal act that has the highest legal force. The constitution defines the foundations of the political, legal, and economic systems of the state. The constitution is the founding document of the state, which sets out the main goals of the creation of the state. In the vast majority of countries, the constitution is adopted by a constituent assembly or by referendum. The constitution is given the following legal designation: a normative legal act of the highest legal force of the state (or state-territorial commonwealth in interstate associations), fixing the foundations of the political, economic, and legal systems of this state or commonwealth, the foundations of the legal status of the state and the individual, their rights and obligations.

The term rule of law is closely related to both constitutionalism and the rule of law, and it refers to the political situation and not to any particular legal law. According to the rule of law, all people are subject to the law, including legislators, law enforcement, and judges. In this sense, it opposes tyranny or oligarchy, where rulers stand above the law. Lack of the rule of law can be found in both democracies and monarchies where laws are not taken into account. The rule of law is at stake where the government does not have the appropriate corrective mechanism to restore it.

The purpose of this chapter is to analyze the international humanitarian law and its effectiveness in contemporary conflicts. In particular, it focuses on the analysis of the challenges that international humanitarian law faces in contemporary international or non-international armed hostilities. While the ongoing progress in the modern world offers new challenges, the issue of the effectiveness of humanitarian law becomes controversial. Therefore, the chapter presents an academic paper, and it is based on the analysis of the various articles, reports, analytical papers, and case studies, depending on which it became possible to answer the main research question and to demonstrate the effectiveness of international humanitarian law enforcement mechanisms in modern conflicts.

Civil and political rights are a class of rights that protect individuals' freedoms from infringement by governments, social organizations, and private individuals. They ensure one's entitlement to participate in the civil and political life of society and the state without discrimination or repression. Civil rights include the ensuring of peoples' physical and mental integrity, life, and safety; protection from discrimination on grounds such as race, gender, national origin, color, sexual orientation, ethnicity, religion, or disability; and individual rights such as privacy, the freedoms of thought and conscience, speech and expression, religion, the press, assembly, and movement. Political rights include natural justice (procedural fairness) in law, such as the rights of the accused, including the right to a fair trial, due process, the right to seek redress or a legal remedy, and rights of participation in civil society and politics such as freedom of association, the right to assemble, the right to petition, the right of self-defense, and the right to vote.

Preface

As it is known, the development of the various states in the world and providing prosperity and stability of our planet is directly dependent on strengthening democratic institutions and providing political, economic, social, legal etc. rights for each citizen of the world.

Democracy (Greek δήμος "demos" - the people; the state "kratos" - law, power) is a form of government in which all power belongs directly to the people or their representatives. The basic requirements of democracy are selectivity and short duration. In addition, the concept of democracy includes a number of rights and freedoms that nature bestows on every person, regardless of his racial, national, confessional, religious, social, ideological or other affiliation.

CHARACTERISTIC FEATURES OF DEMOCRACY

The rule of the poor and needy; A form of government in which the people govern themselves directly and continuously without the help of politicians and government officials; A society based on equal opportunities and personal opportunities, where there is no place for hierarchy and privileges. Majority decision rule. A system that ensures the rights and interests of a minority that exercises control over the power of the majority.

Direct Democracy

Direct, direct and permanent participation of citizens in the activities of government.

Representative Democracy

The limited and indirect form of democracy is limited by the fact that the participation of the people in government is intermittent and short-lived and manifests itself in elections only once every few years.

Classical Democracy

The classic model of democracy is the ancient Greek polis or city-state system of government that developed in Athens in the 6th century BC. 5th-4th centuries The ideal system was the form of direct democracy that prevailed there. Classical democracy is based on the principle of popular government. And it is considered by the people the best form of government.

Defensive Democracy

Democratic ideas gained new life in the 17th and 18th centuries. Democracy was less perceived here as a mechanism for public participation in political life; It was now seen as a means by which citizens could exercise power. Defensive democracy emerged from the individualistic views of liberalism. Protective democracy allows citizens to live fully.

Democracy Promotion

The latest and most radical model for promoting democracy is Jean-Jacques Rousseau.

Developmental Democracy

Embodies the principle of greater participation. Promoting democracy has the merit of promoting participation, demanding more freedom, and promoting personal growth.

People's Democracy

The concept of people's democracy arose after the emergence of Soviet-style regimes. People's democracy attaches particular importance to the redistribution of power between classes. People's democracy is aimed at economic development, not just the expansion of political rights. Marx believed that the overthrow of capitalism would lead to the flowering of genuine democracy.

Human Rights

Human Rights - According to the UN, are inherent rights of all human beings, regardless of race, sex, nationality, ethnicity, language, religion or any other status. Human rights include the rights to life and liberty, freedom from slavery and torture, freedom of expression and speech, the right to work and education, and much more.

The general scope of human rights is governed by international law as well as national and municipal law, as far as international law is concerned, as far as it is reflected in domestic law, although the fundamental legal umbrella is protected by international law, as far as human rights are concerned. On certain standards of human life and behavior agreed upon by international civilization. Human rights doctrine, in addition to international law and the activities of global or regional organizations, also operates and is regulated as a result of measures and policies of states and non-governmental organizations.

Human rights are universally understood as inalienable, fundamental rights that derive only from being human beings, hence they are universal and egalitarian in the sense that they are one for all. It is on the basis of these principles that an understanding of human rights obliges states and individuals to respect the rights of other human beings, including the deprivation of these rights, even in the case of legal liability, as well as in circumstances such as unlawful detention, torture or hanging.

The philosophy of human rights addresses existential, political, and legal issues such as the existence, essence, nature, universality, justice, and legal status of human rights. Evidence of the inalienability and universality of human rights, as well as the very definition of the concept of "right", has often led to critical, skeptical and contradictory philosophical assumptions. These doubts, reflections, and critical responses have created new dimensions of the political and legal philosophy of human rights over time. There is a consensus that human rights include a wide variety of rights, although it is a matter of debate which of these specific rights should be considered in the basic human rights framework. Part argues that the general framework of inalienable rights includes rights such as the right to a fair trial, protection from slavery, the prohibition of genocide or the right to education, while part proposes that the human rights framework be kept to a minimum to avoid extreme manifestations of oppression.

The basic ideas that created the human rights movement developed after World War II, including its reaction to events such as the Holocaust. The culmination of these events was the adoption of the Universal Declaration of Human Rights in Paris in 1948 at the UN General Assembly. Until then, such a universal concept did not exist - although the forerunner of the human rights discourse was "natural rights", which was part of the medieval natural law tradition - these concepts became popular during the European Enlightenment, led by John Locke, Francis Hutchson, Jean-Jacques Burlamac and other philosophers. Which later became the political discourse of the French Revolution and the American Revolution. Contemporary arguments in human rights discourse were developed in the second half of the twentieth century as a response to slavery, torture, genocide, war crimes, etc., as a recognition of human vulnerability to such actions and of taking restrictive measures for a more just society.

The purpose of the book is to introduce the people – who are interested in role of democracy in the world, protection of human rights, scientists, researchers in the field of political sciences, international relations, legal studies, economics etc. representatives of civil society and mass-media means, public sector, students, etc. with the main characters of Democracy and Human Rights, Global Characters of both values and their decisive role for the providing peace, stability, prosperity, tolerance, equality etc.

The book includes 15 chapters. Where the main aspects related to Global Dimensions of Democracy and Human Rights are described and analyzed. Particularly:

The first chapter explains the meaning of democracy, types of democracy, the role of democracy in the socio-economic and political development of the different nations of the world.

With regard to the second chapter, there are reviewed and analyzed the political, social, economic, legal, religious etc. rights of each individual, also the are presented various conventions and declarations, in the field of Human Rights protection issues.

In the third chapter, an author explains that the content of democracy has a different meaning for every ideology, every society and every political system. In particular, ideologies tend to see democracy sometimes as an end and sometimes as a tool used to achieve another ideal.

In the fourth chapter, the researcher presents an idea, according to which democracy enlargement process promotes the peace and stability in the different regions of the world, because as more democratic state is, more peace policy in conducts at the international arena.

As to the fifth chapter, the scholar makes comparative analysis of the three main political regimes in the world, particularly: Totalitarianism, Authoritarianism and Democracy and explains the advantage of democratic political regime for the further development and prosperity of the particular state(s).

The sixth chapter explores the trend of the dialectic nexus between the intensified militarization of the state and the rising levels of corruption in Zimbabwe.

In the seventh chapter, international laws and conventions adopted since the period of the ending the World War II till now and development of the International legal system in the field of democracy and human rights are explained and analyzed.

Chapter 8 is based on focus group discussions reviews pre-service teachers' views about the United Nations (UN) Convention on the Rights of the Child and how teachers perceive their connection to the educational context and their work.

The ninth chapter provides a conceptual understanding of the impact of advanced digital technologies on democracy with a special focus on Artificial Intelligence (AI).

The tenth chapter reveals the tendency of citizens' offline and online political participation.

The author of the eleventh chapter presents research on how the constitution as a supreme law defines the foundations of the political, legal, and economic systems of the state.

Chapter 12 explains that all people despite of their nationality, position, race, religious belief, property, sex etc. are equal before the law, and respect of this principle creates convenient base for the establishment constitutional state.

With regard to the thirteenth chapter, the author, on the base of Geneva and Hague and other conventions, reviews the main laws and rules, which should be respected by the militaries, who are involved in conflict with the purpose to protect the rights of civilians and prisoners of war.

In the fourteenth chapter presents the civil and the political rights of the citizens of the different countries.

In the fifteenth chapter, the author analyzes the principles of free market economy, as a guarantee of providing the economic, business, entrepreneurs and customers rights.

The many academic areas covered in this publication include, but are not limited to:

- Civil Rights
- Constitutional State
- Democracy
- Digital Technologies
- Free Market Economy
- Global Development
- Human Rights
- International Security
- Militarization
- Political Rights
- Socio-Economic Development

Taking into consideration the above-mentioned factors, it should be pointed out that the novelty of the book and its contribution is interrelated with the fact, that for the first time have been presented the combination of the topics, related to the different aspects of Democracy and Human Rights from political, legal, economic, social, educational, historic etc. point of views.

In general, the book *Global Dimensions of Democracy and Human Rights: Problems and Perspectives*, which will be distributed in the different countries and regions of the world, will play significant role in the increasing the knowledge of the International Society – representatives of the different target groups on the issues, related to the Global importance of Democracy and Human Rights issues.

Nika Chitadze
International Black Sea University, Georgia

Acknowledgment

I would like to express my special gratitude to *Ms. Katelyn McLoughlin*, Assistant Development Editor - Book Development of IGI Global for her assistance and attention within the different stages in the framework of the book preparation Process.

At the same time, I would like to dedicate a special thanks to each author of the chapter – citizens of the different countries and representatives of the different nationalities, who took to the Heart the global problems of our planet and implemented very important research in favor of development Democracy and protection of Human Rights. So, without the contributions of such experienced scholars in their fields as *Natalia Beruashvili, Valeria Gonitashvili, Mary Tseruashvili, Irakli Kervalishvili, Ziya Kıraç, Armstrong Mudzengerere, Mürsel Bayram, Merja Paksuniemi, Minna Körkkö, Satu-Maarit Korte, Tanja Joona, Pigga Keskitalo, Arun Teja Polcumpally, Süphan Nasır, Onur Şahin, Merve Kır,* it would be impossible the publishing of the book.

I am too much thankful to my native – International Black Sea University and its Administration, Academic and Administrative personnel for establishing for me an excellent scientific environment and great atmosphere during working over the book.

Chapter 1
The Main Principles of Democracy and Its Role in Global Development

Nika Chitadze
International Black Sea University, Georgia

ABSTRACT

Democracy is a political system based on the method of collective decision-making with the equal influence of participants on the outcome of the processor at its essential stages. Although this method is applicable to any social institution, today its most important application is the state, since it has a lot of power. In this case, the definition of democracy is usually narrowed down to one of the following: 1) The appointment of leaders by the people they govern is through fair and competitive elections. 2) The people are the only legitimate source of power. 3) Society exercises self-government for the common good and the satisfaction of common interests. People's government requires the provision of a number of rights for each member of society. A number of values are associated with modern democracy: legality, political and social equality, freedom, the right to self-determination, human rights, etc.

INTRODUCTION

Democracy (ancient Greek δημοκρατία "people power" from δῆμος "people" + κράτος "power") is a political system based on the method of collective decision-making with equal influence of participants on the outcome of the process or at its essential stages (Oxford University Press, 2021). Although this method is applicable to any social institution, today its most important application is the state, since it has a lot of power. In this case, the definition of democracy is usually narrowed down to one of the following:

1. The appointment of leaders by the people they govern is through fair and competitive elections.
2. The people are the only legitimate source of power
3. Society exercises self-government for the common good and the satisfaction of common interests (Chitadze, 2016).

DOI: 10.4018/978-1-6684-4543-3.ch001

People's government requires the provision of a number of rights for each member of society. A number of values are associated with modern democracy: legality, political and social equality, freedom, the right to self-determination, human rights, etc.

Since the ideal of democracy is difficult to achieve and is subject to different interpretations, many practical models have been proposed. Until the 18th century, the most famous model was direct democracy, where citizens exercise their right to make political decisions directly, through consensus or through procedures for subordinating a minority to a majority (Budge, 2001). In a representative democracy, citizens exercise the same right through their elected deputies and other officials by delegating to them a part of their own rights, while the elected leaders make decisions taking into account the preferences of the governed and are responsible to them for their actions.

One of the main goals of modern democracy is to limit arbitrariness and abuse of power. This goal has often failed to be achieved where human rights and other democratic values were not universally recognized or were not effectively protected by the legal system. Today, in many countries, democracy is equated with liberal democracy, which, along with fair, periodic and general elections of persons vested with supreme power, during which candidates freely compete for votes, includes the rule of law, separation of powers and constitutional restrictions on majority power through guarantees certain personal or group freedoms. On the other hand, left-wing movements, prominent economists, as well as representatives of the Western political elite such as former US President Barack Obama, IMF Managing Director Christine Lagarde argue that the exercise of the right to make political decisions, the influence of ordinary citizens on the country's politics is impossible without ensuring social rights, equality of opportunity and low levels of socio-economic inequality (Chitadze, 2016).

A number of authoritarian regimes had the outward signs of democratic rule, but in them only one party possessed power, and the policy pursued did not depend on the preferences of the voters. Over the last quarter of a century, the world has been characterized by a trend towards the spread of democracy. Among the relatively new problems facing it are separatism, terrorism, population migration, and the growth of social inequality. International organizations such as the UN, OSCE and the EU believe that control over the internal affairs of the state, including issues of democracy and respect for human rights, should be partially in the sphere of influence of the international community.

Democracy Theory

Democracy theory is a collection of descriptive, analytical and normative statements and assumptions that focus on the foundations of democracy and democratic institutions (Britannica, 2022). There are three main streams in modern democracy theory: phenomenological, explanatory, and normative. Phenomenological theory describes and classifies existing democratic systems. Explanatory theory tries to establish whose preferences play a role in a democracy, what decision-making procedures should be, and how to avoid unwanted consequences. The subject of normative theory is the ethical side of democracy: when and why democracy is desirable from the point of view of morality, what principles should be the foundation of democratic institutions, what are the reasonable expectations from citizens in a democratic society.

According to the conclusions of the theory, democracy is not just people's rule, but also a system of citizens' rights. The violation of these rights casts doubt on the democratic nature of government. Equality, compromise and effective participation in political decision-making are central to democracy. Democratization requires a stable state (Britannica, 2022).

There are three main directions in the modern theory of democracy: phenomenological, explanatory and normative (Britannica, 2022). Phenomenological theory describes and classifies existing democratic systems. Explanatory theory tries to establish whose preferences play a role in a democracy, what should be the decision-making procedures, how to avoid undesirable consequences. The subject of normative theory is the ethical side of democracy: when and why democracy is desirable from the point of view of morality, what principles should be the foundation of democratic institutions, what are reasonable expectations from citizens in a democratic society.

An important contribution to the theory was made by Aristotle, John Locke, Charles Louis de Montesquieu, David Hume, Jean-Jacques Rousseau, Alexis de Tocqueville, John Stuart Mill, John Dewey, Jurgen Habermas, John Rawls, Hannah Arendt, Isaiah Berlin and other thinkers (Heywood, 2002).

According to the conclusions of the theory, democracy is not just popular government, but also a system of citizens' rights. Violation of these rights calls into question the democracy of government. The issue of equality and effective participation in political decision-making is central to democracy. Democratization requires a stable state as the only source of legitimate use of force.

In the field of comparative politics, there are projects that seek to measure the level of democracy in the world: Freedom House, Cross-National Time-Series Data Archive, Polity IV, The Economist Democracy Index (Economist), Democracy Barometer.

History of Democratic Thought

Among the currently known philosophical reflections on democracy, one of the earliest is the eulogy of the head of the Athenian state, Pericles, dedicated to the fallen in the Peloponnesian War. In this speech, which Pericles gave in 430 BC. e., he listed the merits of Athenian democracy. In his opinion, laws ensured equality, merit and reputation played a leading role in moving up the social ladder, and freedom became a part of everyday life (Pericles).

In 322 BC. e. Aristotle classified the forms of government in the treatise "Politics". Among the types of popular government, he singled out polity, in which politics is carried out for the sake of the common good, and democracy, in which the poor use their power for their own purposes. In his analysis of real-life regimes, Aristotle noted that freedom lies at the heart of a democratic state. Aristotle considered elections as a trait of the oligarchy, and considered the lot to be a democratic method of filling government posts (Aristotle).

John Locke, in Two Treatises on Government (1690), advocated political equality, personal freedom, and majority rule. According to Locke, the creation of society is preceded by a "natural" state of freedom and equality, so that no one has the natural right to have power over others. Therefore, only a government that leads with the consent of the governed is legitimate. Since it is almost impossible to achieve general agreement, the will of the majority plays a decisive role. According to Locke, the people are the ultimate source of any supreme power, in particular, they have the right to change the government, which abuses the people's trust and violates fundamental rights. By democracy proper, Locke understood a form of government in which citizens legislate and appoint heads of the executive branch (Locke).

Charles Louis de Montesquieu in his work "On the Spirit of Laws" (1748) proposed his own classification of forms of government, while the form in which the entire people has supreme power, he called the republic. Montesquieu believed that for the existence of a republic it is necessary that people strive for the common good. Therefore, he believed that conflicts between various factions pursuing their own narrow interests to the detriment of public interests pose a threat to the stability of the republic. He also believed that elections lead to a kind of aristocratic deviation from the principle of political equality, since MPs are usually richer, more educated and more capable than the majority of the population (Montesquieu).

To mitigate the threat of factional struggles, David Hume proposed increasing the scale of political units where representative government is established. In his opinion, in large formations, each deputy is forced to take into account a wide variety of interests (Hume, 1739).

In The Social Contract (1762), Jean-Jacques Rousseau argued that democracy is incompatible with representative institutions, since the supreme power of the people is inalienable and indivisible. Since direct democracy is possible only in small communities, Rousseau concluded that legitimate democracy is unrealizable on the scale of the nation state. He also believed that democracy leads to acute internal conflicts and civil wars. At the same time, when discussing the political situation in Poland after the establishment of the Russian protectorate, Russo admitted that he saw no alternative to representative government. Rousseau harshly criticized feudalism, defended personal freedom and at the same time called for the subordination of the individual to the "common will". Rousseau proposed to resolve the contradiction between individual freedom and the general will through education and associated political reforms. The result was to be a new free society in which each person strives for the best for himself and for everyone. Subsequently, this theory was repeatedly interpreted as a justification of the perniciousness of autonomous public organizations and the need to manipulate consciousness to achieve harmony between the desires of individuals and the declared needs of society (Rousseau, 1762).

In his work Democracy in America (1835/1840), Alexis de Tocqueville took a position somewhat opposite to Rousseau. He concluded that freedom of political organization was essential to defend against the dictatorship of the majority. At the same time, in his opinion, civil organizations contribute to the development of a civilized society (Alexis de Tocqueville, 1840).

John Stuart Mill developed a utilitarian approach to justifying the value of individual rights and freedoms. In this approach, the criterion is the achievement of maximum well-being for the maximum number of people. In his essay On Freedom (1859), Mill argued that the only ground for limiting personal freedom is to protect others from specific harm done by the individual. He considered illegitimate paternalism, which allows restricting the freedom of people for their own good. He also argued that in order to search for truth, society needs open discussion and a clash of polar points of view. In Reflections on Representative Government (1861), Mill formulated new political ideals and strongly supported the extension of the right to vote to women. At the same time, he believed that for the development of "uncivilized" peoples, monarchy or colonial rule is most suitable, and not democracy, the efficiency of which these peoples will not be able to maintain (Chitadze, 2016).

John Dewey considered democracy the most desirable form of government because it provides the rights necessary for personal development, including free exchange of opinions, freedom to organize to achieve common goals, and the freedom to have and strive for a good life. His work Democracy and Education (1916) emphasizes that in a democratic society, citizens work together in an atmosphere of mutual respect and goodwill to rationally seek solutions to common problems. The system of government must be dynamic: as historical circumstances and public interests change, political institutions must also be revised. For the development of critical thinking, the pursuit of the common good, and the skills of cooperation, Dewey argues, education, in particular the public education system, is necessary. In his work "Society and Its Problems" (1927), he recognized that a person can achieve full development only in a democratic social state (Chitadze, 2016). He also insisted that workers have the right to directly participate in the management of the firms where they work. Dewey was opposed to elitism and the view that the people were incompetent in matters of government. He argued that only society can decide what the public interest is. In order to make informed decisions, people should actively engage in dialogue with other members of local communities.

In a series of papers published in the 1970s, Jürgen Habermas argued that a "perfect speech" environment is necessary to achieve "rational consensus" about values or the validity of facts. In it, participants evaluate the views of others without emotion and outside influence, including without physical or psychological coercion. This ideal serves as the standard for free and open public debate in real democracies.

John Rawls made an attempt to substantiate the desirability of democracy without the use of utilitarianism. In The Theory of Justice (1971), Rawls pointed to the possibility of achieving the well-being of the majority by neglecting the interests of the minority. Since everyone runs the risk of being in such a minority, a purely utilitarian approach is not suitable for choosing a political system. Instead, people strive for the maximum and equal amount of personal freedom, for equal access to political and economic resources and for such a distribution of benefits in society that is most beneficial to the least prosperous strata. And any unequal distribution of social or economic benefits (for example, wealth) should be such that the poorest members of society are in a better position with such a distribution than with any other, including equal distribution (Chitadze, 2016). (It is also assumed that slightly uneven distribution may benefit the poorest by increasing overall productivity.)

The Value of Democracy

John Mill believed that the decision-making process in a democracy is better than in other forms of government, because it forces decision-makers to take into account the interests of the general population and provides them with more complete information. Democracy also has a positive impact on morality, since the awareness of one's own influence on the current policy stimulates the development of personal dignity, responsibility, a sense of justice and the pursuit of the common good. According to Mill, raising the moral level of society and officials also leads to better decisions and laws compared to a society dominated by selfishness, frivolity and servility (Mill, 1863).

On the contrary, Thomas Hobbes argued that government in a democracy is worse than in a monarchy, since democracy encourages irresponsible policies that advance the narrow interests of some at the expense of others, or even push different segments of society against each other. Plato believed that democracy tends to underestimate the importance of knowledge and experience for good governance. Some modern neoliberal philosophers criticize democracy for its economic inefficiency and believe that the market should exercise control over society (Heywood, 2002).

Instrumentalism draws a conclusion about the value of democracy by analyzing its impact on other values. Proponents of this trend believe that political equality and popular sovereignty are not absolute goals. For example, Friedrich Hayek found democracy desirable insofar as it protects personal freedom and private property. The rule of law presupposes the state's monopoly on the lawful use of force within its territory, which makes the question of its democratic accountability extremely important. A similar argument, leading to the value of a democratic method of decision-making, starts from justifying the power of some people over others in terms of protecting the interests and rights of those under control.

On the other hand, there are arguments for democracy as such, based on ideas of freedom and equality. According to Carol Gould, democracy is based on the right of everyone to personal freedom, which on a society scale means the right to self-determination. Human life is influenced by the legal, social and cultural environment. The realization of the reverse influence of a person on this environment is possible only through collective decision-making with an equal contribution from everyone. From this,

Gould concludes that realizing self-government requires democracy. In her opinion, the consequences of a democratic way of making a decision are insignificant, because society, like an individual person, has the right to dispose of its future even to its own detriment. Critics point out that in practice, free individuals are rarely unanimous on any issue, and the political decision-making process cannot fully respect everyone's personal freedom. It turns out that the opponents of the adopted decision find themselves deprived of self-government and, consequently, victims of the dictatorship of the majority (Mkurnalizde, Khamkhadze, 2000).

From the point of view of Joshua Cohen, the policy pursued is legitimate to the extent that it is justified in the eyes of citizens. This attitude is formed as a result of free and reasoned discussion among equals, which requires working democratic institutions. This theory assumes that open public discussion ultimately leads to agreement, at least incomplete (for example, there may be consensus on a list of critical issues, and disagreement may be on priorities).

In Peter Singer's theory, democracy is a way of treating people as equals when it is necessary to organize their life together in a certain way. If people hold different views about the proper organization of this common space, each of them is essentially trying to dictate to others how to live. Hence the need for a peaceful and just compromise between conflicting claims to supremacy. This compromise requires everyone to have an equal opportunity to influence the decision-making process. Democratic decision-making gives everyone an equal voice and thus shows respect for every point of view, even in the face of disagreement. The difficulty of this theory is the question of reaching agreement on a proper democratic procedure for resolving conflicts. This difficulty is circumvented if one considers that democracy should strive to equally respect the interests of citizens. Citizens are also interested in the very existence of democratic procedures, since otherwise they get the impression that the interests of others have more weight in decision-making.

Amartya Sen identifies three advantages of democracy: the self-realization of a person as a member of society, the ability to draw public attention to important issues (and thereby prevent serious problems), and the formation of social values through the exchange of information between citizens (Mkurnalizde, Khamkhadze).

Robert Dahl cites a number of virtues of democracy:

1. It helps prevent despotism
2. Modern representative democracies do not fight each other)
3. Democracies tend to be richer than non-democracies
4. In democratic countries, the level of human development is higher, including health, education and personal income
5. She helps people protect their fundamental interests.
6. It guarantees its citizens a number of rights that non-democratic systems are unable to provide.
7. It provides its citizens with a wider range of personal freedom
8. It provides people with the maximum opportunity to live according to their own laws.
9. It gives citizens moral responsibility for their choices and decisions in the field of public policy
10. Only in a democracy is a relatively high level of political equality possible

Dahl notes that in the above list, items 1-4 are desirable for most people, items 5-7 are secondary for some people, and items 8-10 are disadvantages from the point of view of opponents of democracy (Dahl, 1998).

Critics argue that the listed merits are in part a coincidence. For example, the American Civil War was a conflict between republics, the number of democracies in the 19th and 20th centuries was relatively small, and today nuclear weapons play an important deterrent role. At the same time, democratic countries often fight with undemocratic countries, and countries in transition with each other. For Thucydides, ancient democracy was associated with aggressiveness, and for Machiavelli with imperialism. Today, armed conflicts between democracies and non-democratic regimes often take place under the pretext of humanitarian intervention (Rondeli, 2003).

Larry Diamond points to a number of conflicting demands for democracy, the imbalance between which can have negative consequences. In situations where making any decision will allow some individuals to benefit at the expense of others, democracy can reduce the level of mutual trust and tolerance. Excessive disagreement to the detriment of consensus can have negative consequences for the credibility and stability of government. Democracy also makes it difficult to implement unpopular measures, which will only work in the long term.

During the transition period, democracy sometimes proves to be ineffective compared to other forms of government in terms of economy, governance and order (Dialong, 2000).

The Legitimacy of Democracy

There are three main concepts of the legitimacy of power. According to the first, the legitimacy of power is due to its moral justification in order to rule society. According to the second, legitimacy is determined by the ability of the authorities to shape the responsibilities of citizens. According to the third concept, the government has the right to lead people to the extent that people must comply with the regulations of the government. Unlike the first two interpretations, the latter presupposes that citizens have obligations to the authorities. In this regard, the question arises: since democracy is a collective decision-making process, are those citizens who do not agree with the decisions obliged to execute them?

Some theorists believed that the legitimacy of democracy follows from the very fact that the decision-making process is democratic. Currently, there are almost no supporters of such an argument among philosophers and political scientists.

A number of theories address the issue of the legitimacy of power regardless of the form of government. In particular, most of the instrumentalist arguments in favor of democracy give some reason to respect the decisions made in this way, but these arguments apply not only to democracy. At the same time, in the mainstream of instrumentalism, there is an approach that is closely related precisely to democracy. According to the Condorcet jury theorem, in questions where one of the two decisions is correct, if each participant in the trial more often votes for the correct decision on average, the probability of this decision being made by a majority vote increases with the number of participants and tends to 100%. In this situation, based on the results of the vote, the minority have good reasons to admit their own wrong. The problem with Condorcet's theorem is that it is bounded. First, it presupposes the independence of the voter's opinions from each other, whereas in practice the democratic process is associated with mutual persuasion and coalition-building. Secondly, the theorem assumes that all participants are equally informed, although in practice the minority often has reasons to believe that the majority does not have the information necessary to make a competent decision. Third, the theorem does not take into account the presence of ideological biases common to broad strata of the population. From the theorem, we can conclude that the opposition is unnecessary, which is also the subject of criticism (Chitadze, 2016).

Somewhat different arguments in favor of the legitimacy of democracy are put forward by supporters of theories of consent. Locke believed that a person's consent to the creation of a political community entails his consent to submit to the will of the majority. According to Locke, the primary decision-making process should be based on a natural law, similar to the laws of mechanics, where the movement of a body is determined by the resulting force. Since people are equal in their rights and interests, they equally affect society, from here society should move in the direction where the majority wants to go. Locke emphasized that this "natural" method of decision-making is fully applicable only at the initial stage of the formation of society, and in the future people have the right to establish a monarchy. However, in all circumstances, the authority must enlist the support of a majority of those affected by the decision. For example, the authorities can introduce a new tax only on condition that the majority of owners or their representatives have given their consent to this.

An argument similar to Locke's theory consists in the assertion that people agree to submit to the will of the majority by the very fact of their participation in the democratic process (in particular, in elections). A common problem in all versions of the theory of consent is a fairly free interpretation of human behavior. Participation in a vote may not be a sign of consent to obey the result of the vote, but only an attempt to influence the result. Membership in a society or residence on the territory of a state may not mean a person's consent to the established political procedures or the ruling regime, but only the presence of certain economic and social ties. The notion that voting participants are morally obligated to agree in advance with the outcome contradicts the idea that consent or disagreement is a personal matter (Mkurnalidze, Khamkhadze, 2000).

Some experts believe that a number of principles of political legitimacy can be realized only in a democracy. In the above theory of Carol Gould, the personal freedom of an individual is generalized in the form of the right to self-determination, from which follows the requirement to comply with democratic decisions. According to Peter Singer and Thomas Cristiano, the need to comply with such decisions stems from the special role of equality in democracy. When disagreements arise among citizens about how to achieve substantive equality, the goal of democracy is to make decisions against those disagreements. It achieves this by relying on a more fundamental ideal of equality - that of the participants in the democratic process. Unwillingness to obey decisions made is tantamount to elevating oneself above others and infringing upon this most important form of equality (Shubitidze, 2009). The difficulty of this theory lies in the assumption that any restrictions on democratic power (for example, obliging it to observe certain individual and collective rights) can be deduced from the value of democratic equality.

Limits of Democratic Power

The question of the legitimacy of democracy is accompanied by the question of the limits of its power. Such limits can be internal and external.

Internal limits stem from the demands of the democratic process and fundamental democratic values. For example, there are limits, going beyond which undermines the foundations of democracy and deprives people of the motivation to support the current system. Hence, some political analysts conclude that decisions made with the help of a democratic method must be compatible with the proper functioning of this process. In particular, decisions should not be made that restrict innocent citizens in political rights or in civil rights essential to the democratic process (such as the freedom to express their political views in the media or the freedom to form political groups). Locke goes further and insists that citizens should not accept any violation of fundamental civil rights, including those not related to the electoral process.

Since, according to Locke, consent is the basis for the legitimacy of the political system, democratic authorities have no right to make such decisions.

The outer limits of democratic power flow from principles that are independent of the values and demands of democracy. They can be linked to arguments for non-democratic decision-making methods. They can also be associated with values that are more fundamental than democratic values. For example, some citizens may not recognize the decision of the legislative body to declare war on another state, believing that peace is more important than democracy.

Civic Participation

One of the central problems of the theory is the question of the ability of ordinary people to rule society. First, decisions should be made by people who have the best abilities, knowledge, experience and personality traits. Secondly, in an effective society there must be a division of labor so that human resources are available to solve complex problems, therefore it is unacceptable for each person to spend their time and energy on politics. Third, the contribution of one person to the outcome of the process is extremely insignificant, which deprives people of the motivation to behave responsibly and to seek the necessary information on the eve of voting.

On the basis of these arguments, supporters of elite rule oppose any purely egalitarian form of democracy. They argue that the high degree of civic participation of a poorly informed and emotional population leads to the adoption of mediocre laws promoted by populists and demagogues. James Madison in Vol. 10 "Notes of the Federalist" expressed concern that such laws would jeopardize the rights of some groups. Plato believed that the best form of government would be an aristocracy of "philosopher kings" with outstanding intellectual and moral qualities, that is, meritocracy (Madison, 1982).

A common way to resolve these contradictions is representative democracy, in which civic participation is partly sacrificed for the need for competent government and the need to reduce the time spent by voters. On the contrary, under meritocracy it is impossible to ensure the equality of interests of all people. In addition, meritocracy is accompanied by paternalism, when the state denies people their ability to make the best decisions in their own interests and does not stimulate their self-development in this area.

According to Joseph Schumpeter, in a democracy, the power to make political decisions is acquired through the competition for the votes of the people. This theory focuses on the responsibility of the political leadership to avoid controversial issues and ignore the volatile and vague demands of ordinary citizens. Citizens are charged with the mission of protecting society from irresponsible politicians. Otherwise, Schumpeter believed that the system should encourage civic engagement only among informed segments of the population. However, excessively low civic participation can reduce the government's responsiveness to the wishes of the people. In addition, Schumpeter's theory is incompatible with the idea of equal participation of all citizens in the decision-making process, since in it the function of government is assigned to political elites, whose views should not significantly depend on public discussions (Schumpeter, 1908).

Robert Dahl interprets democratic politics as the pluralism of various groups united by common interests. According to his concept, every citizen belongs to a circle of people who have certain narrow interests closely related to their daily life. Citizens are well informed on these issues and seek to gain influence over others. Although each interest group is a notorious minority, they unite in coalitions to achieve the desired result. In fact, democracy is not becoming the rule of the majority, but of these politically active coalitions. At the same time, excessive civic participation can harm democracy by diluting consensus on social norms and thereby compromising the stability of the system. According to this theory, politics is developed as a result of bargaining between separate interest groups, but not as a result of widespread public discussion, including discussion of issues of the common good and justice (Dahl, 2010).

James Buchanan and Gordon Tullock take a neoliberal approach. They believe that the elites seek to strengthen the role of the state and the bureaucracy in their own interests at the expense of a not overly attentive public. They also point out that the contribution of one rival group to the outcome of the vote is usually not decisive, just like the vote of one citizen. Few circles are able to influence the government, and they do it at the expense of everyone else. Neoliberals argue that trying to organize a democratic state with broad powers will inevitably be ineffective. From this they conclude that the powers of the state should be limited to ensuring fundamental freedoms and property rights, and the rest of the functions of the state should be transferred to the economic market (Shubitidze, 2009). Rights and freedoms are more understandable categories and therefore supervision over them is within the power of ordinary citizens.

In addition, participation in democratic procedures is an important part of political self-education, which can contribute to the strengthening of democratic values. In particular, instilling a sense of personal responsibility for collective decisions requires inner freedom to make erroneous decisions. At the same time, civic participation can grow both by increasing the share of politically active citizens, and by expanding opportunities to influence decision-making.

Moreover, while voters are often reluctant to spend their energy and time gathering the necessary information, research shows that ordinary citizens are able to study complex political issues in depth when they are motivated to do so.

In connection with the division of labor in society, the question arises of what kind of knowledge citizens should have and what standards should their convictions meet. According to Thomas Cristiano, citizens should focus on formulating goals for the development of society, and leave the development of ways to achieve these goals to experts. The implementation of this proposal requires a way to get officials and specialists to work on the implementation of the tasks set by society (Chitadze, 2016).

However, the neoliberal approach faces a number of challenges. First, the ideas about the common good and social justice prevalent in modern society go beyond the minimum state. Secondly, the neoliberal approach ignores the concentration of power and material values in the hands of private individuals, which in a minimal state allows them to impose their will on other people without their consent. The last argument is a mirror image of the neoliberal critique of elite theory.

Most of the above arguments are based on the assumption that people are selfish. This thesis raises objections, and supporters of deliberative democracy, following Mill and Rousseau, argue that citizens are not indifferent to moral issues and therefore are able to act in the name of the common good and justice. This behavior is stimulated by political discussion, provided that the participants are open to other points of view and that there are informed or moral people among the participants in the discussion. Hence, it is concluded that democratic institutions should encourage such discussions.

Public Preference

The problem of civic participation is accompanied by the question of how to reconcile the desire for competent solutions with an equal contribution of the preferences of all participants. In deliberative bodies, deputies can discuss the views of informed circles, but often these circles belong to the political elite.

On the other hand, taking into account the preferences of the masses introduces superficial emotional impressions of ordinary people into the political process.

According to the widespread point of view, the principle of subordination of the minority to the will of the majority is a way of equal consideration of all views. In practice, the implementation of this principle is faced with situations that violate transitivity, when the preference of A over B and B over C does not mean that A is more preferable than C. To avoid such situations, it is necessary to introduce restrictions on the range of acceptable preferences for a given decision-making process. Some political scientists believe that in the process of discussion, citizens come to an understanding and structure their preferences in accordance with transitivity.

In practice, in modern liberal democracies, citizens make their choice from political alternatives directly only in referendums. Elected officials usually make political decisions. The electoral system determines how the preferences of individuals determine the composition of representative bodies. This system is able to better match the outcome to the spectrum of public opinion and can better protect the minority from the dictatorship of the majority (for example, lowering the majority's motivation to vote.

Social Pluralism

In many implementations of democracy, the diversity of public organizations, including informal groups and organized political parties, is considered an important social institution that ensures open competition between different political views. In modern representative systems, parties select candidates for elections to government bodies, mobilize voters, and organize support or opposition to the executive branch. In some countries, the interests of the main social groups (workers, farmers, business) are protected by large public corporations independent of the state.

At the same time, it is widely believed that democracy requires the cohesion of society into a fairly homogeneous nation with a high degree of consensus on basic values. In polyarchy, it is especially important for elites to agree on the norms and rules of political behavior. Moreover, a number of thinkers (including Hobbes, Montesquieu, and Madison) believed that strong factions were a threat to democracy. First, there is a danger that factions will promote the interests of some to the detriment of others and even to the detriment of the common good. Potential consequences of this could be escalation of conflicts or dictatorship of the majority. Second, the fragmentation of power carries a risk to the stability of the political system as a whole. Today, to neutralize such risks, various mechanisms of balances and checks are used. A special role among them is played by the protection of fundamental human rights.

However, a number of problems still need to be addressed. For example, citizens with access to organizations and their resources have an advantage to defend their interests, leading to political inequality. Organizations can exaggerate certain values and distort the civic consciousness of their members. They may focus excessive voter attention on solutions that provide only short-term benefit to a small group. They can also take on the functions of the state, taking these functions out of the control of the people and their representatives. The growing influence of public corporations can lead to the fact that political decisions are made not on the basis of a democratic process, but as a result of negotiations between these corporations and the government.

Dictatorship of the Majority

An important problem in the theory of democracy is the question of how to avoid the dictatorship of the majority. Even if a decision is equally responsive to general preferences that reflect the views of informed people, the decision may have morally or legally unacceptable consequences for a segment of the population. Property rights are of particular concern, as the relatively less affluent majority have the temptation to encroach on the property of the richer minority.

There are situations when, on certain issues, society is divided into two clear camps. In these cases, there is a risk of the emergence of a permanent minority, which always loses in the vote. This situation is somewhat different from the dictatorship of the majority, because the majority can both respect the rights of the minority and, moreover, try to treat them well. However, a permanent minority may have their own interests and ideas about social norms, which they are not able to materialize at the level of politics. According to Thomas Cristiano, permanent minorities are victims of inequality among the participants in the democratic process, which deprives the authorities of the moral right to make decisions that affect the interests of this minority ()Mkurnalizde, Khamkhadze, 2000).

In order to protect the minority, it should first of all be given the right to vote, although this in itself does not provide a majority vote. Secondly, it is necessary to make a reasonable filtering of the preferences of the masses, directing the discussion process in a constructive and devoid of emotions. Third, the adoption of certain measures may require that not only 50% of the participants plus one vote in favor, but a higher percentage. Here, however, one should take into account the risk of negative consequences from undesirable preservation of the status quo. Fourth, it can be specifically stipulated that decisions made by a majority vote that affect certain (constitutional) rights are reviewed by independent courts. It should be borne in mind that this approach narrows the scope of democratic institutions such as referendums and representative government. Fifth, the decentralization of government and the constitutionally guaranteed autonomy of regional governments contribute to the protection of local interests. Sixth, in some electoral systems (for example, proportional) the minority is more fully represented than in others.

A more general question is when the ruling party can pursue an independent policy and when the authorities should strive to agree between parties with different views. Consensus advocates believe that it fosters wider public support for government policies and also enhances the legitimacy and value of democracy. Critics believe that the consensus model allows minorities to veto decisions that are inconvenient for them and inhibits the process of forming government and passing laws.

Electoral System

The subject of controversy is the question of the best system for elections to the legislature for a democratic society. In accordance with the simplest classification, electoral systems are majoritarian, proportional and group-based, although in practice mixed variants are also common.

Under the majoritarian system, the territory is divided into districts with approximately the same population. Each district elects one representative. In a proportional system, seats in a representative body are distributed in proportion to the number of votes cast for parties throughout the territory. In the group system, certain groups of the population (by ethnicity, occupation, class, etc.) directly nominate their deputies in accordance with a previously agreed-upon quota.

The majoritarian system stimulates the formation of a two-party system and therefore, from the point of view of its supporters, is more stable than other forms. Each of the two parties is a broad coalition of different groups and encourages the search for compromise. Parties seek to enlist the support of the typical voter for their profile, hence the tendency to avoid radical elements in their programs. Therefore, the majority system is especially popular in societies that regard moderation and compromise as important democratic values. Critics of this system draw attention to the fact that it tends to ignore the interests of minorities, who are often forced to partially sacrifice their individuality in order to be heard. Minorities are less represented in elected bodies than in society, and the location of the boundaries between electoral districts plays an important role here (Heywood, 2002). In addition, gaining support from a large and diverse sector of the population is often easiest through vague and irrelevant appeals to citizens. As a result, politicians publicly discuss superficial or emotional issues, while they tackle real issues behind the scenes.

In a proportional system, representatives of various groups of the population receive seats in a representative body of government in proportion to the choice of citizens. Clarity of programs is required from parties. Minorities can also afford to express their views more clearly. Therefore, the proportional system is most popular among those who value equality as the moral foundation of democracy. A common criticism of this system is its instability. According to critics, she encourages the division of society into opposing camps based on party preferences. The struggle for power is ongoing, parties are not inclined to compromise, coalitions quickly disintegrate. Combining a proportional system with a presidential republic produces populist leaders and a multitude of parties aligned to them.

Proponents of the group system believe that it better provides representation for historically unpopular groups in the population, who are often poorly organized and wary of expressing their views openly. In addition, even having elected their representatives to the legislature, it is not easy for such minorities to defend their interests, so additional seats should be reserved for them. Critics of this argument believe that such an approach deprives the system of flexibility, since it leads to a shift in emphasis in politics to the same range of issues, even if the majority of citizens consider these issues to be insignificant.

The Transition to Democracy and Its Sustainability

Research into democratic transitions focuses on a period in which a country institutes competitive elections for all key government officials with participatory participation. The emphasis is on procedures that regulate access to power and ensure the accountability of political elites - a historically similar approach to the study of democracy that Schumpeter used academic environment. The main objectives of the research are to determine the reasons for democratic reforms and the criteria for success.

A comparative analysis of political processes in the world shows that the transition to democracy in each case has vivid individual features and largely depends on the previous non-democratic history of the country, the power and strategy of the elites and the masses, as well as the source of the desire for reforms. Nationalist movements in some cases promote democratic change, but in others they hinder the formation of coalitions. Although the field is relatively young and has difficulties with both theory and empirical data, researchers have made an important generalization. It consists in the fact that the processes of decline or disintegration of the state (as the only source of the legitimate use of force) negatively affect the prospects for democratization.

A number of political scientists believe that the prerequisites for a successful democracy are a developed industry, a significant size of the middle class and a high literacy of the population. There is a widespread argument that increased material well-being makes people less receptive to the calls of authoritarian demagogues promising simple and quick solutions to economic problems, and that this increases the chances of survival for newly formed democratic institutions. However, according to studies, the level of economic development alone does not predict whether a country will take the path of democracy and whether democratization will be successful.

According to Robert Dahl, the decentralization of the economy increases the stability of democracy. First, the power of individual officials, including senior officials, is declining. On the contrary, excessive government regulation of the economy entails widespread corruption. Second, the transition to a market economy is accompanied by the development of the rule of law, improved access to information, increased population mobility and an increase in the size of the middle class. These phenomena also contribute to the increased demand for democracy. Dahl also believes that the likelihood of establishing the institutions of polyarchy in a country is higher if the means of violent coercion are dispersed in it, if there is social pluralism in it, if the country is not divided into pronounced subcultures, or there are mechanisms for resolving intercultural conflicts in it, if the beliefs of the politically active part citizens are reinforced by the institutions of polyarchy and if it is not subject to military intervention (Dahl, 2010).

However, Dahl draws attention to the difficulties that arise on the road to democracy. Economic problems include poverty, unemployment, significant inequality in income and capital distribution, inflation and recession. In economically backward countries, the middle class and the well-educated stratum are usually small. Political culture often gives low priority to the values that give resilience to democratic institutions in times of crisis. In many countries, there is no effective legal system, which leaves the norms of a democratic society unprotected and creates grounds for abuse by the executive branch, political elites and criminal groups. In some countries, elected representatives do not determine all government policy, and organizations and individuals play a significant role and are not accountable to any elected body (Dahl, 2010).

Building democracy when a population is divided into opposing regional, ethnic, racial or religious groups is particularly difficult. Although authoritarianism in such conditions is often associated with the domination of some groups at the expense of others, the forced introduction of democracy can lead to deep conflicts, the disintegration of the country and wars. At the same time, a successful solution to this problem, based on compromise and shared values, ultimately leads to stable systems, which are flexible and balanced by political pluralism (for example, India or the United States).

Democratization by itself does not entail political liberalism. An elected government can usurp power held by other branches of government, local governments, or non-governmental organizations. It can strive for a strong state by suppressing opposition, rather than by building coalitions. If such a government pursues economic liberalization, neglecting the legal framework and not guaranteeing property rights, the result is far from the ideal of liberal democracy.

According to the historian Timothy Tilton, democratization was successful in those countries where the aristocracy had a restraining effect on the monarchy, where the weakening of the local nobility and the growth of the bourgeoisie led to the spread of liberal values and where a reactionary alliance of the nobility and the bourgeoisie against the workers and peasants did not arise (Chitadze, 2016).

There is also an opinion that liberal democracy is more stable when the period of authoritarian regime in the state was short, and democratic traditions, customs and institutions have a rich history. Countries with a long history of autocracy and weak spread of trust between people can easily return to autocratic regimes, even with a formally democratic structure of state power.

At the same time, broad support for democracy and negative attitudes towards autocracy are in themselves weakly related to the stability of democratic institutions. More important are interpersonal trust, tolerance towards unpopular groups, support for civil liberties, and political activism. However, elites can make significant adjustments, either suppressing the aspirations of the masses, or, conversely, accelerating the pace of democratization. A sense of economic well-being also contributes to the sustainability of the current regime.

Seymour Martin Lipset analyzed why trust among citizens is essential for a sustainable democracy. According to his theory, some participants in the political process can benefit from breaking democratic rules, which creates an incentive for others to do the same. The legitimacy of a democratic system is essential to sustaining trust. Legitimacy also allows the state (and even obliges it) to use force to protect existing rules (Lipset, 1960).

According to John Higley, liberal democracy is the creation of consensually united political elites. These elites are few in number, and may include high-ranking officials, heads of political parties, managers of private firms, military commanders, the leadership of the media, etc. these norms when making political decisions (Mkurnalizde, Khamkhadze, 2000). At the same time, there should be no complete unity of ideological or religious views among these elites for political competition to exist in the country.

Measuring the Level of Democracy

Ideal democracy is difficult to measure. In practice, comparative political science and sociology use approximations and models such as polyarchy. At the same time, there are two directions in the methodology for measuring the level of democracy. The first seeks to use objective parameters: voter turnout, the composition of legislative bodies, and ensuring the right to vote. The second is based on expert assessments of the integrity of elections, freedom of expression, the availability and security of alternative sources of information, restrictions on the activities of political organizations, etc.

In 1972, Raymond Gastil developed a methodology for polling experts to measure the level of liberal democracy. Gastil's methodology forms the basis of Freedom House's annual Freedom in the World reports (Gastil, 1985). This report contains separate assessments of the state of political and civil rights, in order to measure the level of both political democracy and the rule of law. The methodology of another political scientist, Leonard Sussman, is used to compile the Freedom of the Press report, also published by Freedom House. Arthur Banks developed his own method for calculating the level of democracy based on the analysis of legislative power, and his indicator is included in the Cross-National Time-Series Data Archive database.

In 1974, Ted Robert Guerr developed the Polity classification of political regimes. The project has gone through four stages in its development and still annually publishes a report on the level of democracy in the countries of the world. Polity IV is the current version of this index (Chitadze, 2016).

Since 2007, The Economist magazine has published the Democracy Index annually (Chitadze, 2016).

In 2010, a group of Swiss and German researchers began publishing Democracy Barometer. The index seeks to cover a variety of theoretical concepts, in particular the ideas of liberal and participatory democracy (Democracy Barometer, 2022). The model assumes that democracy is a system of governance that seeks to strike a balance between the normative values of freedom and equality.

Published by the German project Bertelsmann Stiftung since 2003, the Bertelsmann Stiftung's Transformation Index evaluates a number of parameters in developing and transition countries. One of the characteristics is the status of political transformation, which represents the quality of democracy. This parameter is determined by 18 indicators that measure statehood, political participation, rule of law, stability of democratic institutions, political and social integration. At the same time, in order for a country not to be considered an autocracy, it is necessary that six indicators have values that exceed the threshold: free and fair elections, the presence of real power in elected officials, freedom of assembly and association, freedom of speech, separation of powers, and civil rights (Bertelsmann Stiftung, 2022). A similar rating for developed countries (OSCE) is the Sustainable Governance Indicator, which has been published since 2009.

Tatu Vanhanen and Jose Antonio Cheibub (from the University of Illinois at Urbana-Champaign) also compiled their democracy indices (Mkurnalizde, Khamkhadze, 2000).

Critics of methods based on subjective assessments draw attention to their shortcomings. Experts may proceed from inaccurate information about the political situation in the country. They subjectively determine which information is relevant to the rating and which is not. (For example, if a country bans the political activities of "extremists", is this a serious violation of human rights or the number of supporters of such groups should be considered). They can take into account factors that are only indirectly related to democracy. They may also measure differently or have different rating scales. The analysis shows that reports using Gastil's method until 1989 somewhat underestimated the rating of communist regimes and young countries, and at the same time slightly overestimated the rating of traditional monarchies and Christian countries. The Banks methodology reports for the same period showed the opposite trend.

HISTORY OF DEMOCRACY

Since its inception, democracy has been a concept open to interpretation. Its history is, in fact, not only the history of the struggle between supporters of democracy and its opponents, but also the history of discussions among supporters. The subject of discussion was such questions as:

- What is the "people" with power ("demos")?
- What cultural values, rules and institutions are needed for a democracy?
- Is democracy related only to the state or does its implementation require the involvement of all aspects of public life?

Democracy in its modern sense has its origins in Ancient Greece and Ancient Rome, the traditions of medieval city-states and the development of representative authorities in Europe and some British colonies in modern times. In ancient city-states, the assembly, including all citizens, possessed supreme legislative, executive and judicial power. This was possible because the population of these cities rarely exceeded 10,000, and women and slaves did not have political rights. Citizens were eligible to hold various executive and judicial positions, some of which were elective, while others were appointed by lot. In medieval Europe, the concepts of religious, natural and customary law as restrictions on the arbitrariness of power played a key role in the emergence of the principles of democratic government. Of great importance was the spread of the practice when monarchs sought to obtain approval of their orders from various estates. The congresses of representatives of these estates were the prototypes of modern legislative assemblies (Heywood, 2002).

The Age of Enlightenment, the American and French Revolutions stimulated intellectual and social development, especially the development of ideas about civil rights and political equality. Since the 19th century, assemblies of deputies elected in free elections have become the central institutions of democratic government. In many countries, democracy has also come to include adversarial electoral processes, free speech and the rule of law. In countries with communist regimes, the idea of democracy was proclaimed, the structure of which included class unity and mainly state ownership of the means of production. Until the 20th century, democracy assumed that a minority of the population possessed full citizenship on the basis of property qualifications, while the rest were virtually excluded from the political decision-making process. By the beginning of the 21st century, the universality of elections has received worldwide recognition as one of the most important criteria of democracy (Heywood, 2002).

Prehistoric Period

Studies of uncivilized tribes show that in relatively independent and close-knit communities, order is possible when members of the community have a certain independence and when a significant number of its members (for example, elders) collectively make the most important decisions regarding the entire community. From this we can conclude that certain elements of democracy were characteristic of various tribes for thousands of years BC. Later, people shifted from hunting and gathering plants to agriculture and trade, which was accompanied by the growth of communities, as a result, economic and social inequality began to increase, which led to the spread and dominance of authoritarian traditions.

The question of replacing primitive equality with a hierarchically organized society is the subject of research. According to one version, the emergence of leaders in a primitive society is not associated with the subordination of others to themselves by violence, but with the assumption of the function of coordinating joint work, which contributed to the improvement of the situation of the community.

Antiquity

In the 5th and 4th centuries BC. e. in a number of ancient Greek cities, various forms of popular self-government began to arise. The most famous was Athenian democracy, which began to take shape in 507 BC. e. in Athens and which held out for almost two centuries (Heywood, 2002). The object of self-government in this system was the city-state. Citizenship was possessed by the entire non-enslaved population that inherited it from their parents, but only adult men were full-fledged citizens. The supreme organ of power was Ecclesia, where men gathered to vote by show of hands and where the decision was made, for which the majority of those present voted. The questions for the vote were put forward by the bule, which consisted of representatives of territorial districts (demos). The second most important political institution was the people's jury (dicasterium). A feature of Athenian democracy was the close relationship between politics and religion, the small scale of public life, the relatively weak role of writing and the emphasis on the army. In 321 BC. e. Ancient Macedonia imposed property restrictions, thereby depriving the vast majority of the Athenian population of the right to vote (Heywood, 2002).

The attitude towards democracy in Athens was ambiguous from the very beginning. From the point of view of supporters, the will of the people gave legitimacy to the decrees adopted at the meetings, which began with the words of ancient Greek. ἔδοξεν τῆι βουλῆι καὶ τῶι δήμωι - "by the decision of the bule and the people." From the point of view of critics, the people were unreliable, subordinate to momentary interests, subject to emotions and manipulated by the crowd. A well-known example of the arbitrariness committed by the crowd was the death sentence of Socrates. It is no coincidence that Plato in the eighth book of the "States" asserts that excessive democracy inevitably entails tyranny. At the same time, Thucydides, in his History of the Peloponnesian War, cites Pericles' passionate speech in defense of democracy (Plutarch).

The Roman Republic was a contemporary of Athenian democracy. Despite its rapid territorial growth, its rule retained the basic features of a city-state. The legitimacy of the ancient Roman state was also based on the will of the people: its armies fought "on behalf of the Senate and the people of Rome." Citizenship could be obtained through naturalization, by liberation from slavery, or by inheritance from parents. To participate in the vote, a personal presence at the Forum was required, which in fact excluded from the number of full citizens those who lived outside Rome. Voting took place in four representative bodies: the Comitia Tributa was open to all citizens, the Concilium Plebis represented the interests of the plebeians, the Comitia Centuriata consisted of deputies from the army, and the Comitia Curiata included representatives from the nobility from three families and participated in the formation of the Senate. In most cases, deputies were elected by lot, and not by the results of voting. When counting, votes were first grouped (by gender or century), and then a decision was determined, which is supported by most of the groups. Due to the presence of a powerful Senate, which consisted mainly of patricians, the representative bodies did not have supreme power in the republic (Kamenskaya, 2005).

Ancient democracies also existed outside Europe. For several centuries after its conquest by Alexander the Great in 331 BC. BC, the Parthian city of Susa had self-government similar to the Greek city-states (Chitadze, 2016). Some researchers single out the community of property, the obligation to work for all members of the community, etc. among the early Christians as extreme democratic radicalism.

Ancient democracies provided their citizens with the opportunity to participate in self-government, but they did not guarantee freedom of speech or religion, protection of property rights, and did not impose constitutional restrictions on the government. Their institutions disappeared with the fall of the Roman Republic. Although, almost a thousand years later, elements of self-government began to reappear in some city-states and rural communities of the late Middle Ages, it was not associated with the idea of democracy. This idea attracted attention only in the Renaissance, along with other heritage of antiquity, and as a result had a significant impact on Western European thought.

Middle Ages

Beginning in the 9th century, in certain regions of Europe, nobles and honorary citizens began to directly participate in local assemblies and elect deputies to regional assemblies. In the Alps, such areas became self-governing cantons, which became part of the Swiss Confederation in the 13th century. The Scandinavian Vikings gradually developed a multi-level system of representative bodies, and in 930 Iceland, for the first time, arose an analogue of modern national legislative assemblies and parliaments - Althingi. In the cities of the Novgorod land, the most important decisions were made at the veche (Mkurnalidze, Khamkhadze, 2000).

In the 12th century, a number of Italian city-states (such as Venice, Florence, Siena, Pisa) began to hold direct periodic elections for senior leadership positions. At first, only nobles and large landowners could participate in the elections; for example, in Venice, where this order remained until the 16th century, about 2% of the population had the right to vote. In other city-states, over time, this right extended to small merchants, bankers who were in the guilds of artisans, as well as foot soldiers, so that in 14th century Bologna it covered 12% of the population (Kamenskaya, 2005). In the middle of the 14th century, the economic growth of the city-states gave way to decline. Wars, internal conflicts and corruption contributed to the weakening of the republican power, and various authoritarian regimes came to replace them.

In some countries, an elective monarchy became widespread: the Holy Roman Empire, where the emperor was elected by the electors, as well as the Kingdom of Poland (later Rzeczpospolita), where during the 16th-18th centuries "gentry democracy" was characterized by broad rights of the nobility.

New Time

The English Parliament was originally conceived as a royal deliberative judicial body for complaints. In 1215, large landowners obtained from John Landless the signing of the Magna Carta, according to which the monarch could not impose new taxes without the consent of the royal council. Over time, this body finally moved from judicial functions to legislative functions, and by the end of the 15th century, the adoption of a law in England required the approval of not only the king, but also both houses of Parliament (Shubitidze, 2002).

In the course of the Glorious Revolution, English levellers and other radical Puritans demanded broad representation in Parliament, increased powers of the House of Commons and suffrage for the entire male population of the country. Although the republic did not last long, and the monarchy was restored in 1660, the powers of Parliament expanded significantly, especially in matters of the appointment of the prime minister. At the beginning of the 18th century, two political parties arose: the Whigs and the Tories. The adoption of laws became impossible without the support of the leadership of the party majority in the House of Commons, and the monarchs were forced to surrender the formation of the executive branch to this leadership. In 1783, King George III refused to accept the Whigs' proposed prime minister and cabinet members, leading to a constitutional crisis and eventually the king relented. Due to the property qualification, about 5% of the adult population had the right to vote (reforms began only in 1832 and continued until 1928, when women received the right to vote) (Mkurnalizde, Khamkhadze, 2000). The inhabitants of the British colonies had no representation at all in Parliament, although they were obliged to pay taxes to the Crown.

At the same time, due to the remoteness from London, many British colonies received fairly wide autonomy, established local elected bodies of self-government, and in a number of regions gave suffrage to most white adult males. The proliferation of private property and land tenure contributed to the growing popularity of ideas about natural human rights and popular sovereignty.

Bourgeois Democratic Revolutions

The Age of Enlightenment brought a number of new ideological currents: humanism, which considered the personality depending on the abilities and aspirations of a person, and not a place in the social hierarchy; equality, giving each member of society the same rights and responsibilities (although the definition of "society" has varied greatly); the concept of free competition among people, goods and ideas. Although many thinkers were opponents of democracy, they made important contributions to the foundations of modern understanding of this form of government.

The strengthening of nation states shifted the focus of the problems of liberalization and democratization of society from the scale of a city-state to the scale of an entire country. The first step from theory to practice of democracy on this scale was taken in North America, where the struggle for independence from colonial rule was declared in the name of the natural and inalienable right of the people to self-government. At the same time, women, slaves, many free blacks, Indians and, in a number of states, the poor were excluded from the "people". Nevertheless, the legitimacy and institutions of the new republic depended significantly on the will of society.

The revolutionary changes were accompanied by the growing consciousness of Americans as a single nation. This was facilitated by the war with Great Britain, the Declaration of Independence, the flight of opponents of independence to Canada and England, and the rapid strengthening of ties between the states. As a result, it became possible to create a confederation with a single federal government, which grew in strength over time. Due to the enormous size of the country, the system of national self-government has become a representative democracy with federal division. The founders of the United States strove to ensure that social institutions did not reflect all existing views, but only "refined" opinions that could give society a constructive, deliberative character. According to their plan, such a role was to be played by deputies who would gather in small representative bodies to work out well-thought-out decisions in the interests of the common good. At first, the attitude towards political parties was ambivalent: on the one hand, their activities were perceived as destructive for the unity of the nation, on the other hand, they were necessary for an organized electoral process and ensuring open competition in elections. In parallel, in small towns in New England, discussions and voting were practiced at local meetings with the right to direct participation of all citizens.

At the same time, fundamental difficulties of the new political system emerged: only a small proportion of citizens could physically discuss any issue with their representatives (primarily due to the limited time); citizens were distinguished by heterogeneity (regional, ethnic, religious, economic, etc.); conflict became an inevitable and normal aspect of political life, and the concept of the common good required formulations that would suit the entire heterogeneous population. The gradual formation of social institutions necessary to solve these problems contributed to the evolution of the political system towards liberal democracy.

In the summer of 1789, the French National Assembly proclaimed "human and civil rights", which promised political freedom and social equality. According to the declaration, the nation was the source of sovereign power (History of Western Civilization, 2022). Over time, the answer to the question of who has the right to speak on behalf of the nation has changed all the time. At first these were the deputies, then the mobilized in Paris, the committee of public safety, the elite of property owners, and finally General Bonaparte. The moderate revolution was replaced by terror, followed by reaction, a military dictatorship, an imperial monarchy - but each regime claimed to rule on behalf of the people. Both supporters and opponents of the revolution understood that it had irreversibly changed the world. The conclusions were different. Jules Michelet considered the revolution to be the pinnacle of France's devotion to the ideas of freedom. Hippolyt Teng believed that popular sovereignty entails first anarchy and then despotism. A deep analysis of the revolution was done by Alexis de Tocqueville, who viewed it as part of the global historical process of destruction of the institutions of feudal Europe by the democratic forces of the new society (Alexis de Tocqueville).

19th Century

After 1815 and until the end of the century, monarchy continued to be the most common form of government in Europe. The republic survived in Switzerland and several city-states. In 1870, France joined these countries - not of her own free will, because in this way Prussia intended to weaken the enemy defeated in the war. However, representative bodies of power began to play an increasing role. More and more men began to receive the right to vote (Chitadze, 2017). Political parties, trade unions, newspapers provided the infrastructure that stimulated the political activity of the population. The distinction between monarchy and democracy began to blur.

The pressure of the democratic forces affected all political trends. During the first half of the century, the liberals were suspicious of the masses, because of whom, in their opinion, the republic degenerated into a dictatorship. In the middle of the century, the left wing of the liberals began to support universal suffrage for men. Napoleon III, Bismarck, Disraeli and other conservatives also began to resort to democratic means such as plebiscite to more effectively achieve their goals. Even the Roman Catholic Church established a mass movement (Christian democracy) to defend its interests against attacks from the secular state.

The most significant democratic aspirations were not related to public order, but to the national community. The French revolutionaries emphasized that peoples do not belong to rulers and that nations, like individuals, have the right to determine their own destiny. Over time, the idea of self-determination began to mean the right of nations to have their own national state, combining sovereignty with popular self-government, which gave such a state the status of the only legitimate form of organizing political space. Following France and the United States, Italians and Germans became nations in the middle of the century. At the same time, the national liberation struggle of the Irish and Poles was initially unsuccessful. The cultural heterogeneity of the population, especially significant in the Eastern European multinational empires, made it difficult to define a nation itself, which undermined the foundation under the principle of self-determination. Even greater difficulties arose when trying to extend this principle to colonies in the rest of the world. In the middle of the century, even progressive Europeans did not consider the "barbarians" ready for their own independence. However, by the 20th century, the national liberation struggle began to spread throughout the world, and a global movement against colonialism arose.

In the 19th century, there were also processes of rethinking the "people" as a subject of democracy. Initially, for example, in France in the 1830s, out of a population of 30 million, only 200 thousand had the right to participate in elections. Subsequently, the property qualification was weakened and then canceled. Beginning in New Zealand in 1893, one country after another began to empower women with the right to vote (Heywood, 2002). On the other hand, more and more supporters of democracy began to realize that its implementation requires the practical provision of a number of civil rights, in particular the right to organize and to freedom of speech.

By the end of the 1840s. in Western Europe, the concept of the rule of law and the right to property is quite firmly established. During the same period, the view began to gain popularity among Democrats that political reforms were not enough and that deep socio-economic reforms were needed. Karl Marx and Friedrich Engels believed that only a proletarian revolution would lead to the creation of a truly free society of equals (Chitadze, 2016). They viewed democratic procedures as a means for the proletariat to come to power. From their point of view, this opened up the possibility of building a society in which there would be no class contradictions, and therefore, the need for parties would disappear. However, as the labor movement grew, winning elections and pursuing democratic policies were increasingly seen as critical goals rather than a means. By the beginning of the 20th century, this movement, especially the Social Democratic Party of Germany, had become the most consistent and determined supporter of democratic reforms.

Democratization has had a significant impact on European society and culture. Trade unions became legal, free and compulsory schooling was introduced, the construction of a welfare state began, and press circulation increased significantly. At the same time, these processes were far from the only ones, so that at the turn of the 20th century, Western political regimes were a mixture of liberalism, oligarchy, democracy and corruption.

XX Century

The First World War undermined the positions of many influential opponents of democracy. The victors in the war were the Western powers in alliance with the United States, whose President Woodrow Wilson said the goal of the war was to make the world safe for democracy. In line with the views of philosophers such as Immanuel Kant and Jeremy Bentham that democracy is inherently peaceful, the League of Nations was established in 1919 to promote national self-government and good neighborly relations between countries.

In one number of countries (Germany and Austria), democratic revolutions took place, during which dualistic monarchies were replaced by parliamentary democracies, in another number of countries (Poland, Czechoslovakia, Lithuania, Latvia, Estonia, Finland), parliamentary democracy was established in a number of countries that received this period of independence, in the third row of countries (Yugoslavia, Great Britain, the Netherlands, Romania) countries that were already parliamentary democracies, universal suffrage was introduced. All of these countries, as well as Italy, Denmark and Norway, introduced women's suffrage and a proportional electoral system (often with open lists), previously only in Belgium, Sweden and Finland. In an effort to prevent the abuse of power and the dependence of politics on the emotions of voters, constitutions established non-elected bodies, indirect elections, regional inequality, and other mechanisms of balances and checks (Chitadze, 2017).

In 1922, the fascists came to power in Italy. In the early 1930s, the Weimar Republic came under the rule of the Nazis, who established a regime based on racism, extreme nationalism and anti-communism. In parallel, in the USSR, following the brutal suppression of the opposition by the revolutionary regime, the leadership of the All-Union Communist Party of Bolsheviks deployed a system of mass violence and terror for the sake of building socialism (Chanturia, 2000). All three regimes were hostile to representative democracy, but at the same time they combined dictatorship with a number of external attributes of democracy, which in reality were tightly controlled by the regimes themselves: a mass party under a one-party system, demonstrations and plebiscites.

Soviet ideologists characterized the Soviet system as "socialist democracy." However, the elected bodies - the Soviets - did not have real power. Although the Constitution of the USSR declared a number of political and civil rights important for democracy, they were not supported by social institutions and existed only in theory.

The Second World War ended in 1945 with the defeat of the fascist regimes. The extreme right was discredited, outlawed and repressed in some places. Parliamentary democracies were restored in Central and Western Europe. In Eastern Europe, after a short period of democracy by the early 1950s. local communist parties established one-party systems, or multi-party systems with non-free (no alternative) elections, but in 1989 almost all of them were abolished, and democracy was restored.

In the West, democracy came to be understood as liberal democracy, which is characterized not only by free and fair elections, but also by the rule of law, separation of powers and protection of fundamental personal rights and freedoms (speech, conscience, property and association). In a number of countries that called themselves democratic, the struggle of certain groups of the population for the right to vote continued. In the United States, Negroes living in the southern states got a real opportunity to vote in

1964. In Switzerland, women were granted the right to participate in national elections in 1971 (Mkurnalidze, Khamkhadze, 2000).

The post-war years were also marked by the collapse of the colonial system. Although Great Britain and France were against the independence of their colonies, they did not have the strength and capacity to do so in the face of local resistance, pressure from the United States and the USSR, and the unwillingness of their own citizens to defend the empire. By the 1980s, almost all of the former European colonies had gained independence. Although the struggle against colonialism was in the name of national self-determination, the process of establishing democratic institutions in the new states faced serious difficulties. Most of the former colonies came under the rule of authoritarian regimes, often relying on the army.

The end of the 20th century was marked by a new wave of democratization. If after the First World War absolutism, dualistic monarchy and oligarchy lost their attractiveness and were discredited, and after the Second World War fascism and racism, then after the end of the Cold War the Eastern European communist regimes and Latin American military dictatorships suffered the same fate. India has become the most populous country with a democratic system in the world.

MODERN DEMOCRACY

Today, the number of functioning democratic regimes in the world is the largest in the entire history of the world. More than half of the world's population lives in countries where elections are held periodically. The people are widely hailed as the source of political power, and even dictatorships tend to submit their actions on behalf of the people. Elections, even when rigged, have become an essential ritual for legitimizing power. According to political scientists, at the turn of the 21st century, democratic institutions in more than a third of the world's countries were comparable to the institutions of the oldest democracies.

The right to participate in the political decision-making process is reflected in many international documents. For example, the Universal Declaration of Human Rights (Article 21) proclaims that everyone has the right to take part in the government of his country, directly or through freely elected representatives, that everyone has the right to equal access to public service, that the will of the people should be the basis of the power of government, and that freedom to vote must be ensured through universal and equal suffrage (UN, 2022).

In developed democracies, almost the entire adult population of the country has the right to vote. The subject of discussion is the issue of electoral rights for foreigners who have arrived for permanent residence. In some countries (Australia, Brazil), participation in elections is compulsory, but in most countries it is voluntary. Despite the abundance of elections and referendums in countries such as the United States or Switzerland, only a minority of the population constantly participates in them; the rest have little interest in politics.

Several versions have been put forward to explain the reasons for the decline in voter turnout. Political participation requires an investment of time that could be used for personal gain. Some voters are disappointed that politicians are focused on power struggles and self-interest. In the struggle for votes, many parties over time increasingly strive for centrism, which blurs the differences between them. It is believed that the existing parties arose against the background of social and political conflicts of the distant past, and therefore they are poorly adapted to solve modern issues. The media often focuses on political scandals instead of substantive issues. A number of pressing issues (crime, drug addiction, unemployment) are difficult to resolve, no matter what forces are in power. From the perspective of the rich, democracy is a distraction from the problems and opportunities of private life. From the perspective of the poor, democracy is not sufficient to confront poverty, violence and corruption.

The development of mass media, automatic information processing and the theory of artificial intelligence has revived interest in direct forms of democracy.

Problems of Modern Democracy

At the beginning of the 21st century, democracy faced the need to solve a number of problems:

- Inequality. While a market economy indirectly contributes to the spread of democracy, with weak government regulation it can lead to significant inequalities in income, education, social status, and other economic and social resources. Those with more of these resources use them to influence policy. The result is political inequality. Solving this problem requires increasing the democratic accountability of large financial and industrial corporations - not only through external political and economic control, but also within the firms themselves. The latter can take various forms, such as the inclusion of representatives of various groups of employees in the board of directors of a company or self-management of work collectives. Some left-wing movements argue that economic democracy is necessary to ensure political equality, which consists in the distribution of ownership of the means of production among labor collectives.
- Immigration. In developed countries, there are many poor and uneducated people among immigrants with a significant cultural gap from the indigenous population. Some of the immigrants are in the country illegally. They are often accused of hijacking jobs, abusing social benefits and violating accepted norms. Such sentiments contribute to the popularity of radical political movements that are hostile not only to immigration, but also to human rights and sometimes even to democracy itself.
- Terrorism. To combat terrorism on their territory, democratic countries have taken measures to expand the powers of security and law enforcement agencies. At the same time, these measures have imposed restrictions on some of the fundamental freedoms of citizens.
- Nationalism of ethnic minorities. Some ethnic communities strive to create their own states, to which the countries where these communities live (including democratic ones) usually react extremely negatively.
- International organizations. Some problems cannot be solved not only on the scale of an individual city, but also on the scale of the entire country. To solve such problems, a number of international structures have been created, including the UN and the European Community. These structures imply a partial limitation of the sovereignty of the participating countries, in particular, control over the policies pursued is partially beyond the reach of the country's citizens or in the sphere of influence of other countries. Thus, in the OSCE member states, issues of human rights, democracy and the rule of law are discussed at the international level and are not exclusively internal affairs of the respective state. Moreover, these organizations, despite their formal accountability to the participants, have very few political institutions of democracy. In particular, the EU democratization process is faced with the need to answer fundamental questions and determine whether democratic governance of the EU is possible at an acceptable level.

- Transition period. While in some countries the transition to democracy was successful, in others it has not gained or lost its stability. Since the transition period in each country has distinctly individual features, the general methodology of democratization has not yet been developed.

Also, the subjects of discussion are the composition of the empowered people ("demos"), the procedures for democratic representation, the necessary social and cultural conditions, the limits of democratic politics. Relatively new areas of conflict of opinion include the protection of ethnic and cultural minorities from the will of the majority, and the extension of democratic principles to families, religious institutions, schools and hospitals.

Ideal Democracy

The term "ideal democracy" has two meanings. According to the first, the ideal is understood as the best possible system. According to the second, an ideal system is a "cleaned-up" version of real-life systems. The second meaning is discussed in the Basic Institutions of Liberal Democracy section. To formulate the ideal of democracy in the first sense, it is necessary to answer a number of fundamental questions:

- Is democracy better or worse than other forms of government?
- What is the association or territorial unit in which a democracy is established?
- Which members of this association have the right to participate in the decision-making process, that is, are they full citizens?
- What political mechanism do citizens use to govern?
- If there is no consensus among citizens about an issue, whose opinion is decisive?
- If this is the opinion of the majority, how is this majority determined?
- What is needed for the stability of a democratic system?

All of these questions allow for a wide range of answers. For example, a majority can be calculated based on the total number of citizens, the number of voters who voted, the number of representatives from smaller associations or territorial units, etc. Throughout history, the standards of democracy have undergone significant evolution.

According to Robert Dahl, the idea of democracy presupposes the existence of a certain society (demos), where each member is equally competent to participate in the management of this society, has the necessary knowledge about which political choice allows him to protect his interests in the best way. Making political decisions in accordance with this principle requires all members of society to have equal and effective opportunities (Dahl, 1998).

- communicate your political views to others;
- receive information from various sources about alternative proposals and their likely consequences;
- establish how to select proposals for the final decision;
- participate in the final choice of the decision by equal voting.

The listed criteria describe not only the political process, but also the rights of each member of society associated with this process. In particular, a democratic state must ensure the protection of personal freedoms, at least to the extent necessary for an open and competitive electoral process. The most important are the right to vote, the freedom to vote, the right to stand for election, the freedom to express one's political views in the media, the freedom to form political groups and the right to participate in their activities.

One of the fundamental questions of the democratic model is the definition of the circle of persons who are subject to political equality (that is, the demos). If we are talking about a state where all full-fledged citizens have equal opportunities in governing the country, this is the issue of citizenship. According to modern views, all or almost all adults who are subject to the power of a democratic state should be full citizens.

According to Karl Popper, democracy is an open society in which its members are critical of taboos, relying on their own intelligence and critical thinking, as well as on the basis of agreements adopted as a result of discussion (Chitadze, 2016).

According to Daniel Bell, a significant criterion for a democratic society, an indicator of its openness, is the presence of social lifts that allow citizens, regardless of their social origin and only through their personal abilities and efforts to rise to the top of the social ladder, to enter the elite of society (Bell, 1973).

INSTITUTIONS OF DEMOCRACY

Comparison of approaches to the implementation of democracy in different countries shows that each of them is unique in its own way. At the same time, it is possible to carry out different classifications: according to the dominant branch of government, according to the regional hierarchy of power, according to the number of parties, etc. Further generalization allows us to identify the basic political institutions necessary (although, perhaps, insufficient) to achieve ideal democracy.

The practical implementation of democracy depends on many circumstances, in particular the size of the population and the size of the territory. Compared to large administrative units, smaller units are more homogeneous in composition and offer better opportunities for direct political participation. In compact communities, it is possible to organize effective discussions and provide ample opportunities for citizens to influence policy. Therefore, it is easier for smaller structures to meet the criteria of democracy. At the same time, as size decreases, the real amount of power and ability to solve problems decreases, especially in defense and economic matters. One of the ways to solve this contradiction lies in the division of spheres of influence between administrative and public units of various levels, in particular, by endowing cities and regions with autonomy. The most common method is to use representative forms of government in large units.

Typology of Democratic Systems

There are significant differences between political institutions in different democracies. The main types of democratic systems are listed below.
Dominant branch of government

- Parliamentary democracy. The government is appointed by the legislature. The government and its head (prime minister) can also be accountable to the ceremonial head of state (monarch, president, or special body). In a parliamentary republic, the head of state is periodically elected by parliament, or the position is combined by the chairman of the government.

- Presidential republic. The president is directly elected by the people and is the head of the executive branch.
- there are also mixed systems.

Regional hierarchy of power

- Unitary state. Political power is concentrated in the hands of the central government, which determines the scope of the powers of the regional authorities.
- Federation. According to the constitution, power is divided between the central government and the relatively autonomous regional governments.
- Legislative structure
- Unicameral parliament. Normative acts are adopted at meetings with the participation of all members of parliament.
- Bicameral parliament. The Legislative Assembly consists of two chambers, which are formed and function separately. Some regulations may require the approval of only one chamber, others - both chambers.

The system of elections to representative bodies

- Majority electoral system. The territory is divided into districts, each of which has the right to one representative in the legislature. This deputy is the candidate with the majority of votes.
- Proportional electoral system. Political parties in the legislature receive a number of seats proportional to the number of votes they receive.
- Group electoral system. Certain groups of the population nominate their deputies according to a pre-agreed quota.
- Number of leading parties
- Two-party system. The political spectrum is dominated by two large parties.
- Multi-party system. The appointment of a government is usually preceded by the formation of a ruling coalition of two or more parties represented in the legislature.

Basic Institutions of Liberal Democracy

Today, many liberal democracies are characterized by the presence of the following procedural norms (institutions) and adherence to the principle of the rule of law in their observance:

1. Elected government offices. Modern democracies are representative: according to basic laws, elected citizens exercise direct control over the adoption of regulations and political decisions.
2. Free, fair and regularly held elections in which every citizen has the right to participate (as a voter and as a candidate), combined with continuous open political competition between citizens and their associations.
3. Responsiveness of the government. The policy pursued depends on the results of the elections and on the preferences of the voters.

4. Freedom of expression. Citizens have the right to express their thoughts with impunity, including criticizing the government, the political system, the socioeconomic order and the prevailing ideology.
5. Access to alternative and independent sources of information. Citizens have the right to seek and receive information from other citizens, from books, the media, etc. Alternative sources of information must exist, be available and not controlled by any one political group.
6. Developed civil society, the third sector, the autonomy of public organizations and their ability to influence the activities of state institutions. Citizens have the right to establish relatively independent communities or organizations, including political parties.
7. Universal coverage of citizenship. Every adult residing in the country and subject to its laws must have all the rights of a citizen.

The political system, which includes the above seven institutions, is called "polyarchy". The main features of polyarchy are the possibility of political competition, ensuring the right to participate in politics, and coalition-based governance. Such rule is the opposite of a dictatorship, in which the preferences of one group dominate in choosing a political course. An important role is played by the need of competing elites to enlist the support of broad strata of the population, which is not typical for an oligarchy.

The institutions of polyarchy create conditions for the emergence of independent and diverse organizations that play an important role in the political life of the country, which entails political pluralism.

Throughout the 20th century, political scientists were inclined to believe that a significant number of countries supported the institutions listed above to an appropriate extent and therefore, in practice, can be considered democratic. At the same time, a country can meet the standard of polyarchy even if it lacks proportional representation, referendums, party primaries, social equality, or democracy at the local government level. As Robert Dahl notes, the ideal of democracy makes extremely high demands, and over time, polyarchy will probably begin to be considered an insufficiently democratic system.

Jean Baudrillard believes that a modern democratic society is a consumer society, a society of self-deception, where neither true feelings, nor culture, nor any genuine values are possible, where the meaning of human life is reduced to ever-increasing consumption as a justification for the growth of the capitalist economy at any cost (Baudrillard, 1968). From the point of view of Baudrillard, through globalization, democracy, democratic values are transformed into a standardized impersonal product, a kind of product that is sold to other cultures in a package of absolute good as a universal means of solving all problems, which causes various forms of rejection among those who are forcibly imposed on this product. Some researchers argue that the promotion of democracy in the world is one of the consequences of the globalization of the world economy, which also leads to increased international competition, migration flows and a decrease in the social rights of workers in developed countries.

From the point of view of Noam Chomsky, control over the media in the interests of a narrow group of people in modern society makes it possible to manipulate the mass consciousness when the mass is instilled in this or that idea or opinion, which it perceives as its own and the illusion of popular will on the basis of democratic procedures is created (Chomsky, 1979).

Economic Democracy

As the Head of the Department of General Political Science of the Higher School of Economics, Doctor of Philosophy Leonid Polyakov notes: "Today, many of Lenin's ideas are very relevant. For example, criticism of bourgeois democracy as a latent form of the dictatorship of capital. He wrote: who owns, he rules. In such a situation, ranting about the power of the people is just a deception." (Mkurnalizde, Khamkhadze, 2000). A number of socialist authors believe that democratic principles should be developed not only in the political sphere, but also in the economic sphere.

Economic democracy was developed in the writings of Bernstein and his followers. It is defined as a set of measures necessary to correct the inequalities in the distribution of economic power that are detrimental to democracy; as a question of a more even distribution of private property and partial confiscation of economic power from private hands and its gradual transfer in one or another legitimate way (within the existing legal system) under democratically accountable collective control, since some researchers believe that once political democracy was achieved in due to the equalization of political power, then economic democracy will be achieved through a more even distribution of economic power (Chitadze, 2016).

Functionally, economic democracy in enterprises (participation of workers in management, industrial democracy) presupposes wider participation of ordinary workers in the share capital of a company, control of works councils (lower levels of economic democracy) over a significant sphere of production activity: humanization of labor, social policy, policy in the sphere employment and includes the requirement for equal participation of works councils in the management of the enterprise on an equal basis with owners and managers.

There is a point of view (Tom Piketty Capital in the 21st century), which is shared by part of the Western political elite (Barack Obama, IMF Managing Director Christine Lagarde) that the current trend of increasing economic inequality: concentration of income and wealth in the hands of a few is the biggest historical challenge institutions of democracy and leads to the concentration of the power of capital, "patrimonial capitalism" and oligarchy, making senseless democratic procedures that become a means of manipulating the mass consciousness in the hands of financial oligarchs (Chitadze, 2016).

According to the Global Wealth Report, Credit Suisse Bank (2016) property inequality in the world continues to grow: if in 2010 10% of the population owned about 86% of the world's assets, then in 2015 they already owned 89% of all global assets (Chitadze, 2017).

Some researchers (Anthony Giddens) see a way to solve the problem of growing social inequality and the growing power of capital in following the concept of the third way, a form of combining a free capitalist economy with certain social guarantees of the state, the development of economic democracy, the cultivation of social responsibility of business, the introduction of progressive taxation and inheritance tax. capital, the slow evolutionary development of society through institutional reforms based on a critical rethinking of the legacy of Karl Marx and Ferdinand Lassalle in the direction of a non-Marxist form of socialism (Fabian society). Former British Prime Minister Tony Blair considers himself to be supporters of the concept of the third way and the construction of Fabian socialism. Some researchers find elements of the concept of Fabian socialism in the policies of US President Barack Obama (Chitadze, 2016).

Transparency in the field of production and capital movement is considered by researchers as one of the most important elements of modern democracy. The concept of developing democracy, both politically and economically, through the gradual reform of capitalism based on the class world towards greater social justice has been criticized with the Marxists. They read that the power of the oligarchy cannot be seriously limited and placed under public control through progressive taxation and tax on capital, the development of the cooperative movement as one of the ways to evenly distribute economic power (International Cooperative Alliance). The nature of capitalism (Radical geography) is the constant creation of relations of inequality and domination-subordination: between classes, nations and cultures as a basis for achieving maximum profit, which makes it impossible, from the point of view of Marxism, a relatively even distribution of power among all members of society, as in political and economic spheres within the capitalist formation.

THE VALUE OF DEMOCRACY

Abuses in all other forms of government led to a preference for Republican government as the best, because it least imperfect. – James Madison

Democracy was the subject of analysis in terms of its impact on other values and as an independent value. Common arguments in favor of democracy:

- It helps prevent despotism
- She helps people protect their interests
- It helps to reduce the distance between the citizen and the government
- It allows political leadership to be better informed
- It gives people the maximum opportunity to live according to their own laws.
- It allows relatively conflict-free rotation of elites and counter-elites
- It guarantees a wide range of personal freedom and human rights
- It gives citizens moral responsibility for their political decisions.
- It allows all full citizens, regardless of their race, nationality, gender, origin, position in society and beliefs, to participate in the political decision-making process.
- It promotes equality of opportunity, social mobility and the reduction of social inequalities
- Only it is able to ensure political equality, when all citizens have equal opportunities to influence government decisions
- Democracies tend to be richer and have a higher level of human development than non-democracies.
- Democracies relatively rarely go to war with each other (Mkurnalizde, Khamkhadze, 2000).

Democracy is the worst form of government – except for all the others that have been tried. (Winston Churchill, 1947).

Some of these arguments are shortcomings of democracy from the point of view of its opponents. A number of arguments against democracy have also been widely discussed:

- It allows some circles to advance their interests at the expense of others
- It can undermine mutual trust in a situation where the adoption of any decision will allow one person to benefit at the expense of others.
- It opens the possibility for the dictatorship of the majority over the minority
- It encourages dissension, which can negatively affect the authority of the authorities.
- It empowers people who are not competent or fully informed to make decisions.
- It makes it difficult to implement unpopular measures with a likely long-term payoff.
- It distracts people from the problems and opportunities of their private lives.
- In the transition period of democratization, it is inefficient in terms of economy, administration and order

- It can be inefficient compared to the market self-regulation of society

W. Riker criticized what he called the "populist theory of democracy", the origins of which he traces back to J. J. Rousseau. It is based on the idea that there is the will of people as an abstract social phenomenon, and that democracy is the most reliable tool for determining this will. According to William Riker, all voting systems are manipulative and encourage people to be insincere. Since it is impossible to know which voters were dishonest, and to what extent this dishonesty manifested itself in voting, it is impossible to create democratic institutions that would reflect the preferences of all citizens (Chitadze, 2016). Democratic procedures create a free rider problem. This is a situation where the activity of one of the social actors increases the benefits received by others, regardless of their actual activity. The rationality of non-participation is a form of a kind of "blackmail". The advantage is given to the side that is dominated by attitudes towards achieving other goals. By virtue of less interest in democratic procedure, it can gain more from the market exchange of participation for alternative goods.

Dictatorship of the Majority

Even if the decision made equally takes into account the preferences of all citizens, for a part of society it may have unacceptable consequences in terms of morality or law. In many theories, such decisions are considered illegitimate. The implementation of universal suffrage and a proportional electoral system contribute to a more accurate representation of interests, but do not solve the problem. The way out lies in the creation of some additional system of checks and balances, which protects the minority from arbitrariness on the part of the majority and at the same time does not contradict democracy. The following approaches have been proposed:

- Qualified majority or consensus as a condition for a decision
- Separation of powers into executive, legislative and judicial branches
- Possibility of annulment by an independent court if it violates constitutional rights and freedoms
- Decentralization of power, its division according to the territorial level
- Filtering the preferences of the masses in order to direct the discussion in a constructive direction, for example, by delegating direct decision-making powers to deputies

It should be noted that some of the above measures may also have negative consequences, such as political stagnation or the narrowing of the scope of democratic institutions.

The Sustainability of Democracy

For the stability of the state, it is necessary that citizens carry out even those decisions of the authorities against which they object. In the case of democracy, this means that the minority obeys the will of the majority, the change of power proceeds peacefully, and the opposition not only has the right to express public disagreement with state policy, but also acts strictly within the law. Therefore, one of the most important conditions for the stability of democracy is its legitimacy in the eyes of citizens. The legitimacy of the implementation of democracy can be justified by its value and the equality of all participants in the process. The presence of common basic values plays an important role here, which allows reaching agreement on the principles of political behavior. This builds trust between citizens, encourages them to abide by existing rules, and justifies the use of force to protect those rules.

A number of authors believe that the recognition by society of democratic principles and constitutional rights as cultural values gives stability to the state during a crisis. At the same time, the absence of an effective legal system leaves the norms of a democratic society unprotected and creates the basis for abuse by the authorities, political elites and criminal groups.

These arguments are supported by sociological studies, according to which the stability of democracy correlates with interpersonal trust, tolerance towards unpopular groups, support for civil liberties and the political activity of the population.

Authoritarianism and Democracy

In authoritarian states, power is concentrated in the hands of the ruling group, which in its actions is not limited by responsibility to the ruled. Most authoritarian regimes of the past differed from representative democracy in a number of ways:

- elections to the authorities were either not held, or had no alternative, or did not lead to a change of power even in the event of a formal victory of the opposition
- the power of elected persons was often limited by powerful non-elected organizations (army, church, party)
- opposition openly persecuted
- the media were controlled by the state, subjected to censorship and systemic repression

At the same time, political scientists note that at the turn of the 1990s, the number of hybrid regimes in the world (which received the names "imitation democracy", "authoritarian democracy", "electoral authoritarianism", etc.) grew in the world, having signs of both authoritarianism and democracy (Lebedeva, 2007). In such regimes, there are periodic elections and elements of political competition, so that the opposition is able to challenge, weaken and sometimes even defeat the ruling forces in elections, in the legislature, in the courts and in the media. However, the conditions of competition for the ruling forces and the opposition are unequal due to systemic abuse of administrative resources and violations of the rights of opposition supporters.

Autocrats can use nominally democratic institutions to legitimize themselves and mobilize society in their support. Individuals who agree to cooperate with the regime receive rewards and concessions in exchange. Related negotiations often take place in special, government-controlled, restricted forums, such as parliaments.

An essential indicator is the degree of development of the rule of law. According to political scientist Adam Przeworski, democracy is first of all the certainty of procedures with the uncertainty of results. According to political scientists and public figures, in a liberal-democratic country, citizens, through democratic procedures, develop rules for the interaction of various subjects of society and form the mechanisms of state power that acts in accordance with these rules (Przeworski, 1991).

Such a model is fundamentally different from a system in which the government itself establishes the order of interaction between the subjects of society and forms the necessary management mechanisms for this. In a non-ruleal state, individual authorities may override or circumvent laws that regulate the powers of these authorities. This, in particular, opens up opportunities for manipulation of the justice system and the media in order to reward those loyal to the regime and punish the opposition without regard to legal procedures.

According to political scientists at Freedom House and Radio Liberty, modern authoritarian regimes also deliberately distort the essence of democracy, interpret it as the imposition of alien values by the West, hinder the work of international organizations engaged in human rights activities (UN, OSCE, ECHR) and instill in young people a hostile attitude towards democratic values.

Some political scientists distinguish delegative democracy as a separate category, in which the executive branch partly subordinates the legislative branch and poorly takes into account the preferences of voters in the policy pursued, however, the change of power remains possible, and civil rights are protected.

Varieties of Democracy

Political Regime

Historically, ideas about democracy have been dominated by two basic models. In a direct democracy, full-fledged citizens make political decisions directly by voting, with the minority further subjugated to the will of the majority, or by achieving full consent. In a representative democracy, citizens delegate this function to their elected representatives, who are accountable to voters for their actions. The practical implementation of democracy became the development of these ideas, and the early models were discredited over time and today are considered only as stages towards modern forms of democracy:

Oligarchic democracy allows only large owners to take a direct part in government and guarantees their civil rights. The right to vote is subject to property restrictions. A related model is a plutocracy, where the ruling class pursues policy primarily in the interests of big capital.

Egalitarian democracy aims to achieve political equality. Egalitarian politics presupposes equal participation in the political process, equal representation, equal protection of rights and freedoms, and equal access to politically significant resources. Proponents of this approach usually call for the implementation of policies in the interests of the whole nation and put them above the interests of a minority or an individual citizen. Nationalist versions of this model interpret the nation in an ethnic sense, not a civil one, and give full rights only to persons of certain nationalities.

Socialist democracy is similar to egalitarian, but focused on the will of the common people. It involves the gradual elimination of class society and predominantly state ownership of the means of production. The term "socialist democracy" was enshrined in the Program of the Russian Communist Party of 1919. In the late 1940s, another term was introduced by the communist parties - "people's democracy" - as a type of socialist democracy (Chitadze, 2016).

Liberal (also bourgeois and constitutional) democracy is based on a number of principles:

- Government with the consent of the people based on the will of the majority
- Peaceful change of power through periodic elections
- Public compromise and search for consensus
- Information openness of the political decision-making process
- Influence of citizens on decision making
- A system of checks and balances to prevent arbitrariness on the part of the majority
- The rule of law
- Guarantees of political, civil and social human rights

- Guarantees of the opposition's rights

Imitative democracy has a number of external attributes of democracy, but in fact, the influence of citizens on the decision-making process is extremely small. This may be due to the fact that some citizens are deprived of the right to vote, or the elected representatives do not determine the entire policy of the government, or the executive branch subjugates the legislative and judicial branches, or the justice system is not able to enforce the principles laid down in the constitution. A variation of this model is the dominant party system.

Theory

In the modern literature on political science, several theoretical concepts of democracy have also developed:

The aggregative model considers democracy as a set of legal mechanisms that ensure a stable balance in society by reaching a compromise between the interests of different circles.

Deliberative (deliberative) theory focuses on the role of public discussions in decision making and the striving of participants for the common good. She argues that the democratic nature of the system is proportional to its information openness.

Institutional theory sees the main role of the democratic state in the implementation and protection of public ideas about political and civil rights.

Consensual democracy seeks to make decisions that take into account the widest possible range of preferences, and not just the preferences of the majority.

The majority concept combines the requirement of competitive elections with the thesis of the rule of will of the majority, for which political institutions should contribute to the concentration of power, rather than its decentralization.

The minimalist concept sees democracy as a system of government in which citizens delegate their rights to exercise political power to elected officials, since they themselves do not have enough time and knowledge. In this theory, the susceptibility of the leadership to the wishes of the ruled is ensured mainly by the competitive struggle for the votes of the electorate.

Participatory democracy proceeds from the need for broad and, if possible, direct participation of citizens in the development of legal norms. The subject of her attention is political activism and the willingness of citizens to bear responsibility for the consequences of their decisions.

The plebiscitary model reduces the participation of citizens to the periodic issuance of a "vote of confidence" in one candidate or another and is usually studied from the point of view of the degradation of the institution of elections.

Economic democracy argues that for the participation of the broad masses in political decision-making, it is necessary to distribute private and state property among public shareholders, for example, in the form of cooperative property.

Social Movements

The term "democracy" is sometimes used in the name of social movements:

Social Democracy stands for the transition to a socially just society within the framework of democracy.

Christian Democracy seeks to solve socio-economic problems while respecting Christian principles.

Democracy and Republic

Until the 18th century, the term "democracy" meant direct democracy in small towns where the entire population was able to come together. In the same sense, this word was used by one of the ideologists of the United States, James Madison, who called the system of representative government a "republic". Other US leaders (James Wilson, John Marshall, Thomas Jefferson) began to refer to the American system as "democracy" because the source of power was ultimately the people, and thus used the two terms interchangeably. Destutt de Tracy and James Mill spoke of representative government as a revolutionary invention that opened up the possibility of building democracy over a large area (Mkurnalizde, Khamkhadze, 2000). After visiting the United States in 1831-1832, Alexis de Tocqueville also proclaimed it a democracy, where government is based on popular sovereignty (Alexis de Tocqueville, 2017).

Immanuel Kant called a "republic" a legal state with separation of powers, a system of balances and checks, protection of individual rights and some level of representation in government. He contrasted the republic with democracy as a system with universal suffrage and unlimited majority rule, which he considered prone to tyranny. Kant considered the goal of human history to be the achievement of a universal legal civil society, where the greatest freedom of each will be compatible with the freedom of others and the natural inclinations, the destiny of man, will receive their maximum development. According to modern dictionary definitions of a republic, this concept acts as an antipode to a monarchy and is incompatible with the head of state, who is elected for life or not elected at all. On the contrary, the concept of democracy does not contradict parliamentary monarchy (Kant, 1795).

Some modern political scientists believe that the concepts of "democracy" and "republic" are no different.

Democracy and Religion

The list of major religions by country with representative democracy covers all world and many national religions. In a number of countries it is Christianity, in Indonesia it is Islam, in Mongolia it is Buddhism. Hinduism predominates in today's most populous democratic state, India. Many religions assert the ability of each person to make moral choices, which historically contributed to the spread of ideas about equality and, as a result, about democracy.

Since its inception, the Christian Church has been based on important democratic principles: the election of the highest church hierarchs (bishops) by secret ballot, the highest church body is a collegiate body (Local Council, Ecumenical Councils), the highest positions in the church hierarchy can be occupied by Christians, regardless of their nationality. and class origin. Islam is also based on significant democratic principles: the election of the imam, the head of the religious community on the basis of authority and regardless of his social origin, the absence of a strict hierarchy in the religious structure; according to Islamic Sharia law, the most correct way to transfer power is to elect the head of state directly by the population or with the help of electors. Any Muslim, regardless of his origin, can become the highest spiritual authority, a sheikh.

Some Christians express doubt that this religion is compatible with democracy, on the grounds that all authority is from God, the flock must obey the shepherds, and only the monarch is accountable to God as the anointed one. On the other hand, Protestantism teaches that all people are equal before God, and hence before authority; that God called people to be priests and kings, and therefore endowed them with the right to self-government; that God gave people life and faith, and hence inalienable rights and freedoms. Catholicism claims that society and the state exist to create the conditions necessary for the self-realization of man (personalism), and that power should be as close as possible to citizens (the principle of subsidiarity). The Orthodox theologian Feofan (Prokopovich) believed that power was initially divided among the people, who had the right to establish any form of government. The philosopher G. P. Fedotov saw Orthodox democracy as a continuation of the traditions of the Novgorod Republic (Chitadze, 2016). In Orthodoxy, the concept of catholicity is also widespread, which encourages everyone to participate in the search for truth, although it considers only unanimous consent, based on love and respect for others, as an acceptable method of decision-making.

CONCLUSION

Democracy as a civilizational phenomenon acts as a specific product of Western civilization, which by the end of the 20th century had succeeded. receive the status of a universal value. Today, in political sciences, the idea of democracy prevails not only as a proper political institution (or system of institutions), but as a more complex phenomenon that includes cultural (democratic political culture), socio-psychological, and ideological aspects.

Human rights and freedoms are the universally recognized social opportunities of the individual, the provision of which is real in the conditions of the progress achieved by mankind. As a rule, they in their modern form are proclaimed and enshrined in international legal documents1.

The difference between human rights and the rights of a citizen, due to the difference between law and law, is a progressive democratic idea that has a long history. The Constitution legally enshrined this idea as a constitutional principle, the basis of the constitutional order. The constitutional and legal doctrine and universal human practice have developed a difference in the concepts of human rights and freedoms. Freedom is the independent behavior of the bearer of freedom, which must have an adequate form of using it. Human freedom is ensured and protected by the state, but is not regulated by it. In using freedom, a person should not only abuse it, i.e. harm others. The right is the possibility of free behavior clearly outlined by the state within the limits defined by law. A person, realizing the right, should not go beyond the boundaries of this right. In the realization of human rights, the role of the state is more active than when a person uses freedom.

The topic concerning the rights and freedoms of the individual does not lose its relevance, despite the rapid development of the institutions of the state and law, the rooting of democracy, the strengthening of mechanisms for protecting the rights and freedoms of man and citizen. The personality has always striven and will strive for the highest point of freedom, therefore there is no limit to the development of the institution of the rights and freedoms of the individual.

REFERENCES

Alexis de Tocqueville. (1840). *Democracy in America*. Retrieved from: https://www.history.com/topics/france/alexis-de-tocqueville#:~:text=As%20%E2%80%9CDemocracy%20in%20America%E2%80%9D%20revealed,example%20of%20equality%20in%20action

Alexis de Tocqueville. (2017). *The State of Society in France Before the Revolution of 1789*. Retrieved from: https://www.gutenberg.org/ebooks/54187

Aristotle. (2022). *Politics*. Retrieved from: https://iep.utm.edu/aris-pol/

Baudrillard, J. (1968). *The System of Objects*. Retrieved from: https://arthistoryunstuffed.com/jean-baudrillard-system-of-objects/

Bell, D. (1976). *The Coming of Post-Industrial Society: A Venture in Social Forecasting*. Basic Books. doi:10.1080/00131727609336501

Bertelsmanstiftung. (2022). *Democracy under pressure worldwide*. https://www.bertelsmann-stiftung.de/de/startseite

Britannica. (2022). *The theory of democracy. Democratic ideas from Pericles to Rawls*. Retrieved from: https://www.britannica.com/topic/democracy/The-theory-of-democracy

Budge, I. (2001). Direct democracy. In P. A. B. Clarke & J. Foweraker (Eds.), *Encyclopedia of Political Thought*. Taylor & Francis.

Chanturia, G. (2000). *World Geography*. Editing House Meridiani.

Charles Louis de Montesquieu. (1748). *On the Spirit of Laws*. Retrieved from: https://www.goodreads.com/book/show/141958.The_Spirit_of_the_Laws

Chitadze, N. (2016). *Political Sciences*. International Black Sea University.

Chomsky, N. (1979). *The Political Economy of Human Rights*. Academic Press.

Dahl, R. A. (1998). *On Democracy*. Yale University Press.

Dahl, R. A. (2010). *On Democracy*. Audibooks.com

Democracy Barometer. (2020). *The Democracy Barometer is a new instrument to measure the quality of established democracies*. Retrieved from: https://democracybarometer.org/

Diamond, L. (2000). *Developing Democracy*. JHU Press.

Freedom House. (1984). *Freedom in the World. 1983-1984*. Retrieved from: https://freedomhouse.org/sites/default/files/2020-02/Freedom_in_the_World_1983-1984_complete_book.pdf

Hamilton, A., Madison, J., & Jay, J. (1982). *The Federalist* (J. E. Cooke, Ed.). Wesleyan University Press.

Heywood, A. (2021). *Political ideologies* (7th ed.). Bloomsbury Publishing.

History. (2022). *Pericles*. Retrieved from: https://www.history.com/topics/ancient-history/pericles

Hume, D. 1739–1740. A Treatise of Human Nature: Being an Attempt to introduce the experimental Method of Reasoning into Moral Subjects. Floating Press International Churchill Society. (2022). *The worst form of government*. https://winstonchurchill.org/resources/quotes/the-worst-form-of-government/

Kamenskaya. (2005). *Politology*. Aspect Press.

Kant, I. (1795). *Perpetual Peace: A Philosophical Sketch*. Retrieved from: https://www.mtholyoke.edu/acad/intrel/kant/kant1.htm

Lebedeva, M. (2007). *World Politics*. Aspect Press.

Lipset, M. (1960). *Political Man: The Social Bases of Politics*. The Johns Hopkins University Press.

Locke, J. (1690). *Two Treatises on Government*. Retrieved from: https://www.yorku.ca/comninel/courses/3025pdf/Locke.pdf

Mill, J. S. (1863). *Utilitarianism*. Retrieved from: https://books.google.ge/books?id=ujgIAAAAQAAJ&dq=editions:OCLC38110333&lr=&source=gbs_summary_s&redir_esc=y

Mkurnalidze, K. (2000). *Political Sciences*. Tsodna.

Plutarch. (n.d.). *Complete Works. — Volume 3: Essays and Miscellanies by Plutarch*. Retrieved from: https://www.gutenberg.org/ebooks/3052

Przeworski, A. (1991). *Democracy and the Market: Political and Economic Reforms in Eastern Europe and Latin America*. Cambridge University Press. doi:10.1017/CBO9781139172493

Reference, O. (2022). *Democracy*. Retrieved from: https://www.oxfordreference.com/view/10.1093/acref/9780195148909.001.0001/acref-9780195148909-e-241

Rondeli, A. (2003). *International Relations*. Nekeri.

Rousseau. (1762). *The Social Contract. Or Principles of Political Right*. Retrieved from: https://www.marxists.org/reference/subject/economics/rousseau/social-contract/

Schumpeter, J. A. (1908). *Methodological Individualism*. Germany. OCLC 5455469.

Services, O. E. R. (2020). *History of Western civilization*. Retrieved from: https://courses.lumenlearning.com/suny-hccc-worldhistory2/chapter/establishment-of-the-national-assembly/

Shubitidze, V. (2009). *Political science*. Georgian Technical University.

United Nations. (2022). *Universal Declaration of Human Rights*. Retrieved from: https://www.un.org/en/about-us/universal-declaration-of-human-rights

KEY TERMS AND DEFINITIONS

Civil Society: A community that embraces shared norms and ethical standards to collectively manage problems without coercion and through peaceful and democratic procedures for decision making aimed at improving human welfare.

Classical Liberal Economic Theory: A body of thought based on Adam Smith's ideas about the forces of supply and demand in the marketplace, emphasizing the benefits of minimal government regulation of the economy and trade.

Collective Good: A public good, such as safe drinking water, from which everyone benefits.

Commercial Liberalism: An economic theory advocating free markets and the removal of barriers to the flow of trade and capital as a locomotive for prosperity.

Comparative Advantage: The concept in liberal economics that a state will benefit if it specializes in the production of those goods which it can produce at a lower opportunity cost.

Complex Interdependence: A model of world politics based on the assumptions that states are not the only important actors, security is not the dominant national goal, and military force is not the only significant instrument of foreign policy. This theory stresses cross-cutting ways in which the growing ties among transnational actors make them vulnerable to each other's actions and sensitive to each other's needs.

Constitutional Democracy: Government processes that allow people, through their elected representatives, to exercise power and influence the state's policies.

Democracy: a form of government in which the people have the authority to deliberate and decide legislation ("direct democracy"), or to choose governing officials to do so ("representative democracy"). Who is considered part of "the people" and how authority is shared among or delegated by the people has changed over time and at different rates in different countries, but over time more and more of a democratic country's inhabitants have generally been included. Cornerstones of democracy include freedom of assembly, association and speech, inclusiveness and equality, citizenship, consent of the governed, voting rights, freedom from unwarranted governmental deprivation of the right to life and liberty, and minority rights.

Democratic Peace: The theory that although democratic states sometimes wage wars against non-democratic states, they do not fight one another.

Development: The processes, economic and political, through which a country develops to increase its capacity to meet its citizen's basic human needs and raise their standard of living.

End of History: Francis Fukuyama`s thesis that the end-point in the ideological debate about the best form of government and economy had been reached, with liberal capitalism and democracy prevailing throughout the world without serious competition from advocates of either communism or autocracy.

European Union (EU): A regional organization created by the merger of the European Coal and Steel Community, the European Atomic Energy Community and the European Economic Community (called the European Community until 1993) that has since expanded geographically and in its authority.

Gender Empowerment Measure (GEM): The UN Development Programs attempt to measure the extent of gender equality across the globe`s countries, based on estimates of women's relative economic income, high paying position, and access to professional and parliamentary positions.

Human Development Index (HDI): An index that uses life expectancy literacy, average number of years of schooling and income to assess a country's performance in providing for its people's welfare and security.

Human Needs: Those basic physical, social, and political needs, such as food and freedom that are required for survival and security.

Human Rights: The political rights and civil liberties recognized by the international community as inalienable and valid for individuals in all countries by virtue of their humanity.

Human Security: A measure popular in liberal theory of the degree to which the welfare of individuals is protected and promoted in contrast to realist theory's emphasis on putting the states interests in military and national security ahead of all other goals.

Humanitarian Intervention: The use of peacekeeping troops by foreign states or international organizations to protect endangered people from gross violations of their human rights and from mass murder.

Information Age: The era in which the rapid creation and global transfer of information through mass communication contributes to the globalization of knowledge.

Information Technology (IT): The techniques for storing, retrieving, and disseminating through computerization of the internet recorded data and research knowledge.

Intellectual Property: Inventions created by the use of human intelligence in publications art and design by individuals that are often illegally used for commercial purposes without credits or royalties to their creators in violation of GAT`s agreement.

Interdependence: A situation in which the behavior of international actors greatly affects others with whom they have contact, making all parties mutually sensitive and vulnerable to the others actions.

Intergovernmental Organization (IGOs): Institutions created and joined by state governments which give them authority to make collective decisions to manage particular problems on the global agenda.

International Court of Justice (ICJ): The primary court established by the United Nations for resolving legal disputes between states and providing advisory opinions to international agencies and the UN General Assembly.

International Regime: Embodies the norms, principles and rules. An institution around which global expectations unite regarding a specific international problem.

Liberal International Economic Order (LIEO): The set of regimes created after World War II designed to promote monetary stability and reduce barriers to the free flow of trade and capital.

Liberalism: A paradigm predicated on the hope that the application of reason and universal ethics international relations can lead to a more orderly, just, and cooperative world. liberalism assumes that anarchy and war can be policed by institutional reforms that empower international organizations and law.

Morality: Principles about the norms for behavior that should govern an actor's interactions.

Morals: Principles clarifying the difference between good and evil and the situations in which they are opposed.

Neoliberalism: The new liberal theoretical perspective that accounts for the way international institutions promote global change, cooperation, peace, and prosperity through collective programs for reforms.

Nongovernmental Organizations: Transnational organizations of private citizens maintaining consultative status with the UN. They include professional associations, foundations, multinational corporations, or simply internationally active groups in different states joined together to work toward common interests.

Norms: Generalized standards of behavior that once accepted shape collective expectations about appropriate conduct.

Pacifism: The liberal idealist school of ethical thought that recognizes no conditions that justify the taking of another human's life even when authorized by a head of state.

Peace Building: Post-conflict actions predominantly diplomatic and economic that strengthen and rebuild governmental infrastructure and institutions in order to avoid renewed recourse to armed conflict.

Transparency: With regard to the GATT the principle that barriers to trade must be visible and thus easy to target.

Chapter 2
The Universality of the Human Rights Principles

Nika Chitadze
International Black Sea University, Georgia

ABSTRACT

Human rights are rules that protect the dignity and freedom of each individual. In their totality, fundamental rights form the basis of the legal status of an individual. The specific expression and scope of these rights, both in the positive law of different states and countries and in various international legal treaties, may differ. In public international law, the most famous document that enshrines them is the UN Universal Declaration of Human Rights. In OSCE member states, issues of human rights, fundamental freedoms, democracy, and the rule of law are international in nature and do not belong exclusively to the internal affairs of the state concerned.

INTRODUCTION

Human Rights - According to the UN, are inherent rights of all human beings, regardless of race, sex, nationality, ethnicity, language, religion or any other status. Human rights include the rights to life and liberty, freedom from slavery and torture, freedom of expression and speech, the right to work and education, and much more (UN, 1948).

The general scope of human rights is governed by international law as well as national and municipal law, as far as international law is concerned, as far as it is reflected in domestic law, although the fundamental legal umbrella is protected by international law, as far as human rights are concerned. On certain standards of human life and behavior agreed upon by international civilization. Human rights doctrine, in addition to international law and the activities of global or regional organizations, also operates and is regulated as a result of measures and policies of states and non-governmental organizations.

Human rights are universally understood as inalienable, fundamental rights that derive only from being human beings, hence they are universal and egalitarian in the sense that they are one for all. It is on the basis of these principles that an understanding of human rights obliges states and individuals to

DOI: 10.4018/978-1-6684-4543-3.ch002

respect the rights of other human beings, including the deprivation of these rights, even in the case of legal liability, as well as in circumstances such as unlawful detention, torture or Hanging.

The philosophy of human rights addresses existential, political, and legal issues such as the existence, essence, nature, universality, justice, and legal status of human rights. Evidence of the inalienability and universality of human rights, as well as the very definition of the concept of "right", has often led to critical, skeptical and contradictory philosophical assumptions. These doubts, reflections, and critical responses have created new dimensions of the political and legal philosophy of human rights over time. There is a consensus that human rights include a wide variety of rights, although it is a matter of debate which of these specific rights should be considered in the basic human rights framework. Part argues that the general framework of inalienable rights includes rights such as the right to a fair trial, protection from slavery, the prohibition of genocide or the right to education, while part proposes that the human rights framework be kept to a minimum to avoid extreme manifestations of oppression.

The basic ideas that created the human rights movement developed after World War II, including its reaction to events such as the Holocaust. The culmination of these events was the adoption of the Universal Declaration of Human Rights in Paris in 1948 at the UN General Assembly (UN, 1948). Until then, such a universal concept did not exist - although the forerunner of the human rights discourse was "natural rights", which was part of the medieval natural law tradition - these concepts became popular during the European Enlightenment, led by John Locke, Francis Hutchson, Jean-Jacques Burlamac and other philosophers. Which later became the political discourse of the French Revolution and the American Revolution. Contemporary arguments in human rights discourse were developed in the second half of the twentieth century as a response to slavery, torture, genocide, war crimes, etc., as a recognition of human vulnerability to such actions and of taking restrictive measures for a more just society.

HISTORY

Human Rights in Antiquity

The Cyrus Manifesto is a clay cylinder on which Cyrus the Great ordered to engrave in cuneiform a list of his victories and merciful deeds, as well as a list of ancestors. The artifact was discovered during the excavations of Babylon in 1879 and entered the British Museum (Chitadze, 2016).

The cylinder became widely known after the last Shah of Iran in the 1960s proclaimed the text applied to it as the first ever declaration of human rights: Cyrus spoke out for the abolition of slavery and freedom of religion. The Shah promised to build his policy in accordance with the precepts of Cyrus, the founder of Persian statehood.

Later, the concept of human rights in their modern sense dates back to the Renaissance and Reformation in Europe, the time of the gradual disappearance of feudal authoritarianism and religious conservatism, which dominated throughout the Middle Ages. During this period, European scholars attempted to form a kind of secular version of religious ethics. Although the ideas of individual rights and freedoms have existed in one form or another for a significant part of human history, they have not been characterized by a noticeable resemblance to the modern concept of human rights. As researcher J. Donnelly noted, in the ancient world, "traditional communities usually had a developed system of duties ... concepts of justice, political legitimacy and prosperity, which were an attempt to ensure human dignity, well-being and success in complete isolation from human rights. The relevant institutions and practices represent an alternative to these rights rather than a different formulation of them." More often than others, there is an opinion that the concept of human rights originated in the West; although other, earlier cultures had significant moral and ethical codes, it was the concept of human rights that they generally lacked. Some researchers, for example, are convinced that the word "law" itself does not occur in any languages until the 15th century. Medieval freedom charters, such as the English Magna Carta, were not inherently documents of human rights, but rather the basis and form of a limited political and legal agreement intended to regulate certain circumstances in the state. Subsequently, some of these documents, including the said Charter, were considered in the early stages of modern discussions about human rights. Some researchers, however, believe that the relevant rights were partly described already in the Kalisz Statute of 1265 (Levin, 1985).

The origins of the development of human rights in Europe can be traced to the Twelve Articles of 1525, the manifesto of the Reformation and the Peasants' War in Germany, which formed part of the demands of the peasants in the struggle for their rights. The first article of the document echoes the ideas of M. Luther, set forth in his treatise on the right of the Christian community to evaluate the doctrine and choose a spiritual mentor; to some extent, it can be said that the entire document as a whole owes its appearance to the Reformation movement (Stahl, 1957). In addition to social and political demands, the authors claimed the right to freedom of conscience; this right was at the center of active discussions already then, in the 16th century, when the actual term "human rights" did not yet exist.

Subsequently, in the early seventeenth century, Baptist theologians, including J. Smith, T. Helwys, and R. Williams, wrote tracts in which they actively advocated freedom of conscience. Their ideas influenced the views of J. Milton and J. Locke on religious tolerance (Müller-Schwefe, 1961). In addition, in the then emerging American colonies - Rhode Island, Connecticut, Pennsylvania - there were conditions for the support of religious freedom, and various religious minorities found refuge in them (Clifton, 1961). The Declaration of Independence, the US Constitution and the American Bill of Rights then formalized and legalized the respective traditions (Middlekauff, 2005). These documents, inspired by the American Revolution, influenced, among other things, the UN Universal Declaration of Human Rights.

For the first time, the concept of "human rights" is found in the French "Declaration of the Rights of Man and Citizen", adopted in 1789, although before that the idea of innate rights had come a long way in development, the English Magna Carta (1215), the English Bill of Rights (1689) and the American Bill of Rights (1791).

In the 19th century, in different states, the initial liberal set of civil and political rights (freedom and equality, inviolability of the person, property rights, suffrage, etc.) was formed in different ways, which in the modern sense are very limited (property electoral qualifications, political prohibitions, inequality of men and women, racial restrictions, etc.). One of the central socio-political problems directly related to human rights at that time was the problem of slavery; a number of figures, such as the Briton William Wilberforce, made efforts to abolish it.

As early as 1807, the Slave Trade Act appeared in the British Empire, prohibiting, accordingly, the slave trade, and in 1833, the Slavery Abolition Act. In the US, the northern states abolished the institution of slavery between 1777 and 1804, while the southern states were reluctant to abandon it; this ultimately led to conflicts and disputes over the expansion of slavery into new territories and became one of the reasons for the split of the country and the civil war that followed. Subsequently, a series of amendments to the US Constitution was adopted, which prohibited slavery, guaranteed full citizenship and a full set of related rights to all who were born in the state, and also provided black Americans with the right to vote (Shubitidze, 2009).

In the 20th century, under the strong influence of socialist movements, social and economic rights were added to civil and political rights (as a rule, the rights of workers: the right to join trade unions, work, rest, social assistance, etc.).

In 1922, at the initiative of the German and French leagues for human rights, two dozen organizations in different countries create the International Federation for Human Rights (FIDH), the world's first international organization for the protection of human rights.

The Second World War and the tragic experience of totalitarian regimes initiated a qualitative leap in the development of the institution of human and civil rights, the leading role in the development of which is played by international law.

On December 10, 1948, by resolution 217 A (III), the UN General Assembly adopted and proclaimed the "Universal Declaration of Human Rights":

as a task to which all peoples and states must aspire, so that every individual and every organ of society, keeping this Declaration constantly in mind, should strive, through enlightenment and education, to promote respect for these rights and freedoms and to ensure, through national and international progressive measures, universal and effective recognition and implementation of them both among the peoples of the Member States of the Organization, and among the peoples of the territories under their jurisdiction. — Universal Declaration of Human Rights, Preamble

Since 1950, every year December 10th has been celebrated as International Human Rights Day (UN, 1948).

Also in 1950, the European Convention for the Protection of Human Rights and Fundamental Freedoms was signed in Europe. The main difference between this Convention and other international treaties in the field of human rights is the creation of a real mechanism for the protection of declared rights - the European Court of Human Rights (Karumidze, 2005).

In 1966, under the auspices of the UN, the International Covenant on Civil and Political Rights and the International Covenant on Economic, Social and Cultural Rights were adopted. These and subsequent international agreements approved the international standard of human and civil rights and the guarantees for ensuring these rights, with the aim of incorporation (reflection) in the constitutional system of the participating states. It is not exhaustive: "the inclusion of some rights does not mean a derogation, much less a denial of other rights and freedoms of man and citizen" (Karumidze, 2003).

Equality Is a Universal Principle of the Legal Status of an Individual

The idea of human equality has its roots in the mists of time. But it took centuries to prohibit discrimination against groups of people on one or another basis.

Like the Declaration of the Rights of Man and the Citizen of 1789, the Universal Declaration of Human Rights proclaimed that all human beings are born free and equal in dignity and rights.
However, it was further noted:

every human being shall have all the rights and all freedoms (proclaimed by the Declaration) without distinction of any kind, such as race, colour, sex, language, religion, political or other opinion, national or social origin, property, estate or other position.

Furthermore, no distinction shall be made on the basis of the political, legal or international status of the country or territory to which a person belongs, whether that territory is independent, trust, non-self-governing or otherwise limited in its sovereignty. — Universal Declaration of Human Rights, Art. 2 (UN, 1948)

Equality of Women and Men

Women require special attention in this respect. For the first time, the issue of equality of rights between men and women began to be addressed by the ideologists of the Great French Revolution. In 1791, the Women's Education Act was passed and some civil rights were granted. But during the years of the Thermidorian reaction, these positions were pushed back. At the end of the 19th - beginning of the 20th centuries. in Germany, the theory of "three K" - Kinder, Küche, Kirche (children, kitchen, church) spread, but other areas of public opinion developed in parallel. In Great Britain, in 1847, the 10-Hour Working Day for Women Act was passed and access to the teaching profession was opened. In the United States, since 1848, married women have received the right to property, and since 1880, the opportunity to be members of trade unions. Suffrage was first used by New Zealand women in 1893 (Heywwod, 2002).

Human Rights Law

Legal Instruments and Jurisdiction

The human rights enshrined in the Universal Declaration of Human Rights, the Geneva Conventions and various UN treaties, while legally binding, are very difficult to enforce in practice due to a lack of consensus on the application of certain rights, lack of appropriate national legislation, or authorities authorized to take measures to ensure them.

There are a number of internationally recognized organizations that have a worldwide mandate or jurisdiction over certain aspects of human rights:

- The International Court of Justice is the main judicial body of the United Nations, has worldwide jurisdiction, and is governed by the UN Security Council (ICJ, 2022). The International Court of Justice resolves disputes between nations, but has no jurisdiction over individuals.
- The International Criminal Court is the body responsible for investigating and punishing war crimes and crimes against humanity when they occur within its jurisdiction and has the power to prosecute those responsible for such crimes that have occurred since its establishment in 2002. A number of UN members have not joined the court, and this court does not have jurisdiction over citizens of these countries, while others have signed but not yet ratified the Rome Statute, which established the court (Rome Statute of the International Criminal Court, 2002).

Democratic Principles of Securing and Ensuring the Rights and Freedoms of Man and Citizen

The concepts of democracy and the rule of law are to a certain extent connected with the understanding of the relationship between human rights and freedoms and state power.

Every individual is endowed with a certain degree of freedom. However, when realizing his interests, an individual must take into account the interests of other individuals - the same members of society as he is. This is the restriction of the freedom of the individual by law to a certain extent.

Freedom is the ability and possibility of a consciously-volitional choice by an individual of his behavior. It implies a certain independence of a person from external conditions and circumstances.

Law is always a partial restriction of individual freedom necessary for the coexistence of free citizens.

Categories of law exist in three main types: inalienable rights (basic), temporally inalienable and fully derogable (Mkurnalizde, Khamkhadze, 2000).

CLASSIFICATION OF THE RIGHTS AND FREEDOMS OF MAN AND CITIZEN

In the legal doctrine, according to the main sphere of manifestation in public relations, human rights are usually divided into personal, political, socio-economic and cultural, however, to a large extent, such a division is also symbolic. For a number of them, only the difference between human rights and the rights of a citizen is essential. Human rights can also be divided into 1) personal + political; 2) socio-economic; 3) cultural + collective. Below is a popular theory of classification of human and civil rights and freedoms (Chitadze, 2016).

Personal

Personal rights are the rights of everyone, and although often referred to as civil, are not directly related to belonging to the citizenship of the state, do not follow from it. They are considered innate and inalienable for every person, regardless of his citizenship, gender, age, race, ethnicity or religion. Necessary for the protection of human life, dignity and freedom. Personal rights usually include:

- The right to live;
- Punish ability only in court - the prohibition of extrajudicial reprisals;
- Inviolability of the person;
- Freedom of movement and choice of residence;
- Inviolability of the home;
- Inviolability of correspondence;
- Prohibition of forced labor;
- Inviolability of property (some jurists refer to economic; in France it is recognized as one of the main personal rights since the Great French Revolution.
- Dignity of the individual
- Freedom of conscience and religion
- The right of the individual to recognition of his legal personality
- Right to asylum
- Right to citizenship
- The right to marry and found a family
- The right to own property

The Right to Live

The right to life is an inalienable right of every person, protected by law. Its content is that no one can be deliberately deprived of life. Also, the right to life imposes on the state an obligation to do everything to ensure that human life is out of danger and to undertake an effective investigation of murders.

Origins of the Concept

The right to life was first proclaimed as a natural right in the US Declaration of Independence of July 4, 1776, but this right is not found either in the US Constitution, adopted in 1787, or in the constitutions of other states adopted until the middle of the 20th century.

Only after World War II, in 1948, did the UN General Assembly adopt the Universal Declaration of Human Rights, Article 3 of which reads: "Everyone has the right to life, liberty and security of person."

Somewhat later, in 1950, within the framework of the Council of Europe, the Convention for the Protection of Human Rights and Fundamental Freedoms was concluded.

Multilateral human rights instruments relating to the right to life have also been adopted in other parts of the world. Such, for example, was the Inter-American Convention on Human Rights adopted in 1969.

Another important document was the International Covenant on Civil and Political Rights concluded in 1966 within the framework of the UN. Article 6 of this document proclaims the right to life as an inalienable right of every person, protected by law (Karumidze, 2003).

Deprivation of Life: The Death Penalty

According to Article 2 of the Convention for the Protection of Human Rights and Fundamental Freedoms mentioned above, the application of the death penalty in certain cases is allowed:

No one may be intentionally deprived of life except in execution of a death sentence passed by a court for a crime for which the law provides for such punishment.

However, the International Covenant on Civil and Political Rights stipulates that in the case of the death penalty, "death sentences may be imposed only for the most serious crimes"; at the same time, everyone who is sentenced to death "has the right to ask for pardon or commutation of the sentence." It should be added that the death penalty cannot be imposed "for crimes committed by persons under eighteen years of age, and is not carried out against pregnant women" (Karumidze, 2003).

Other Grounds for Deprivation of Life

Deprivation of life, according to the Convention for the Protection of Human Rights and Fundamental Freedoms, is also possible "when it is the result of an absolutely necessary use of force" in the following cases:

- protecting any person from unlawful violence;
- lawfully arresting or preventing the escape of a person lawfully detained;
- suppression, in accordance with the law, rebellion or insurrection.

Inviolability of the Person

the principle that a person cannot be arbitrarily deprived of liberty. Article 9 of the Universal Declaration of Human Rights provides that "no one shall be subjected to arbitrary arrest, detention or exile."

Freedom of Movement and Choice of Residence

the right of a person to freely move around the country, choose his place of residence and stay, leave the country and return to it. It is one of the fundamental personal human rights and is included in the Universal Declaration of Human Rights, adopted by the UN General Assembly in 1948. Usually, this freedom is fully granted only to citizens of the country, and various restrictions may be imposed on the movement of foreign citizens.

Privacy

Privacy (in legal science) is the value provided by the right to privacy.
The right to privacy includes:

- a ban on the collection, storage, use and dissemination of information about the private life of a person without his consent;
- the right to control information about yourself;
- the right to protection of honor and good name;
- the right to protection of personal data;
- the right to secrecy of communications (sometimes formalized as a separate right);
- the right to the inviolability of the home (sometimes formalized as a separate right);
- medical secrecy, adoption secrecy, confessional secrecy and other types of professional secrecy.

In socialist states, the term "private life" is used, not "private life" (similar to "personal property" instead of "private property").

In many countries formally declared human rights are not always implemented in practice. Privacy, even guaranteed by laws and the constitution, often remains on paper.

History

This right became widespread in Europe during the period of bourgeois revolutions. It was normatively enshrined in French legislation, it is still not positively enshrined in the US Constitution and the US Bill of Rights, but is derived from a number of amendments to the Constitution.

It was scientifically developed for the first time in an article by well-known legal scholars S. D. Warren and L. D. Brandeis "The Right to Private Life", published in 1890 in the USA (Utrech Journal, 2015).

Subsequently, the right to privacy was upheld by a series of US Supreme Court precedents that justified its existence and removed it from a series of amendments to the US Constitution (Bill of Rights).

In the post-war period (40-50s) it was enshrined in a number of international treaties, the norms of which were implemented by the legislation of many countries, including the USSR (the right to privacy), and later Russia.

The right to privacy was further developed in a number of precedents of the European Court of Human Rights in Strasbourg (the well-known precedents are Princess Hanover against Germany, Znamenskaya against Russia, Fadeyeva against Russia, etc.).

Communication Mystery

The secret of communication (in legal science) is the value provided by the right to the secret of communication. Currently, the right to secrecy of communication is considered an integral part of human rights - the natural and inalienable rights of the individual, recognized at the international level. A violation of the secrecy of communication is recognized as familiarization with a protected message by any person other than the sender and recipient (or his authorized representative). In some types of communication, due to their technical features, it is allowed to get acquainted with the message of individual communication workers, as, for example, when transmitting a telegram. In such cases, it will be considered a violation not to familiarize, but to disclose the content of the message. Along with the message itself, information about the message is also protected; for telephone conversations, these are the numbers of the calling and called subscribers, the time of the call and its duration.

The very concept of "human rights" arose in the 18th century and was based on the European philosophical traditions of five or six previous centuries. The French Declaration of the Rights of Man and of the Citizen of 1789 is considered the first document that officially proclaimed "human rights" in their modern form. Some researchers consider the US Declaration of Independence of 1776, which also proclaimed a set of individual rights, more or less similar to the modern one, to be the founder of modern "human rights". These two documents formed the foundation of the modern legal paradigm, which at first operated only in Europe and the New World, and later spread to the whole world. However, the right to privacy of correspondence was not included in these documents. It appeared as part of "human rights" later - in UN documents in 1945-1948 (Chitadze, 2016).

There is evidence of Inca mail in Peru. Here, until the beginning of the 16th century, there were postal messengers who, in addition to state messages, delivered fresh fish, fruits and other products to the king's table. As Ciesa de Leon points out in the Chronicle of Peru, the Inca laws provided for the preservation of the secrecy of the information contained in the forwarded messages:, they never talked about what they were going to convey in the message, even if the notification had already gone further (by mail)" (Chitadze, 2016).

The concept of secrecy of correspondence has been included in various decrees and job descriptions since the 17th century and becomes a universal part of the laws by the 19th century. Systematic violations of the secrecy of communication by this time are perceived precisely as violations, and the involved officials of the postal departments and black offices are forced to justify themselves before public opinion and even before their superiors.

Forced Labor

Forced labor is the performance of work under the threat of any punishment (violent influence).
Under international law, forced labor does not include:

- work, the performance of which is conditioned by the legislation on conscription and military service or alternative civilian service that replaces it;

- work performed under emergency conditions;
- work performed as a result of a court verdict that has entered into legal force.
- The prohibition of forced labor is established:
- Universal Declaration of Human Rights, articles 4, 23 (December 10, 1948)
- International Covenant on Civil and Political Rights, Article 8 (December 16, 1966)
- European Convention for the Protection of Human Rights and Fundamental Freedoms, Article 4 (November 4, 1950)
- Slavery Convention (September 25, 1926)
- Supplementary Convention for the Abolition of Slavery, the Slave Trade and Institutions and Practices Similar to Slavery (September 7, 1956)
- International Labor Organization Convention No. 29 concerning Forced and Compulsory Labor (May 1, 1932) (Karumidze, 2003).

History

One form of forced labor is slavery. It is associated with the absolute control of one person over another. After the prohibition of slavery in the 19th and 20th centuries, such a form of forced labor as debt bondage was widely practiced in colonial and developing countries. Massive use of forced labor by states occurred during and after World War II.

Currently

- Forced into prostitution (sexual slavery)
- Kidnapping people (usually the homeless, unemployed, lonely) and using them as slaves.
- The use of military personnel in jobs not related to military service.
- Forcing prisoners to work not related to the tasks of rehabilitation and maintaining order in places of deprivation of liberty.
- Engagement in work that is not part of official duties, as well as violation of other norms of labor legislation under the threat of violence or punishment (dismissal).

Right of Private Property

The right to private property is usually considered among the fundamental human rights.

The Universal Declaration of Human Rights (Article 17) provides that everyone has the right to own property either alone or in community with others, and no one shall be arbitrarily deprived of his property (UN, 1948).

Article 1 of Protocol No. 1 to the European Convention on Human Rights of 20.03.1952 provides that every natural or legal person has the right to respect for his property (possessions). No one may be deprived of his property except in the public interest and under the conditions prescribed by law and the general principles of international law. It is stated, however, that the foregoing provisions do not derogate from the power of the State to enforce such laws as it deems necessary to exercise control over the use of property in accordance with the general interest or to secure the payment of taxes or other charges or penalties (Council of Europe, 1952).

Confiscation, forced purchase of a land plot for state and municipal needs, seizure of a land plot used in violation of the law, forced purchase of mismanaged cultural property and domestic animals in case of improper handling of them, foreclosure of property on obligations are carried out in a judicial proceeding.

Nationalization and requisition are carried out of court. Foreclosure on property can also be carried out of court, according to the executive inscription of a notary.

However, in all the above cases, except for confiscation, which is a punishment for a crime or an administrative offense, and foreclosure on property for the obligations of the owner, the owner must receive monetary compensation.

A fine, which is also a deprivation of property, can also be imposed as a punishment for an administrative offense out of court, but in this case, the person on whom the fine is imposed, if he does not want to pay it voluntarily, has the right to appeal against the decision to impose it in court.

The European Court of Human Rights has pointed out, in particular in the case of Butsev v. Russia (2005), that a "claim" may constitute "property" within the meaning of Article 1 of Protocol No. 1 to the European Convention on Human Rights if, in it has been sufficiently established that it can be legally enforced and therefore the applicant's failure within a reasonable time to enforce the judgment awarding him compensation for the injury sustained as a result of his participation in the liquidation of the consequences of the Chernobyl accident constitutes an interference with his the right to free use of their property (Chitadze, 2016).

Dignity

Dignity is respect and self-respect of the human person as a moral category, a characteristic of a person from the side of his inner value, conformity to his purpose, the basis for the formation of legal awareness and the acquisition of material and non-material rights.

Early ideas of dignity were determined by social status. At present, dignity means "inner nobility", regardless of origin and position in society.

Dignity as a moral concept - characterizes the individual as a person and is determined not by external conventions, but by the freedom inherent in a person as an individual person and citizen, acts as the basis for the expression of will, opposing self-interest and other practical motives (according to I. Kant). From the greatest value of human life follows the presence of dignity in every person who does not even suspect it.

In contrast to merit, dignity is an imperative concept (a person should be worthy, while merit is imputed to a person as a sign of approval of his successes).

Right

In ancient Roman society, "dignitas" (Latin) is the influence that a male citizen acquired throughout his life, including personal reputation, moral position and ethical value. And also the right of a man to be respected and treated appropriately by virtue of the reputation and position of his family. The definition does not have a direct translation, so some interpretations include the concepts of "prestige", "charisma", "respect", "the power of personal influence" in this term. Octavian August associated it with the established term "auctoritas" (authority), defining the latter as an expression of the dignity of a man.

In the monarchical system, the sovereign was called the source of honor ("the source of dignity"), from which all dignity comes, expressed in the exclusive right to assign legitimate titles of nobility and knightly orders to other persons. The system of titles of nobility implied, first of all, the designation of the rights of ownership and management of the lands of the sovereign, who is the "supreme owner" of the land. Therefore, the bestowed titles (English titles, estates) did not just mark the "worthiness" of the person bestowed, but led to the emergence of quite specific property rights and obligations to the sovereign.

In constitutional law, "the dignity of the individual" is a criterion for the attitude of the state to the individual and his legal status. In the moral and legal sense, dignity is considered as the source and cause of the emergence of human rights. Therefore, the Charter of the United Nations, the Universal Declaration of Human Rights, the Charter of the European Union on Human Rights and many other documents that have the highest legal force and establish fundamental rights, consider human dignity as one of the fundamental values.

In civil law, "dignity" is one of the intangible benefits that belong to a person from birth. It is inalienable and intransferrable.

Freedom of Religion

Freedom of religion is the right to profess and practice any religion. Historically, the meaning of the term has expanded, and today freedom of religion is usually understood as also the right not to profess or practice any religion, to profess and/or advocate the rejection of religious or other worldviews.

History

- Ancient Persia (VI century BC) - Cyrus, Ancient India (III century BC) - Ashoka. Rome - tolerance for those who recognized, along with their own, the Roman gods.
- 313 - Edict of Milan: a letter from the emperors Constantine and Licinius proclaiming religious tolerance in the territory of the Roman Empire.
- after 1206 - the Great Yasa of Genghis Khan, which, among other things, proclaimed limited religious tolerance: it was not forbidden to believe in their gods, but it was required to believe in one God.
- 1568 - the law on freedom of conscience and religion, adopted by the Hungarian Parliament in the city of Torda.
- 1573 - Warsaw Confederation in the Commonwealth.
- 1598-1685 - the effect of the Edict of Nantes on religious tolerance (towards the Huguenots) in France.
- 1689 - The Toleration Act in England.
- 1789 - Declaration of the rights of man and citizen in France.
- 1791 - Freedom of religion is enshrined in the First Amendment to the US Constitution.
- 1844 - Edict on religious tolerance in the Holy Land (Chitadze, 2016).

Freedom of Religion in the International Law

In modern times, it developed in the system of bilateral relations as a protection of the rights of minorities (for example, the protection of the rights of the Orthodox in the Ottoman Empire was guaranteed by its agreements with the Russian Empire); in multilateral relations since 1878 (Chitadze, 2016).

Enshrined in the Universal Declaration of Human Rights, the International Covenant on Civil and Political Rights, the European Convention for the Protection of Human Rights and Fundamental Freedoms.

- The right of the individual to recognition of his legal personality
- The essence of a person as a legal person is manifested in the fact that he can be the subject of the rights and obligations provided for by law. Legislation, endowing it with the ability to acquire, implement and protect them by its actions, establishes the conditions under which a citizen can become such a subject. Participants in civil legal relations, if there are grounds (legal facts) provided for by law, become bearers of rights and obligations. However, before the latter arise, it is required that the relevant persons be able to participate in certain civil legal relations. In other words, in order to have rights and obligations, an individual must be to a certain extent a legal entity, have the legal ability to participate in civil legal relations.
- The institution of legal personality is one of the most important in civil law. O. S. Ioffe expressed the opinion that "legal personality" is an institution of civil law on a par with a contract, the right of ownership. J. R. Webers noted that in the field of civil law, the institution of legal personality forms not only the norms that directly regulate the civil legal capacity and legal capacity of a citizen, but also the norms created by individual institutions regarding the ability of the latter to be a subject in specific legal relations (Karumidze, 2003).
- International human rights instruments (art. 6 of the Universal Declaration of Human Rights, art. 16 of the International Covenant on Civil and Political Rights) proclaim that every person, wherever he is, has the right to recognition of his legal personality.
- states, c) to own property both individually and jointly with others, d) to freedom of peaceful assembly and association, e) to participate freely in the cultural life of society, to enjoy the arts, f) to participate in scientific progress and enjoy its benefits, g) the right to protect their moral and material interests, which are the result of personal copyright scientific, literary or artistic works.
- The term "legal personality" is used in the theory of law to characterize a person as a subject of law. recognition of a person as a subject of civil law means endowing him with civil legal personality. The emergence, change and termination of the latter is associated by the legislator with the facts of immediate life, since they are given a certain legal significance.

Right of Asylum

The right of asylum (French droit d'asile) is a human right recognized by the world community to seek asylum from persecution, as well as the right of states to provide asylum on their territory.

The right of asylum in the history of mankind was of two kinds: 1) internal, when the persecuted received asylum and protection from punishment within the same state; 2) external, or on the basis of international law, when the territory of another state serves as asylum.

Modern international law recognizes two types of asylum: territorial (on the territory of a state) and diplomatic (within the walls of a diplomatic mission on the territory of a foreign state). Also, a number of Latin American states grant diplomatic asylum on their territory on the basis of the 1928 Havana Convention on the right of asylum.

Historic Right of Asylum

In Antiquity

First Refuges:

Under the conditions of the peculiarities of the structure of a number of ancient societies, ancient customs and religion could resist the force of laws that existed only in favor of the social elites. The offender in many cases, by virtue of natural law and customs, was only an innocently persecuted victim, who aspired under the protection of religion and found in its sanctuaries an inviolable refuge. And the very existence of such a right of asylum served not only to strengthen respect for religion, but was often enshrined in law.

The effectiveness of such protection is considered controversial, since such protection was provided without distinction to both illegally prosecuted and overt criminals, therefore, in the case of criminals, the benefit to society was not always:

- on the one hand, the offender was hidden from the deserved punishment, increasing the number of crimes.;
- on the other hand, a criminal guilty of a minor crime could avoid unreasonable reprisals (this is especially useful if the specified criminal who is being prosecuted was a witness to a serious crime committed by other criminals).

Shelters of the Ancient East

According to the law of Moses, in ancient Israel and later in Judea, several cities were appointed for refuge, but not for all criminals, but only for those guilty of blood feuds and those who feared the same from the relatives of the murdered by them. It was an attempt to put an end to the endless "flywheel spinning", as they say now, blood feud from generation to generation, since this, in particular, also threatened the well-being and internal security of ancient Israel as a state.

Shelters in Ancient Greece and Ancient Rome

In Greece and Rome, temples, statues of emperors (because of their deification), and other sacred buildings served as a refuge.

The right of asylum has been most widespread since the triumph of Christianity. The idea of pardon, the doctrine of complete cleansing through repentance and faith in Christ, the fear of retribution for bloodshed - all this prompted the clergy to protect those who resorted to God's house. Christian churches became a refuge not only for persecuted criminals and innocents, but also for slaves who fled from the cruelty of the slave-owning law, which pursued them in the unconditional power of their masters.

The Roman Christian emperors, who officially legalized the right of church asylum, at the same time established a number of restrictions for it. So Theodosius I (392) and Flavius Arcadius decided that debtors should be either extradited or bishops should repay their debts to creditors. According to the law of Theodosius II (432), a runaway slave could be sheltered only for one day, the next day he was to be handed over to the master, but with the obligatory taking from the latter an oath promise to forgive the slave. Jews (more precisely, Jews) enjoyed the right of asylum only if they accepted Christianity. Justinian (535) forbade giving refuge to murderers, perjurers, and kidnappers (Karumidze, 2003). According to the law of Theodosius II, the place of refuge was not only the altar and the inside of the temple, but the entire territory of the temple (everything in the church fence): - gardens, squares, baths, buildings, so that the fugitives were not forced to eat and sleep in churches.

Into the Middle Ages

In the Middle Ages, the popes, using their authority, extended the ecclesiastical right of asylum to cemeteries, monasteries, bishops' houses and church almshouses. Whoever violated the inviolability of the asylum was anathematized and subjected to civil punishment. Asylum-seekers could be extradited to civilian judges, but with the condition that they not be executed or mutilated. Following the example of the church asylum, kings and emperors, and then specific rulers, gave some cities the right to be a place of refuge for a certain kind of criminals. For example, the city of Reutlingen served as a refuge for those who committed murder in the heat of anger (that is, in a state of passion - in modern legal terminology).

The Christian temple was the main refuge for quite a long time. Such a shelter was of great importance in the so-called. barbarian states that adopted Christianity, but gradually the pure ecclesiastical refuge began to lose its significance for three reasons:

- some popes indirectly denied the right of church asylum for persons who have committed particularly serious crimes;
- the decline of the authority of the church in the second half of the Middle Ages;
- the spread of other forms of refuge - partly religious (for example, French councils) and purely secular.

With the establishment of firm order and legality in the Western states, and with the assertion of the beginning of the independence of the state from the interference of papal power, the ecclesiastical right of asylum and the similar right of privileged cities gradually fell into oblivion. The ordinance (decree) of Francis I (1539) in France and the law of 1624 in England destroyed the ecclesiastical right of asylum (Karumidze, 2003).

XVIII-XIX Centuries

In 1760, in Bavaria, on the basis of a papal bull, an order was issued for the extradition of deserters from asylums on the condition that they would not be put to death or other severe punishment. A similar order was issued in 1788 by the Elector-Archbishop of Trier and by a general order in Prussia in 1794, in Württemberg (1804) and in Saxony (1827) (Davitashvili, 2002).

In 1850, the Siccardi law (Italian: leggi Siccardi) was required in Turin to terminate the ecclesiastical right of asylum. A papal circular of 1852 limited the right of asylum to three days, and completely abolished it in some cases. The right of asylum lasted longer than others in embassy houses (Gudushauri, 2002).

The Modern Right of Asylum: Political Asylum

Political asylum is a special legal status granted to a person who, for certain reasons, is persecuted in his homeland: usually, for political, religious and other beliefs, as well as for actions that are not qualified in the international and national law of the host state as an offense, and the right to entry and stay in the territory of this state. Under the laws of most countries, including the United States and Russia, an applicant can only apply for asylum while in the territory of the state in which the applicant is seeking asylum.

Nansen Passport

In 1922, at the initiative of the Norwegian navigator and explorer Fridtjof Nansen, then Commissioner of the League of Nations for Refugees, an international document was established that certifies the identity of a stateless person. Initially, it was issued to the so-called white émigrés, and later to other refugees who could not get a regular passport. In 1942, this passport was recognized by the governments of 52 states, and it became the first travel document for refugees. In total, about 450,000 Nansen passports were issued to help stateless refugees find shelter in other countries (Gaiamo, 2017).

Havana Conventions of 1928

At the VI Pan-American Conference, which took place in Havana in January-February 1928, conventions on diplomatic law were adopted:

1. about diplomatic officials;
2. about consular officials;
3. on the right of asylum (Convention on Asylum, 1928).

1948 Universal Declaration of Human Rights

On December 10, 1948, the UN General Assembly approved the "Universal Declaration of Human Rights", taking into account many factors, including "that the disregard and contempt for human rights have led to barbaric acts that revolt the conscience of mankind." The 14th article of the Universal Declaration is devoted to the right of asylum:
Article 14:

1. Everyone has the right to seek and enjoy asylum from persecution in other countries.
2. This right cannot be exercised in the event of prosecution based in reality on the commission of a non-political crime, or an act contrary to the purposes and principles of the United Nations (UN, 1948).

Convention Relating to the Status of Refugees 1951

On July 28, 1951 in Geneva, at a conference convened in accordance with resolution 429 (V) of the UN General Assembly of December 14, 1950, with the participation of plenipotentiaries of countries, an international treaty was adopted - the "Convention relating to the Status of Refugees", which entered into force on April 22, 1954 of the year (The 1951 Refugee Convention).

The convention gave definitions of the term "refugee" and established general rules on the basis of which refugee status is granted. The Convention forbade any discrimination against refugees who receive rights partly on an equal footing with nationals of their host country and partly under the same conditions as foreigners. The convention allows the expulsion of refugees in the interests of national security, but prohibits their return to the state from which they fled for fear of persecution.

Subsequent Acts of International Law

On December 14, 1967, the UN General Assembly adopted as a recommendation the "Declaration on Territorial Asylum" (UN, 1967). A conference on territorial asylum was held in 1977, but failed to reach a convention. However, there are asylum provisions in the 1954 OAS Caracas Convention and the 1969 OAU Convention on Specific Aspects of Refugee Problems in Africa. The Council of Europe adopted a declaration on territorial asylum in 1977 (Council of Europe, 1977).

Citizenship

Citizenship is a legal relationship between a person and the state, expressed in the totality of their mutual rights, duties and responsibilities.

Citizenship is one of the institutions of constitutional and administrative law and is usually enshrined in the constitution (basic law) or constitutional act of the state and other legal acts. It manifests itself as a relationship between the state and persons under its care, the constitutional and social protection of every person in the state: the state recognizes and guarantees the rights and freedoms of a citizen, protects and patronizes him abroad; in turn, the citizen unconditionally observes the laws and regulations of the state, fulfills the duties established by him. The totality of these rights and obligations constitutes the political and legal status of a citizen, which distinguishes him from foreign citizens and stateless persons.

In monarchical countries, the connection of a person with the state is expressed not in the form of citizenship, but in the form of citizenship. Unlike citizenship, citizenship embodies the direct connection of a person with the monarch, and not with the state as a whole.

Citizenship or nationality is certified in the manner established in the state. However, practice in different states varies widely: from the right to have no documents at all in the UK to mandatory ID cards in the countries of the European Union or even an internal multi-page passport in some countries that were formerly part of the Soviet Union.

Acquisition of Citizenship

There are several ways to acquire citizenship:

- Filiation (by birth) - the acquisition of citizenship by birth. There are three forms of filiation:
    - By right of blood (lat. Jus sanguinis) - obtaining citizenship through the marriage of parents. The child acquires citizenship if his parents (or one of them) has the citizenship of this state;
    - By the right of the soil (land) (lat. Jus soli) - the child acquires the citizenship of the state in whose territory he was born. A birth certificate practically guarantees a certificate of citizenship. Renunciation of citizenship and deprivation of citizenship are impossible or difficult, and vice versa, it can be easily restored (USA et al.;
    - By inheritance - a rare form that is available in the legislation of several European countries. Thus, persons who were citizens of the Republic of Latvia before June 17, 1940 transfer their citizenship rights to their descendants. The difference from the "right of blood" can be traced in a situation where the parents of the child, citizens of the Republic of Latvia, legally died before his birth. The civil status of the newborn in this case depends on the status of his ancestors on the day of June 17, 1940. This practice is also observed in Romania (Aleksidze, 2016).
- Naturalization (rooting) - entry into the citizenship of a person at will. The procedure for admission to citizenship is regulated by the legislation of the state. Usually, in order to acquire citizenship, a number of conditions must be met (knowledge of the language, housing, etc.). The term

"naturalization" (naturalization) historically means the acquisition of the rights of natural (natural) citizens (or subjects). As part of naturalization, sometimes allocate:

- ◦ Registration - the acquisition of citizenship at the request of a person without any additional conditions (usually, the categories of persons entitled to use this method are specified by law);
- ◦ Citizenship is usually an honorary gift of citizenship to a person by the head of state for some merit (if such is provided for by law).

- Option - a person's choice of citizenship when changing the borders of states. The option procedure is regulated by international treaties of such states.
- Transfer - the transition of the population of any territory from one citizenship to another in connection with the transfer of the territory in which they live, one state to another.

In some countries (Antigua and Barbuda, Saint Lucia, Dominica, etc.) it is possible to obtain citizenship by purchasing real estate or by investing in the country's economy. This form of acquiring citizenship is called citizenship by investment and is widespread in Europe (the so-called "Golden Visas" of Portugal, the UK, Latvia, etc.) and the Caribbean (St. Kitts and Nevis, Grenada, etc.) . To obtain citizenship, the applicant goes through several stages - a residence permit (residence permit), permanent residence (permanent residence), the naturalization procedure itself (obtaining citizenship). The procedure for obtaining citizenship varies depending on the legislation of the country (Aleksidze, 2016).

Restoration of Citizenship

- Reintegration - the restoration of the citizenship of any state of persons who previously had it and then lost it. The meaning of reintegration most often lies in the procedure that is applied in these cases. May be provided for in special laws and in ordinary nationality legislation. In the latter case, it can be considered as a kind of naturalization.
- Repatriation (lat. repatriate) - return to their homeland. The term is usually used in relation to prisoners of war, displaced persons, refugees, emigrants with restoration of citizenship rights or return to the country of residence of the insured in the event of an insured event.

Termination of Citizenship

The legislation of most countries provides for the possibility of termination (withdrawal from) citizenship:

- Renunciation of citizenship - termination of citizenship at the initiative of a citizen.
- Deprivation of citizenship - termination of citizenship at the initiative of the state.
- Change of citizenship - the transition from one citizenship to another citizenship. (According to modern Russian legislation, only dual nationals, as well as persons who may find themselves in the territory transferred to another state in connection with a change in the state border, actually have such an opportunity).
- Expatriation (from Latin ex - from and patria - homeland, fatherland) - temporary or permanent expulsion of a person from the country (his geographical or cultural homeland), usually associated with deprivation of citizenship (Aleksidze, 2016).

Stateless and Bipatride

- Constitutional law knows situations when a person can have citizenship of several states or not have citizenship at all:
- stateless (stateless person) - a person who is not considered as a citizen by any state by virtue of its law.
- bipatride - a person who has evidence of his citizenship of two states. Bipatrides are also commonly referred to as persons with more than one citizenship (Aleksidze, 2016).

The Importance of Citizenship

While fundamental human rights and freedoms are inviolable in relation to all people, a country usually grants only its citizens such additional rights as: to elect and be elected (active and passive suffrage), participate in a referendum, hold public office, etc. d.

In addition to these rights, granted only to citizens, citizens also bear a certain, inherent only to them, range of duties. Usually, the duties of citizens include the passage of military service.

The rights of persons having the citizenship of more than one State are usually somewhat different from those of other citizens. This issue is regulated by international treaties and agreements.

The Right to Marry and Found a Family_

Discussing the importance about marriage rights, it can be better to present the Convention on Consent to Marriage, Age for Marriage and Registration of Marriages, Opened for signature and ratification by General Assembly resolution 1763 A (XVII) of November 7, 1962

Contracting States

Desiring, in accordance with the Charter of the United Nations, to promote universal respect for and observance of human rights and fundamental freedoms for all without distinction as to race, sex, language or religion,
Bearing in mind that Article 16 of the Universal Declaration of Human Rights provides as follows:

"1) Men and women who have reached the age of majority have the right, without any restriction on grounds of race, nationality or religion, to marry and found a family. They enjoy the same rights in relation to entering into marriage, during the state of marriage and upon its dissolution.

2) Marriage may be entered into only with the free and full consent of both parties to the marriage,

Bearing in mind also that the General Assembly of the United Nations, in resolution 843 (IX) of 17 December 1954, indicated that certain customs, obsolete laws and practices relating to marriage and the family were contrary to the principles set forth in the Charter of the United Nations and in the Universal Declaration of Human Rights,*Affirming* that all States, including those bearing or assuming responsibility for the administration of Non-Self-Governing and Trust Territories pending their independence, should take all appropriate measures to abolish such customs, obsolete laws and practices by ensuring, in particular, full freedom the choice of a spouse, the complete abolition of child marriage and pre-puberty marriage contracts for girls, the establishment, where necessary, of appropriate penalties and the establishment of a civil status register or other register in which all marriages are registered, *hereby agree* as follows:

- Article 1:
    - Marriage is not allowed without the full and free consent of both parties, which must be expressed by them personally, in accordance with the law, after proper announcement, in the presence of a representative of the authority having the right to formalize the marriage, and in the presence of witnesses.
    - Notwithstanding the provisions of paragraph 1 of this article, the presence of one of the parties is not required if the appropriate competent authority is satisfied that there are exceptional circumstances and that this party, before any competent authority and in the manner prescribed by law, has expressed consent and didn't take it back.
- Article 2:
    - The States Parties to this Convention shall enact legislation establishing a minimum age for marriage. Marriage shall not be entered into with a person under the prescribed age, unless the competent authority, in the interest of the parties to the marriage, authorizes an exception to this rule for serious reasons.
- Article 3:
    - All marriages are registered by the competent authority in the relevant official registry.
- Article 4:
    - This Convention is open until 31 December 1963 for signature by all States Members of the United Nations or of any specialized agency and by any other States invited by the General Assembly of the United Nations to participate in this Convention.
    - This Convention is subject to ratification. Instruments of ratification shall be deposited with the Secretary General of the United Nations.
- Article 5:
    - This Convention is open for accession to all States referred to in paragraph 1 of Article 4.
    - Accession is effected by the deposit of an instrument of accession with the Secretary General of the United Nations.
- Article 6:
    - This Convention shall enter into force on the ninetieth day after the date of the deposit of the eighth instrument of ratification or accession.
    - For each State which ratifies or accedes to this Convention after the eighth instrument of ratification or accession has been deposited, this Convention shall enter into force on the ninetieth day after the deposit by that State of its instrument of ratification or accession.
- Article 7:
    - Any Contracting State may denounce this Convention by written notification addressed to the Secretary General of the United Nations. The denunciation shall take effect one year from the date of receipt of this notification by the Secretary General.
    - This Convention shall cease to be in force on the date of entry into force of a denunciation which reduces the number of Parties to eight.
- Article 8:
    - Any dispute arising between any two or more Contracting States concerning the interpretation or application of this Convention not settled by negotiation shall, at the request of all

parties to the dispute, be submitted to the International Court of Justice for decision, unless the parties agree otherwise.

- Article 9:
    - The Secretary-General of the United Nations shall notify all States which are Members of the United Nations and States which are not Members of that Organization referred to in paragraph 1 of Article 4 of this Convention of the following:
        - (signing the Convention and receiving instruments of ratification in accordance with article 4;
        - receipt of instruments of accession in accordance with Article 5;
        - the date on which this Convention enters into force in accordance with Article 6;
        - notices of denunciation received under Article 7, paragraph 1;
        - that the Convention ceases to be in force in accordance with article 7, paragraph 2.
- Article 10:
    - This Convention, of which the Chinese, English, French, Russian and Spanish texts are equally authentic, shall be deposited in the archives of the United Nations.
    - The Secretary-General of the United Nations shall transmit certified copies of this Convention to all States Members of the United Nations and non-Members of this Organization referred to in Article 4, paragraph 1 (UN, 1962).

Political Rights

Overview

Although political freedoms are usually enshrined in the legal acts of the highest legal force of the state, between the proclamation of rights and freedoms and their conscious implementation there can be a "great distance".

The person himself must be ready for the conscious exercise of these rights and freedoms. Therefore, an important role is played by the political culture of a person, that is, the ability to make a political choice, find a compromise, reach consensus, understand the possibility and legitimacy of conscious actions in each specific situation.

In a legal society, unlike a totalitarian one, only legal freedom can exist. However, freedom, not supported by law and practice of implementation, can turn into its opposite - arbitrariness, tyranny, violence.

There are two aspects to the definition of political freedom. The first - negative - freedom from coercion and pressure of the state in relation to a person, the second - positive - the goal of providing freedom (for what? Why?). In the latter sense, political freedom is presented as an opportunity to reveal the potential of the individual in the relationship between the individual, strata of society and the state.

History

The first reasoning about political freedoms we find in Aristotle's "Politics", where he talks about the contradictions between the category of "freedom" and the democratic form of government (Aristotle).

The first partial reflection in the legislation of political freedoms is found (although without the use of this term) in the English Magna Carta in 1215 (Magna Carta, 1215).

Subsequently, important milestones on the way of formalizing this concept and its classification were the English Bill of Rights, adopted in 1689, the French "Declaration of the Rights of Man and Citizen" of 1789 and the American Bill of Rights of 1791 (Held, 2000).

In the 19th century and at the beginning of the 20th century, the situation with political freedoms in different states develops differently. The original liberal set of civil and political rights (freedom and equality, suffrage, etc.) is still, in the modern sense, very limited (property electoral qualifications, political prohibitions, inequality of men and women, racial restrictions, etc.).

Only after the Second World War there was a qualitative leap in the development of the institution of human and civil rights, the leading role in the development of which is acquired by international law. On December 10, 1948, the UN General Assembly adopted the "Universal Declaration of Human Rights". In 1950, the European Convention for the Protection of Human Rights and Fundamental Freedoms was signed in Europe, creating a real mechanism for protecting declared rights - the European Court of Human Rights. In 1966, under the auspices of the UN, the International Covenant on Civil and Political Rights and the International Covenant on Economic, Social and Cultural Rights were adopted (Karumidze, 2003). These and subsequent documents approved the international standard of human and civil rights and guarantees for the provision of these rights with the aim of incorporation (reflection) in the constitutional system of the participating states.

The Difference in Interpretations

There is a significant difference in the understanding of "true" political freedoms by different philosophical schools and political currents.

The left ranks as such freedom from poverty, hunger, incurable diseases, etc., but right-liberal politicians, in particular Friedrich August von Hayek and Milton Friedman, object to such an abuse of the concept. Anarchists have their own view on this, calling the freedom supported by the capitalists "selfish" (Heywood, 2002).

Some people see political freedom as synonymous with democracy, while others find significant differences between the two concepts.

Ecologists argue that political freedoms should include restrictions on the use of ecosystems.

There are many philosophical discussions about the nature of political freedom, the different types of freedoms, and the degree to which freedom is desirable. For example, determinists argue that all human actions are predetermined and, therefore, freedom is an illusion, and Isaiah Berlin distinguished between the negative and positive sides of political freedom.

To date, discussions continue, and the meaning of the term, its nature and components is continuously refined.

In general, Political rights and freedoms differ from personal, social, economic and other rights in that, as a rule, they are closely related to belonging to the citizenship of a given state. They are one of the groups of fundamental constitutional rights and freedoms of citizens, as they determine their participation in the public and political life of the country. Political rights typically include:

- Equality before the law - the absence of estates;
- Freedom of conscience - the right to have any beliefs, including to profess any religion or not to profess any;
- Freedom of speech and press - prohibition of censorship;

- Freedom of assembly - the right to hold meetings both indoors and outdoors;
- Freedom of association - the right to form unions without asking permission;
- Freedom to strike;
- The right to apply.
- The right to take part in the government of one's country (Chitadze, 2016).

Equality Before the Law

Equality before the law, equality of rights is the most important principle of democracy and classical liberalism, according to which all citizens are equal before the law, regardless of their race, nationality, gender, sexual orientation, place of residence, position in society, religious and political beliefs. Violation of this principle is called discrimination.

Equality focuses on human rights and their limitations. The subject of special attention is the legislative protection of rights and equal access of all citizens to the legal system.

Equality before the law includes the equal duty of citizens to abide by the law and the equal treatment of law enforcement agencies towards various violators of the same norms. The latter is closely related to the principle of the rule of law, since it requires that laws be treated equally by those who make them and those who have supreme power. Justice should not take into account the origin, power, wealth or social position of the persons standing before it. The jurisdiction of the courts that rule in the cases of ordinary citizens should extend to all citizens.

Emergence

The concept of equality of citizens before the law arose in ancient Greece during the formation of city-states. The Greeks abandoned the reverence for royal power as a key value of social organization, which was characteristic of most civilizations of that time. In the city-states, the most important decisions were made with the participation of all male citizens, who received this right in exchange for participation in hostilities. At the same time, the principle of equality applied only to the citizens of the city (they were also members of the phalanx during the wars), without touching women and slaves.

Generalization of Legal Norms

Laws should formulate the conditions for their applicability in general terms, without pointing to specific individuals, organizations or small social groups. They should not be published to solve specific problems, if under other circumstances similar actions of the authorities would be illegal. However, in some cases the generalization requirement runs into difficulties. For example, in welfare states, some rules apply to persons of a clearly defined socio-economic status, and because part of society does not consider these laws justified, from the point of view of critics, they represent a form of legal discrimination.

Equal Access to the Legal System

Due to social inequality, some people have better access to resources to protect their interests and, therefore, a better chance of winning a lawsuit. Correction of such trends is often associated with objective difficulties, which are complicated by the above requirement for the generalization of legal norms and procedures.

In History

Legalism (beginning of the 8th century BC). Guan Zhong, the prime minister of the State of Qi proclaimed the principle "The ruler and officials, high and low, noble and vile, everyone must follow the law. This is what is called the great art of government." (Mkurnalizde, Khamkhadze, 2000).

The Athenian politician Solon (beginning of the 6th century BC), one of the famous ancient Greek "Seven Wise Men", took credit for his ability to maintain equality (Mkurnalizde, Khamkhadze, 2000).

In the World

Article 7 of the Universal Declaration of Human Rights states:

All people are equal before the law and are entitled, without distinction, to the equal protection of the law. All human beings are entitled to equal protection against any form of discrimination in violation of this Declaration and against any incitement to such discrimination (UN, 1949).

Freedom of Conscience

Freedom of conscience is a natural right to independently form beliefs and values that contribute to self-actualization. The concept of "freedom of conscience" includes a wider range of issues than the concept of "freedom of religion". The essence of freedom of conscience is usually studied from the point of view of philosophy, ethics, political science and religious studies.

History - Reformation

The 15th century was marked in Europe by the beginning of the Reformation, within which, according to a number of researchers, "the very idea of freedom of conscience came to light." The famous 95 Wittenberg theses of Martin Luther, which became the main document of the Reformation, linked the freedom of conscience of a Christian with the demand for free preaching and the unhindered dissemination of Holy Scripture, which was traditionally considered the prerogative of the Church. Thus, the main task of the Reformation was to eliminate the dominant influence of the Catholic Church as an adherent of the reaction, which, among other things, was the largest feudal lord in Europe. Sebastian Castellio was one of the first to raise the question of freedom of conscience in his pamphlet De haereticis, an sint persequendi (1554), published under a pseudonym (Chitadze, 2016).

Bill of Rights

The British Bill of Rights of 1689 recognized the right of a person to have his own opinions and beliefs, to follow his beliefs, no matter what others advise, etc. (Shubitidze, 2009)

Declaration of the Rights of Man and Citizen

In France, the principle of freedom of conscience was first proclaimed in Article 10 of the Declaration of the Rights of Man and of the Citizen (1789), which states that "no one may be persecuted for his convictions, even religious ones, provided that their promulgation is not threatens public order." The Constitution proclaimed "freedom of religious worship" (September 1791). The French Civil Code of

1804 - the Napoleonic code does not deal with religious issues at all, thus demonstrating that the state is in its fundamental foundations secular (Chitadze, 2016).

US Constitution

The first US Constitution of 1787 did not contain a list of inalienable rights, since the founding fathers proceeded from the fact that the rights naturally belonging to a person do not need to be confirmed in the text of the Basic Law. Their enumeration could be perceived as an exhaustive list of rights and freedoms, which could lead to infringement of rights not included in the list. The lack of a list of federally enshrined rights and freedoms in the Constitution caused criticism of this document. The newly elected US Congress in 1789 was proposed draft amendments containing provisions on political and personal rights. The first ten amendments to the US Constitution, which constituted the federal Bill of Rights, were ratified by the end of 1791 (Chitadze, 2016). Amendments were adopted providing for freedom of religion, freedom of speech and the press, the right of the people to peacefully assemble and petition the government, the inviolability of the person, home, papers and property, and other rights.

Universal Declaration of Human Rights

The Universal Declaration of Human Rights was adopted at the third session of the UN General Assembly by resolution 217 A (III) of December 10, 1948 and defined basic human rights. Article 18 of the Declaration states:

"Everyone has the right to freedom of thought, conscience and religion; this right includes freedom to change his religion or belief and freedom, either alone or in community with others and in public or private, to manifest his religion or belief in teaching, worship and observance of religious and ritual rites" (UN, 1948).

Modernity: Freedom of Conscience and Separation of Church and State

The relationship between freedom of conscience and the separation of church and state seems to be ambiguous. On the one hand, there is a positive correlation between the separation of church and state and the provision of freedom of conscience in this state. For example, Sharia includes both legal and religious norms. For example, in 2006, the Sharia court of Afghanistan sentenced Abdul Rahman, a Muslim who changed his religion, to death. On the other hand, the separation of church and state does not guarantee freedom of conscience, and non-separation does not exclude it. Thus, countries with a state church are known (for example, Great Britain and most other monarchical states of Europe), nevertheless, providing their subjects with the right to profess a religion of their choice or not to profess any. On the contrary, in some states with a separated church (all communist regimes, Iraq, Turkey), adherents of many religions were discriminated against.

The separation of the church from the state took place: in Russia - 1918 (Decree on the separation of the church from the state and the school from the church), France - ratified in 1905. Columbia - 1853. USA – 1787 (Chitadze, 2016).

Freedom of Speech

Freedom of speech is the right of a person to freely express his opinion. This right includes freedom to hold opinions and freedom to receive and impart information and ideas without any interference from public authorities and regardless of frontiers. The exercise of these freedoms, which imposes duties and responsibilities, may be subject to such formalities, conditions, restrictions or sanctions as are prescribed by law and are necessary in a democratic society in the interests of national security, territorial integrity or public order, for the prevention of disorder or crime, for the protection health and morals, to protect the reputation or rights of others, to prevent the disclosure of information received in confidence, or to maintain the authority and impartiality of the judiciary.

This right is mentioned in a number of international ones, including: the Universal Declaration of Human Rights (Article 19), the European Convention for the Protection of Human Rights and Fundamental Freedoms (Article 10) (Un, 1948).

Utilitarian and Liberal Approaches

Freedom of speech is closely related to issues of establishing the truth, self-government, ensuring the flexibility of the political system, self-realization of the individual, natural human rights and their protection.

Historically, it has emerged as a tool to ensure awareness and maintain a high level of competence in public authorities. Thus, the English Bill of Rights of 1689 guaranteed members of Parliament complete freedom to discuss the affairs of the kingdom and officials, without which his work would be ineffective. This feature of freedom of speech is still valued even by some authoritarian regimes that leave small and safe for their stability "islands of freedom" (for example, uncensored small-circulation newspapers) in order to have an objective idea of what is really happening in the region and beyond. outside. More broadly, this freedom has come to be seen as one of the essential conditions for seeking and establishing truth. As J. Mill wrote, "the special evil of the suppression of opinions is that all of humanity is destitute, and those who are against this idea are even more than its supporters. If the thought is right, they are deprived of the opportunity to replace the lie with the truth; if it is false, they lose ... the clear appearance and lively impression of truth tinged with lies ... Complete freedom of expression is a necessary condition to justify claims to truth (Held, 2000).

Another aspect of the 1689 Bill of Rights was that it regarded Parliament as the highest representative body of national self-government, and therefore that the right to know the workings of government came from the people. With the development of democracy, the latter has acquired particular relevance (Held, 2000).

From the point of view of this political system, the most important aspect of freedom of speech is the freedom to disseminate such information that may affect the outcome of elections or the work of government. Here, in most modern liberal democracies, legislative restrictions are low and are imposed only for the duration of election campaigns: publications in the media should make it clear whether their goal is to influence elections and who is really responsible for them. In order for people to be sufficiently informed on the eve of elections, they must familiarize themselves with various points of view. This primarily applies to the main sources of information for voters (today it is television) and is ensured either by access to a wide range of uncensored and independent sources, or by a policy of pluralism in the media holding a monopoly position.

When combined with democratic procedures that hold the government accountable to the electorate, freedom of speech becomes one of the most important tools for protecting all human rights. As Karl Popper noted, it also plays a key role in ensuring the stability of liberal democracy, since it makes it possible to adjust the work of the government and even the political system as a whole to the objective needs of society.

Immanuel Kant

Liberalism revealed the ethical side of freedom of speech, which on an emotional level began to dominate the utilitarian view outlined above. Here, human dignity and objective needs (natural rights), given to a person from birth, come to the fore. The concept has Christian roots, and its early popularizers (beginning with Hugo Grotius) often referred to the biblical quotation: "And God created man in his own image" (Gen. 1:27). However, it was later reformulated by Kant in terms of the secular theory that the principles of human society have a fundamental natural nature. This approach, first reflected in the American "Bill of Rights" and the French "Declaration of the Rights of Man and Citizen" (1789), means that only such restrictions on freedom of speech that are forced and morally justified are permissible:

Free expression of thoughts and opinions is one of the most precious human rights; every citizen, therefore, can freely speak, write, print, answering only for the abuse of this freedom in cases provided for by law. ("Declaration of the Rights of Man and Citizen", art. 11)

Today, legitimate restrictions include the protection of national security, public order, health and morals, the reputation and rights of others (including copyright), confidential information, and justice (Heywood, 2002).

Parenting and Self-censorship

Many liberal thinkers, beginning with J. J. Rousseau, have noted the importance of teaching a culture of free speech. In their opinion, conducting a discussion in order to establish the truth and a tolerant attitude towards alternative points of view contributes to progress and harmony in society. However, the political and cultural aspects of liberalism are in some conflict with each other (Chitadze, 2011).

From a cultural point of view, freedom of speech strives for the independent development of one's own convictions for each person, the independent formulation of standards and life goals by him. On the other hand, the people, endowed with the power of self-government, must use it reasonably and for the good of society. Thus, people should not only have the freedom to discuss all public issues, but also be able to use it to make an informed choice.

However, the upbringing of "responsible citizens" goes beyond pure education and is in fact a kind of censorship, since it makes personal beliefs dependent on public morality (A. de Tocqueville). A number of modern critics point out that the loss of independent thinking increases the risk of manipulation of public consciousness. Nevertheless, the majority of the population of democratic countries (especially conservatives) find such interference in the sphere of the individual to some extent justified and necessary.

The other side of this issue is the regulation of private enterprises. This is especially true of advertising, which is a form of "commercial free speech" and is often subject to numerous legal restrictions in the name of consumer protection, public order and fair competition.

However, even with regard to ordinary freedom of speech, government regulation of the media and leading advertisers, as well as the high share of government sources in the information market, leads to "self-censorship", when private media impose preemptive restrictions for fear of losing significant sources of income. Self-censorship is also subject to industries whose income is largely dependent on public opinion, such as the film industry.

Because of this, neo-liberalists believe that the key to ensuring freedom of speech is private property and non-interference of the state in private business activities. They argue that this not only puts a barrier to state censorship and removes most of the grounds for self-censorship, but also opens up additional opportunities for the dissemination of independent opinions, including private publishing houses and press advertising. Neo-liberals disagree with left-liberal supporters of state funding of the media (as well as election campaigns, education, etc.). They believe that guaranteed support for the media is necessary for them to function independently of both public opinion and capital.

Press and Media Freedom Ratings

In the field of comparative politics, there are organizations and projects that seek to measure the level of freedom of speech in the world or in certain regions:

- Freedom of the Press: An annual study and accompanying rating of the state of press freedom in countries around the world, published by the international non-governmental organization Freedom House.
- Worldwide Press Freedom Index - “Worldwide Press Freedom Index”: an annual study and accompanying rating on the state of press freedom in countries around the world, published by the international non-governmental organization Reporters Without Borders.
- Media Sustainability Index - published by IREX
- African Media Barometer: published by Friedrich-Ebert-Stiftung

The methodologies for these ratings have been published and include both objective parameters (for example, the number of journalists killed in connection with their professional activities) and subjective assessments of experts (for example, the level of self-censorship in the media). Quantitative indicators are usually considered more reliable, but after statistical processing they do not always reflect the full picture, so they are often supplemented with qualitative parameters. For example, a high number of media outlets does not necessarily indicate that they are diverse and reflect a wide range of opinions. The dissemination of biased or unverified information discredits the very concept of media freedom. According to some analysts, in the long run, the most important criterion is whether the media listens to citizens and acts on their behalf (Chitadze, 2016).

An analysis of the methods used in these indices revealed a number of shortcomings. Some parameters are normative, such as considering state media ownership or state subsidies to private media as a negative contribution to freedom of expression. This has often served as the basis for accusations of bias, as well as advancing American or European political interests. Further, the main subject of study is usually television, press and radio, while digital media receive little attention. Despite these shortcomings, many experts believe that the methodologies are statistically consistent and come to similar conclusions, so they are an important, useful, and credible tool for studying media freedom around the world (Chitadze, 2016).

To further improve methodologies, UNESCO has developed a set of indicators that the organization considers to be culturally and politically neutral. The organization itself does not currently measure the level of freedom of speech.

Freedom of Assembly

Freedom of assembly - the right to hold rallies, pickets, demonstrations, as well as to gather indoors; belongs to the human rights of the "first generation" (civil and political). Freedom of assembly is enshrined in Article 20 of the Universal Declaration of Human Rights, Article 21 of the International Covenant on Civil and Political Rights, Article 11 of the European Convention for the Protection of Human Rights and Fundamental Freedoms (UN, 1948). Usually only the freedom of peaceful assembly is protected.

Basic Principles

In 2007, under the auspices of the OSCE Office for Democratic Institutions and Human Rights, the Guidelines on Freedom of Peaceful Assembly were developed (Karumidze, 2003). The document notes the impossibility of creating a single model law on freedom of assembly that could be adopted by all participating countries, but it formulated the minimum standards that should be observed by the authorities of participating countries in the process of regulating the right to freedom of assembly. The following are the main provisions of this document.

Only peaceful gatherings of citizens are subject to state protection. An assembly is defined as peaceful if its organizers pursue peaceful intentions. At the same time, the concept of "peaceful" includes such behavior that may irritate those who do not agree with the ideas of the participants in this meeting, and also includes such behavior that may be aimed at preventing the actions of third parties.

Principle 1. Presumption in Favor of Holding Assemblies

Since the right to freedom of peaceful assembly is a fundamental right, its implementation should be carried out without external regulation, as far as possible. Those wishing to participate in the assembly do not have to ask permission to do so. Legislation should clearly define the presumption in favor of freedom of assembly. At any opportunity to interpret the norms of the law in favor of holding an assembly, it should not be hindered.

Principle 2. Duty of the State to Protect a Peaceful Assembly

The state is obliged to provide a full set of mechanisms and procedures for the effective practical implementation of freedom of assembly without excessive bureaucratic regulation.

Principle 3. Legality

Any restrictions must be based on the provisions of the law, and the law itself must comply with international human rights law and its rules must be clearly formulated and not cause discrepancies. Everyone should be able to unequivocally determine whether his behavior is contrary to the law or not.

Principle 4. Proportionality

Any restrictions on freedom of assembly must be proportionate. When pursuing legitimate aims, the authorities should give preference to measures that provide the least level of interference with the conduct of an assembly. Limitations provided for by law should not be applied automatically, but only taking into account the specific situation in each specific case. Forced cessation of assemblies should be taken as a last resort when it is impossible to achieve legitimate goals in other ways.

Principle 5. Good Administrative Practice

Legislation should clearly state which body has the power to regulate freedom of assembly. The general public should be given free access to complete and reliable information about the activities of this body, and its decision-making procedures should be transparent.

Principle 6. Non-Discrimination

When regulating the freedom of assembly, the authorities are obliged to provide an equal opportunity to exercise this right to any person or groups of persons. No restrictions are allowed on the basis of race, gender, nationality, religion, political views, belonging to certain social groups, and the like (Karumidze, 2003).

The Role of High Technologies

According to experts, the development of artificial intelligence technology and face recognition poses a potential threat to freedom of assembly. The government can use facial recognition to identify those participating in a peaceful rally and then harass them and thus suppress freedom of speech and assembly.

The Right to Take Part in the Government of One's Country

Article 21 of the Universal Declaration of Human Rights

Article 21:

1. Everyone has the right to take part in the government of his country, directly or through freely chosen representatives.
2. Everyone has the right of equal access to public service in his country.
3. The will of the people must be the basis of the authority of the government; this will must find expression in periodic and non-falsified elections, which must be held with universal and equal suffrage, by secret ballot or by other equivalent forms ensuring freedom of voting (UN, 1948).

Socio-Economic Rights

These are the possibilities of the individual in the sphere of production and distribution of material goods, designed to ensure the satisfaction of economic and closely related spiritual needs and interests of a person. Socio-economic rights include:

- Labor rights (the right to work and freedom of work);
- The right to protection of the family, motherhood, fatherhood and childhood;
- The right to social security;

- The right to housing;
- The right to education;
- The right to health care and medical care;
- The right to an eight-hour day, fair working conditions, equal pay for work of equal value, etc.

Labor Law

Labor law is an independent branch of legislation that regulates relations in the sphere of labor. It is a relatively young branch of law (the moment of origin refers to the turn of the 19th-20th centuries).

Recently, public law blocks have been distinguished from labor law, such as the right to social security (in relation to public non-budgetary "social funds") or the specifics of hiring labor for the performance of exclusively public (state and municipal) service functions.

Subject

The subject of labor law is labor and other directly related relations. Thus, we can distinguish:

- individual labor relations (ITO)
- public relations closely related to labor (OOTT) in terms of:
    - labor organization and labor management;
    - employment with this employer;
    - training and additional professional education of employees directly from this employer;
    - social partnership, collective bargaining, conclusion of collective agreements and agreements;
    - the participation of workers and trade unions in the establishment of working conditions and the application of labor legislation in cases provided for by law;
    - liability of employers and employees in the labor sphere;
    - state control (supervision), trade union control over compliance with labor legislation (including labor protection legislation) and other regulatory legal acts containing labor law norms;
    - resolution of labor disputes;
    - compulsory social insurance in cases stipulated by federal laws.

Employment Contract as a Source of Law

A number of scholars consider it extremely controversial to single out an employment contract as a source of law, which by its nature is an act of realization of a right. The legalization of labor contracts as a source of law is fraught with dispersion or confusion of key legal categories. Recognition of an individual contract as legal would automatically mean recognition of the status of a lawmaker for its participants.

Morality in the System of Sources of Labor Law

Moral standards have a special impact on the legal regulation of labor relations. By themselves, they are not sources of law, but they have two forms of consolidation: as legal norms in legal acts and as customs and traditions.

Custom

At present, a number of scientists in the field of labour are advocating the recognition of a legal custom (customs of law enforcement practice) in labor relations as a source of law. Examples of such peculiar real regulators of labor relations are written applications for employment that have become widespread in practice, drawing up bypass sheets upon dismissal, examples of the interpretation by judicial practice of the "free expression of the employee's will" upon dismissal of their own free will, etc. The examples cited by supporters of the labor law custom indicate either about cases of essentially reducing the level of labor rights established by law, or about the interpretation of labor law norms by courts.

International Sources of Labor Law

With regard to the generally recognized principles and norms of international law and international treaties, a special place in the system of sources of labor law of these acts is due to the fact that they provide guarantees for the implementation of international legal standards of the labor rights of an employee.

- Acts of the United Nations Organization. The main contribution of the UN to the international legal regulation of social protection is the definition of a catalog of basic human rights that must be provided in the legislation of any country that claims to be considered civilized. The Universal Declaration of Human Rights (1948) is primarily a programmatic political document that formulates a package of basic inalienable and inalienable social and labor human rights: the right to work, the right to free choice of work, the right to protection from unemployment, the right to fair and favorable working conditions, etc.;
- Covenants and conventions of the United Nations, ratified by the state, are legally binding. According to the International Covenant on Economic, Social and Cultural Rights (1966), the states participating in the Covenant recognize the right of every person to work, safe and healthy working conditions, the right to rest, to join trade unions, etc. (Karumidze, 1966);
- Acts of the International Labor Organization. The leading source of international legal regulation of social and labor rights are the acts of the ILO. One of the main activities of the ILO is rule-making - the development and adoption of international legal acts (declarations, conventions, recommendations) containing international social and labor standards. As of July 1, 2022, the ILO unites 187 states, in which more than 98% of the world's population lives (ILO, 2022). The ILO conventions and recommendations, as a result of its standard-setting activities, remain the main means of implementing the policy of this organization, its goals and objectives. By early 2008, 188 conventions and 199 ILO recommendations had been adopted (Aleksidze, 2016). At present, the ILO is concentrating its efforts and the efforts of its members on the active ratification and application of the fundamental conventions. These include eight conventions: "On Freedom of Association and Protection of the Right to Organize" 1948 (No. 87), "On the Application of the Principles of the Right to Organize and Collective Bargaining" 1949 (No. 98), "On Forced or Compulsory Labor 1930 (No. 29), "On the Abolition of Forced Labor" 1957 (No. 105), "On Discrimination in Labor and Employment" 1958 (No. 111), "On Equal Remuneration" 1951 (No. 100), "On the Minimum Age for Employment" 1973 (No. 138), "On the Prohibition and Measures for the Elimination of the Worst Forms of Child Labor" 1999 (No. 182) (Aleksidze, 2016);
- International regional acts in the sphere of labor - acts adopted by regional organizations of states, such as the Council of Europe, the European Union, etc. Conventions of regional international

organizations of states are a kind of multilateral international treaties of a regional nature with a limited number of participants. The Council of Europe has adopted more than 150 human rights conventions, including those containing social and labor standards. Among them, the leading place is occupied by the Council of Europe Convention "For the Protection of Human Rights and Fundamental Freedoms", the European Social Charter of 1961 (as amended in 1996). The main regional European labor standards are enshrined mainly in these two acts (Karumidze, 2003);

- International legal customs is precisely an international norm, which is designed to regulate the relationship of subjects of international law.

Labor Relations

There are several theories. The first concept of "non-independent" or "dependent" labor was developed by L. S. Tal at the beginning of the 20th century. Formally, a free and equal worker is included in the economic activity of an enterprise alien to him and becomes a non-independent worker (Chitadze, 2016).

Labor Law. Labor law is a set of legal norms, administrative decisions and precedents that establish rights and obligations for employees and employers (individual entrepreneurs and organizations). Essentially, it regulates labor relations between trade unions, employers and workers. In Canada, the labor laws governing the rights and obligations of unionized workers and employers are different from the laws governing the rights and obligations of employers and non-unionized workers. In most countries, however, no such distinction is made. However, there are two main categories in labor law. The first is collective labor law, which regulates relations between the employee, the employer and the trade union (collective labor agreement). The second is individual labor law, which establishes the rights of employees to work when concluding an employment contract (individual labor contract). The labor movement played a key role in the process of passing laws regarding the protection of labor rights in the 19th and 20th centuries. Since the beginning of the industrial revolution, labor rights have been an integral part of social and economic development. The emergence of labor law is the result of both the struggle of the working class for better working conditions, obtaining the right to association, and the demands of employers to limit the powers of workers' associations, to prevent an increase in labor costs. Employers' spending could be increased as union demands for higher wages are met, as well as legislation that places high demands on health, safety and equal working conditions. Workers' associations, such as trade unions, can also participate in the resolution of labor disputes and gain political power that employers can oppose. As a result, the state of labor legislation in any period of time reflects the result of the struggle of various strata of society.

Work Time. With the development of industrialization and the introduction of technology, the number of working hours has decreased significantly. The 14-15 hour working day was the norm, and the 16 hour working day was not considered an exception. The use of child labor, usually in factories, was common. In 1788, in England and Scotland, about 2/3 of the workers in the new water textile mills were children. The struggle of the movement for an eight-hour day eventually led to the fact that in 1833 in England a law was passed limiting the working day of miners to 12 hours, for children to 8 hours. In 1848, a 10-hour working day was established, in the future, the duration of working hours with the preservation of wages was reduced even more. The first Labor Act was passed in Great Britain in 1802. After England, Germany became the first European country to change its labor laws; Chancellor Bismarck's main goal was to undermine the foundations of the Social Democratic Party of Germany (SPD). In 1878, various anti-socialist measures were taken by Bismarck, but despite this, the socialists continued to win the majority of seats in the Reichstag. Then the Chancellor changed his approach to solving the problem of socialism. In order to calm the discontent of the working class, he introduced a series of paternalistic social reforms, in which social security was guaranteed for the first time. In 1883, the Compulsory Hospital Insurance Act was passed, providing for the right of workers to health insurance; while the employee paid 2/3, and the employer 1/3 of the amount of money. In 1884 the Accident Insurance Act was passed, while in 1889 old-age and disability pensions were established. Other laws restricted the employment of women and children. These efforts have not been fully successful; the working class never became the backbone of Bismarck's conservative government. In 1841, the first Labor Law was passed in France. However, it only limited the working hours of underage miners, and was practically not applied until the period of the Third Republic (Gudushauri, 2010).

Health and safety at work. Labor legislation also provides for provisions relating to the right to work in conditions that meet safety requirements. In 1802, the first factory law was drafted to protect the safety and health of children working in weaving mills.

Fight against discrimination. This provision means that discrimination based on race or gender is unacceptable. Unfair Dismissal International Labor Organization Convention No. 158 provides that "employment relations with workers shall not be terminated without legitimate grounds and until such time as he has been given the opportunity to defend himself in connection with the charges against him." Thus, on April 28, 2006, after the unofficial cancellation of the First French Employment Contract, the Labor Court recognized the New Employment Contract, which was contrary to international law and therefore illegal and null and void (Gudushauri, 2010).

Child Labour. Child labor is the engagement of children in work before they reach the age prescribed by law or custom. Most countries and international organizations view child labor as a form of exploitation. In the past, child labor was widespread, but after the advent of universal schooling, the recognition of the concepts of work safety and children's rights, the areas of child labor gradually began to decrease. Forms of child labor include working in factories, mines, mining or mining, working in agriculture, helping parents develop small businesses (such as selling food), or doing odd jobs. Some children work as tour guides, sometimes combined with work in shops and restaurants (where they may also work as waiters). Other children are forced to do tedious and repetitive tasks such as assembling boxes or polishing shoes. However, the number of children working in factories in difficult conditions is not so large compared to the same indicator of employment in the so-called informal sector - "sales on the street, work in agriculture or at home" - that is, everything that is beyond the reach of official inspectors and media control.

Collective Labor Law. Collective labor law governs tripartite relations between the employer, employee and trade union organizations. Trade unions are a form of association of workers whose activities are regulated by the norms of labor legislation. However, this is not the only existing form of public association of citizens. In the United States, for example, workers' association centers are associations that are not covered by all the rules of labor union law.

Unions. Legislation in some countries provides for the compliance of trade unions with a number of requirements in the conduct of their activities. For example, voting is mandatory in cases of organizing a strike and collecting membership fees for the implementation of political projects. The right to join a trade union (prohibition of the employer's side) is not always legally enshrined. Under the terms of some codes, certain obligations may be imposed on union members, for example, to support the opinion of the majority when going on strike.

Strikes. Strikes are one of the most effective means of resolving labor disputes. In most countries, strikes are legal when a number of conditions are met, including the following:

1. holding a strike must comply with democratic processes ("wild strike" is recognized as illegal);
2. "Strike of solidarity", that is, not officially employed workers are prohibited from taking part in strikes;
3. a general strike may be prohibited in order to maintain public order;
4. workers in a number of professions may be prohibited from participating in strikes (airport workers, medical workers, teachers, policemen, firefighters, etc.);
5. Strikes may be carried out without interruption by employees of their duties. Such strikes take place in hospitals, or, for example, in Japan, when workers, increasing labor productivity, violate the established production plan.

A boycott is a refusal to carry out purchases, sales, other trade transactions from the trade turnover as a protest against their immoral behavior. Throughout history, workers have resorted to such forms as slowdowns, sabotage in order to gain greater freedom to regulate labor issues or reduce working hours.

Pickets. Picketing is a spread of action among employees, often popping up during strikes. Persons of wage labor gather outside production growth, where there is a strike, the opportunity to acquire as many workers as possible, to make it difficult to get to a worker who does not want to join a trade union. In many of these countries, action is limited to labor laws, laws prohibiting demonstrations, or the imposition of a ban on picket elections. For example, labor legislation may provide for a ban on secondary picketing (picketing arranged by employees of one employer at another enterprise not directly involved in the disputed situation of the employer, for example, carried out with the aim of disrupting the supply of raw materials to an enterprise where workers and employer) or flying pickets. The legislation may provide for rules prohibiting obstruction of the legitimate interests of others (refusal to work in a trade union, for example, is legal).

Participation of Employees in Conflict Management. The right to participate in the discussion, the introduction of what is enshrined in German lawmaking, is provided in one form or another in all countries of continental Europe, such as Holland and the Czech Republic. It includes the right to be elected to represent workers on the board of registrars. In Germany, at the level of the conference, it is fixed, according to the statement made at the meeting of the meeting of the trade union body. However, the German model provides for a bicameral board in which the supervisory board visits the executive board. Members of the Supervisory Board are elected by shareholders and trade unions in equal numbers, except in cases where the head of the Supervisory Board, in accordance with the law, is a representative of the shareholders. If full recognition is not achieved, a bipartisan consensus is established between them, established by the social democratic agreement of Helmut Schmidt in 1976. In the United Kingdom, recommendations were made, which were enshrined in the Bullock Report (Industrial Democracy). Published in 1977 by Callaghan's Labor backbone, they provided for a bicameral council (Chitadze, 2016). However, the results of such a proposal were to become more radical. Due to the lack of a bicameral board requirement in the British legislature, board members were to be elected by the unions. However, no action was taken and Britain "plunged into a winter of discontent." This was due to the commission's proposal for the Fifth Company Law Project, which was never implemented.

The International Labour Organization

The International Labor Organization (ILO), headquartered in Geneva, is one of the oldest international organizations and a surviving body created within the League that followed the First World War. Her position is that "labor is not a commodity", items that can be disposed of in the same way as goods, services or capital, and that respect for human dignity requires equality and fairness in the workplace. The ILO has adopted many Conventions applied by member countries, which are the main standards in the field of labor. Countries demand to ratify the Convention and consider national legislation as part of the investigation with it. However, their performance is not secured by stress resistance; even if the provisions are strictly observed, it should be taken into account that they are not harmonized with each other.

European Labor Law

The European Working Time Directive limits the working week to 48 hours and provides for a maximum of 11 hours of rest in every 24-hour hours. As with all EU Directives, its inclusion in national law is mandatory. While the Directive applies to all Member States, the UK may be able to extend the 48-hour workweek. In France, by contrast, the legislation is stricter, limiting the working week to 35 hours (but optional hours are still allowed). In 2006, the controversial Securities Services Directive (the so-called Blockstein Directive) was adopted (Neil, 2010).

National Labor Law

- **UK Labor Law:** The first labor laws in Great Britain were the Factory Laws (first 1802, then 1833) and the Master and Servant Act 1832. In the UK until 1960, the employment contract served as the main element of legal regulation. Since then, this regulatory framework has been greatly expanded by the "equality movement" and influence from the European Union. There are three sources of law: acts of Parliament, called statutes, other regulations (issued by the Secretary of State and Parliament) and case law (which is the result of the activities of the courts). The first major act in the field of labor law was the Equal Pay Act of 1970, although it did not enter into force until 1972 because it was radical. This Law was adopted in order to develop coordinated positions on the issue of ensuring equality between male and female labor. Since the election of the Labor government in 1997, there have been many changes in UK labor law. These were related to the increase in maternity and paternity rights, the introduction of a national minimum wage, the adoption of the Working Hours Directive, establishing working hours, rest breaks and the right to paid annual leave. In order to tighten discrimination laws, a ban was introduced on discrimination based on age, religion or belief, sexual orientation, and gender, race, and disability (Mkurnalizde, Khamkhadze, 2000).
- **Labor Law of the People's Republic of China:** The basis of the labor legislation of the People's Republic of China is the Law of the People's Republic of China "On Labor" (05.07.1994). This law regulates a wide range of issues: state promotion of employment, conclusion of individual and collective labor contracts, determination of working and rest periods, payment of wages, labor protection for women and minors, labor safety, vocational education and training, social insurance, resolution of labor disputes, state control in the sphere of labor, legal liability for violations of labor legislation.

Another important law, the Law of the People's Republic of China "On Employment Contracts" (current version - dated December 28, 2012) - is dedicated to the employment contract. This law regulates the conclusion, execution, termination and termination of individual labor contracts, and also establishes special rules on collective labor agreements, part-time labor relations, the use of agency work, and the payment of severance pay upon dismissal (Chitadze, 2016).

The regulation of labor relations in the PRC is also carried out by by-laws (administrative legal acts, departmental acts) and judicial clarifications (clarifications of the Supreme People's Court of the PRC). The activity of trade unions is carried out in accordance with the Law of the People's Republic of China "On Trade Unions". In practice, strikes are strictly prohibited, although they are legally permitted by law.

- **Labor Law in France:** The first labor laws in France are the Laws of Waldeck Rousseau, adopted in 1884. In the period from 1936 to 1938. thanks to the efforts of the Popular Front, laws were passed on the introduction of 2-week paid holidays, a 40-hour working week, not counting overtime hours. The result of the so-called Grenelle negotiations, held on May 25 and 26, 1968, was the reduction of the working week to 44 hours and the creation of trade unions in every enterprise. The minimum wage was increased by 25%. In 2000, the government of Prime Minister Lionel Jospin passed a law reducing the working week from 39 to 35 hours. Five years later, the Conservative government of Prime Minister Dominique de Villepin adopted a "new model of employment contract" (the so-called contract of first employment). By giving employers more latitude in labor law, the first-hire contract drew criticism from unions and other opponents who argued that it infringed on part-time work rights. In 2006, he failed to pass the First Hire Contract Act through an emergency ballot, due to massive protests from students and unions. President Jacques Chirac had no choice but to cancel it (Alber, 2010).
- **Mexican Labor Law:** Mexican labor law grants workers the right to organize trade unions, participate in collective bargaining and strikes. The current state of the legislation reflects the historical relationship of the state with the confederation of Mexican workers. The Confederation of Labor is closely associated with the Institutional Revolutionary Party, which has been the ruling party under various names for more than seventy years. Although the law recognizes the rights of workers to strike and organize, the implementation of these rights in practice is hindered by corrupt ties between trade unions and employers.
- **US Labor Law:** In the United States, the length of the working day agreed with employers does not exceed 8 hours, which was established back in 1912. The provisions of the Wages and Hours Act of 1938 limited the maximum working week to 44 hours, and in 1950 the number of hours was reduced to 40. Green Cards entitle legal immigrants to work, as well as US citizens without a work permit. However, as a result of bureaucratic organization, illegal immigrants also have the opportunity to work in the US. Despite the established 40-hour working week, some professions require more working hours in order to complete the assigned tasks. For example, when preparing products for sale in the market, it is allowed to work more than 72 hours a week. However, this is not a duty, but a right. During the harvest period, a 24 hour rest is provided for every 72 hours of work for 7 days. Office workers, technical and medical staff cannot be fired for refusing to work more than 72 hours a week. The Fifth and Fourteenth Amendments to the US Constitution limit the powers of the federal and state governments to counter discrimination. The scope of private law is not subject to limitation by the Constitution. The Fifth Amendment prohibits the federal government from taking a person's life, liberty, or property without due process of law and pro-

vides for equal protection of the state. The Fourteenth Amendment prohibits states from violating human rights without due process of law and denying the equal protection of the law. Equal legal protection provides for limiting the powers of the federal and state governments to discriminate against employees, ex-employees, or job seekers on the basis of race, religion, and gender. Legal protection requires following a dismissal procedure before being dismissed if the employment relationship is terminated due to violation of human rights and freedoms, such as the right to freedom of speech or the right to property. The Employment Act of 1967 protects the rights of persons aged 40 and over against age discrimination. The objectives of the law are: - to promote the employment of older people on the basis of their abilities, and not to prohibit arbitrary discrimination on the basis of age in employment; — helping employers and employees find ways to address the impact of age on employment. The growth of labor productivity, the increase in the level of well-being leads to the fact that the preservation of the place of work and the restoration of work are impossible for older workers; It is common practice to impose arbitrary restrictions on age criteria, regardless of competence, which negatively affects the employment of older workers. The level of unemployment, especially long-term unemployment, among this age group of the population is quite high and leads to a loss of skills and self-esteem. Title VII of the Civil Rights Act is the primary federal law that prohibits discrimination by public and private employers, labor organizations, and employment agencies on the basis of race, color, religion, sex, and national origin (Gilbert, 2010).

Liability for Violation of Labor Law

Distinguish responsibility in the field of human labor:

1. According to the subject of responsibility:
    a. Responsibility of the employee to the employer
    b. Responsibility of the employer to the employee
2. According to the content of the violation of labor law:
    a. Violation of labor discipline by an employee
    b. Liability of the parties to labor relations

Parental Rights

Parental rights are the civil rights of a person acquired simultaneously with the assumption of duties for the upbringing and maintenance of the child.

The owner of parental rights can be both the biological parent of the child and the one who adopted him. parental rights include:

- The right to raise a child (priority over all other persons), to choose the form of his education and a specific educational institution;
- The right to represent the interests of the child in relations with any individuals and legal entities;
- The right of a parent living separately to communicate with the child, to receive information about him from educational, medical and other institutions;
- The right of minor parents to live together with the child and participate in his upbringing

- The right of disabled parents to receive maintenance from able-bodied children

When a child reaches the age of 18, parental rights terminate (except for the right of disabled parents to support). Termination of parental rights also occurs if children acquire full legal capacity before this age.

Deprivation of parental rights is carried out by a court decision in relation to each child separately and does not release from parental responsibilities (except in the case of adoption (adoption) of a child, when the child loses rights and is released from obligations in relation to his biological parent.

Establishing Paternity

Legal rights and obligations between parents and children arise on the basis of state registration of the origin of the child. By itself, the fact of consanguinity, not confirmed by law in the procedure for establishing paternity, does not give rise to legal rights and obligations of parents and children.

Paternity is usually established by the court in the following cases:

- One of the parents avoids submitting a joint application to the authorities registering the birth of the child;
- The actual father cannot be recognized as a father.

Moreover, if the actual father found out that another person was recorded as the father of the child, then the actual father can challenge this entry in court.

The established origin of the child from a particular person is the basis for the rights and obligations of both the parent and his children.

Deprivation of Parental Rights

If the parents, or one of them, evade their duties, abuse children, exercise mental or physical violence against them, are addicted to drugs or chronic alcoholism, have committed a crime against the health or life of their children, then they may be deprived of parental rights. Children whose parents are alive but deprived or limited in parental rights are called social orphans. In Russia, the most common causes of social orphanhood include parental alcoholism, extremely difficult financial situation, failure to fulfill parental responsibilities (for example, if parents leave the child alone for a long time, force the children to wander, do not maintain normal living conditions at home).

Social Security

Social security is a form of assistance organized by the state for an approved circle of persons, provided upon the occurrence of certain legal facts, in situations established by law, in order to equalize the social status of citizens.

Essential Features

- The state nature of the organizational and legal methods of distribution of the total social product established in society through the social security system. Sources of financing: at the expense of the state budget and special off-budget funds formed by the state (pension, medical insurance).

- Legislative consolidation of the list of social risks recognized by the state as grounds for providing certain types of social security. That is, the right to social security is established for a certain group of citizens only upon the occurrence of circumstances specified in the law; these are mainly events, for example, reaching a certain age, disability, death, birth.
- Fixing in the norms of law or in agreements sanctioned by the state, the circle of persons to be provided, that is, certain categories of citizens established by law (the disabled, those who have lost their breadwinner, children, families with children, the unemployed, victims of political repression, veterans, etc.).
- Rationing by the state of the social standard of security, below which it cannot be, by legislatively fixing the types of security, its level and conditions of provision.

Definition

There is no official definition of social security as a multidimensional phenomenon in the legislation. In the scientific and educational literature, the concept of social security is formulated by the authors in different ways, depending on what signs are taken as basic, basic for this phenomenon (see above).

Social Security Means:

- a form of distribution that guarantees citizens a normal level of living and cultural standards in excess of remuneration for work in old age, in the event of disability and the loss of a breadwinner;
- a system of material support and services for citizens due to age, illness, disability, unemployment, loss of a breadwinner, upbringing of children and in other cases established by law;
- the totality of public relations that develop between citizens, on the one hand, and state bodies, local governments, organizations, on the other hand, regarding the provision of medical care, pensions, benefits and other types of support to citizens at the expense of special funds, budgetary funds in the event of life circumstances entailing loss or decrease in income, increased expenses, low income, poverty, or on the distribution of extra-budgetary funds for social purposes and the redistribution of part of the state budget in order to meet the needs of citizens in the event of loss of a source of livelihood, incurring additional expenses or lack of the necessary subsistence minimum for objective socially significant reasons.

Essence of Social Security

The purpose of the social security system is manifested in its functions. The legal literature identifies four main functions of social security: economic, political, demographic, social and rehabilitation.

1. Economic function. The economic function is expressed in the provision of material support to citizens in a difficult life situation, in promoting the development of social production in general and in individual sectors of the national economy, the economic rise of priority development zones, etc.
2. Political function. The political function is aimed at bringing together the social level of various segments of the population, creating conditions that ensure a decent life for every person. It is designed to stabilize social relations in the field of social protection of the population.

3. Demographic function. The demographic function contributes to stimulating the growth of the country's population, the reproduction of a healthy generation, the growth of life expectancy of citizens, etc.
4. Social rehabilitation function. The social rehabilitation function of social security is associated with meeting the specific needs of the elderly and disabled citizens. It is expressed in the creation of conditions conducive to the preservation of their legal status and the protection of the health of all citizens.
5. Social security performs another very important function - protective. First of all, it is precisely this task that society sets for itself by providing social security to its citizens, because protecting them in a difficult life situation, helping them solve various problems (material, physical, psychological, age, etc.) are the main purpose of social security.

Subject of Social Security

The subject of social security is the types of social relations that are divided into three groups:

1. The first group is relations regarding monetary payments, including various pensions, allowances and compensations.
2. The second group - relations regarding medical care, treatment, drug care, socio-cultural treatment, services for the disabled and people of retirement age
3. The third group - procedural and procedural relations (in connection with the established legal form, the basis for the emergence, change and termination of social security relations).

The Main Stages of Formation

The need for social security appeared simultaneously with the emergence of human society. In any society, regardless of its economic and political structure, there are always people who, due to natural reasons beyond their control, cannot acquire the source of their livelihood by their own efforts. These people are primarily children and the elderly. In addition, every person who has lost the ability to work temporarily or permanently due to a health disorder can join the ranks of the disabled. As society develops and social ties become more complex, the number of reasons for a person's need for social assistance are added to those that are due to the nature of the economic relations prevailing in society, which give rise to unemployment, inflation, and poverty.

Social security as a certain form of life support for people has specific historical types, since it is carried out within the framework of a particular socio-economic formation.

Primitive Communal, Slaveholding and Feudal Periods

The content of the elderly and the disabled in the primitive communal system was most likely carried out by virtue of custom. In a slave-owning society, there were no forms of providing for slaves in old age or in case of disability, but for veterans of military service, pensions were already introduced in Ancient Greece; in ancient Rome, service was rewarded by the provision of land.

The feudal period is characterized by the dominance of subsistence farming, the basis of which is the family, which is responsible for the material provision of the elderly and the disabled. In the same period, other forms of social support for those who cannot work and do not have a household appear, for example, charity, sanctioned begging. State pensions are beginning to be distributed to major dignitaries, bishops, prefects and other persons who have meritorious services to the monarch. Thus, the pension at that time had the character of a reward, and not a type of provision for the able-bodied.

Fundamentally New Stage

At the end of the 19th century, the social security of employees began to be carried out on a legal basis, fixed by the state. As a way of organizing it, state social insurance of hired workers is being introduced. In the future, national social security systems begin to form, covering the entire population and guaranteeing social assistance regardless of the payment of insurance premiums.

Germany

On June 15, 1883, the Reichstag passed a law on compulsory state insurance in case of illness; in July 1884 - the law on insurance against accidents. The law of July 22, 1889 introduced compulsory insurance for disability and old age. Following Germany, laws on compulsory social insurance are adopted in other European countries.

The essence of this system was that every person who met the conditions specified in the law was subject to compulsory insurance; premiums for insurance were made not only by employees themselves, but also by entrepreneurs; provision was provided on the basis of legal norms, which made the state social insurance system guaranteed; through the rules of law, uniform conditions and amounts of security were fixed, not depending on the specifics of the industry in which the insured worked.

According to the insurance laws of Germany, the insured was provided with free treatment, free medicines and cash benefits, the amount of which depended on the basis of payment (to all insured; women in connection with childbirth or within six weeks after childbirth; for funerals in case of death of the patient; in case of industrial injury; in case of illness; in case of partial or complete disability; family in case of loss of a breadwinner due to an accident at work).

The old-age pension was appointed when the employee reached 70 years of age. It consisted of two parts: the principal amount and a fixed amount paid from public funds. A special mechanism was envisaged for determining the amount of disability pensions from a general illness. This amount was formed from three parts: 1) a constant annual amount, the amount of which depended on the category of the insured according to the level of wages; 2) state surcharge in a fixed amount; 3) a constantly increasing amount, calculated taking into account the duration of the insurance period (Papashvili, 2010).

England

The insurance laws of 1911-1913 introduced sickness and disability insurance. The English insurance system was distinguished by the wide participation of representatives of the insured in the work of the insurance authorities. In addition, part of the contributions was paid by the state itself. Differentiation of insurance payments was carried out according to gender and age. In the order of social insurance, benefits, pensions, medical care, medicines, and sanatorium treatment were provided. Old-age pensions were awarded upon reaching the age of 69.

In 1946-1948, a major reform was carried out in the field of social security. It provided for: coverage of all persons of hired labor and members of their families, as well as persons who independently provide themselves with work; the establishment of pensions and benefits in fixed amounts without taking into account earnings, but at the level of the national minimum standard; giving the entire population the right to treatment; introduction of family allowances, pensions. Medical care began to be provided free of charge at the expense of the state, and not in the form of social insurance (Kveselava, 2010).

France

In France, the old-age insurance law was introduced in 1911, and the sickness insurance law only in 1928. The right to an old-age pension arose from the age of 65, under certain conditions it could be obtained from 60, and even 55 years, but at a lower rate. The disability pension consisted of a fixed amount, and the old-age pension consisted of a fixed amount and a state supplement (Kveselava, 2010).

Sweden

Compulsory social insurance for old age was introduced by law in 1913-1915. The fund for the payment of pensions was formed from the contributions of the insured and state subsidies. The amount of the insured's contribution was low and depended on the amount of income. Contributions were paid in the communities, and the community was responsible for their non-payment. The retirement age was 67 years (Papashvili, 2010).

Australia

In 1908, a law was passed under which men acquired the right to an old-age pension from the age of 65, and women from the age of 60. One of the conditions for receiving this pension was living in Australia for 25 years and owning property of no more than a certain value. With the onset of complete disability, men could receive a pension from the age of 60. The pension was also assigned to persons who became disabled due to an accident (Gudushauri, 2010).

USA

In the United States, the state social security system arose much later than in European countries. Compulsory or voluntary accident insurance legislation began to take shape in 1908, and by 1920 such laws were in place in 43 states. The first federal old-age insurance law was passed in 1920, but it only applied to federal employees. At the federal level, war veterans were also covered by pensions. The federal law on social security did not appear in the United States until August 1935. He introduced old-age pensions, as well as state assistance to certain categories of those in need - the elderly, the blind, children from poor families. In 1935, a program was also created to help needy families with dependent children (Shubitidze, 2010).

Right to Housing

The right to housing is one of the social and economic human rights ("second generation" rights). Foundations in international law - Article 11 of the International Covenant on Economic, Social and Cultural Rights, Article 16 of the European Social Charter, Article 31 of the Revised European Social Charter. The right to housing, although not expressis verbis, is also recognized as enshrined in the African Charter on Human and Peoples' Rights by virtue of its articles 14, 16 and 18(1). According to the UN Committee on Economic, Social and Cultural Rights, aspects of this right under the ICESCR include:

legal security of residence; availability of services, materials, facilities and infrastructure; affordability in terms of costs; habitability; availability; location; cultural relevance (Karumidze, 2003).

The right to housing is the right of a person to have, receive, or in any other way acquire housing that meets the requirements of housing, as well as to freely choose housing for living.

The right to housing is a negative human right and consists in the choice of one of the types of housing in the chosen place of residence.

From the position developed by the European Court of Human Rights within the meaning of Art. 8 of the European Convention. The concept of "dwelling" is not limited to a dwelling (housing) that is occupied or created legally or in the manner prescribed by law. "Dwelling" is an autonomous concept that does not depend on the classification in national law. The retention of the right to a dwelling and the presence of registration in such a dwelling does not mean that it is a valid dwelling. The European Court of Human Rights has determined the criteria for the concept of "dwelling": a) the existence of sufficient ongoing links with a particular place of residence; b) there is no other housing or intention to acquire it; c) purpose - residence; d) long period of residence (Judgment of the European Court of Human Rights "Buckley v. United Kingdom" of August 25, 1996; Judgment of the European Court of Human Rights of June 20, 2006; Judgment of the European Court of Human Rights of November 18, 2004) (Aleksizde, 2016).

Right to Education

The right to education is one of the "second generation" human rights (socio-economic and cultural; the aspect of non-discrimination can also be considered as a civil right of the first generation). The UN Committee on Economic, Social and Cultural Rights identifies four main characteristics of the right to education: availability, accessibility (non-discrimination, physical and economic accessibility), acceptability and adaptability of education, and also indicates that "the right to education can only be exercised if teachers have and students of academic freedom. The scope of the right to education may be different for different levels of education - for example, the International Covenant on Economic, Social and Cultural Rights provides for compulsory and free primary education, but only the gradual introduction of free higher education. Separately, freedom of education can stand out (UN, 2005).

Regulatory Framework

The right to education is declared in article 26 of the Universal Declaration of Human Rights, enshrined in articles 13 and 14 of the International Covenant on Economic, Social and Cultural Rights, articles 28 and 29 of the Convention on the Rights of the Child, in article 2 of the First Protocol of the European Convention for the Protection of Human and Fundamental freedoms, article 17 of the Revised European Social Charter, article 13 of the San Salvador Protocol to the American Convention on Human Rights, article 17 of the African Charter on Human and Peoples' Rights, article 11 of the African Charter on the Rights and Welfare of the Child (Aleksidze, 2016).

History

Article 22 of the Declaration of the Rights of Man and Citizen of the Jacobin Constitution of Year I (1793) set the society's task of making education accessible to everyone. Article 157 of the German Paulskirche Constitution of 1848 provided for free primary education.

Mexico was the first to establish the right to education at the constitutional level (in 1917) (Chitadze, 2016).

Right to Health Care

The right to health care, the right to medical care (UDHR term) or the right to the highest attainable standard of physical and mental health (ICESCR term) is one of the second generation human rights. It is also enshrined in the European Social Charter (Article 11) (Alber, 2010).

The Committee on Economic, Social and Cultural Rights identifies the following elements of the right to health:

- Availability of facilities, goods, services, related programs including infrastructure, trained and paid staff, essential medicines.
- accessibility (non-discrimination, physical accessibility, economic accessibility, information accessibility)
- acceptability (in terms of medical ethics, cultural criteria, gender and lifestyle requirements, as well as focus on confidentiality and health improvement)
- quality (scientifically and medically acceptable and of high quality, including the availability of qualified medical personnel, scientifically proven and suitable medicines and medical equipment, safe drinking water and adequate sanitation services)

US President F. Roosevelt in 1944 called for legislating the right to medical care in the "Second Bill of Rights" (Alber, 2010).

Cultural Rights

Cultural rights ensure the spiritual development of the individual. These include:

- Freedom of sciences and arts (freedom of literary, scientific and other forms of creativity and teaching);
- Freedom of teaching.

Freedom of Creativity

Freedom of creativity is the natural right to freely choose one's creativity, themes, objects for description, the use of any visual means and artistic techniques that the author considers appropriate to achieve the chosen creative goal. It is considered as one of the manifestations of the fundamental principle of freedom of speech, which implies the right of everyone to freely express their thoughts.

The principle of freedom of creativity proposes to proceed from the fact that the presence of any taboos on topics or visual means, on the one hand, limits the possibilities of self-expression of the author, on the other hand, deprives society of truly artistic works. Therefore, from the point of view of supporters of the principle of freedom of creativity, the possibility of creativity without restrictions is more valuable than political or moral principles, for the observance of which the freedom of creativity is limited.

The principle of freedom of creativity is in a rather complex and ambiguous relationship with public morality, religion and public policy, in particular, with the principle of tolerance. Moral and religious principles include prohibitions on certain topics and means of expression (a ban on the use of taboo vocabulary, insults, a ban on nudity, a ban on describing sexual acts in many religions, religious prohibitions proper, such as a ban on the image of Muhammad in Islam and a ban on "offensive to God" statements in many religions, and so on). Some topics are not recommended for coverage for political reasons. The problem with all the motives for restricting the freedom of creativity is that their validity in each particular case is usually obvious only to supporters, so that in the event of a conflict between "defenders of moral values" and "fighters for freedom of speech", it is extremely rare to find a compromise.

A case in point is the story of Salman Rushdie's The Satanic Verses. For this book, the writer was sentenced to death in 1989 by Ayatollah Khomeini. The Ayatollah saw in the book blasphemous allusions to the Prophet Muhammad and his wives, after which he issued a fatwa (a religious order that any Muslim must follow), according to which Rushdie should be killed (Mkurnalizde, 2000). Since that time, Rushdie has been living under the constant protection of the British Secret Service. Despite the fact that in almost any context, the death penalty for a literary work is perceived as something unacceptable, you can still find expressions that approve of it, and not only from Muslims.

Academic Freedoms

Academic freedom (university autonomy) - the principles according to which the teaching staff and researchers of higher educational institutions and research organizations are given the right to present the academic subject at their own discretion, choose a topic and methodology for scientific research, and students - to acquire knowledge according to their inclinations and needs. Academic freedoms are closely related to the autonomy of universities, which the European University Association defines in 4 areas: organizational, financial, freedom of recruitment and academic autonomy proper (Chitadze, 2016).

Academic freedoms also imply academic responsibility for creating optimal conditions for the free search for truth, its free presentation and dissemination.

Characteristic

The international association "Academy for Academic Freedoms" has formulated two main principles of such freedoms:

1. Both inside and outside an educational institution or research organization, there is complete freedom to raise any questions and seek the truth, including about controversial and unpopular views, regardless of whether or not someone is offended by one or another point of view.
2. Educational institutions and research organizations may not restrict the academic freedoms of their staff members, or use their public statements as a reason for disciplinary action or dismissal.

However, in practice, in most European countries, the state still regulates academic freedoms, since universities receive funding from the budget, their employees are civil servants and are subject to general legislation even in such purely internal matters as the selection, appointment and dismissal of senior officials, the time of their office and the size of the salary. The duration of the financial cycle, both in relation to targeted programs and grants, has a great influence on the solution of strategic issues of universities. Only in three European countries the financial cycle of universities exceeds one year, in 24 countries their activities are planned only for a year.

In most European countries, universities have the right to choose the language of instruction for all undergraduate programs. In France, teaching is conducted only in the national language, in Belgium (Flanders) and Latvia, the number of programs that can be taught in foreign languages is regulated by the state (Chitadze, 2021).

Restrictions

Of course, academic freedoms have their limits. In the United States, under the 1940 Statement of Principles on Academic Freedom and Academic Career, professors are limited in their ability to disseminate information that is not related to their professional activities. In public speeches, it is allowed to express personal opinion without regard to the position of the leadership, but it should be stipulated that the speaker is making a statement on his own behalf, and not on behalf of his institution. An academic career should also depend solely on professional competence, and dismissal can be due either to incompetence or to unseemly behavior that provokes protest from the entire faculty.

Academic Freedoms for Professors

The concept of academic freedom (Lehrfreiheit in Germany) is an integral part of academic culture in Germany, France, the UK and the USA. In all these countries, the teaching staff can conduct scientific research and publish their results without any restrictions, but there are some national peculiarities regarding teaching.

In Germany

Freedom of study (German: Freiheit des Studiums): within the limits of the established rules, students can freely choose which courses they will attend and, in some cases, the date of the exam. It is allowed to set your own focus (specialization) within the course.

These freedoms are partly limited by study rules and mandatory schedules, which, especially in the first semesters, prescribe teaching the basics of the subject and thus ensure that all students will build on a solid foundation of skills and knowledge in the later course of study. These restrictions are sometimes criticized; this applies in particular to undergraduate and state examination courses. Labor market-oriented training can also reinforce the structure of the course.

Students can develop their own scientific opinion and must also express it. If it is contrary to doctrine, it is an opportunity to practice the art of reasoning.

According to the German academic tradition, professors can promote their personal point of view and philosophical views among students. However, outside the educational institution, the dissemination of one's views is undesirable or even prohibited. In teaching activities, the professor is not limited by anything and is not bound by any officially approved program or schedule (Chitadze, 2021).

In France

Like all civil servants, a professor of an educational institution or a researcher in a research laboratory must maintain a neutral point of view and during the performance of his duties and not reveal any political or religious views. However, the academic freedom of a university professor is confirmed by law and the Constitutional Council of France: "the research and teaching staff (university professors and their assistants) in the course of their research and teaching activities are completely independent and enjoy freedom of speech on the condition that they respect university traditions, the requirements of the law, the principles of tolerance and objectivity". Career advancement in France mostly requires peer review and is not limited to ordinary administrative decisions (Chitadze, 2021).

In USA

In the United States, the basic principles of academic freedom are set forth in the 1940 Statement of Principles on Academic Freedom and Academic Career, jointly adopted by the "American Association of University Professors" and the "Association of American Colleges" (now the "American Association of Colleges and Universities"). According to these principles, "Teaching staff, in the course of performing their duties, shall enjoy the freedom to express their views on the subject." The "application" authorizes the administration to impose "restrictions on academic freedoms on religious and other matters," which must be clearly stated in writing at the time of hiring. The implementation of this agreement is monitored by six regional commissioners working in all colleges and universities in the United States, including private and religious institutions. All identified cases of violations are subject to publicity in the media (Chitadze, 2021).

Academic Freedoms for Universities and Colleges

A characteristic feature of the English university is its freedom in hiring faculty, setting standards for education and rules for admitting students. This set of principles is called institutional autonomy, and it is different from the freedoms that an educational institution gives to students and teachers.

In the United States, the meaning of the term academic freedom of the university is defined by the Supreme Court and means that the university "itself determines who has the right to teach and learn, how to teach and how to organize the admission of students." In 2008, a federal court in the state of Virginia ruled that professors should not have special academic freedoms, and all academic freedoms belong only to the educational institution as an institution. The judge, referring to earlier court decisions, argued that "there is no such constitutional right to academic freedom that could prohibit the leadership (of the university) from changing the assessment given by (a professor) to one of its students." However, the court stated that one should distinguish between cases where the administration forces the teacher to change the grade (which clearly violates the law) and when it establishes an appeal committee that can change the grade following an appeal by the student. This decision is considered an important precedent by the American academic community (Chitadze, 2021).

Environmental Rights

- The right to a healthy environment;
- The right to reliable information about the state of the environment;
- The right to compensation for damage caused to health or property by an environmental offence.

Right to a Healthy Environment

The right to a healthy environment or the right to a sustainable and healthy environment is a human right advocated by human rights and public environmental organizations to protect ecological systems that ensure human health. This right is interrelated with other health-oriented human rights such as the human right to water and sanitation, the right to food and the right to health.

The right creates a duty for the state to regulate and enforce environmental regulations, control pollution, and otherwise ensure justice and protection for communities affected by environmental problems. The right to a healthy environment has been an important right for setting environmental legal precedents for litigation on climate change and other environmental issues.

The right to a healthy environment is at the heart of the international approach to human rights and climate change. International agreements supporting this right include the 1972 Stockholm Declaration, the 1992 Rio Declaration, and the recently adopted Global Environment Pact. More than 150 states at the UN have recognized this right in one form or another through national legislation, litigation, constitutional law, contract law, and others. Two regional treaties, the African Charter on Human and Peoples' Rights and the American Convention on Human Rights, include the right to a favorable environment. Wednesday. Other human rights instruments, such as the Convention on the Rights of the Child, refer to environmental issues to the extent that they are related to the main directions of this document, in this case it refers to the rights of children (Lebedeva, 2007).

Special Rapporteurs on Human Rights and the Environment John Knox (2012-2018) and David Boyd (2018-present) have made recommendations on how to formalize these rights in international law. This was approved by a number of committees at the level of the UN and local legal communities (for example, the New York Bar Association) in 2020 (Chitadze, 2021)

Digital Rights

Digital rights are human rights, consisting in the right of people to access, use, create and publish digital works, access and use computers and other electronic devices, as well as communication networks, in particular, the Internet. Internet access is recognized as a right under the laws of a number of countries.

According to Konrad Becker's Dictionary of Tactical Reality, "digital human rights are the extension and application of universal human rights to the needs of an information-based society... Basic digital human rights include the right to access the electronic network, the right to freely communicate and express opinions online, and the right to privacy" (Becker, 2010). In 1997, at the Documenta art festival in Kassel, The People's Communication Charter was presented for the first time by a group of Amsterdam activists from the De Waag media center. It formulated demands relating to the preservation of public public space as a public good and to protect it from encroachment by commercial and police interests. Since 1997, the code of human communication rights has been seriously improved, and work to protect them has been consistently carried out by the public initiative CRIS (Communication Rights in the Information Society), in cooperation with UNESCO, various NGOs and other structures of international importance (Chitadze, 2016).

The concept of digital law is inextricably linked with the concept of digital services. If there are no digital services in the required volume, then there can be no digital right to use them. In the days of analog phones, there was no right to telephone communication, since society could not provide telephone lines to everyone. The transition to digital mobile communications made it possible to provide everyone with mobile phones. Everyone has the right to digital telephone communication, but a citizen can lose this right. When arrested, mobile phones are confiscated.

The digital rights of a citizen can be infringed by the state (for example, by law enforcement agencies), as well as the digital rights of a citizen can be infringed by a provider that has announced its readiness to provide digital services, has entered into an agreement, but does not want to fulfill it. Various kinds of scammers can attack the digital rights of a citizen. One of the ways to infringe on the digital civil rights of a person is to impose completely unnecessary digital services on him (for example, spam).

CONCLUSION

In general, it should be pointed out, that Human rights are rules that ensure the protection of the dignity and freedom of each individual person.

Taken together, fundamental rights form the basis of the legal status of an individual. The specific expression and scope of these rights, both in the positive law of various states and countries, and in various international legal treaties, may differ. In international public law, the most famous document fixing them is the UN Universal Declaration of Human Rights. In the OSCE member states, issues of human rights, fundamental freedoms, democracy and the rule of law are of an international nature and do not belong exclusively to the internal affairs of the respective state.

REFERENCES

Alber, J., & Gilbert, N. (2010). *United in Diversity? Comparing Social Models in Europe and America*. Oxford Scholarship.

Aleksidze, L. (2016). *Dictionary of International Law*. Tbilisi State University. Retrieved from: https://www.britannica.com/topic/hylomorphism

Becker, K. (2010). *Tactical Reality Dictionary: Cultural Intelligence and Social Control Paperback* (1st ed.). Autonomedia.

Chitadze. (2011). *Geopolitics*. Universali.

Chitadze. (2016). *Political Sciences*. International Black Sea University.

Chitadze. (2021). *European values*. https://eu-gs.ge/wp-content/uploads/2021/12/EU-GS-%E1%83%9E%E1%83%9D%E1%83%9A%E1%83%98%E1%83%A2%E1%83%98%E1%83%99%E1%83%98%E1%83%A1-%E1%83%93%E1%83%9D%E1%83%99%E1%83%A3%E1%83%9B%E1%83%94%E1%83%9C%E1%83%A2%E1%83%98.pdf?fbclid=IwAR0vJVJFskKyWq98LN6JHHDv8OU0L4NZAyEl4qD5FJK6UH-kxkFvymgsfSQ

Council of Europe. (1950). *European Convention for the Protection of Human Rights and Fundamental Freedoms, Article 4*. Retrieved from: https://www.echr.coe.int/documents/convention_eng.pdf

Council of Europe, Committee of Ministers. (1977). *A Declaration on territorial asylum in 1977*. Retrieved from: https://www.refworld.org/pdfid/3ae6b3611c.pdf

European Commission. (2022). *Slavery Convention*. Retrieved from: https://ec.europa.eu/anti-trafficking/1926-slavery-convention_en

Held, D. (2000). *Models of Democracy*. Biddles.

Heritage. (2022). *Origins of Parliament*. Retrieved from: heritage/evolutionofparliament/originsofparliament/birthofparliament/overview/magnacarta/#:~:text=Magna%20Carta%20was%20issued%20in,as%20a%20power%20in%20itself

Heywood, A. (2021). *Political Ideologies* (5th ed.). Retrieved from https://www.pdfdrive.com/andrew-heywood-political-ideologies-5th-edition-pdf-e18896250.html

History. (2022). *The British Bill of Rights of 1689*. Retrieved from: https://www.history.com/topics/british-history/english-bill-of-rights#:~:text=The%20English%20Bill%20of%20Rights%20was%20an%20act%20signed%20into,Parliament%20power%20over%20the%20monarchy

ILO. (2022). *Member States*. Retrieved from: https://www.ilo.org/global/about-the-ilo/how-the-ilo-works/member-states/lang--en/index.htm

International Labor Organization. (2022). *International Labor Organization Convention No. 29 concerning Forced and Compulsory Labor*. Retrieved from: https://www.ilo.org/dyn/normlex/en/f?p=NORMLEXPUB:12100:0:NO:P12100_ILO_CODE:C029

Karumidze, V. (2003). *International Organizations*. Tbilisi State University.

Kveselava, S., & Papashvili, G. (2003). *Political Sciences*. Georgian Technical University.

Lewin, I. (1985). *The Jewish community in Poland*. Philosophical Library, the University of Michigan.

Middlekauff, R. (2005). *The Glorious Cause: The American Revolution, 1763—1789, Revised and Expanded Edition*. Oxford University Press.

Mkurnalizde, K. (2000). *Political Sciences*. Lega.

Müller-Schwefe, M. J. (1961). In Die Religion in Geschichte und Gegenwart, 3. Auflage, Band IV.

Obscura, A. (2017). *The Little-Known Passport That Protected 450,000 Refugees*. Retrieved from: https://www.atlasobscura.com/articles/nansen-passport-refugees

Olmstead, C. E. (1960). *History of Religion in the United States*. Retrieved from: https://academic.oup.com/jcs/article-abstract/4/2/222/810658?redirectedFrom=fulltext

Regional Refugee Instruments & Related. (2022). *Convention on Asylum. Havana, 1928*. Retrieved from: https://www.refworld.org/docid/3ae6b37923.html

Stahl, H. B. (1957). *Die Religion in Geschichte und Gegenwart* (Vol. I). Auflage.

UK Government. (2022). *Bill of Rights 1688. note X1*. Retrieved from: https://www.legislation.gov.uk/aep/WillandMarSess2/1/2/data.pdf

UK Parliament. (2022). *English Magna Carta in 1215*. Retrieved from: https://www.parliament.uk/about/living-

UN. (1948). *Universal Declaration on Human Rights*. Retrieved from: https://www.un.org/en/about-us/universal-declaration-of-human-rights

UN. (2005). *Basic Facts about the United Nations*. United Nations Department of Public Information.

UN. (2022a). *On December 14, 1967, the UN General Assembly adopted as a recommendation the "Declaration on Territorial Asylum"*. Retrieved from: https://legal.un.org/avl/ha/dta/dta.html

UN. (2022b). *UN General Assembly resolution 1763 A (XVII) of November 7, 1962*. Retrieved from: https://www.refworld.org/docid/456d89064.html

UNHCR. (2022). *The 1951 Refugee Convention*. Retrieved from: https://www.unhcr.org/1951-refugee-convention.html

United Nation Treaty Collection. (2022). *Supplementary Convention for the Abolition of Slavery, the Slave Trade and Institutions and Practices Similar to Slavery. September 7, 1956*. Retrieved from: https://treaties.un.org/pages/ViewDetailsIII.aspx?src=TREATY&mtdsg_no=XVIII-4&chapter=18&Temp=mtdsg3&clang=_en

United Nations. (2007). *Multilateral treaties deposited with the Secretary-General: Rome Statute of the International Criminal Court*. Retrieved from: https://treaties.un.org/pages/ViewDetails.aspx?src=IND&mtdsg_no=XVIII-10&chapter=18&clang=_en

Warren, D., & Brandeis, L. D. (1890). *The Right to Private Life*. Retrieved from: https://utrechtjournal.org/articles/10.5334/ujiel.cp/

KEY TERMS AND DEFINITIONS

Age of Enlightenment: (Also known as the Age of Reason or simply the Enlightenment) is an intellectual and philosophical movement that dominated Europe in the 17th and 18th centuries with global influences and effects.

Civil Society: A community that embraces shared norms and ethical standards to collectively manage problems without coercion and through peaceful and democratic procedures for decision making aimed at improving human welfare.

Constitutional Democracy: Government processes that allow people, through their elected representatives, to exercise power and influence the state's policies.

Council of Europe (CoE): An international organisation founded in the wake of World War II to uphold human rights, democracy, and the rule of law in Europe.[3] Founded in 1949, it has 46 member states, with a population of approximately 675 million, and operates with an annual budget of approximately 500 million euros.

Democracy: A form of government in which the people have the authority to deliberate and decide legislation ("direct democracy"), or to choose governing officials to do so ("representative democracy"). Who is considered part of "the people" and how authority is shared among or delegated by the people has changed over time and at different rates in different countries, but over time more and more of a democratic country's inhabitants have generally been included. Cornerstones of democracy include freedom of assembly, association and speech, inclusiveness and equality, citizenship, consent of the governed, voting rights, freedom from unwarranted governmental deprivation of the right to life and liberty, and minority rights.

European Convention on Human Rights (ECHR; formally the Convention for the Protection of Human Rights and Fundamental Freedoms): An international convention to protect human rights and political freedoms in Europe.

Human Rights: The political rights and civil liberties recognized by the international community as inalienable and valid for individuals in all countries by virtue of their humanity.

Human Rights Movement: Refers to a nongovernmental social movement engaged in activism related to the issues of human rights. The foundations of the global human rights movement involve resistance to colonialism, imperialism, slavery, racism, segregation, patriarchy, and oppression of indigenous peoples.

Human Security: A measure popular in liberal theory of the degree to which the welfare of individuals is protected and promoted in contrast to realist theory's emphasis on putting the states interests in military and national security ahead of all other goals.

International Court of Justice (ICJ): The primary court established by the United Nations for resolving legal disputes between states and providing advisory opinions to international agencies and the UN General Assembly.

International Human Rights Law (IHRL): The body of international law designed to promote human rights on social, regional, and domestic levels.

International Law: Also known as International Ethics, public international law, and law of nations, is the set of rules, norms, and standards generally recognized as binding between nations.

Legal Rights: Those rights bestowed onto a person by a given legal system (they can be modified, repealed, and restrained by human laws). The concept of positive law is related to the concept of legal rights.

Liberalism: A paradigm predicated on the hope that the application of reason and universal ethics international relations can lead to a more orderly, just, and cooperative world. liberalism assumes that anarchy and war can be policed by institutional reforms that empower international organizations and law.

Morality: Principles about the norms for behavior that should govern an actor's interactions.

Morals: Principles clarifying the difference between good and evil and the situations in which they are opposed.

National Human Rights Institution (NHRI): An independent state-based institution with the responsibility to broadly protect and promote human rights in a given country.

Natural Rights: Those rights that are not dependent on the laws or customs of any particular culture or government, and so are *universal*, *fundamental* and *inalienable* (they cannot be repealed by human laws, though one can forfeit their enjoyment through one's actions, such as by violating someone else's rights). Natural law is the law of natural rights.

Office of the United Nations High Commissioner for Human Rights: Commonly known as the Office of the High Commissioner for Human Rights (OHCHR) or the United Nations Human Rights Office, is a department of the Secretariat of the United Nations that works to promote and protect human rights that are guaranteed under international law and stipulated in the Universal Declaration of Human Rights of 1948. The office was established by the United Nations General Assembly on 20 December 1993[3] in the wake of the 1993 World Conference on Human Rights.

Rule of Law: The political philosophy that all citizens and institutions within a country, state, or community are accountable to the same laws.

UN Human Rights Council: Created in 2005, has a mandate to investigate alleged human rights violations.

Universal Declaration of Human Rights (UDHR): An international document adopted by the United Nations General Assembly that enshrines the rights and freedoms of all human beings. Drafted by a UN committee chaired by Eleanor Roosevelt, it was accepted by the General Assembly as Resolution 217 during its third session on 10 December 1948 at the Palais de Chaillot in Paris, France.

Chapter 3
Ideologies and Democracy:
A Symbolic Approach

Ziya Kıvanç Kıraç
https://orcid.org/0000-0002-8728-2834
Firat University, Turkey

ABSTRACT

Since democracy is accepted as one of the basic human values, some states and societies have accepted democracy as an ideal. However, the content of democracy has a different meaning for every ideology, every society, and every political system. In particular, ideologies tend to see democracy sometimes as an end and sometimes as a tool used to achieve another ideal. The mental worlds of cultures are conveyed by symbols that create simple shortcuts. Political symbolism is an important motif that draws the route of the bridge connecting a country's past to its future. Different perceptions of concepts such as democracy, human rights, freedom, and equality are related to the political culture codes of the relevant society. A liberal dimension of symbolism was examined in the example of the USA and its social dimension in the Soviet Union. France, as the father of nationalism, is also discussed with its experience of democracy. As one of the young nations, Turkey has been examined in terms of symbolism and democracy.

INTRODUCTION

In the post-Cold War world, democracy has become a universal principle desired by almost all countries. But confusion reigns when talking about democracy in everyday life. Because it is complex that the issue of exactly what the concept includes and what it is about. Is democracy individual freedoms, is it a multi-party system, is it the rights of minorities, equal voice or something else? Is a strong civil society against the central influence of the state a factor in the development of democracy? Undoubtedly, it is possible to answer these questions by having a good command of both political science and constitutional law. In addition, the concept is also connected with sociology. Because when people talk about democracy, the concept actually means something different to each of them. One of the possible reasons for this is that we are members of different groups in terms of scope and content, such as family, neighbor environment, association, club, working environment, nation and state. Each affiliation develops

DOI: 10.4018/978-1-6684-4543-3.ch003

a system of meaning based on its own worldview. Of course, we do not claim that the meanings differ as much as black and white according to their point of view. However, the networks we are in are open to debate on agreed meanings. If we think that our imagination is formed by what we learn, we can say that we can construct even very basic subjects and concepts in our minds in different ways. Because the meaning has been broken with modern times and the decisive role of religion on meaning has been lost. Modern thought, which has turned into idolaters, has given certain rational answers about the place of man in this world. The institutional structure of modernism claimed to have an inclusive world of meanings about nature and society. However, when we look at the dark corridors of the human mind, many studies that show that symbolic wholes such as myths, religious predictions, mystical thoughts and stereotyped perspectives are much more decisive in human life will come to the fore. Ideologies also frequently make use of symbols and symbolic forms as a set of political beliefs. Because ideologies interpret the current situation in the form of worldview. They argue that there can be a good society. They have arguments about what political progress will look like. Ideologies that make up the language of political discourse develop approaches to concepts that are woven with symbols. In a sense, they form a direct link between action and meaning. Whether nationalism or liberalism, fascism, communism, or different versions of nationalism, they seek to create a symbolic framework that they can use to reexamine and respond to political issues and concepts. For example, the French Revolution, which caused the emergence of ideologies like many social changes, was transformed by the ideologies themselves as progressive, reactionary, despotic, extremist, etc. labeled as. Because the established political images have been replaced by the symbolic concepts of ideologies in modern times. Ideology, which emerges as a map of reality, allows the creation of collective consciousness. It is known that group affiliations play an important role in the formation of individuals' opinions. In this sense, ideologies are a symbol of community mind and memory. Like other political concepts, democracy is a symbol used in politics. It is also a political symbol interpreted by ideology. Every ideology's view of democracy is attributed to cultural or formal symbols. Democracy can sometimes be the reflection of a historical freedom struggle on the statue, or it can be the driving force of a transformation that supports two other motifs such as equality and fraternity. Sometimes it is a sapling that can only be kept alive with the power of a gun. Sometimes it is a discourse that will serve equality. This study tries to deal with the phenomena of democracy in different cultures. In the content of the study, examples of liberalism, nationalism, conservatism and socialism are discussed. How democracy is handled in the aforementioned ideologies is examined through symbols. The first part focused on the ideology-symbol relationship, and the second part focused on the relationship between democracy and ideology. The main body of the subject is the symbolic reflections of the perspectives on democracy with country examples.

1. Ideology and Symbol

The direction of the relationship between human and meaning has historically been determined by various breaks. Modernization has caused changes not only in the developments in the outside world, but also in the understanding and interpretation of the world. In the process of perceiving the world, the dominance of religious and mythical knowledge has ended, and a more factual and abstract way of thinking has been replaced. Modern man has passed to an empirically-based cognition and has perceived the events in the environment with its scientific dimension. Precise information can be obtained by reflecting on what has been seen. This development has been possible when people have developed the concepts of perception and cognition in scientific terminology and differentiated between looking and thinking. This separation has led people to think what they see instead of seeing what they think. In other words, during the Renaissance, people discovered the difference between thinking and looking (Mitchell, 1986). This situation is defined by Max Weber as "the disenchantment of the world". The fall of man in the void of meaning has opened the door to ideologies and the meaning has begun to be knitted in the form of an ideological network. Nearly two hundred years later, a situation occurred that initiated a new change in the status of knowledge in post-industrial societies. This new situation came to be known as Postmodernism. The defining feature of this situation, according to Lyotard, was that meta-narratives lost their explanatory features and disappeared (Lyotard, 1997). Jean Baudrillard, in his work In the Shadow of the Silent Masses, claims that the meaning ceases to be the ideal line that drags the society away. The masses demand a demonstration against the constancy and imposition of meaning. What fascinates people is not thinking, which works as a construction process in this sense, but rather being fascinated by imagination (Baudrillard, 2009). In the postmodern era, time has accelerated and lost its function as a tool to make sense of the world. The present has become important and history has become just a nostalgic look. Every day there has been a collection of images. Culture is also formed by images that turn into photographic analogies. This is a situation that weakens historicity and affects the formation of meaning (Jameson, 1992). Undoubtedly, it is clear that this interpretation includes a post-modern point of view. But on the other hand, it still ironically refers to the modern. Because what happens in societies is not the disappearance of meaning, but its pluralization. How, for example, are we to explain the still vigorous circulation of ideologies? The suspicion against the truth has also reduced the ideological sharpness. Rather than disappear, there are now intertwined ideologies with no definite boundaries.

The ideology has many definitions. However, in terms of setting an example for the study, it would be appropriate to define it through the relations between ideology, meaning, culture and symbol. Clifford Geertz proposed two approaches in his study of ideology: the first is the interest theory and the second is the coercion theory. According to the interest theory, ideologies form the basis of the struggle between competing groups for power. The strongest group is the one who can institutionalize their own ideology. The compulsion theory, on the other hand, argues that ideology develops against the contradictions of modern society. People agree with the views of ideologies against the discontinuous structure of norms in society. Because ideologies develop ways of thinking and reaction that will add meaning to life. Ultimately, what both theories should focus on is the relationship between ideologies and symbols in the formation of a social group's worldview. Ideologies should be considered as symbol systems that interact and construct meaning (Geertz, 1977). Studies focusing on the relations between meaning and symbol have generally increased in the last century. In this field, especially the weight of semiology is seen. Semiology, which tries to solve the universe of meaning and focuses on areas such as the formation of meaning and creating meaning, deals with social functioning in a structural context in defining the world (Barthes, 1977). Both structuralism, Frankfurt School and semiology, which developed through independent initiatives, argue that meaning is formed within a cultural system and that everything is a sign. A sign means a situation, action or entity that replaces a concept in our mind. However, "semiotics, languages, codes, tokens, etc. It is a science that examines sign systems such as (Guiraud, 1975). Therefore, a sign is anything that replaces something else it describes or represents. Indicators have both a literal meaning and a connotation of what they implicitly point to. While the sign itself is a referrer as it is, what it actually points to is the sent meaning (Gottdeiner, 1995).

Language is both a large sign system that helps us understand the world and a cultural system based on it. Words and grammar are considered as a result of intertwined networks of culture. Similarly, there are opinions that ideology is a semiotic system. For example, Barthes argues that the first meanings of words in the dictionary are actually connotations. In this sense, language itself is like a reflection of the established ideology (Barthes, 1974). Rather, it is the ideological approach of the government that controls the production and dissemination of not only goods but also ideas. Ideological concepts, like all other production and consumption products, are part of social reality. They also represent or pervert a reality other than itself in relation to other concepts. So the ideological thing is the sign. There is no ideology without a sign. Meaning arises in the semiotic interaction between people, and therefore individual consciousness is shaped in the materiality of signs created by an organized group. Therefore, individual consciousness appears as a social ideological phenomenon (Volosinov, 1986). Ideologies belong to the world of social belief and are therefore embedded in social memory. They are shared by group members or human communities. As a special kind, they are socially shared mental representations. In this sense, knowledge is controlled by group ideology. It is relative in nature and true to a group or to a whole culture according to its own criteria (VanDijk, 1998). What is important at this point is the relationship of a mental representation with imagination. Althusser talks about the meaning-making function of images between the real world and the world of belief. Ideology is strengthened through material practices embedded in the rituals that exist within the ideological apparatus of the state. Subjects are invoked through these rituals. Over time, they become carriers of ideological meanings. This is how the dynamics of ideologies as cultural structures constructed through symbolic representations are determined (Althusser, 2014). Althusser's point of view can be interpreted as the fact that the established ideology is articulated to the vital practices of individuals through symbols, and in this way, the hegemonic discourse creates the chance to reproduce itself continuously. This issue is also related to legitimacy theories on a national basis. At the same time, it can be said that all other ideologies are the sum of such signification practices within themselves. However, the semiotic dimension of ideology and the dimension of political symbolism are intertwined. Symbols are actually indicators. However, while there is a similarity between the signifier and the signified in the signs, the symbols form completely arbitrarily. However, both construct a mnemonic image through a communication (Guiraud, 1975). While images can change over time through perceptions, in Walter Lippman's words, they can become fixed by turning into "pictures in our minds", that is, prejudices (Lippmann, 1998).

2. Democracies and Ideologies

Lacan says that the three things that hold the human mind together are imaginary, symbolic and real. What is called the real is the outside world that we can never reach due to the phenomenon of language. In this sense, language is an obstacle to reaching reality. We learn the language primarily in our family. Therefore, our thoughts about the world are determined by the "other". The interaction between reality and meaning begins here. Meaning is more constructed. In adulthood, one wants to break this first meaning (Lacan, 2001). It is a gateway for other ideologies. In daily life, when you look at something within the cultural patterns, when you talk about something or when you are in a practice, meaning is actually formed through ideological memory. Political symbolism establishes meanings in ideological shortcuts. In this way, even the most difficult political situations or concepts to think about are settled in certain image planes in the memories. Especially in nation-building processes, founding ideologies frequently use national symbols. Symbols can be a monument, statue or building as a sign, or they can take the form of a poem anthem or discourse.

Culture is a structure based on common symbols. Social structure and political systems are formed by the complex configuration of symbols. In this sense, the distinctive features of societies can be explained by Kertzer's discourse, understanding how symbolic things exist in politics, how political actors manipulate symbols, and how they are related to the material foundations of political power (Kertzer, 1988). At this point, it is necessary to pay attention to the difference between political symbols and symbols in politics. Anything in the normal course of life can be turned into a political symbol with an ideological embellishment. Or concepts in politics can be reconstructed from the point of view of an ideology (especially the founding ideology). In this sense, democracy has become the most important universal principle of the world after the French Revolution. However, the struggles for independence and democracy have also developed in such a way that they affect the political system, the constitutional system and the legal systems on very different scales. The perspectives of nations on basic concepts in politics have also been formed by the interaction of both founding ideologies and political cultures. It is possible to consider all these as an extension of political communication. Political communication is basically based on the logic of persuasion. Persuasion and consent requires compromise on complex concepts. Cultural symbols serve this more in a country. Certain stereotypes and forms of discourse are effective as a symbol in the process of forming public opinion. It makes use of many techniques of political communication, as the lack of consensus poses a threat to the legitimacy of power and dominant thought. The most effective of these is known as propaganda. Consensus on political concepts is also established through symbolic forms.

Democracy has passed through various experiences since ancient times and has become one of the most important universal values today. Especially in his adventure after the French Revolution, he was sometimes identified with freedom, sometimes with equality, and sometimes with the government of the people. In fact, if we look at the French flag, we can see that it is equalized with all three. The basic principles of today's modern democracies can come to the fore as different motifs in the political history of the countries. Today there are as many different forms of democracy as there are democratic nations in the world. No two systems are exactly the same and no one system can be taken as a "model". There are presidential and parliamentary democracies, democracies that are federal or unitary, democracies that use a proportional voting system, and ones that use a majoritarian system, democracies which are also monarchies, and so on. The history of democracy, on the other hand, has also been shaped by an ideological perspective. Each ideology has dominant or recessive approaches to democracy. It is possible to trace the meaning loaded with ideological symbols in this sense.

The basis of the principles of liberalism is about citizenship and democracy. Liberals see democracy in individualistic terms as consent meaning at the ballot box. That is, democracy is seen as the same thing as regular and competitive elections. On the one hand, democracy prevents the abuse of power. On the other hand, it should always be supported by a constitution in order to prevent the tyranny of the majority. However, in addition to consent and participation, the tendency to emphasize the need for greater reconciliation in society is also a prominent feature of liberalism (Vincent, 2003). Since the liberal stance contains an objection and rebellion against the old system, it does not go to glorify the old periods, traditions and legends. It projects a better world by criticizing the old. Socialism similarly begins with a critique of the present. It moves because history should be a leap forward. It supports the idea of a radical democracy based on popular participation. By criticizing the capitalist dimension of liberal democracy, he shifts to a line that gives more importance to public control (Baradat, 2012). In this sense, the road to democracy is built on the idea of equality. While conservatism embraces liberal democracy, they avoid putting property and traditions into the hands of the masses. They tend to see democracy as an unconventional field. The most complex of political ties between the past and the future is seen in nationalism. Nationalism, which is the driving force of the nation-state logic, approaches democracy with the concepts of nation and majority, although the tones are different in itself (Vincent, 2003). Considering for today, it will be seen that the borders between ideologies do not remain as clear as before. Especially with the effect of post-modernism, ideological mixtures are known by many different names today. For example, liberalism has both right and left versions. It can be said that these intertwinings are actually a factor in the fact that democracy is seen as a basic universal value by all ideologies. On the other hand, ideologies approach democracy with different intonations. Particularly, It is possible to see this in the dominant ideologies in the nation-building process.

3. Ideologic Symbols and Democracy

It is possible to find the ancient roots of democracy in Ancient Greece, and its modern roots in the enlightenment period. The effects of liberalism in the emergence of the nation-state and its inspiration for the form of the state are known. The modern understanding of democracy is under the influence of electoral democracy, which has developed in the industrialized west and is known as liberal democracy (Heywood, 2003). Sartori argues that the democratic state is the new version of liberalism with a new name (Sartori, 1987). Liberalism's emphasis on freedom is undeniable in the founding of the United States of America, which is one of the first examples of the modern state. The Declaration of Independence was prepared by Thomas Jefferson in 1776, which became a guide to freedom defenders around the world. In the declaration, which is based on the fact that nature gives certain rights to everyone, "the right to life, the right to freedom and the right to be happy" is mostly emphasized. Jefferson's approach is close to what John Locke describes as "life, liberty, and property". It is generally accepted that this school, namely liberal democracy, dominated American political history (Baradat, 2012). Tocqueville emphasized that the basic desire in America is equality. Turning to the idea of equality is the principle of equality in human history. However, over time, the desire for equality may shift to individualism. This is an issue that needs to be addressed with different aspects for democracy (Tocqueville, 2006). On the other hand, how the state will implement democracy is another issue. Based on the saying that the best state is the least governing state, liberal democracy, at least in America, does not seem to interfere with religion, press and free speech (Roskin, 2000). The tones of liberalism have been in different tones in the American political history journey. It has also been criticized by the conservative movement from time to time regarding the position of the state and the individual. For example, the most important themes of the Progressive Movement, which emerged in the 1890s and determined American political life until the 1920s, were social reforms, promotion of democracy and the expansion of women's rights. Its ultimate goal is to reduce the inequalities and social problems caused by the uncontrolled capitalism that developed after the civil war. However, American liberalism also interacted with other factors. (Lustig, 1982). On the other hand, it can be said that the American political culture has produced unique symbols in the process of nationalization. The liberty bell, known as the symbol of freedom and symbolizing the reading of the declaration of independence in the states, and the 4th of July celebrations, which was declared as the Independence Day, are two of them. Another example is that thirteen colonies and fifty states are symbolized by lines and stars on their flags. However, none of these examples had as much impact as the Statue of Liberty. One of the first things that come to mind when America is mentioned today is the Statue of Liberty. Although it is defined as a national symbol, it also contains some historical and political symbols. It is located on Liberty Island in New York City, USA. The Statue of Liberty, officially known as Liberty Enlightening the World, is a monumental statue and observation tower that has been the symbol of America since 1886, on Liberty Island in New York

City, USA. The Statue of Liberty, made of copper, was gifted to the USA by France on the occasion of its 100th anniversary. It was built between 1884-1886. She is a tall, calm and strong woman. She wore loose dresses and sandals, like the clothes of an ancient Greek goddess. This shows that United States democracy can be traced back to the ideas of ancient Greek democracy. The seven pointed ends of the crown on the head of the statue symbolize the seven continents or the seven seas. The torch means path lighting and is also a symbol of hope. It is said that immigrants who flocked to New York gave hope when they saw this statue. Undoubtedly it is about a mental acceptance that they have stepped into a new world. Because in the poem written by the poet Emma Lazarus and placed on the ground part of the statue, there is a promise to be a home where they can breathe freely for the homeless, immigrants and the poor. It has often been referred to as a symbol of America's promised freedoms (Staton, 2010). As a result, the Statue of Liberty has become a part of Amierkan democracy history with its meanings. Treating the established new order, individualism, rights and freedoms as concepts that form the basis of democracy is a summary of American-style liberalism.

A long time after the American experience, this time in 1848, the beginning of a long revolutionary process took place. The Industrial Revolution was completed and capitalism developed very rapidly. The crisis of this growth was the troubles of the oppressed working class. Workers' work in both long hours and unsanitary conditions has created deep discontent. The Communist Manifesto, written by Marx and Engels in 1848, is believed to have caused mass protests. Because a propertyless society and a classless order were envisaged in the declaration. The opinion, which gathered a lot of supporters, triggered workers' uprisings in many countries. (Rosenberg, 1965). It is known that the dimension of Marxism split into two main branches over time and the radical part was called communism and the remaining part was called social democracy. Although the basic principles of Communism after the Bolshevik revolution matched the official ideology, the social dimension of democracy has always existed as a counterforce in the system. Social democracy, particularly in the 20th century, has shaped the liberal theory's "limited state" principle with the "social state of law" and directed the state to take more responsibility and to positive interventionism. The understanding of the "social state of law" advocated by social democracy is based on the understanding that social equality can be realized through state intervention. At the same time, the welfare state advocates the spread of democracy to a wide base and its provision in the social sense. However, in case the state intervention is beyond the borders, it is important to bring the rule of law principle to the fore. Thus, the social state and the rule of law are emphasized as two separate concepts. Social democracy also attaches importance to the understanding of statism. However, it can be stated that this statism is a "reformist" state that strives for the development of social state principles in a moderate manner. At the same time, the state acts with some balancing elements.

It is seen that it is limited by the liberal theory and in this respect, it stands out with its closeness to liberal theory. This understanding of statism is defended by parties that adopted reform policies, mostly in the 19th and 20th centuries. (Schmidt & Ritter, 2013). It is known that during the establishment of the Soviets, there was opposition to social democracy. In Lenin's speeches, social democrats are mostly shown as those who are on the side of the petty bourgeoisie. Since the 1920s, it has been seen that democracy was established not with freedom but with the concept of equality. It is normal for this to happen. Because what needs to be done is to explain the real life conditions to the oppressed and persuade them to create a society where equality reigns. As a matter of fact, Constructivism, which emerged as an important art movement of the time, attempted to produce realistic and development-oriented works instead of mythology or incomprehensible symbolic works. Although the four corners of the Soviet Union were paved with monuments, this progressed along a line that depicts the prevailing ideology and heroism of the period. Since communism is essentially built on real life conditions and the future, just like liberalism, it tries to design what is current and future-oriented, not great events or mythologies in history. Communist governments' attempts to suppress popular culture and maintain an official high culture were often unsuccessful. The will to local popular culture in the West eventually prevailed. Theories have also been developed that the spread of popular culture reduces the quality of civilization and actually transforms the masses into audiences by means of mass persuasion used by demagogues (Gans, 1999). For the Soviets, the reflection of this was mostly in the form of commemoration days, marches and the official delivery of the ideology to the people. On the other hand, it would not be wrong to say that Soviet-type democracy emerged when the Soviet Union was sinking. The symbols of social democracy in Russia today are neither a monument nor a poem. As a result of the realistic policy, the two main policies "Glasnost" and "Perestroika" symbolized the new regime. According to Gorbachev, perestroika represents the comprehensive development of socialist rule, removing the congestion, giving dynamism to the economy. At the same time, it is supporting entrepreneurship, reconsidering the centralized structure, and implementing transparency and openness. According to the restructuring policy, everything on which social progress depends, political and ideological methods must be renewed, socialist democracy must be strengthened and conservatism must be driven away (Gorbachev, 2007). Although the Soviets produced famous ideologues and strong leaders, they were not as effective as Glasnost and Perestroika, which symbolized the weakest moment of the Soviets, namely the end. As Kessler said, what is symbolic is real politics, which is often expressed in a powerful way (Kessler, 1978). This historical break, perhaps representing the beginning of social democracy, occurred with the implementation of two policies.

The country where democracy can be considered as a spiral along with freedom and equality is France. Having the most important political developments of both the French Revolution and the Enlightenment period, the country is one of the first examples of the nation-building process. While the Enlightenment period highlights the nation-state model as a rational form of government, it is also known for the destruction of existing old orders and its iconoclast feature. Enlightenment, rejecting the symbolic world of the Middle Ages full of myths and rituals, replaced superstition and superstition with positive knowledge. Divided into dynasties on the verge of the modern era, Europe is a mosaic of different ethnic groups. Building a nation-state necessitated the establishment of monolithic models by ministries instead of discarding the customs and dialects of local and ethnic groups (Baumann, 2005). Throughout the radical phase of the French Revolution, iconoclasm was supported by members of government and citizens alike. Numerous monuments, religious artifacts and other historically significant items were destroyed in an attempt to destroy any memory of the Old Regime. King XV, located in the square of Paris and bearing his name until then. The statue of Louis was destroyed. Therefore, revolutions usually start by demolishing old idols. However, after a certain time, ideological symbols become the driving force of the new system. National holidays and rituals invented after the French Revolution can be given as an example (Idzerda, 1959). The French have historically had many national symbols, such as Marianne, the Gallic rooster. However, French democracy proceeds with the meanings represented by the three colors on its flag. The Declaration of 1789 is a text that determines the public principles of the new era and abolishes the old regime. First of all, equality before the law was mentioned in the declaration. The proclamation that put an end to arbitrary rule instead spoke of the rights of society. It also refers to rights and freedoms. Accordingly, they are natural, inalienable and sacred rights of man. The two basic human values that dominate the text are freedom and equality (Roskin, 2000). Fraternity, on the other hand, is more about citizenship laws. In France, which is more liberal than European countries in this regard, it is not obligatory for a foreigner who is granted citizenship to renounce his previous citizenship. In addition, birth and residence facts in France directly accept second-generation immigrants as citizens (Brubaker, 1990). Therefore, “Liberty, Equality, Fraternity” has been used to mean the universalization of the legal system with pluralism and human rights, which is the basis of the nation-state and its mode of government, democracy. Institutionalizing these three important dimensions of democracy has never been easy. This issue is more about the existence of a strong army. According to Billig, societies that have an army believe that some things are more valuable than life itself. The national anthem of France, Marseillaise, which is the source of democracy, speaks of the tireless struggle with the enemies. The struggle for nation building is as much a struggle for monopoly over the means of violence as for independence (Billig, 1995). At the entrance of the Paris courthouse, there is the phrase “The sword is the guardian of the law”. This expression means that, as Castoriadis states, discourse is a form of the symbolic. Discourse is a meaning that can be perceived and thought (Castoriadis, 1987). Even in the cradle of democracy, the necessity of the military and decision-making institutions to protect the law was considered.

Turkey is one of the younger generation countries where the process of nationalization and democracy experience go hand in hand. The views that sprouted in the last period of the Ottoman Empire and were shaped by Mustafa Kemal formed the driving force of the new state. The transition from monarchy to republic is most marked by the tone of democracy. Mustafa Kemal’s views are mostly related to the French Revolution. Turkish modernization symbolizes a radical break with almost all the traditions of the old state. It has also attracted attention with its applications far ahead of its time. Granting women the right to vote and be elected as early as 1934 showed the new state’s faith in democracy. Although the transition to multi-party life took time, Mustafa Kemal’s revolutions were tried to be made gradually under the protection of military intellectuals. Therefore, Mustafa Kemal and his friends became both the soldiers who determined the fate of a new nation and the political leaders of the new state. The new period is equipped with both a new history thesis and modern political concepts. The concepts of secularism and democracy were undoubtedly the most striking of the mentioned revolutions (Karpat, 2001). In addition, citizenship rights and a new civil law initiatives are also important moves. In the light of science, targeting the western life for the Turkish youth has also been one of the extraordinary moves. The radical and rapid establishment of these concepts has been influential in the implementation of democracy after Mustafa Kemal for many years under the tutelage of an army. Rather, the enlightenment model, which proceeds from the ceiling to the bottom, needed this kind of support. The experience of this process by the masses who have not yet adapted to the idea of democracy has been supported by various institutional structures (Tachau & Heper: 1983). The army, which founded the state and is considered to be above politics, has always seen itself as the protector of democracy and retained the authority to intervene in the system when necessary. The debate over the founding and protective role of the army is sometimes referred to as militarism. With the definition of Vagts, militarism includes all kinds of thought and value systems and emotions, by carrying the military mentality, military behavior and decision-making styles to the civilian sphere, and putting military institutions and procedures above civilian ones (Vagts, 1959). In Turkey, the army took over the administration with a military intervention on May 27, 1960 and declared this new period as the second republic. It was argued that the experience after the transition to the multi-party system represented a break with the basic principles of democracy and dictatorship, and it was said that there would be a return to democracy with military intervention. With this date, as the institutions representing the power of the army in politics increased, a dual parliamentary system was envisaged to be formed by those elected and appointed together with those who were close to the French system. The justifications for legitimizing the intervention to the public were carried out through objects that would make Mustafa Kemal and his revolutions more visual. Turkish youth, human rights, a western-oriented modernity have always been portrayed. In addition, Mustafa Kemal monuments were made visible in many parts of the country as a leader cult. However, the general view of the Turkish military is that Turkish democracy is going through a period of gentle growth. As a matter of fact, a bayonet monument adorned with ivy was erected in Taksim Square in Istanbul. This monument remained in the square until another military coup, that is, until 1980. Many pictures similar to the bayonet monument were drawn in political magazines. The emphasis is on the fact that democracy is such a gentle sapling that it cannot grow in the absence of the army. In a new nation, Turkey, the army is symbolized in this sense not as a potential enemy of democracy but as its protector. Although the name of the regime is interpreted as Kemalism from time to time, it has also been discussed as a militarist modernization type in other studies. Although it is absolutely necessary to have strong armies for the formation of new nations, its identification with democracy in the case of Turkey is an important situation. Although the relations between the army and civil society in Turkey have been the subject of many studies, especially in the legitimization of democracy and its becoming an established concept, the army's acting as an intellectual class and taking it under its protection requires many sociological studies. Because Mustafa Kemal remained the great leader and symbol of the new republic, but the position of the army in the system led to different interpretations. Although, this period is the time period that Huntington interprets as the second reverse wave for democracies. Because throughout the process, the worldwide departure from democracy is striking. Because most democracies have turned into an authoritarian system with military coups (Huntington, 1993). The place of the soldier in the historical experience of Turkish democracy has sometimes resembled the French adventure with certain intonations.

CONCLUSION

The idea of democracy emerges as the universal value of humankind's long historical experience. It has definitions such as a good and moral system or defending the national interest. In addition, it also includes meanings such as the collective self-government of the people and the will of the majority. Along with the modern period, ideologies have dealt with different dimensions of democracy and formed their views. However, it is not possible for a concept to be considered independent of political culture and placed on the mind map of a society. Although democracy is used almost in the same sense, the adventure of establishing democracy has progressed quite differently. It is possible to construct democracy, which stands as a universal basic political principle before us, from the perspective of the founding ideology and the nation-state, both through institutional and newly invented traditions. Political symbolism is a way of thinking about how concepts should be placed in the memory of nations. The ideologies that were effective in the establishment of countries have handled democracy in different ways and symbolized it. Democracy, like other political concepts, often emerges in the form of a monument, a visual, a flag and a discourse. Today, political symbolism has the power to transmit, change and even manipulate a nation's history, ideology and culture. It is possible to trace the place of democracy in the construction of collective memory through the symbols of nations. Political history is the accumulation of human experience. In this sense, it is also a collection of symbols.

REFERENCES

Althusser, L. (2014). Ideology and Ideological State Apparatuses (G. M. Gosgharian, Trans.). Verso Publish.

Baradat, L. (2012). *Political Ideologies*. Routledge.

Barthes, R. (1974). *S/Z: An Essay*. Farrar, Straus and Giroux.

Barthes, R. (1977). *Music Text Image*. Fontana Press.

Baudrillard, J. (2009). *The Transparency of Evil: Essays on Extreme Phenomena*. Verso Books.

Baumann, Z. (2005). *Liquid Life*. Polity Press.

Billig, M. (1995). *Banal Nationalism*. Sage Publications.

Brubaker, R. (1990). Immigration, Citizenship, and the Nation-State in France and Germany: A Comparative Historical Analysıs. *International Sociology, 5*.

Castoriadis, C. (1987). *The Imaginary Institution of Society*. The MIT Press.

Gans, H. (1999). *Popular Culture & High Culture*. Basic Books.

Geertz, C. (1977). *The Interpretation of Culture*. Basic Books.

Gorbhacev, M. (2007). *Memoirs*. Transworld Publishers Limited.

Gottdiener, M. (1995). *Postmodern Semiotics: Material Culture and the Forms of Postmodern Life*. Blackwell.

Guiraud, P. (1975). *Semiology*. Routledge.

Heywood, A. (2003). *Political Ideologies* (3rd ed.). MacMillan.

Huntington, S. (1993). *The Third Wave: Democratization in the Late Twentieth Century*. Oklohama University Press.

Idzerda, S. (1959). *The Background of the French Revolution*. American Historical Association.

Jameson, F. (1992). *Postmodernism, or, The Cultural Logic of Late Capitalism*. Duke University Press. doi:10.1215/9780822378419

Karpat, K. (2001). The Rise of Modern Turkey. *The Journal of Military History, 65*(3).

Kertzer, D. (1988). *Ritual Politics and Power*. Yale University Press.

Kessler, C. S. (1978). *Islam and Politics in Malay State*. Cornel University Press.

Lacan, J. (2001). *Ecrits: A Selection*. Routledge. doi:10.4324/9780203995839

Lippmann, W. (1998). *Public Opinion: With a New Introduction by Micheal Curtis*. Transaction Publishers. (Orginal work published 1922)

Lustig, J. (1982). *Corporate Liberalism: The Origins of Modern American Political Theory, 1890-1920*. University of California Press.

Lyotard, J-F. (1997). *The Postmodern Condition: a Report on Knowledge*. University Press.

Mitchell, W. J. (1986). *Iconology: Image, Text, Ideology*. The University of Chicago Press.

Rosenberg, A. (1965). *Democracy and Socialism*. Beacon Press.

Roskin, M. (2000). *Countries and Concepts* (7th ed.). Pearson Press.

Sartori, G. (1987). *Democratic Theory*. Greenwood Press.

Schmidt, M., & Ritter, G. A. (1990). *The Rise and Fall of a Socialist Welfare State*. Springer.

Staton, H. (2010). *The Statue of Liberty*. Chelsea Clubhouse.

Tachau & Heper. (1983). The State, Politics, and the Military in Turkey. *Comparative Politics, 16*(1).

Tocqueville, A. (2006). *Democracy in America*. Harper Classics. (Orginal work published 1835)

Vagts, A. (1959). *A History of Militarism*. Meridian Books.

Van, D., & Teun, A. (1998). Ideology. Sage Publications.

Vincent, A. (2003). *Modern Political Ideologies*. Blackwell.

Volosinov, V. (1986). Marxism and the Philosophy of Language (L. Mateska & I. Tutunik, Trans.). Harvard University Press.

KEY TERMS AND DEFINITIONS

Democracy: A way of governing which depends on the will of the people. Its two main principles are individual autonomy and equality.

Ideology: The narratives that emerged after the Enlightenment and claimed to offer guides to understanding life.

Indicator: Any object, situation or event that points to something other than itself, is representative and can be interpreted.

Meaning: The stage of understanding what is happening around us.

Political Communication: A method of effectively using symbols and other conductors to deliver political messages to the masses.

Political Symbolism: Manipulating the use of symbols to reinforce the identity of groups.

Symbols: Signs that convey meanings in a short way.

Chapter 4
Democratic Peace Theory and Its Role in Practice on the Way of Providing International Security and Cooperation

Natalia Beruashvili
Independent Researcher, Georgia

ABSTRACT

The theory of democratic peace was first invented by the German philosopher Immanuel Kant in his 1795 article "Permanent Peace." In this paper, Kant argues that states with governments of constitutional republics are less likely to go to war because doing so requires the consent of the people who would be at war. While monarch kings and queens can unilaterally declare war, given the security of their subjects, a government elected by the people takes the decision more seriously. The United States first promoted the concepts of democratic peace theory in 1832 by adopting the Monroe Doctrine. In this historic part of international politics, the US has affirmed that it will not tolerate the attempts of European monarchies to colonize any democratic nation in North or South America.

INTRODUCTION

Democratic peace theory (or liberal democratic theory, or simply democratic peace) is a popular theory that democratic regimes, or more narrowly liberal democratic regimes, do not go to war with each other.

Proponents of the theory of democratic peace identify several factors that contribute to the onset of peace between democratic states:

- Democratic leaders are forced to admit guilt for the defeat in the war before the voting public;
- Publicly accountable statesmen tend to create diplomatic institutions to resolve international tensions;

DOI: 10.4018/978-1-6684-4543-3.ch004

- Democracies do not tend to view countries with related policies and governance doctrines as hostile;
- Democracies tend to have more public wealth than other states and therefore avoid war in order to preserve infrastructure and resources.

Main Principles of the Theory of Democratic Peace (TDP)

The special interest in world politics as a scientific discipline is the analysis of the interaction of democratic states, which is reflected in the theory of the democratic world, which was mentioned when considering the theories of international relations. The origins of this theory go back to the thesis of Immanuel Kant about "perpetual peace." The philosopher put forward the hypothesis that democratic states will behave differently than non-democratic states in the international arena. Focusing on better moral principles, these countries will establish peace with each other (Kant, 1795). The idea of I. Kant was developed in the twentieth century, has emerged as a theory of a democratic world. First, several authors engaged in studying the problems of the world drew attention to the fact that developed democracies are not at war with each other, confirming this based on statistical analysis. But immediately began to raise objections. In general, they boiled down to the following provisions.

1. The history of the interaction of democracies is too small to draw general conclusions based on statistical data.
2. There is no clear definition of which states can be called developed democratic, and it is not always clear what does it mean, "they do not fight with each other."

Discussing within the framework of these two main arguments, opponents of the theory of a democratic world cite historical examples, which, in their opinion, contradict the thesis that "democracies do not fight each other." For example, during the Second World War, Great Britain declared war on Finland, although there was no armed action. Is it possible to consider this fact of declaring war as its actual conduct? There is no answer to this question.

Germany, during the outbreak of the First World War, is often referred to as another historical example of hostilities between democracies. The question here is how far Germany can be viewed as a democratic state if we take into account such features of its government as the de facto independent role of the Kaiser in decision-making. There are other examples too.

In all cases, supporters and opponents of the theory of democratic peace put forward their arguments and counterarguments. In general, at least as a general pattern with possible exceptions, the theory of the democratic world justifies itself. Therefore, discussions are of greater interest not as to whether this is the case and what the exceptions maybe, but why developed democracies do not enter into war with each other.

In general, the analysis of the theory of the democratic world can be presented in full detail by giving a comparative analysis of two main concepts - M. Doyle and B. Russet. The first, based on the ideas of I. Kant, argues that in foreign policy, developed democracies rely on the same principles as in internal ones (Doyle, 1983). Governments of democratic countries, including when entering a war, must justify themselves in front of their citizens. The presence of common principles and values among democratic countries forms their "peaceful union" and at the same time aggressive behavior towards autocracies. B. Russet offers a different explanation of the phenomenon of a democratic world. It comes from the cultural and structural features of democratic states and argues that citizens in democratic countries see themselves as free people who are accustomed to respecting the rights of others (Russet, 1998). The openness of borders, the free exchange of information in democratic states reinforce this perception. These cultural characteristics, which are absorbed by man since childhood, limit the manifestation of aggression against other humans. In addition, people in democratic countries are used to resolving conflicts peacefully - through negotiations, agreements, judicial procedures.

The second factor explaining the phenomenon of a democratic world, according to B. Russet, is the principle of decision-making in democratic countries, including the beginning of the war. War-oriented leaders must conduct these decisions through appropriate legitimate procedures. In the event of a conflict, democratic countries are forced to spend more on making decisions about the start of hostilities. As a result, a "cooling" period arises, allowing to pay off the first emotional reactions and look for a rational way out of the conflict.

In principle, both concepts do not contradict each other. Rather, the latter is only a more developed approach. Nevertheless, many questions remain. For example, why is the aggression of democratic countries towards non-democratic states possible? Is there always a response, or defensive, reaction? If so, what is perceived as a threat? Why did democratic countries wage imperialist wars? If these were not mature democracies, then where is the maturity criterion?

Influence of Democracy on Politics in the World

With the coming to power of the 1st administration of Bill Clinton, the theory of democratic peace acquired the status of an axiom in US foreign policy, without affecting the domestic one. The high degree of adherence to this concept has prompted its apologists to claim that it has "acquired the status of law in the social sciences."

This theory is one of the key prerequisites for building the US foreign policy doctrine. Thus, presidents representing both dominant political parties have spoken out in support of this theory. In one of Democrat Clinton's speeches:

By far the best strategy for securing security and building lasting peace is to support the spread of democracy around the world. Democracies do not attack each other.
Republican George W. Bush after meeting with British Prime Minister Tony Blair:

The reason I advocate democracy so strongly is because democracies don't go to war with each other. The reason is that people from most democratic societies do not like war, they understand what war means... I believe that democracy can bring peace. And that is why I believe so strongly that our path in the Middle East is the spread of democracy.

Also, Tony Blair alone spoke out in support of this theory (Chitadze, 2016).

Theory

Liberalists are convinced that their values are tolerant and universal. The main interests of the individual are self-preservation and material well-being. Thus, according to their own selfish interests, people should stop violence and begin to cooperate. Liberal ideas laid the foundation for a liberal ideology that differentiates states by form of government.

In the process of improving the theory, its adherents modified the main postulate of TDP (democracies do not fight each other) to the statement "wars between democracies are less likely." This amendment attracted the attention of critics, who raised the question of the possibility of competition between democracies if one of them claims to be strengthened to the detriment of US interests.

In his article The Study of Democratic Peace and Progress in International Relations, Chernoff conducted a methodological study and came to the conclusion that at the present stage of the development of science, the liberal democratic postulate that two democratic states will be more peaceful towards each other than any other the combination of states with other forms of government is generally accepted (Mkurnalidze, 2000).

There are three types of evidence for TDM: institutional, normative, and economic interdependence.

Institutional Approach

A state with a liberal democratic regime is characterized by the separation of branches of power, institutions representing the interests of citizens, the presence of a developed institution of civil society, which impose restrictions on decision-making and adjust government preferences. The leaders of this type of state are not in a position to go against the opinion of the most common sentiments of the electorate if they want to be re-elected to their post. If the leaders nevertheless take the risk and unleash a war, they will try to win it at all costs, since a political miscalculation or failure will affect their ratings, and hence the chances of re-election (Rondeli, 2003).

Regulatory Approach

TDP advocates testify that democracies are rational, predictable and trustworthy participants in international relations. Democracies perceive each other as peace-loving states. In order for a state to be recognized as democratic, an appropriate perception of it by neighbors with a democratic form of government is required (Rondeli, 2003).

Economic Interdependence

The market liberal economy of democratic states and trade between them contribute to the strengthening of trusting relationships and mutual understanding (Chitadze, 2011). According to the theory, trade and finance ties are mutually beneficial for the participants, and wars lead to the termination of transactions and, thus, the impoverishment of the population, which voters cannot themselves wish for. Wealthy countries are seen as less hostile because they have something to lose in case of war. Supporters of TDP actively promote the creation of new and expansion of existing financial, economic and trade international organizations (for example, the WTO, the International Monetary Fund) in order to achieve the greatest interdependence between the participating countries. Close economic interdependence prevents the outbreak of wars.

Criticism

A survey among high-ranking US foreign policy and security officials conducted at the beginning of the 21st century showed that they do not believe in the usefulness of this theory. Thus, the more important the positions of officials were, the less they valued (or knew about) the theory of democratic peace, but the more they knew and appreciated structural realism, the opposite theory of democratic peace.

Realists

- Criticize the empirical basis of TDP. For example, 1815-1850. Was a period of stability in Europe, but it was supported by the Holy Alliance (Russia, Austria, Prussia), that is, a group of non-democratic (monarchist) countries. Denying peacefulness between democracies, realists cite examples when democratic countries deliberately, in accordance with their military or economic interests, sought to escalate the internal situation in democratic countries (for example, the overthrow of left-wing democratic regimes (Chile (1973), Iran (early 1950s).), Indonesia (mid-1960s)) in order to contain Soviet influence), as well as the escalation of tension between themselves (the threat of British intervention in the USA in 1861, the Venezuelan crisis between Great Britain and the USA in 1895-1896, the crisis around Fashoda between France and Great Britain, Ruhr Crisis between France and the Weimar Republic of 1923) (Rondeli, 2003).
- They state that the economic, political, military potentials of democratic countries are not the same, which provokes rivalry between them, the struggle for control over sources of raw materials, and putting pressure on each other. Stronger democracies used this to their advantage and tried to subjugate the weaker ones, provoking disagreements that almost escalated into armed clashes (Rondeli, 2003). In addition, the economic interdependence of democracies is not evenly distributed among the participants.
- The behavior of states where democratization has recently taken place is criticized. Realists point out that this type of country is more aggressive than non-democratic ones and argue that this is inevitable (Chitadze, 2011). On the contrary, realists point out that non-democratic states are quite capable of being peaceful. For example, the countries of the former socialist camp in the second half of the 20th century, where nationalism and revanchist sentiments towards each other were suppressed, were quite peaceful. In addition, the USSR watched over the unity of the socialist bloc.
- Identification of problems of causation. Historical examples are indicated (for example, wars for colonies) that contradict the postulate of the peacefulness of democratic countries, but confirm that for the sake of their interests they are ready to violate liberal democratic values. Realists also take into account the factor of territorial position and its influence on the nature of foreign policy: the safer the environment, the more unpredictable the foreign policy behavior of states (Chitadze, 2011).
- The argument that the very political and civic arrangement of democratic regimes limits the behavior of their governments is questioned. Opponents of the TDP point out that authoritarian leaders also tend to soberly assess their chances before unleashing a war, since in case of defeat they will lose not only power, but also their lives. Meanwhile, the public in democracies often thinks irrationally and thus becomes the target of populist and war-interested groups.
- Realists question what states will think about how their actions will affect the joint benefit when the risks are high, on the contrary, according to realists, they will be concerned with the question of who will get more.

Constructivists

An essential aspect of constructivist criticism is the neglect of the sociocultural context. They put forward the thesis that interests are set socially, not intellectually. Since TDP and the very concept of democracy were formulated in the Western socio-political environment, they reflect the interests of Western political scientists and leaders of Western countries, therefore, democratic values are not universal. Thus, constructivists deny the possibility of a harmonious implementation of democracy in isolation from historical conditioning. In their opinion, forced democratization only exacerbates the situation in the region. An example is the former countries of the socialist camp.

- Draw attention to the meaning of the terms "war" and "peace". "War" now means not only armed conflicts, but also covert wars supported by democratic states through the supply of weapons, etc. (for example, US intelligence assistance to the Taliban in Afghanistan in 1993-1997).
- Criticism of the attempts of TDP supporters to extrapolate ideas about modern "democracy" to phenomena in retrospect. Constructivists demonstrate the evolution of the concept of "democracy" over the course of US history. At the beginning of the 20th century in the United States, liberal-minded politicians did not see a contradiction between the principles of democracy and the lack of rights of the black population or the fact that the US Senate was not directly elected.
- Constructivists also believe that democracies are not peaceful in and of themselves. Denial of any determinism and focusing on the worldview of the persons of the political process. Liberal-democratic norms are not capable of influencing the head of state if they are not shared by him. Decision makers contribute their interpretation of existing norms. Consequently, democratic states are not immune from the cases when aggressive and fanatical persons come to power. In addition, there is always the possibility of a change from a democratic system to an authoritarian one (Chitadze, 2011).
- "Democracy" is a symbol that draws a dividing line between "us" and "them", which is ethnocentrism and discrimination against other peoples.
- Constructivists show that just because democracies are less militant among themselves, this does not mean at all that the same will be true between democratic and non-democratic countries. On the contrary, they suggest greater aggressiveness of the former towards the latter. In addition, it is pointed out that democratic countries do not have a clear understanding of which states are authoritarian and which are democratic. For example, the United States changed its mind several times about the nature of the Hitler regime.

Liberals

Some liberals criticize TDP mainly on the grounds that the "quality of democracy" has changed. In the world, modern democracies are being modified into oligarchic ones. For example, the Arab-Israeli war of 1967, the Israeli intervention in Lebanon in 1982 cannot be regarded as defensive, and therefore do not quite correspond to the spirit of democratic states (Chitadze, 2011).

Integration and Democratization of the World as Tendencies of the Modern Stage of Its Development

Integrating Processes in the Modern World - Approaches for Understanding the Integration Processes

Globalization, being the central trend of the modern stage of world development, is accompanied by integration processes, or by integration. It's not by chance that one of the approaches to globalization suggests considering it as continuous in the historical plan expansion of that space, on which happens the intensive interaction of people. Nevertheless, integration is only a part of the globalization process, albeit one of the most significant. First of all, speaking about integration, it's necessary to keep in mind that it implies the rapprochement of state actors. Non-state actors usually are not considered when studying integration processes or at least they end up on the periphery of research attention. In this regard more accurately will be arguments about the inclusion of this or that country in integration, rather than globalization processes, as the state is integrated entirely based on the signing of the intergovernmental agreements. Globalization, firstly, does not imply such agreements, and secondly, it can flow differently for various regions of one state. Alone internal regions of the state are successfully included in globalization processes, others end up as outsiders. With extreme differences, the inclusion of different internal regions in globalization raises a threat of breakdown of the state.

Another important point when analyzing integration is that this process involves cooperation between states in different spheres, areas, and forms. Respectively, there's division and different kinds of cooperation. Thus, it can be indicated on the following basis for identifying the concrete types of integration:

- Political, economic, scientific-technical, etc. (by subject);
- Global, regional, sub-regional integration (on a geographic basis).

In this case, it can be noted another version, that cooperation and integration can go "in breadth", as a result of an increase in the number of participants in the process, also "in-depth", through intensification of interaction in different spheres among the same participants.

The practice of interstate cooperation has been existing for a long time. However, only in the second half of the twentieth century did interstate cooperation on a large scale acquire constant forms. This, in the first place, is connected with the intensification of cooperation, enlargement of its spheres, and development of integrational processes, which demanded the establishment of intergovernmental formations and institutions. Therefore, another important point, characterizing integration, is not only cooperation, but the creation of a mechanism for interstate cooperation, in other words – the institutionalization of cooperation. In this case, integration is, firstly, closely related to the development of intergovernmental organizations (IGOs), which offer the formation of interstate decision-making mechanisms. Through joint institutions, the integration processes are carried out. Secondly, integration is considered in two points of view: as a process and as a result of the interaction of the states.

What encourages states to integrate? First of all – the existence of common problems, which are easier to solve and only possible, by joint efforts. The development of the world at the end of the twentieth century and the beginning of the twenty-first century led to the strengthening of international contacts, the interdependence of the world, especially in the economic field, which contributes to integration processes and promotes the creation of various kinds of intergovernmental organizations. This interdependence is closely tied to the growth of global problems, and for its solving the concerted action by various states is required.

Another reason encouraging integration processes is the interest of "medium" and "small" states in increasing their international influence. For these countries, it's easier to impact the international processes with combined efforts rather than by acting alone. With the example of the European Union, it can be indicated, that if the founder members of the European community were 3 "small" and 3 "big" states, from 1973 – 5 "small" and 4 "big", in the 1980s – respectively, 8 and 4, in 1995 – 11 "small" and 4 "big", then among the new members, who joined EU in 2004, 9 countries were "small", except Poland, which can be regarded as "medium" state. In 2007, and later in 2013 all three new members of the EU were "small" states. The State, by joining the international organization formally loses several functions, but simultaneously acquires an additional number of other functions, which is especially important for the "small" states (Chitadze, 2016).

What is integration? The Realist school is prone to considering the integration processes and activity of international organizations as a certain product of state interactions, which fundamentally does not go beyond their external politics. In other words, the emergence and development of intergovernmental organizations, according to this view, did not fundamentally change the nature of international relations.

Unlike realism, the approaches to integration and international organizations were formed in the framework of the liberal tradition, where these questions received the most development. In them IGOs act by new formations. Theoretical understanding of the integration processes starts in the middle of the twentieth century and is connected with the liberal tradition, in the framework of which two theoretical schools (approaches) were formed: *Functionalism/neo-functionalism and federalism.*

David Mitrany is considered to be the father of functionalism, who in 1943 published his work: "A Working Peace System". In it, he analyzed the reasons, because which the League of Nations failed, and concluded that integration processes cannot start with political aspects. In this case, the state begins to fear for their sovereignty. D. Mitrany focuses on the development of economic, social, scientific, and technical integration that has to be from the start. Political integration remains at the second level. D. Mitrany and his followers insisted that it's important for people to work out the habit of cooperation and show the benefits of joint actions (Mitrany, 1966).

Initially, functionalism was not connected with the analysis of how transnational corporations develop and focused attention on interstate cooperation. However, afterward, several types of research have concluded that the activity of TNC, which not often leads to the economic integration of various states, was developing in fact according to the logic of functionalism. Representatives of TNC often perceive the world holistically and see themselves as cosmopolitans. All this contributes, according to the functionalist point of view, to expanding of national boundaries and creation of a single economic culture, in the conclusion of which state policy more and more becomes at the same time both - internal and external, thus, *intermestic.*

Until recently, the process of economic integration was considered by many scholars as a passage strictly "ascending" to several steps. It has been determined the following aspects:

1. The creation of a free trade zone, when member countries remove customs barriers and quantitative restrictions in mutual trade. Usually, is taken into account the gradual mutual cancellation of custom fees and other restrictions.
2. The formation of the customs union, within which happens the movement of goods and services at a single customs tariff and by a uniform foreign trade policy about the third countries.

3. Formation of the single market, which includes the elimination of barriers between countries not only in mutual trade but also in the movement of capital and labor. At this stage happens the development of policies for the development of industries and sectors of the economy, common to all integrating countries. Also, general funds form for social and regional development of backward regions, including in the integration association.
4. Organization of economic and monetary union. Previously existing forms of integration are complemented by member countries conducting the unified economic and monetary policy, by the creation of systems of international regulations of social-economic processes.
5. Final, fifth, stage was defined as the transition to political integration and creation of common political institutions.

In recent times, this integration scheme is referred to with more care, meaning that this process, firstly, is not necessarily going in the progressive direction – it can be "slowed down" on this or that stage; Secondly, economic integration does not always lead to political, as many thoughts earlier, highlighting the fifth stage. Exactly the political sphere turns out to be the most complicated and painful in processes of integration, which can be seen in the example of EU, where the question about Common Foreign and Security Policy (CFSP) was fixed in the document of Maastricht Treaty, signed in 1992 (EU, 1990-1999). But still, this area in the EU remains less developed compared to others, although, in recent years significant shifts are emerging.

All these points are marked by the opponents of functionalism. Also, the thesis of functionalism, that political differences will disappear as cooperation develops is criticized. In practice, quite often it's the other way around – it's not technical and economic cooperation that affects policy, but a political decision leads to the development of cooperation in a particular area. For example, it was precisely for political reasons that the USA left UNESCO during the concrete period.

Representatives of the federalism school, opposite from the previous one, moved political integration to the forefront, believing that international relations must be built on transferring some of the powers to supranational entities from the outset. This direction is characterized by a special emphasis on the creation of political institutions. If the integration process of functionalists is about the principle of "from down-up" then according to federalists, on the contrary – "From top to down".

Federalists, representatives of which are, in particular, researchers like A. Etzioni, A. Spinelli, etc. generally received the least distribution (Etzioni, 2001). Nevertheless, the ideas of federalism became noticeable from the first general elections of the European Parliament in 1979 (1979 Direct Elections).

Within the frameworks of federalism, the ideas of "world governance" were actively developing at one time, which had to unite in the common state and remove, in the opinion of the adherents of this school, inter-state conflicts from the agenda. Ideas about world governance met stiff resistance from the side of different kinds of researchers and politicians, who emphasized the necessity to preserve national and state identity. Later, many works appeared, which showed the failure, at least shortly, to implement these ideas. At the same time the concept of "world governance" stays popular among several non-governmental organizations, which see its realization as their task.

Under the influence of Federalism, functionalism received further development and it exists in the modern world in the form of neo-functionalism. This direction, based on the main premises of functionalism, included some features of federalism. In neo-functionalism practical problems are prioritized in the spheres of health, technological change, legal and other issues that matter to the whole of humanity. Under this, the importance of political decisions is emphasized. Exactly they – the issues that are important on the global scale – contribute, according to this point of view, to integration processes and push the members to the further unification in the sphere of economy. Neo-functionalists usually use the development of the European Union as a model to illustrate their theoretical views.

The integration processes themselves are far from simple ones. The national interest of some states clashes with the interest of other states, units, regions. To this should be added that levels of integration are usually on the different stages of economic and social development. Therefore, despite the mutual benefit from integration, the contribution of some in particular spheres is greater than others. The heterogeneity of interests of various groups within integrating countries means that someone benefits from integration to a greater degree, therefore is interested in it, while other segments of the population or groups are losers. The latter oppose integration processes and put pressure on government structures.

There are other costs of integration. As in the case of globalization, not only the positive aspects that countries possess are integrated, but also the negative ones. So, in the early 1990s, Venezuela discovered that after the opening of the border with Colombia, its territory was used for drug trafficking.

All this compels, along with the traditional theories of integration: functionalism, neo-functionalism, federalism, to discuss problems and, accordingly, to propose theoretical schemes related to the limitation of integration processes. S. Huntington, in an article published in 1996 in the journal "Foreign Affairs", "The West Unique, Not Universal," expressed doubt about the possibility and expediency of any kind of universal "integration" (Huntington, 1996). In his opinion, integration processes should be limited within the framework of civilization. The world, according to the researcher, is becoming more modernized (using modern technologies, with an emphasis on economic development, etc.), but at the same timeless "western", does not accept the values inherent in Western European civilization, as well as its culture and religion. Based on this premise, the United States, for example, as the author believes, should closely cooperate and, accordingly, be part of integration formations with its West European partners, which will help preserve and develop this civilization and to which they all belong, and keep their distance from other civilizations. In a narrower sense, if we are talking for example, about the enlargement of NATO, this organization, according to S. Huntington, should closely cooperate and include such countries close in civilizational relations as the Baltic countries, Slovenia, but not those oriented to Islam or Orthodoxy. In the future, NATO's relations with the "distant" in civilizational terms - Turkey and Greece, according to S. Huntington, will become weakened (Huntington, 1996).

Is the principle of civilization a limiting factor in the processes of development and integration? It seems that such a statement would be a simplification of modern international processes. Moreover, several facts, such as the active role of Japan in the activities of the seven leading countries of the world, according to S. Huntington, belonging to different civilizations, are poorly explained (Huntington, 1996).

At the same time, it is obvious that on the path of increasing integration, when these processes in one area stimulate it in others, which can be called spillover, the opposite processes are also possible, which can be named as spillback, when the regional integration scheme fails, as happened in the case of attempts of integration in East Africa. A regional integration structure can also stagnate, which can be called spill around. Under these conditions, integration in certain areas begins to contradict the processes which are taking place in other areas.

Box 1.

It is important!
For the development of the regional integration processes its necessary the following conditions: geographic location, the stable economic development, similarities of the political systems, positive view of the population on integration – public support of the integration processes, internal political stability, similarity of the historic and social development, comparative forms of governance and economic systems, comparative uniformity in the field of culture, close level of the military development and economic resources, common understanding of the foreign threats, comparative structure of the governmental agencies, possessing the experience for cooperation.

Different processes, leading to the opposite in comparison with the integration of the results – the disintegration of the states or interstate formations, is described in the literature as "disintegration". It's important to underline that it, just like the term "integration", refers primarily to interstate relations. In 1991 when the USSR collapsed, in the place of which 15 new states emerged (Chitadze, 2017), some international organizations also collapsed, in which the Soviet Union played a key role (in particular the Council for Mutual Economic Assistance, Warsaw Treaty Organization). In the 1990s the states such as Yugoslavia, Czechoslovakia also disintegrated. In the first case, the disintegration was painful, with several armed conflicts, in the second case it was held gently - peacefully, getting the name of "velvet divorce". Among newly formed countries, strong separatist tendencies were observed, for example, in the case of Moldova (problem of Transnistria), Georgia (Abkhazia and Tskhinvali District - so-called South Ossetia), Crimea and Donbass Region (Ukraine), Azerbaijan (Nagorno Karabakh), Russia (Chechnya), etc.

Relations between integration and disintegration processes should rather be viewed similarly to the existing one between globalization and regionalization. The world after the Cold War is characterized by many intrastate and interstate relations. This restructuring proceeds primarily along the path of integration processes, which is especially clearly seen in the example of the development of the European Union, but at the same time does not exclude the disintegration of the former unions and formations.

Democratization of the World

The Concept of Democratization and Democratic "Wave"

Various authors indicate democratization as a tendency of modern world development. At the same time, the concept itself in political science is mainly used in two meanings. The democratization, firstly, is understood as the indication of raising the number of democratic states; secondly, strengthening and developing democratic institutions and processes in different countries. The latter has special value for states that are in the process of transition to building a democratic state i.e., democratic transition. G. O'Donnel and Ph. Schmitter distinguishes the following steps in democratic transition: Liberalization, democratization, and consolidation (Schmitter, 2017).

And yet, in world politics, in contrast to political science, the notion of "democratization" is more often used in the first sense, as an increase in the number of democratic states. A more understanding of the democratization of the modern world is possible – as an expansion of the circle of participants in international cooperation. However, this approach is not yet well established in world politics.

There are different views and procedures for assessing which countries can be considered democratic. Disputes are often caused related to the states who are in the transition period, in which several signs of democratic development are present, while some other signs are not evident. However, in the most general form, according to the data of American researcher D. Caldwell, in 1941 approximately 25% of the states could be considered as democratic, and in 1996 their number already reached 40%, and in the second decade of the XXI Century – about 50%. If we take into account countries that are in the process of democratic transition, then this figure, according to the American institute Freedom House, which analyses democratic development in the world, can reach about 75% in the third and fourth decade of the XXI century (Freedom House, 2019). American researcher and editor-in-chief of Foreign Affairs, F. Zakaria, was writing that at the beginning of the 21-st century, 118 countries were democratic (Zakaria, 2003). In any case, no matter what specific figures will be taken as a basis, almost all authors agree with the fact that the number of democratic countries in the world is increasing. In this case, however, many researchers have several doubts, which will be discussed later.

The emergence of democratic states in the world was not linear. S. Huntington published in the "Journal of Democracy" an article called "Democracy's Third Wave", as well as a book "The Third Wave: Democratization in the Late of Twentieth Century", distinguishing periods in world history, associated with the development of democratization processes (Waves of Democratization), and peculiar democratic backsliding (Huntington, 1993). Some authors, such as R. Dix, pushing away from some specific events, indicate slightly different dates for the development of waves of democratization than S. Huntington. Or the events of late 1989 – early 1991 in Eastern Europe are distinguished in another fourth separate wave of democratization, for example by Ph. Schmitter (Schmitter, 1991). Nevertheless, in general, if we do not take into account the differences in approaches of various researchers, we can distinguish the following waves, or stages, of democratization.

The first wave of democratization is the longest, it lasted for a century and dates back to S. Huntington 1820-1920. During this "wave" more than 20 democratic states were formed (29 – according to S. Huntington and 21 – according to R. Dix) (Chitadze, 2016). These countries were characterized by parliamentary and party systems with wide voting rights. The first "wave" was followed by a "backsliding" from the main road of democratic development, which lasted from the second half of the 1920s through the first half of the 1940s. and is associated with the advent of fascism in several countries around the world (Huntington, 1991).

The second "wave" (mid-1940 – early 1960s) was caused by the defeat of fascism in the Second World War and the collapse of the colonial system after it comes, according to S. Huntington, a new regressive wave, during which several military and authoritarian regimes were formed (including in 1967 in Greece and 1973 – in Chile). In general, the second backsliding lasts from the early 1960s through the early 1970s (Huntington, 1991).

Finally, a new, third "wave" begins in the first half of the 1970s. democratic processes grip the Wester Europe (Greece – 1974, Portugal – 1975, Spain – 1977); Latin America (Dominican Republic – 1975, Honduras – 1982, Brazil – 1985, Peru – 1988, Chile – 1990 and others); Asia (Turkey – 1988, Philippines – 1986, South Korea – 1988); Eastern Europe (Hungary – 1989, Czechoslovakia – 1989, Poland – 1989, Bulgaria – 1989 Baltic states in 1991, etc.); Africa (In South Africa the first general elections were held in 1994) (Chitadze, 2016).

What causes the democratization processes? Different authors give different answers to the question about the cases contributing to this. Political scientists usually consider two groups of factors, variables:

- Structural (independent variables) – the level of economic and social development, social–class processes, dominant values in society, etc.

- Procedural (dependent variables) – accepted decisions, personal characteristics of politicians, etc.

A detailed analysis of these two groups of factors is conducted by the researcher A. Y. Melville. Modified in the "funnel of causality" model, which was proposed by American author D. Campbell and his colleagues to analyze the behavior of the voter, he used it to study transition problems. At the same time in the very process of democratic transition A., Y. Melville highlighted the phases of the establishment and consolidation of democracy (Chitadze, 2016). Further, in the study of factors influencing the institution of democracy, he proposes "a gradual transition from predominantly structural to predominantly procedural analysis", and while studying the second phase - from micro to macro factors.

In political science, the external environment, the trends of world development are usually considered as one of the structural variables of the democratization process: how much does it contribute (or not) to this process? However, in the modern world, with an ever-closer interweaving of foreign and domestic policy, the international environment can act as a structural and procedural variable. And the latter seems to be more and more significant. Decision-making (which is a procedural variable) by the world community about this or that country can lead to the development of democratic processes in them. The UN has repeatedly adopted resolutions regarding the apartheid regime in South Africa, as well as the decision on sanctions, which was the factor influencing the country's refusal from the policy of apartheid and the holding of democratic elections in 1994.

The end of the twentieth century, which coincided with the third "wave" of democratization, which by several states, and by the degree of their involvement in democratic processes, is, perhaps, particularly turbulent, brought with its other trend of world development – globalization and integration of the world. All these processes strengthen each other. Following democratic principles and traditions for the big number of participants is a vital example. Staying out of the world "democratic club" in the modern globalizing world means to be a kind of an outcast. This encourages more and more new associations to be guided by democratic values.

Figure 1. Democracy index, 2019
Source: https://blog.pressreader.com/public-libraries-have-an-important-role-in-sustaining-democracy

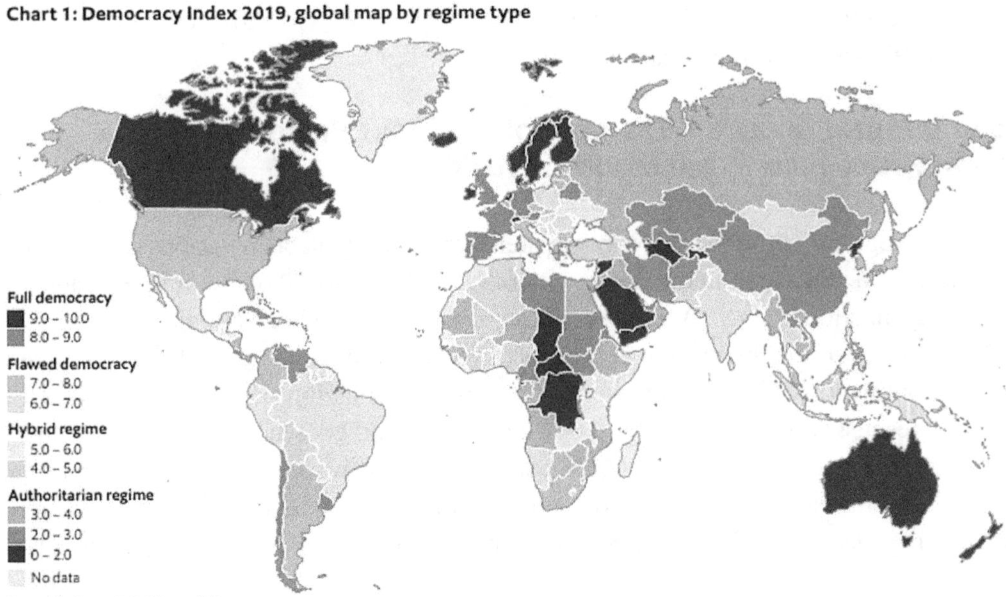

To deny the democratic path of development, state leaders are deliberately going, opposing their country to the rest of the world. In this context, one can view the process of democratic transformation at the end of the twentieth century precisely as a tendency of the political development of the world, in the implementation of which the non - endogenous (internal) factors are becoming more important (level of social-economic development, political processes in society, etc.) and exogenous regarding this state, i.e. international environment. Exactly this encourages democratic transformation.

The democratization of the late twentieth century gave the foundation to F. Fukuyama to talk about the end of history. In the sense that the historical development of humanity has made its choice in favor of democracy enlargement. His article has been criticized a lot. Objections were made by such statements as the forecast about the ending of the conflicts in the world in connection with the ending of ideological confrontation between East and West, linearity and uniformity of historical development, etc. however, the thesis about the processes of democratization as a common tendency, perhaps, was least contested. Indeed, if at the beginning of the twentieth century, a relatively small number of states could be considered as democratic, they not always take responsibility for the electoral and other rights (in several countries the rights of women and national minorities, also people without property were limited) in the start of the twenty-first century these problems turned out to be if not solve, solvable (Fukuyama, 1989).

However, it should be emphasized that democratization is not an unambiguous process. With particular clarity, this appeared as a result of the last "wave" of democratization, when illiberal democracies, hybrid regimes, and imitation of democracies were formed. Their essence lies in the fact that democratic institutions and processes in various states are used as an external form, sometimes used as a way to cover the undemocratic mechanisms for the realization of power. Perhaps, the term "illiberal democracies" has received the greatest distribution due to the work of F. Zakaria, published in 1997, in "Foreign Policy" journal. F. Zakaria pushes away the statement of R. Holbrooke, who in 1996, offered to imagine the example, that during free democratic elections in the country the candidate who openly confesses racist, fascists or separatists' views and opposes a peaceful solution of the conflict, particularly in Yugoslavia is elected by population (Holbrooke, 1998). This leader democratically comes to power, but he professes undemocratic views and pursues a corresponding policy. F. Zakaria breaks this logic of reasoning and draws attention to the fact that the emergence of the so-called illiberal democracies is possible i.e., those who took only external attributes of democratic transformation. In addition, the number of these kinds of countries, as he wrote, had been increasing. In 1990 they were 22% of the total number of democratic states, and in 1997 – already 35% (Zakaria, 1997).

European Integration as an Example of the Most Profound Integration Processes in the Modern World

In recent years integration processes have been intensively taking place in various regions of the world – in North America, in particular, in the framework of NAFTA (North American Free Trade Agreement), in Asia such organizations as ASEAN (Association of Southeast Asian Nations) was established (Karumidze, 2004). However, the integration processes have achieved the greatest degree of development on the European continent within the framework of the European Union (EU). The main discussion in the EU countries goes just about how far integration can and should go: what should remain under the jurisdiction of the national state, and what should be included in the responsibility of supranational entities.

The idea of the unification of Europe to prevent war was expressed even during the Second World War. After its finishing, one of the active supporters of integration processes in Europe was French foreign minister R. Schumann, who, together with another French author, political analyst J. Monnet, largely laid the foundations for the future development of Europe. The first practical step was the creation of the European Coal and Steel Community (ECSC), designed to coordinate and stimulate the economic development of six European countries – Belgium, Germany, Luxembourg, Netherlands, and France. The strengths of these countries were directed at facilitating the trade of coal and steel inside the "six" (Kapanadze, Gogolashvili, 2006).

The next step in the development of European integration is connected to the Rome Treaty of 1957 when the same six countries decided to transfer the principles of cooperation that were laid earlier to a different sphere – nuclear energy – and formed the European Atomic Energy Community (EURATOM). The European Economic Community (EEC) was created as well, having a name known as the Common Market. A free trade zone was formed, where tariffs and restrictions on the movement of goods within the borders of the EEC were abolished. ECSC, Euratom, and EEC formed the European Community (EC), which at the beginning of the 90th gained the name European Union (Kapanadze, Gogolashvili, 2006).

In 1981 the single European act was adopted, which set a goal for 1992 to create a real common market with free movement of goods, capital, and labor and services (Kapanadze, Gogolashvili, 2006).

Especially intensively went through the integration processes in Europe after the end of the Cold War (the end of 1980s – the beginning of the 1990s). A significant event in this period was the signing of the Maastricht Treaty, determining a new stage of development of European integration. of great importance was the creation of the Schengen group (zone), which facilitated visa and customs movements inside Europe, and also the transformation of the European Economic Community into a more integrated structure – the European Union (Chochua, 2007).

All the processes of modern European integration is characterized by multidimensionality. They simultaneously cover various spheres – economic, political, humanitarian, etc. in addition, they are characterized by a feature such as a tendency to expand the integration members.

The crisis in Kosovo gave impetus to the development of the EU in the field of common foreign and security policy. There was a decision to create expeditionary forces numbering 60,000 people. Agreement in Nice in 2001 envisaged the formation of European rapid reaction force by 2003 (NATO, 2006).

Box 2.

It is interesting!

The **European Union (EU)** is a political and economic union of 27 (the UK officially left the organization in 2020) member states that are located primarily in Europe. It has an area of 4,475,757 km2 (1,728,099 miles2) and an estimated population of about 513 million. The EU has developed an internal single market through a standardized system of laws that apply in all member states in those matters, and only those matters, where members have agreed to act as one. EU policies aim to ensure the free movement of people, goods, services, and capital within the internal market, enact legislation in justice and home affairs and maintain common policies on trade, agriculture, fisheries, and regional development. For travel within the Schengen Area, passport controls have been abolished. A monetary union was established in 1999 and came into full force in 2002 and is composed of 19 EU member states which use the euro currency. The EU and European citizenship were established when the Maastricht Treaty came into force in 1993. The EU traces its origins to the European Coal and Steel Community (ECSC) and the European Economic Community (EEC), established, respectively, by the 1951 Treaty of Paris and the 1957 Treaty of Rome. The original members of what came to be known as the European Communities were the Inner Six: Belgium, France, Italy, Luxembourg, the Netherlands, and West Germany. The Communities and their successors have grown in size by the accession of new member states and in power by the addition of policy areas to their remit. The latest major amendment to the constitutional basis of the EU, the Treaty of Lisbon, came into force in 2009. No member state has left the EU or its antecedent organizations (Greenland, an autonomous territory within Denmark, left the Communities in 1985). However, the United Kingdom signified its intention to leave after a membership referendum in June 2016 and is negotiating its withdrawal.
Containing 7.3% of the world population, the EU in 2017 generated a nominal gross domestic product (GDP) of 19.670 trillion US dollars, constituting approximately 24.6% of global nominal GDP. Additionally, all 27 EU countries have a very high Human Development Index, according to the United Nations Development Program. In 2012, the EU was awarded the Nobel Peace Prize. Through the Common Foreign and Security Policy, the EU has developed a role in external relations and defense. The union maintains permanent diplomatic missions throughout the world and represents itself at the United Nations, the World Trade Organization, the G7, and the G20. Because of its global influence, the European Union was described in 2006 as an emerging superpower.
Through successive enlargements, the European Union has grown from the six founding states (Belgium, France, West Germany, Italy, Luxembourg, and the Netherlands) to the current 27. Countries accede to the union by becoming a party to the founding treaties, thereby subjecting themselves to the privileges and obligations of EU membership. This entails a partial delegation of sovereignty to the institutions in return for representation within those institutions, a practice often referred to as "pooling of sovereignty".
To become a member, a country must meet the Copenhagen criteria, defined at the 1993 meeting of the European Council in Copenhagen. These require a stable democracy that respects human rights and the rule of law; a functioning market economy; and the acceptance of the obligations of membership, including EU law. Evaluation of a country's fulfillment of the criteria is the responsibility of the European Council. No member state has yet left the Union, although Greenland (an autonomous province of Denmark) withdrew in 1985. Article 50 of the Lisbon Treaty provides the basis for a member to leave the Union. Since mid-2017, the United Kingdom has been negotiating terms for its withdrawal from the EU.
Six countries are recognized as candidates for membership: Albania, Iceland, North Macedonia, Montenegro, Serbia, and Turkey, though Iceland suspended negotiations in 2013. Bosnia and Herzegovina and Kosovo are officially recognized as potential candidates, with Bosnia and Herzegovina having submitted a membership application.
The four countries forming the European Free Trade Association (EFTA) are not EU members but have partly committed to the EU's economy and regulations: Iceland, Liechtenstein, and Norway, which are a part of the single market through the European Economic Area, and Switzerland, which has similar ties through bilateral treaties. The relationships of the European microstates, Andorra, Monaco, San Marino, and Vatican City include the use of the euro and other areas of cooperation.

A half-century history of the development of European integration gives us materials for the theoretical understanding of this experience. It can be identified three fundamental principles of the concept and practice of EU integration construction:

- Integration is not a goal but a means.
- Integration requires gradualism.
- Integration needs an adequate mechanism.

Figure 2. EU Member states
Source: https://op.europa.eu/en/web/general-publications/maps

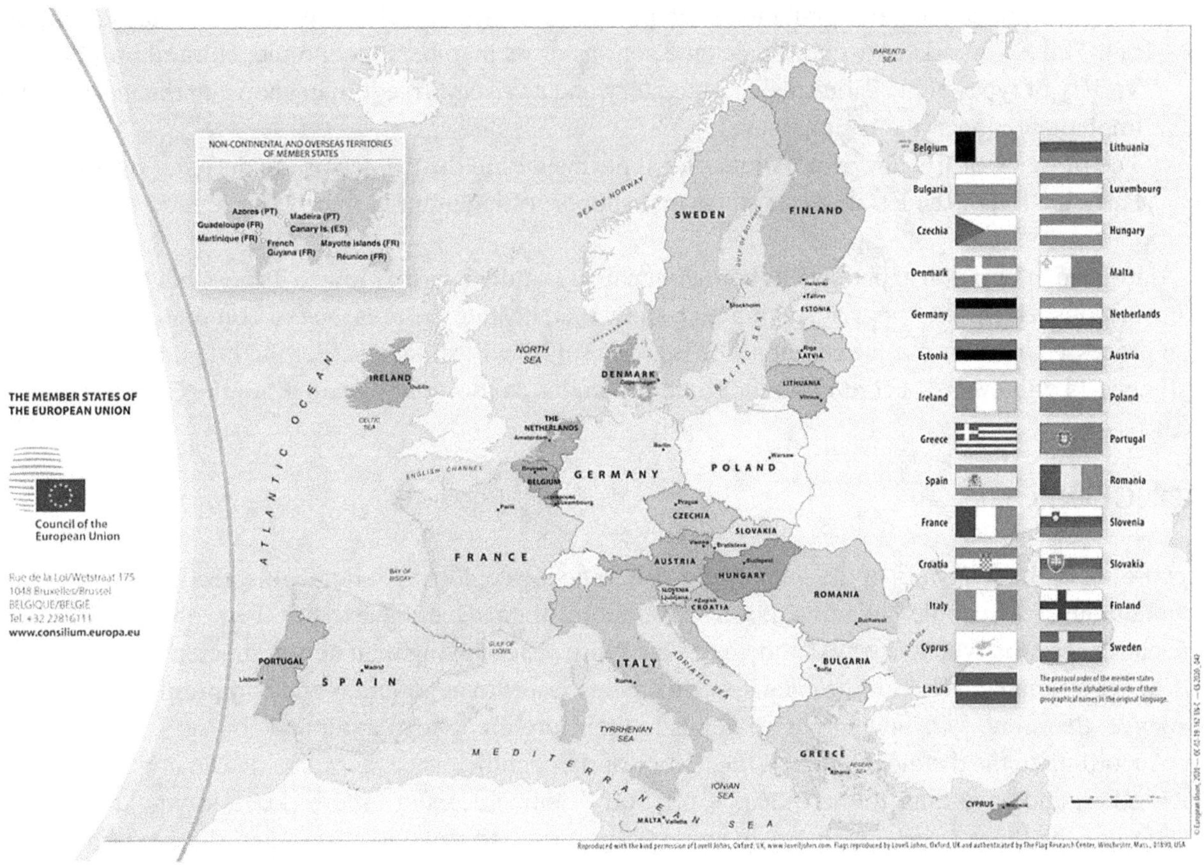

In the framework of the first principle, there are 2 aspects. Firstly, integration implies that all participants benefit, since their interests are easier to realize with joint efforts. In addition, they also contribute to the general construction, jointly use products, and exclude coercive methods of decision-making. Secondly, integration does not solve all existing problems. It's a means, it can only help in solving the problem.

The principle of gradual integration implies that this process is long and consists of several stages. In the economic field, they are the same as were listed, but with the reservations made: the creation of a free trade zone of the customs union; the formation of a common market; the formation of economic and monetary union. Haste in the transition to the next phase turns into failures, which is also shown by the experience of the EU. For example, in 1970, a plan for the formation of a monetary union was proposed, providing for the introduction of a single currency in 1980. But it was never destined to come true precisely because the EU was not ready for such steps.

It is also important to formulate five basic principles for the functioning of EU institutions:

- The presence of interstate and supranational institutions, which allows maintaining a balance between national and common interests;

- Separation between EU competencies and national institutions. The decision in some areas is determined by supranational institutions (agriculture, trade, monetary policy), in others – at the same time national and supranational (in particular, regional. Scientific and technical, social policy). Third – the EU only coordinates the actions of its members (economic, cultural policy).
- Variety of types of decisions made: obligatory and advisory, freedom in choosing the means of the implementation at the national level;
- The primacy of EU law over national legal norms within the framework underlying treaties;
- Participation of the EU member states and support of its integration processes.

European integration experience is being intensively studied with a view to its possible application in other regions. However, research and practice show that, despite the presence of common laws, integration processes in each case have their specifics. The future will show whether the integration processes in the world will evolve according to the same principles as this took place within the EU.

CONCLUSION

According to the followers of the theory of democratic peace: Democratically elected governments are accountable to the people, therefore, because the people themselves have to test themselves for the damage caused by war, which is why democracies are more peace-loving than non-democracies. Also, when resolving internal conflicts or problems, democracies resort to negotiation and compromise rather than violence; therefore, such an approach extends to their foreign policy nature and course.

According to the dyadic relation of the theory of democratic peace, democracies do not fight against each other, and according to the monadic relation - democracies are more peace-loving. The dyadic relation of the theory explains that democracies are open and trusting each other, their external problematic issues are resolved in a similar way to their internal dispute resolution approach, i.e. through negotiation and compromise. Since and because non-democratic states are characterized by opacity and their internal processes are permeated with violence and pressure, it is therefore impossible to trust an undemocratic regime. The dyadic view holds that the nature of domestic and foreign policy management by democracies is the same. Monad's claim argues that democracies do not start wars against each other, and moreover, democracies very rarely engage in war with non-democracies.

REFERENCES

Chitadze, N. (2016). *Political Sciences*. International Black Sea University.

Chitadze, N. (2017). *World Geography*. Scholars Press.

Chochua, D. (2007). *EU Institutes*. GFSIS.

Doyle, M. (1986). *Empires*. Cornell University Press.

Etzioni. (2015). *Political Unification Revisited: On Building Supranational Communities*. Retrieved from: https://rowman.com/ISBN/9780739102732/Political-Unification-Revisited-On-Building-Supranational-Communities

EU Publications. (2022). *Maps*. Retrieved from: https://op.europa.eu/en/web/general-publications/maps

Francis, F. (1992). *The End of History and the Last Man*. Retrieved from: https://www.scribd.com/doc/52275991/Book-Summary-Fukuyama-The-End-of-History-or-the-Last-Man?

Freedom House. (2019). *Global Freedom Status*. Retrieved from: https://freedomhouse.org/explore-the-map?type=fiw&year=2020&status[free]=free

Huntington. (1991). Democracy`s Third Wave. *Journal of Democracy*.

Huntington. (1993). *The Clash of Civilizations*. Retrieved from: https://www.jstor.org/stable/20045621

Kant, I. (1795). *Perpetual Peace: A Philosophic Essay* (W. Hastie, Trans.). Retrieved from: https://librivox.org/perpetual-peace-by-immanuel-kant/

Kapanadze, G. (2006). *Policy of the European Union*. GFSIS.

Karumidze. (2004). *International Organization*. Tbilisi State University.

Mitrany, D. (1996). A working peace system. Chicago: Quadrangle Books.

NATO. (2006). *NATO Handbook*. NATO Public Diplomacy Division.

Pressreader. (2019). *Public libraries have an important role in sustaining democracy*. Retrieved from: https://blog.pressreader.com/public-libraries-have-an-important-role-in-sustaining-democracy

Russet. (1998). *The Third Leg of the Kantian Tripod for Peace: International Organizations and Militarized Disputes, 1950–85*. Cambridge University Press.

Schmitter, P., & Karl, T. (1991). *What Democracy Is...and Is Not*. Retrieved from: https://www.journalofdemocracy.org/articles/what-democracy-is-and-is-not/

Schmitter. (2017). *Democratization in the Middle East and North Africa: A More Ambidextrous Process?* Retrieved from: https://www.tandfonline.com/doi/abs/10.1080/13629395.2016.1220109

Zakaria, F. (2003). *The Future of Freedom: Illiberal Democracy at Home and Abroad*. W.W. Norton & Company.

KEY TERMS AND DEFINITIONS

Democracy: A form of government in which the people have the authority to deliberate and decide legislation ("direct democracy"), or to choose governing officials to do so ("representative democracy"). Who is considered part of "the people" and how authority is shared among or delegated by the people has changed over time and at different rates in different countries, but over time more and more of a democratic country's inhabitants have generally been included. Cornerstones of democracy include freedom of assembly, association and speech, inclusiveness and equality, citizenship, consent of the governed, voting rights, freedom from unwarranted governmental deprivation of the right to life and liberty, and minority rights.

Democratic Peace: The proposition that democracies are more peaceful in their foreign relations.

Democratic Peace Theory: Posits that democracies are hesitant to engage in armed conflict with other identified democracies. Among proponents of the democratic peace theory, several factors are held as motivating peace between democratic states.

European Union: A political and economic union of 27 member states that are located primarily in Europe.

Integration: Implies the adoption of policies by separate countries as if they were a single political unit. The degree of integration is often tested by seeing whether interest rates or share prices or the prices of goods are the same in different national markets.

Liberalism: A political and moral philosophy based on the rights of the individual, liberty, consent of the governed and equality before the law.

Waves of Democracy: The term, popularized by Huntington (1991), can be conceptualized in at least three ways: as rises in the global level of democracy, as periods of positive net transitions to democracy, and as linked sets of transitions to democracy.

Chapter 5
The Democratic Political Regime and Its Role in State Development

Irakli Kervalishvili
Georgian Technical University, Georgia

ABSTRACT

Political regime (fr. régime from lat. regimen – management, command, leadership) is a set of means and methods by which political power is exercised in the state. The political regime characterizes the models of appointing persons to managerial positions, exercising and transferring power, the role of violence in the political process, as well as the activities of political subjects: the level of political competition, the degree of closeness of political elites, the degree of participation of citizens in governance, institutional restrictions imposed on actors. Sometimes the concept of a political regime also includes the degree of political freedom in society and the observance of human rights. In the case of democracy, the following issues represent the main characteristics of a democratic political regime: 1) The appointment of leaders by the people they govern takes place through fair and competitive elections. 2) The people are the only legitimate source of power. 3) The society exercises self-government for the common good and satisfaction of common interests.

INTRODUCTION

The political regime is a set of methods and forms of exercising state power, which determines the nature of political life in the country and the functioning of the political system of society.

The nature of the political regime depends on the functioning of the structures within the specified political system (state, party, public organizations). On the degree of development of democratic principles in society, the features of political culture and traditions.

The political regime of this or that state is characterized not only by the peculiarities of the country's constitution but also the focus should be on the real means and methods of exercising state power, which often does not coincide with the content of the country's constitution.

DOI: 10.4018/978-1-6684-4543-3.ch005

A particular political regime is ultimately characterized by the interaction of existing institutions between the public and civil society. It is necessary to focus on the following relations: interpersonal, social strata, etc. It is necessary to take into account the correspondence of political power to the values recognized by the majority of the people.

When determining the essential characteristics of the political regime in political science, two directions have been formed that are associated with an explanation of the nature of political science itself. First, it is a legal definition. In such a characteristic, the features of the political regime are determined by the official legal forms of government, which, in turn, are based on the formal legal criteria for the functioning of the state, which, in turn, are associated with the legal norms proclaimed in the Constitution. Based on these approaches, the system of constitutional (legal) norms under the political regime and the principles of their implementation in practice is determined.

The second - the sociological direction - focuses on the interaction of government, society, and citizens. In this sense, the political regime is a special social mechanism - a means of managing society, combining, on the one hand, the main models of the formation of state bodies and means of making political decisions, on the other hand, aspects of the participation of various political entities. These actors include the ruling elite, party leaders, and individual citizens. Based on this position, the political regime includes the following parameters:

- the degree of political participation of people and their involvement in the process of making government decisions, reflecting the degree of public representation and public control, and civic engagement;
- the nature of the functional connection of state institutions and its connection with fundamental human rights and freedoms;
- the degree of freedom of competition between the ruling and opposition forces in the process of formation of public authorities;
- compliance of the measures taken by the administrative bodies with the legal foundations, expressed in observance and respect for constitutional norms and laws;
- The role and place of state ideology, relations with opposition ideological trends, the level of media freedom;
- Ways of implementing public administration, the level of public support for the policy pursued by the government, the degree of establishment of institutional order in society (Britannica, 2022).

Three main types of political regimes are widely known: totalitarian, authoritarian, and democratic.

Both classical and modern types of political regimes existed and exist in different modifications in different states. They have always embodied and represented the qualitative state of civil society in a given political system, the nature of state institutions and the interaction between them, the mechanism of functioning of political power, and management in general.

Let's take a quick look at each of the political regimes and compare them with their democratic political regimes.

Totalitarian Regime

The totalitarian regime is characterized by the desire of the state to establish state control over all spheres of public life, the ultimate goal of which is the complete subordination of a person to political power and the dominant ideology.

The concept of "totalitarianism" was introduced into circulation by the Italian fascist ideologist G. Gentile in the early 20th century. In 1925, this concept was first used in the Italian Parliament. The political leader of Italian fascism, Benito Mussolini, included it in his political vocabulary. From this time begins the establishment of a totalitarian regime in Italy. Around the same time, a totalitarian-communist regime was established in the USSR, which assumed a particularly cruel character under Stalinism. Later, in 1933, the Nazi regime was established in Nazi Germany (Kamenskaya, 2005).

In each of the countries in which a totalitarian regime was established and developed, this system had its characteristics. In addition, there are common features that are characteristic of all forms of totalitarianism and embody their essence. These include the following signs:

1. High concentration of power, penetration of the ruling apparatus into all spheres of public life. There is no problem with "power and society" in the totalitarian consciousness: the power and the people think as a single, indivisible organism. In this case, other problems become relevant, namely: the state and the people against internal enemies, the people and the environment against the external hostile environment. Paradoxically, under the conditions of totalitarianism, people who are alienated from power believe that the government expresses its interests deeper and more comprehensively than it can do.
2. Totalitarian regimes are characterized by a one-party system. There is only one ruling party led by a charismatic leader. What guides their activities and what governs them, the party cells of the party penetrate all the production and organizational structures of society.
3. Ideologization of public life. All totalitarian ideologies are considered in history as a legitimate movement towards a certain goal (world domination, building communism, etc.), which justifies all means. This ideology introduces several different myths (about the dominant role of the working class, the superiority of the Aryan race, etc.), which symbolize the power of magical symbols. In the direction of the ideological indoctrination of the population, totalitarian society is making large-scale efforts.
4. Totalitarianism is characterized by a monopoly of power over information resources and complete control over the media. All this information has one general direction - the glorification of the existing multitude, and its achievements. Through the media, it is planned to raise the enthusiasm of the masses to achieve the goals set by the totalitarian regime.
5. State monopoly on the use of all means by the armed forces. The army, police, and all other law enforcement agencies report directly to the center of political power.
6. The presence of a processing system of universal control over human behavior, a system of violence. For these purposes, concentration camps, and ghettos are created, where hard labor is used, people are tortured, their will to resist is suppressed, and innocent people are being mass repressed. For example, in the USSR a whole network of camps, the Gulag, was created. By 1941, it included 53 concentration camps, 425 correctional labor colonies, and up to 50 juvenile camps. Over the years, up to 40 million people died in these camps. In a totalitarian society, the entire resource of the repressive apparatus is involved. Through it, fear is introduced, pressure is exerted on a particu-

lar citizen and his family members, rumors and suspicions arise, and anonymous letters are sent. Everything is being done to ensure that there are no disagreements and opposition in the country. The state controls the life and behavior of the population through law enforcement operations.

7. All totalitarian regimes are characterized by the following principle: "Everything is prohibited except what the government orders." Guided by this principle, society carries out the education of a person acceptable to one or another government. Totalitarianism needs especially modest people, modest in everything: in desires, in clothes, in behavior. Any individualism is suppressed, it should be like everyone else, with no originality in reasoning. Listening is widely developed, etc.

The main features of totalitarian political regimes are listed above, creating the preconditions for their unification into one group (SparkNotes, 2022).

At the same time, there are specific features that make it possible to single out in this group various types of totalitarianism known to world history. These are communist totalitarianism, fascism, and national socialism.

Communist totalitarianism embodies the characteristic features of the regime with particular clarity. Here everything, including economic life, is represented by total control. Private property is being abolished and, consequently, all the foundations of individualism—the autonomy of members of society—are lost.

Fascism is a totalitarian political regime characterized by anti-democratism, racism, and chauvinism. Fascism is based on the need for a strong, ruthless government, which in turn is based on the universal dominance of an authoritarian party, a cult of personality. The countries where fascist organizations were first created were Germany and Italy. In 1922, fascism dominated Italy. Italian fascism is characterized by a desire to revive the Roman Empire.

National Socialism is the third type of totalitarian political regime. It was created in Germany in 1933 and absorbed the features of both fascism and communist totalitarianism. In addition, it differs from the two above types in its goals and social priorities. The goal of National Socialism is to dominate the Aryan race, to declare the German nation a nation of the highest rank.

Authoritarianism

Authoritarianism - (from the Latin word authorities - power) - is the state-political structure of society, formed by one person or political group. At the same time, state control does not extend to foreign policy spheres, as well as to the economy, culture and religion, and so on. Historical experience shows that authoritarian regimes, as a rule, are formed in states where there is a change in the social system, which is accompanied by a sharp polarization of political forces. Authoritarianism can also spread to countries with protracted economic and political crises that cannot be resolved through democratic norms. Since such phenomena are often observed in the process of development of the world community, it becomes clear that authoritarianism belongs to fairly common political regimes. There are many examples of authoritarian regimes in world history. In many countries, this regime is not even alien to the modern period. In particular, in the second half of the twentieth century, authoritarian regimes were established in several countries free from the colonial yoke - Africa, Asia, and Latin America. According to some scientists, in the USSR after 1953 there was an authoritarian change of the totalitarian regime.

The special conditions in which an authoritarian political regime is being created determine the main goal put forward by it - restoring order in the country and ensuring normal conditions for public life. This goal, in turn, determines the means to achieve it (first of all, it is the concentration of political power in

a single decision-making center), and also takes into account specific opportunities and all spheres of public life and all social strata, to which the existence of this regime.
The following general characteristics of authoritarian regimes include:

1. Separation of people from power. In this case, the subject of management is either one person or a group of people. A particular person can be a charismatic leader, a monarch, a dictator, or a populist leader. A specific group is a military junta or a ruling, political party. They have uncontrolled and unlimited power. An authoritarian society creates a huge gap between political power and the people. Both the state and the people do not fill this gap.
2. Lack of a single ideology. Authoritarian leaders (unlike totalitarianism) do not try to justify their political actions with lofty goals, such as convincing the population that they are changing the world. They are simply trying to present to the public the fact that the country is on the brink of an abyss, and they are taking it upon themselves to save it. After that, they claim, they express their readiness to transfer power to other political forces.
3. Reliance on the force, which is a sufficient condition to force those who do not obey the regime, if necessary, to become "supporters" of power. But such a regime does not resort to mass repression, as under totalitarianism. Moreover, it can be popular with the population, especially when the positive results of its activities are visible.
4. Monopolization of politics. All political activity is carried out by political authorities with a concentration of power. Accordingly, the activity of other subjects of politics is prohibited: such subjects include the political opposition, political parties, and other public organizations. In some cases, authoritarianism allows a limited number of trade unions and political parties, although they operate under strict government control.
5. Refusal of complete control over society. The most authoritarian regime is most often built on the principle - that "everything is possible, except for politics." The government gives up general control over society and leaves several areas in its control zone: its security, national defense, public order, and foreign policy. In addition, political power actively intervenes in the organization of social welfare and the overall development strategy. The economy, culture, religion, and private life remain outside the control of the state.
6. Formation of the ruling elite in a non-democratic way, namely by appointment from above. As a result, the circle of an authoritarian leader is chosen based on personal sympathies and loyalty to the leader, and not based on business qualities and abilities (Kamenskaya, 2005).

The above components are common features that characterize authoritarian regimes. However, these modes also have specific properties by which they are differentiated and typologies. Let's consider some types of authoritarian regimes that the famous Polish political scientist E. Viatri proposes (Study.Com. 2022).

- Military government. It happens, when the militaries take the power. Within this type of ruling, political activity is either completely banned or severely restricted. For example, after the military junta led by Pinochet came to power in Chile in 1973, all political parties were banned.
- Another type of authoritarian military regime is the period before the Second World War in Poland under Marshal Piłsudski when the activities and existence of political parties were allowed, but their activities were limited.

- Theocratic authoritarian regime. In this case, there is a concentration of political power in the hands of a fanatical religious clan. This regime was established in Iran after the 1979 revolution. At the same time, according to some features, the theocratic regime is close to totalitarian.
- a personalized regime in which power belongs to a political leader, although state institutions (except for the police) are weak. Such regimes generally do not exist for a long time, because the leader is not allowed to stay in power for a long time.
- Monarchist authoritarian regimes are functioning in Jordan, Morocco, Saudi Arabia, etc.
- Partially authoritarian regimes - are characterized by a multi-party system (for example, in Mexico), the presence of opposition, and elections. However, there are electoral fraud and high levels of corruption.

Democratic Political Regime

The term democracy (in Greek - demos - people and Kratos - power) means the power of the people (Kamenskaya. 2005). But a situation where political power is exercised by the whole people or direct democracy is an idealistic approach to the issue. True democracy is carried out under a government elected by the people. It's called a representative democracy. This circumstance must be taken into account when considering a democratic political regime.

This mode is characterized by the following features:

The source of power in a democratic state is the people. He elects his representatives, giving them the authority to work in the relevant elected body to protect the interests of the population. If the people whom the voters wanted to see in power are not successful, it will be possible to correct the situation only in the next elections. In a democracy, the law protects not only the citizens but also the government from the citizens. The mistakes of a deputy (if he did not violate the law) or the loss of his powers are not a reason for his recall.

In a democracy, the government has a high degree of legitimacy, and the country's policies are carried out following the adopted laws. By law, the state also provides ample opportunities for the realization of their interests and needs. The democratic regime is characterized by the principle - that "everything that is not prohibited by law is allowed." Therefore, in democratic states, there is ample opportunity for citizens to participate in all areas, create various unions, manage the funds of organizations, etc. This, in turn, testifies to the high quality of civil society.

1. A democratic regime is characterized by the division of different branches of government. This means the separation of legislative, executive, and judicial powers. The highest legislative body of the country - the parliament, has the exclusive right to pass laws. There are known cases when the power of this or that branch has been abused, therefore, there is a danger of excessive concentration of political power in this or that institution of government. Therefore, under a democratic political regime, the three branches of government balance each other. In particular, the supreme executive power (president, government) has only legislative, budgetary, and personnel initiatives. The president has the power to veto decisions made by the legislature. The Supreme Judicial Authority has the right to determine the compliance of the issued laws with the constitutional norms.
2. A democratic regime is characterized by the participation of the people in the process of making political decisions. This process is manifested in the expression of opinion in the mass media,

participation in demonstrations or lobbying activities, etc. The political participation of the people in the decision-making process is guaranteed by the Constitution.

3. An important characteristic of a democratic political regime is political pluralism, which offers the possibility of creating a multi-party system based on the principles of political rivalry between political parties, as well as a legitimate political opposition both inside and outside parliament. In carrying out its mission, the opposition has become a critic of the activities of government agencies, offering an alternative program. The parliamentary opposition controls the government through its factions and blocs and also presents its position in the media.
4. A democratic political regime is characterized by a high degree of protection of human rights. It includes the norms, rules, and principles of interaction between the state and its citizens. Human rights are in the spotlight of the international community. There are about 50 political-legal documents that ensure human rights and facilitate their legal process. These include the Universal Declaration of Human Rights, adopted by the United Nations General Assembly on December 10, 1948, the European Convention for the Protection of Human Rights and Fundamental Freedoms (1950), the African Charter on Human and Peoples' Rights (1984), and the Paris Charter for a New Europe (1990). Legal norms, human rights, and freedoms are reflected in these and other documents (Chitadze, 2016).

In modern times there are three types of democratic political regimes: presidential, parliamentary, and mixed.

The presidential system of government is carried out in conditions of strict adherence to the democratic principle of sovereignty when great importance is attached to the level of legitimacy. The president himself forms the government (team) based on his views - often on the principle of personal loyalty, but more often on the principle of professional qualities. At the same time, all presidential candidates (ministers - advisers, heads of departments) are approved, for example, in the case of the US Senate, which has the right to reject some of the candidates. Neither the ministers nor the president has the right to be members of parliament at this time.

The Cabinet of Ministers is subject only to the President and has the status of a deliberative body with the Head of State. Parliament can not express a vote of no confidence and overthrow the government. The influence of the parliament on the activities of the president and the government during the approval of the state budget and the adoption of laws can take place.

In the case of the US, the president has the power to introduce legislation (for example, a draft budget), but only members of the US Congress have the right to initiate legislation. All laws passed by Congress (US Parliament) are sent to the President for signature, and the latter may not approve (veto) this or that bill. For its part, parliament can overcome the president's veto during a re-run by both chambers if the legislature can vote by a qualified majority on a law rejected by the president.

The President has the right to issue decrees, but only in the field of activity of the state authorities. He has no right to dissolve Congress and call new elections to the supreme legislature. The president is the supreme commander-in-chief and subordinates to the armed forces. But the right to declare war and truce belongs to Parliament.

The supreme body of the US judiciary is the Supreme Court - which consists of 9 people (3 of whom are women). The position of a judge is permanent.

Given the fact that the president has broad powers, the US Constitution allows Congress to impeach the president. This process is possible in several cases: if there have been cases of violations of the constitution or treason by the president, or actions - which undermine the authority of the government. The impeachment mechanism is a kind of brake to prevent the state from abusing its authority and turning a democratic political system into an authoritarian one.

Parliamentary Democracy - is the most common form of democratic political regime, prevalent mainly in European countries. Its characteristic features are: the legislative power belongs to the parliament, and the government is formed by the parliamentary majority. The government is accountable to Parliament, which can declare a vote of no confidence in it (the government). If the parliament expresses a vote of no confidence, the whole government headed by the Prime Minister will resign. The Prime Minister becomes the leader of the parliamentary majority as a whole. He is in the government only among the "first among the equals", and all decisions are made on a collegial basis.

Parliamentary elections have a major impact on the formation of the government: it is formed either by representatives of the party that won the majority of seats or by representatives of several parties that are united in a united coalition to form a parliamentary majority.

One-party governments are typical in the United Kingdom, Japan, Canada, Italy, Belgium, and the Federal Republic of Germany, and the formation of government in Israel often ends with the formation of coalition governments.

In a parliamentary democracy, the head of state is often a monarch with limited but important powers (Great Britain, Japan, Sweden, Spain). Under certain conditions, he can dissolve parliament and call new elections, and sign laws. If the monarch refuses to sign the law, the document is returned to Parliament for further consideration.

In some countries where the parliamentary system operates, the president is the head of state, elected by parliament. Such countries are - Germany, Italy, and Israel.

The mixed principle of a democratic regime is characterized by the following principle: the head of state is the generally current president, and the government is appointed by parliament. This type of political system is stable in France. Within this system, a paradoxical situation can be created that took place in France. Within this system, a paradoxical situation can be created, which took place in France: in the 80s and 90s of the last century, the president was a socialist and the prime minister was a representative of the right-wing.

CONCLUSION

Political regime (fr. régime from lat. regimen - management, command, leadership) - a set of means and methods by which political power is exercised in the state.

The political regime characterizes the models of appointing persons to managerial positions, exercising and transferring power, the role of violence in the political process, as well as the activities of political subjects: the level of political competition, the degree of closeness of political elites, the degree of participation of citizens in governance, institutional restrictions imposed on actors. Sometimes the concept of a political regime also includes the degree of political freedom in society and the observance of human rights.

There are various approaches to the classification of political regimes (for example, the schemes of Robert Dahl, Juan Linz) and the democracy indices based on them; they use different criteria for comparison and infer different types of political regimes (or regime types). Among the main types, as a rule, there are democracy, autocracy, and totalitarianism, although the key distinction in modern political science is the dichotomy of democratic and non-democratic regimes.

In modern political science, the political regime is one of the main categories that is used to describe political reality. Political scientists use this concept in cross-country comparisons to explore national differences in policy design; study how different regimes affect the economy, and public institutions; establish the causes and "trajectories" of regime transformations - transitions from one regime type to another (for example, democratization). The concept can also be used to describe international and regional politics. At the same time, the formation of precisely the "regime" as a descriptive category of politics took place in political science in the 2nd half of the 20th century. The commonplace of the modern approach to this concept is the emphasis on the method (method) of the actual exercise of power and the functioning of specific political institutions, including contrary to the existing de jure constitutional provisions, which distinguishes the concept of a regime from the concept of a form of government.

It is believed that the political regime is a more dynamic concept than the "state" or "statehood" (several political regimes can change in one state) and less dynamic than the "government", specific leaders, or the state policy undertaken by them (within one political regime during authorities can be replaced by different governments and various political decisions can be made). Speaking of "regime change", they mean not only regime transformations, but also a change in key parameters of the political order - for example, a significant change in the composition of the group that exercises power: since 1925, several rulers and governments have changed in Iran, but the regime type remained authoritarian, and in terms of the composition of the ruling group there were two regimes: the Shah state of the Pahlavi dynasty (1925-1979) and the Islamic Republic of Iran (since 1979). The mode acts not only as a category but also as a unit of observation in cross-country comparisons.

About the concept of "political system", French-speaking and English-speaking traditions diverge. In the former, the concept of a system is considered more stable (during the evolution of one political system, several political regimes may change), while in the latter, the concepts of system and regime often do not differ, and the change of the political system as a system (form) of government (English system of government) does not mean a change of political regime.

The concept of a political regime is widely used not only in comparative politics, but also in other social disciplines (for example, in political sociology or jurisprudence), and therefore the content of this concept is disputed. So, in the theory of state and law and constitutional law, the political regime, firstly, is attributed to the forms of the state (along with the form of government and the form of territorial structure), and secondly, they are correlated with the concepts of state regime and political system, which emphasize the natural exercise of state power and its legal design.

Cover of Tocqueville's 1866 edition of The Old Order and Revolution

The modern conventional understanding of the political regime in political science is based, on the one hand, on the separation of this concept from the concepts of "government" and "state" ("regime" is considered a more mobile concept than "state" or "statehood", and less mobile than a separate "government", politicians occupying their positions), and on the other hand, it is connected not so much with formal state institutions as with the actual way of exercising power. This understanding, as well as in general the tradition of using the term "regime" as a self-sufficient concept with independent content, appears in political science relatively recently, although, in the course of the development of socio-political thought, certain typologies of the political structure were introduced, starting from antiquity.

As such, the phrase “political regime” appeared in Western political-theoretical literature as early as the 19th century. The word “regime” goes back to the French “Ancien Régime”, i.e. The old order of pre-revolutionary France began to be used for a theoretical understanding of the political order thanks to the work of Alexis de Tocqueville’s “The Old Order and Revolution”.

Initially, the word “regime” was not used as a term with certain independent content and, in fact, did not differ from such concepts as the form of government or the state system as a whole. Thus, in the tradition of French constitutional law, the distinction between “regimes” correlated with the distinction between the following forms (“regimes”) of government, i.e. essentially types of government structures:

- The “regime” of the merging of powers - absolute monarchy
- The “regime” of separation of powers - the presidential system
- “Mode” of cooperation between authorities - parliamentary system (parliamentary republic or monarchy)

Within the framework of this approach, the formal structure of the institutions of state power comes to the fore, and the subject of study is the attitude of the state to legislative norms, the legal status of citizens, constitutional restrictions on government bodies, and guarantees of human and civil rights and freedoms established in the state. This tradition is preserved in the theory of state and law, in which the concepts of “political” and “state regime” can differ, and at the same time, emphasis is placed on the de jure elements of the political order. The concepts of “political regime” and “state regime” in the literature can be identified and can be separated by different authors.

Among modern definitions, there are two main approaches to this concept. On the one hand, this is a legal approach that is closely related to the legal tradition of constitutional law and early definitions of the concept and focuses on the formal structure of government institutions. On the other hand, the more modern tradition of viewing the regime as the actual arrangement of political processes, the de facto distribution of power in society, and the relationship between political institutions is often summarized as a sociological approach to the concept. This approach pays special attention to the activities of social groups, features of the social structure, and social norms and excludes the possibility of changing the political regime by changing only legal norms, which brings it closer to the modern idea of political regimes in political science.

REFERENCES

Britannica. (2022). *Regime. Political Science*. Retrieved from: https://www.britannica.com/topic/regime

Chitadze, N. (2016). *Political Sciences*. International Black Sea University.

Kamenskaya, N. (2005). *Political Sciences*. Aspect Press.

SparkNotes. (2022). *Types of Regimes*. Retrieved from: https://www.sparknotes.com/us-government-and-politics/political-science/politics-and-political-science/section3/

Study.Com. (2022). *Political Regimes: Characteristics and Examples*. Retrieved from: https://study.com/learn/lesson/regime-types-characteristics-example.html

KEY TERMS AND DEFINITIONS

Autocratic Regime: Rulers do not originate from free and fair elections but reach power via other means (election rigging, coup, revolutions, hereditary succession, or appointment by the ruling oligarchy). Various forms of repression (dismissal from work, imprisonment, exile, assassination) are used against political opponents. Civil liberties are restricted to prevent opponents from reaching power. Yet, the government does not force people to participate politically through simulated shows of support, and people not interested in politics are left alone. There are some spheres of social activity that are independent of the government, like churches and professional associations. Some examples of autocratic regimes include contemporary Russia, Singapore, China, Saudi Arabia, Venezuela, and Rwanda.

Democratic Regime: Government institutions originate from free and fair elections while civil liberties (speech, religion, association, press, assembly, and due process rights) and political rights are respected. The key characteristics of politics are the people's ability to peacefully change the government using the electoral process. Some examples of democratic regimes include contemporary France, Germany, the United States, Ghana, Japan, and India.

Political Regime: The concept of a political regime refers to the formal and informal structure and nature of political power in a country, including the method of determining office holders and the relations between the office holders and the society at large.

Totalitarian Regime: Shares most features of autocracies but are even more repressive and controlling. Repression is applied not only against political enemies but also, in order to create fear in the society, entirely innocent people. Even slight political disobedience, like telling a political joke, may be severely punished. A totalitarian regime does not permit any independent social activity by controlling non-government associations and businesses (which are politicized) and even most aspects of private life. The population is forced to participate in shows of (fake) political support like obligatory marches and meetings. A totalitarian regime is guided by a clearly specified ideology (Communism, Fascism, Islamism) and led by a charismatic leader (Hitler, Stalin, Mao) who enforces a cult of personality.

Chapter 6
Corruption and Militarization as Obstacles to Development and Democracy:
The Case of Zimbabwe

Armstrong Mudzengerere
Social Sciences University of Ankara, Turkey

Mürsel Bayram
Social Sciences University of Ankara, Turkey

ABSTRACT

The menace of institutionalized corruption accounts for the stalled development of Zimbabwe despite the country being ranked among the economic giants in Southern Africa in the early 1980s. The chapter explores the trend of the dialectic nexus between the intensified militarization of the state and the rising levels of corruption in Zimbabwe. The nation's fragility is typical of the perpetual decay of norms-based governance at the mercy of the military. Consequently, a fragile state with a militarised executive tends to neutralize and weaken good governance structures such as the judiciary, military, and civil society. Corruption is not new in Zimbabwe, but after the 2017 military coup, the evident military cronyism in political appointments serving economic interests of the elite, which was somewhat clandestine under Mugabe's rule, coincides with high and rising levels of corruption without legitimate checks.

INTRODUCTION

Ending corruption and moving towards governance that prioritizes and serves the basic socio-economic rights of citizens is one of Africa's longest and pending struggles in the post-colonial era. Corruption has evolved to become more dynamic, opaque, and complex, and in more ways, resistant to solutions and attempts to address it (Hoffmann & Hendricks, 2018). Zimbabwe is not an exception in Sub-Saharan Africa (SSA). The SSA region had the lowest ranking in the 2019 Corruption Perceptions Index (CPI),

DOI: 10.4018/978-1-6684-4543-3.ch006

scoring a regional mark of 32 out of 100. In Southern Africa, South Africa, which continues to grapple with state capture, public sector procurement corruption and local authority's corruption scored 44, Zambia 34 and Mozambique 26; with Zimbabwe scoring 24, the worst in comparison to its counterparts.

Corruption has manifested and evolved in a post-independent state that had a strong socioeconomic base at independence that would have catapulted it to be a top regional economic performer, had it kept corruption declining the past four decades. The Zimbabwe liberation struggle, which ended with the 1979 ceasefire and elections in 1980 based on the Lancaster House Constitution, focused on fighting white minority monopolism and corruption. White supremacist nepotism and unequal distribution of wealth were dominant corruption domains. After independence, under the Zimbabwe African National Union-Patriotic Front (ZANU-PF) led government for the first four years, Zimbabwe was a stable state politically and economically compared to its neighbors (Riddell, 1984). The government led by the then Prime Minister Robert Mugabe worked to engender equality by implementing socialist policies. Zimbabwe was a relatively corruption free welfare state committed to highly effective poverty reduction, with evident potential for growth and transformation.

In 1987 Zimbabwe changed to executive presidency under Mugabe, centralization was implemented, and military obsession became more apparent. Zimbabwe became a securocracy beyond a de-facto military state. Ever since, Zimbabwe has degenerated into a perpetually unstable economic state characterized by economic failure. These failures paved way for the implementation of Structural Adjustment Programs (SAPs) in the early 1990s with the currency devaluation reforms greatly depleting its purchasing value, despite SAP's promises for recovery. By the time of the rise of opposition politics in 1999 and the land reforms in the early 2000, Zimbabwe was failing both politically and economically. The post-independence stability of the state was shaking and grand corruption cases had been recorded. ZANU PF policies of forced land takeover were broadly criticized, both the 2005, and later the 2008 elections were marred with electoral corruption violence, deaths, and high military involvement and the label 'military state' was revived in scholarly discourse.

A Unity Government was formed with the main opposition Movement for Democratic Change (MDC) in 2009 and 'the most democratic constitution' was enacted in 2013. Past the unity government, Zimbabwe further plunged into instability because good governance and obedience to democratic principles had failed to take root, three decades after independence, as though the call to arms that ignited the flame of the liberation struggle had been long forgotten with its lessons unlearned. At this point it is important to mention that the post-independence state can be seen as similar in morph and form to the pre-independent state, especially in the context of institutional cultures and governance philosophy, an argument warranting the assertion that colonialism merely changed color and race in Zimbabwe.

The occurrence of the November 2017 coup was a culmination of party factionalism rooted in corruption and struggle for avenues for extraction of kickbacks using public office. The military effectively took over and mutated from being a stakeholder to a stockholder in the Zimbabwean political matrix. Apparent in this historical synopsis is the assertion that political corruption is the root of corruption in Zimbabwe.

In literature, corruption has been discussed in its many forms (Mubangizi & Sewpersadh, 2017). Ranging from petit, systematic, and systemic corruption. Different causes and loopholes have been proffered as the sources of corruption, including nepotism (Apata, 2019), lack of constitutionalism, good governance and bureaucracy (Joslyn, 2019). This has caused a high compliance cost and political instability. Some authors have argued that state fragility arising from armed conflict is a permissive condition for corruption. However, this piece contributes to literature by arguing that when state institutions are militarized, it increases rampant corruption which leads to state failure. This is manifest in Zimbabwe where corruption has escalated since the military coup in November 2017, despite the president's pledge to uproot corruption. Ever since, corruption has been facilitated by retired or active military individuals thereby plunging Zimbabwe into abject status of perpetuating state failure.

This chapter does not argue that state failure, corruption nor military obsession were absent in pre-coup Zimbabwe. Instead, it focuses on the impact of the pronounced military takeover of the helm of government structures in the "Second Republic" under the presidency of Emerson Mnangagwa, himself a securocrat par excellence. While corruption in the first republic had strong military underpinnings, its continuation, dynamics, and evolution in the Second Republic makes for a strong case worthy of analysis. One key reason is that the Second Republic's key pledge to Zimbabweans towards a socioeconomic transformation that benefitted all citizens was built on the pretext of purging corruption, which seemed and sounded genuine, transformative. Though this promise became an electoral buy-in, a key to democratic validation of a coup government, which the citizenry counted on, corruption become more pronounced in the Second Republic in comparison to the first.

The authors argue that there is an associative relationship between militarization and corruption, debilitating corruption, and dilapidation of strategic and key sectors crucial to social and economic development in the country. Through a qualitative explanatory case study approach rooted in Critical Discourse Analysis, we examine media content (print and electronic), legal and policy documents as well as journal articles to present a case on the nexus between militarization and corruption with the state failure as the ultimate outcome. This context sets the qualitative epistemological basis upon which the quest for practical policy proposals can be pursued to deconstruct the militarization-corruption nexus which reflects and solidifies Zimbabwe's political hierarchy. Since the rule of law has been reduced to 'rule by law', this chapter proffers that constitutionalism and legalism alone will be inadequate to address Zimbabwean problems. It will be equally impossible without sustained regional and international diplomatic pressure on Zimbabwean politicians to act in the best interest of their citizens.

THEORETICAL FRAMEWORK

The basic conception of corruption is the mis-governance and a disease of weak institutions; thus, the move from "functional good to dysfunctional bad" (Nichols, 2017). However, such simplicity in characterization does not imply the non-existence of complexity surrounding definitions and characterizations of corruption. Complexity is inevitable since corruption is an anthropological phenomenon tied to context with socio-political implications (Torsello & Venard, 2016). The Oxford English Dictionary describes corruption as "dishonest or fraudulent conduct of those in power, typically involving bribery". The shortfall in this definition is twofold: first, it describes corruption as akin to the public office occupant's personal benefit, second fraudulent conduct or abuse is broad (Rothstein & Varraich, 2017).

Characterization of corruption should capture its evolution and scope. Definitions fall into three major categories; public office centered, market centered (corrupt civil or private service worker treating their job as a market, and people centered (Rothstein & Varraich, 2017). In support of this view, Khan, 2006 notes that definition is much more relevant to Zimbabwe since it states corruption as a product of a malfunctioning governance system. Despite this characterization, corruption and how its manifestation and evolution unfolds is unique to a specific country or the smallest possible government unit invaded by it. Further, the phenomenon of corruption is also visible in the private sector between individuals and between domestic and foreign actors in their dealings.

To understand the full corruption spectrum, the levels of corruption, "grand, petty and state capture" levels can be used since all three are evidently existent in Zimbabwe (Shah & Schacter, 2004). Firstly, grand (systemic) corruption is purposive and secretive disregard of standards of moral behavior in a polity by politicians and other parties to corrupt acts (Africa, 2016). It can be the embezzlement of public funds, clientelism and patronage which are acts that contradict the constitution, and different law regimes such as the African Union laws on corruption or the United Nations prescribed legal morals (Otaluka, 2017). In such a system, leaders maximize self-aggrandizement at the expense of the general populace. Petty corruption involves the use of public office for smaller economic gain in smaller transactions. It is prevalent in the middle to low grade public office holders.

Lastly on state capture, Zimbabwe perfectly fits the descriptive underpinnings of the practice, where instead of being granted a consensual right to govern, violence and if necessary, death is used to extract, marshal and deploy resources of an economy and society, in the process asserting raw power to control the state (Bratton, 2015). State capture alone warrants an independent inquiry which this research does not intend to commit to, yet its magnitude and prominence demands the explanation hereunder given considering the intricate relationship with the sector capable of monopolizing violence, fear, force, death and the forms of control through which a nation's citizenry can almost or truly become subservient to the military.

In Africa and in Zimbabwe specifically, corruption has evolved and intensified to the extent of no return, the intensity of which has enabled it to evade succinct measure by the conventional tools for measurement currently in use (UN, 2016). Corruption has been massively sector based and these trends have worsened in the past four decades. Since 1980 Zimbabwe has become a survivalist state sustained by corrupt activities of the political elite to preserve their power (Nyoni, 2017). To date corruption has been normalized as a top-to-bottom phenomenon. The lack of will to enforce anti-corruption measures in the form of laws or public administration ethics which constitute a good governance package at the political level has immensely catalyzed corruption (Maguchu & Maja, 2019). As constitutionalism and the rule of law declined in the past decade, corruption infested the Zimbabwean polity. Corruption has evolved from being predominantly political to encompass all state related sectors; for instance, the banking, mining, tendering and procurement, construction and local governance. Principal of these other sectors the driving force is politics since extracts from the corrupt dealings are used for political financing.

Since Zimbabwe's independence, there has emerged a complex network of corruption built by patronage networks that rely on co-opting strategies used at low levels of the bureaucratic structure to keep the positions of political elites (Wellington Garikai et al., 2015). It has been done by strategic recruitments and appointment of associates, this in turn compromises policies consistent with commitment to good governance and public administration ethics. It is imperative to the inquiry to note that corruption has become so engrained in the public sector that officials have become more powerful than the law and justifications of corrupt practices or the muzzling of voices that speak up about or against it are the key precepts to the normalization earlier stated.

MILITARIZATION OF STATE INSTITUTIONS IN ZIMBABWE

Active military engagement in civil affairs in Zimbabwe is based on the complex patronage systems and networks built around the ZANU-PF's liberation struggle ideologies (Zimbabwe Democratic Institute Report 2017). Anchored in the military, since independence, ZANU-PF has established an octopus state far reaching in all government agencies blurring the conventional dichotomy of political party and state. ZANU-PF has assumed the role of the state and therefore the two are conflated and through the aid of military backing of the stated ideological origins. In Africa, the military has been used as a tool for promoting political interest rather than adhering to their moral duties (Houngnikpo, 2016). Hence this reflects the militarisation of the state in Zimbabwe with the use of the military to protect its political interests which is political longevity.

With the political origin, it suffices to mention that the military is totally ZANU-PF (with internal liberation-originating factions of course), despite any attempts of denial by any of the military, ZANU-PF or the state, a trinity whose autonomy is merely symbolic. Recruitments into government parastatals has been done under the auspices of patronage lines based on liberation war credentials, showing that the idea of disentangling the military from government structures remains an exotic conception, one which even bends the nature and form of the elusively adopted and conjured democracy, which the militarization of governance continues to make all the more difficulty to attain. Just as Zimbabwe has had a currency that is not a currency, a coup that is not a coup, the country has in equal measure a democracy that is not one.

The question then becomes when did this problem start? There is no clear distinction between the party, the military and the state due to integration of the military into governance structures (Hlatywayo & Mangongera, 2020). In comprehending how the military has disconnected from its military duties and apolitical role to become active in Zimbabwean politics, it is important to give a brief historical background.

Following the liberation of Zimbabwe, a decision was made to from a national army which comprised of three groups namely Zimbabwe National Liberation Army (ZANLA) which was under ZANU-PF led by Mugabe, the Rhodesian army and the Zimbabwe People's Revolutionary Army (ZIPRA) under the Zimbabwe African People's Union (ZAPU) led by Joshua Nkomo (Tendi, 2013). The heterogenous nature of ethnic groups within the army led to suspicions amongst themselves which culminated into the Gukurahundi massacres which targeted the ZIPRA forces as they were perceived to be rebels. From this event, rose the active use of the military to drive the one-party state agenda by ZANU-PF earmarking the beginning of the unbridled dominance of military, party, and state alliance under Mugabe. Opposition would emerge at the turn of the millennium from within the trade unions when state failures mounted.

From 2000-2020 Zimbabwe has experienced an observable penetrability of key state parastatals and infiltration by the military. Generals and brigadiers from the liberation struggle became executives of parastatals, majority without the academic or managerial credence that most of these parastatals demanded from the seat of a chief executive. As part of his political strategy Mugabe did this to create an interdependence alliance between the state, ZANU-PF and the military which reflected power politics and power consolidation during his tenure. For example, in 2009 in the media sector members of the military through the Ministry of Information were appointed into media related boards notably Brigadier General Epmarcus Kanhanga into ZIMPAPERS, Brigadier General Benjamin Mabenge and Major General Gibson Mashingaidze to ZBC (Ndlovu-Gatsheni & Ruhanya, 2020). The same infiltration can be attributed to other state institutions and independent commissions such as the Zimbabwe Electoral Commission (ZEC). The Zimbabwe Democratic Institute Report 2017 observed that democratic principles in Zimbabwe and institutions that promote democracy are being suffocated my militarisation, of these include the media, the rule of law, electoral processes, the land paradox and constitutionalism.

In consequence, ZANU-PF maintained strong military presence in politically premeditated operations like land reform (2000), Operation Murambatsvina (2004) and Operation Makavhotera Papi (2008) (Ndlovu-Gatsheni & Ruhanya, 2020). These manoeuvres evidenced the use of the military for political gains. Military involvement in politics and key state institutions favoured Mugabe from 1980-2017, however the same structures that he created worked against him, ushering a new administration under Mnangagwa through a planned military aided coup, all under the guise of leadership change (Hlatywayo & Mangongera, 2020). From these events it can be clearly stated that the gradual militarisation of the state led to the capture and subsequent failure of the political economy of Zimbabwe.

In his analysis of corruption in Zimbabwe, Yamamoto, 2014 highlighted how the political elite have unceasingly operationalized power to amass wealth without facing the wrath of the law. He argues that "the scandals have been popping out of the bottle one after another." To name but a few, these include:

Table 1. Popular corruption scandals in Zimbabwe post-independence, post-coup and lost values

No.	Name of Scandal	Involved Institution/Person	Year	Amount/Value
1.	Paweni Scandal	Samson Bernard Paweni	1982	USD$6 Mil
2.	NRZ Housing Scandal	National Railways of Zimbabwe	1986	Unknown
3.	Zisco Blast Furnace Scandal	Zimbabwe Iron and Steel Company	1987	100 000 tonnes iron ore
4.	Fokker Plane Scandal	Air Zimbabwe	1987	US$100 Mil
5.	Willowgate Scandal		1988	USD$65Mil
6.	ZRP Santana Scandal	Zimbabwe Republic Police	1989	
7.	War Victims Compensation Scandal		1994	USD$300Mil
8.	Grain Scandal	Grain Marketing Board (Zim)	1995	USD$ 6Mil
9.	Soltran Scandal	Zimbabwe Electricity Supply Authority	1998	Unknown
10.	Chinese Tender Scandal	Ministry of Water and Rural Development	1999	USD$196Mil
11.	Harare Airport Scandal	Air Zimbabwe	2000, 2008,	ZWD7Bil USD$54Mil
12.	Chiadzwa Scandal	Zimbabwe Revenue Authority, Zimbabwe Mining Development Corporation, Kimberly Process	2006-2016	US$ 15Bil
13.	Command Agriculture Scandal	Office of the President and Cabinet Ministry of Agriculture		USD$3Bil
14.	Chivhayo Scandal	Zimbabwe Electricity Supply Authority	2017-2018	USD45Mil
15.	CovidGate Scandal	Minister of Health and Child Welfare Obert Moyo	2020	USD$60Mil

Source: Compiled by the authors based on data from Yamamoto 2014, Transparency International 2019.

Notably, the Covidgate scandal of 2020 involves those currently in power. What is apparent is that during Mugabe's reign this neo-patrimonial state (where those involved in the echelons of power continue to use state wealth for selfish gains) survived, ironically no minister implicated in corruption was arrested and most of them hold positions in the Second Republic. With the increasing presence of military officials in state institutions corruption has been permitted to further perpetuate in Zimbabwe, contrary to the ideals of military office that command order, discipline, and honesty among other moral obligations to a republic.

THE MILITARIZATION-STATE FRAGILITY NEXUS

One of the leading tools in explaining and measuring state fragility is the Fragile States Index (FSI) produced by the Fund for Peace (OECD, 2020) in the (Fragile State Annual Report 2019). Though it has many criticisms like simplifying a complex concept into statistics and indicators, it provides the basis for seeing the magnitude of fragility by descriptive statistics which triggers curiosity to explore the subject. In the 2019 FSI report for instance, Zimbabwe was ranked a failed state in the "alert" category with a score of 99.5 and in the 2020 FSI report it has remained in the alert category with a score of 99.2. Though there is a slight improvement, remaining in the same category points to weakness of the Zimbabwean state.

According to the Organisation for Economic Cooperation and Development (OECD: 2020) state fragility is a crucial factor to development given the target for Agenda 2030 on Sustainable Development Goals (SDGs) (OECD, 2020). With the advent of coronavirus (COVID-19), state fragility has been exacerbated where it has been already existent, not just in Zimbabwe but globally. Thus, there are also strong external factors aggravating fragility where there are weaker governments and institutions, although they are not key to this inquiry. From these categories, Zimbabwe can be classified as a deteriorating state since the willingness to perform state functions is in decline. High levels of corruption and self-enrichment are also visible, compounded by chronic or low capacity for rule of law, decreased cooperation with the civil society and rising possibilities of localised conflict (Brinkerhoff, 2007).

A critical analysis reveals that in the past decade Zimbabwe has performed poorly in the three pillars of a functional and stable state (authority, legitimacy and capacity). The Zimbabwean state has questionable authority as the ruling party which has been in power since 1980 has been accused of rigging elections. The state has excessively exercised its authority and ability to use violence over its sovereign territory. However, the problem is the composition of such authority as it is derived from military elements who are backing civilian leadership in a leadership union where the republic cannot make a distinction of who is leading them, of where the military, the party, and the state begins and ends (Masunungure, 2011).

The army in Zimbabwe holds a strong influence on the presidential candidate in elections. For instance, in 2002 the army declared that it was not going to accept anyone without liberation struggle credentials to lead the country (*Army Deals Blow to Mugabe Rival*, 2002). The 2017 military coup which was carried out in the name of "restoring the liberation legacy" and "targeting criminals around the president (Chando 2020). Evidently, the military in Zimbabwe is not confined to the barracks as it meddles in ruling party politics thereby increasing the fragility of the state. There are also allegations that the security sector in Zimbabwe is deeply involved in the planning and implementation of election rigging strategies, which have manifested in violence sometimes including the 2000, 2008 and 2018 post-election violence where the military shot several protesting citizens (Ndlovu-Gatsheni & Ruhanya, 2020).

The existence of vested military interests explains the undoing of the Zimbabwean government, or more precisely, of the citizens since the effects of the government's undoing are felt and transferred to the ordinary citizen. In Zimbabwe state authority is vested in military authority and this dispels the importance of democratic processes as well as democratic institutions. In the same vein, there are no supportive relationships between the state authorities and civil society, further exacerbated by the perceived danger of civil society organizations as threats to national security through intent to effect regime change. While the confrontations between civil society and the state calling itself the second republic warrants an independent analysis, on a fundamental level the battle can be written down as a tag of war on the status quo which we have in part been describing in this paper. With strong power, or perhaps the strongest of all institutions, the existence of unquestionable military authority accounts for failure to generate economic performance needed to transform the lives of citizens. Essentially, transformation and its prospects are a threat to the militarized state governing Zimbabwe.

In Zimbabwe, the military occupies the echelons of power and simultaneously the financial sector, social and health services sector, local governance, agricultural and other sectors which have significantly collapsed. Most of the Southern African countries in general and Zimbabwe in particular, have not been at war in the past decade, but still experience unprecedented high levels of poverty, hyperinflation, unemployment, gross corruption, inequality, and massive 'survival' migration (Masunungure, 2011). Of particular interest in Zimbabwe as a country without an active war is the persistent high national, annual expenditure wherein for many years on record, funds allocated to the military and therefore defence are higher than what is allocated to health, education and sometimes to production sectors that enable the economy such as agriculture. A fundamental question in this light lingers, Expenditure in military and defence against who, or what, and for defending who, or what?

Guided by gauging the former question against where the military is playing its notable role in the second republic, evidence has sufficiently mounted to validate a nexus between militarization and state fragility in Zimbabwe, contrary to the conception that fragility is mainly induced by civil conflicts. Clearly, there is fragility in peace since sub-national level weaknesses are a common feature without armed struggle (Grävingholt et al., 2012). This situation has been persistent from the Mugabe regime from 1980 to November 2017 when the state was primarily securocratic and until the military took over where currently under the regime of Emmerson Mnangagwa it has become fundamentally militarized, albeit without shedding to the securocratic nature, but merely increasing to it and evolving from it.

KEY FINDINGS AND DISCUSSION

To comprehend the Zimbabwean crisis, conceptualizing the interconnectedness between the inception of military interest, involvement into the civilian business, the ensuing political-economic structure and the subsequent gradual predatory nature which has led to state fragility in Zimbabwe, it is key to go back in history once more. In 1998, the Zimbabwean military intervened in the DRC crisis, which prompted unbridled access of military personnel to diamonds. This in our perception, would be the true inception of military involvement in civilian affairs and fraudulent activities such as looting. With the taste of the loot too good to give up, to the extent that it had to be domesticated on resources at home in Zimbabwe, a marriage of predatory conveniences had to be finalized with the military. Thus, during the Mugabe era the military played a significant role in strengthening his longevity in power, to the conveniences of benefits enjoyed there under with the consequences transferred to the citizenry. For example, the historically lavish state expenditure in the country has been bankrolled by and through taxing of civilians on one side while benefits from billions worth of mineral resources never made it to the public sector to benefit the same civilian.

2017 heralded a novel trajectory in Zimbabwean politics as the military entrenched its prominence as not only a game changer by ousting Mugabe but also aiding the preeminence of Mnangagwa's administration. By disregarding the coup due to fatigue over Mugabeism, a period stained with overt violence, electoral misconduct, and administrative lawlessness; the citizenry, opposition parties, western countries and government structures became complicit to the unconstitutional transference of power, which would be infamously labelled, "a coup that was not a coup". This earmarked hope for a new interlayered period in Zimbabwean governance history, one detached from Mugabe and Mugabeism. In it, Mnangagwa promised to further good governance and reconfigure the political spectrum to be amenable to democracy, a feature which was alien during the previous modus operandi.

Despite the euphoria, grand promises and speeches which had begot hope for a new chapter, the purported democratic transition of the post-Mugabe government began deeply rooted in patronage and nepotism as the capture of the executive branch of the government laid the foundation of the unbridled dialectically interwoven militarisation of the state and institutionalised corruption. The transition and ascendance of senior military commanders to key government positions heralded the first principal step which ushered in cronyism to preserve loyalty. In fact, one would argue it was business as usual, despite it being labelled and packaged differently; the era of Mugabeism would be gone, yet the governance that followed was merely a mirror of it albeit with new evolved features that sought to present it as a democracy, an illusory one considering the takeover of power and its later attempted legitimization which was heavily contested.

Mnangagwa to invest in his political longevity began ingraining the military in public affairs through rewarding the generals who spearheaded the 2017 coup with key government positions. Notably he appointed retired general Chiwenga as the vice president and in 2020 as the new minister of health to solve major issues affecting the health sector in Zimbabwe after the advent of the Covid 19 virus (Herald, 2022). In addition, the late Sibusiso B. Moyo, a retired major general in the military was also appointed as the minister of foreign affairs and international trade and the late Perence Shiri a former general of the Air Force of Zimbabwe was the minister for land, agriculture, and rural resettlement. Therefore, these appointments depict a steady increase in the number of military personnel's occupying key executive positions, albeit without unquestionable meritorious credibility to occupy the positions despite the military power they bring to the table to control the key sectors that hold Zimbabwe together.

During the Mugabe regime sophistry and a clandestine approach guided the appointment of military personnel in public affairs as he deployed them to government parastatals, however this cannot be said for the Mnangagwa administration. Regulating key government decisions has become prone to abuse due to the military takeover of the executive. A key example that comes to the fold is at one point the threat to if not the firing of all nurses who had gone on strike, in a country with a longstanding human resources deficit in the health sector. To follow the trend of the rampant frequency in the capture of the executive, Air Commodore Jasper Chimedza was appointed as the secretary for the ministry of health. These cases illuminate premeditated structural, administrative capture and control by and through military power, the highest possible and strategic national institutions; from which corruption is enabled, constitutionalism rescinded, professionalism and democratic values put into disarray in the process undermining both government structures and daily civil life.

Evidently in Zimbabwe the military has become a stockholder and central in national decision making entrenching a patrimonial, hegemonic socioeconomic culture, where the elites and their spawn benefit from the key economic opportunities availed by the state. In a tweet, member of parliament Themba Mliswa said "I applaud Hon Chiwenga's vision for the Health sector, I have confidence in the professionalism and discipline of military personnel to formulate successful strategies, the health sector desperately needs a restore legacy approach". His words came to fruition as the vice president militarized the health system as all aspiring health professionals in Zimbabwe are now obliged to join the Zimbabwe National Army (ZNA) first through the Défense Forces Service Commission as Junior Resident Medical Officers (Tweet et al., 2020). The perpetuation of uncontrolled military influence is now weakening professionalism and constitutionalism illustrating the levels of the militarization of the state. The above characteristics underscore an authoritarian regime which seeks to eliminate democratic processes such as the right to demonstrate, as the militarisation of the health sector was meant to stem strikes by health professionals over poor personal protective clothing during Covid -19.

To maintain its hegemony, ZANU-PF in tandem with the military has habitually used terror campaigns to instil fear on the rural populace to influence electoral procedures, mainly the outcome. Compounded with the deliberate appointment of military personnel within the Zimbabwe Electoral Commission (ZEC) which is responsible for administering elections, this was meant to buttress the cancerous political corruption, another signature of the Mugabe regime (ZDI Report 2017). The 2018 elections saw a similar trajectory, though in this instance choreographing the election process to appear more democratic than all prior included a complex militarization of the electoral process and judiciary system (Ndlovu-Gatsheni & Ruhanya, 2020). Ultimately the constitutional court announced Mnangagwa as victorious with 50.6%. Despite the presence of international observers and a new government under Mnangagwa, the commandeering of the 2018 electoral process showed the skewed favour of the military towards ZANU PF. Mnangagwa had failed to validate his "Zimbabwe is open for business" mantra which hovered around promises for a democratic transition, and the perpetuation of political corruption reflects his government as a surrogate of a militaristic takeover, an evolution and upgrade of Mugabeist securocracy.

Cynicism towards the Mnangagwa administration has emanated from the marriage of convenience between ZANU PF, the military and a seemingly captured judiciary system which is an irrefutable game changer in power politics as it stifles any attempts to eradicate systemic corruption. Fast forward to 2020 the security apparatus and the judiciary have been used to weaken the opposition in a fashion that signals a potential to exterminate competitive politics. From the raiding and subsequent seizure of the opposition MDC Alliance headquarters to constant arbitrary arrests of government critics the political meddling and shrinking democratic space mirrors a militarised state. A purported democratic transition proved to be skimmed process to prolong ZANU PF's longevity in power and this has polarised the nation permeating fragility. Inversely Muronzi (2020) argues that a disconcerting feature arousing from the political instability is that global interest over Zimbabwe has declined as the constant subjugation of human rights has dented the image of Zimbabwe dissuading foreign direct investment. The political fiasco has exhibited itself as a sole reason for the economic malaise and state fragility in Zimbabwe.

International integration and reengagement efforts have been stifled because of this political corruption as antagonism with countries like the US and UK has continued with Zimbabwe being tagged as a "foreign adversary" (Banda, 2020). State fragility in Zimbabwe can be attributed to the unbridled militarisation of government structures and systemic corruption which has become complexly rooted in all sectors. Whether it is the allocation of tenders to companies and individuals that cannot deliver for example in the procurement of PPEs in response to Covid-19 or the procurement of snow graders for a country temperate country that experiences snow by accident, the complicit of the military and benefitting of individuals connected to it resembles a country not fit for business despite being touted as open for business. Inevitably the transference of burdens of misgovernance axe basic human rights both directly and indirectly. With the government culpable, this has caused the continued ostracization of Zimbabwe from the international stage.

The new dispensation through the "Zimbabwe is open for business" mantra aspired to resuscitate the economy. However, with the current trajectory, the cartelised, militarised state with its cancerous systemic corruption at its core, this aspiration will remain a pipeline dream. Aljazeera (2020) reported that with high annual inflation rates fluctuating from 500%-837%, 7.7 million people being food insecure, a health system reeling from the Covid 19 pandemic and with Zimbabwe barred from debt relief, it remains a disturbing feature in Mnangagwa's regime that corruption remains unabated (Muronzi, 2020). Signalled as the driver for the purported economic recovery agenda, the mining sector also blankets the bribery and extortions mirroring state fragility in Zimbabwe. The militarisation of the state instead of curbing the smuggling of natural wealth from Zimbabwe has generally heightened and permeated the haemorrhaging of mineral resources.

Njini and Marawanyika (2020) reported that Zimbabwe loses approximately $100 million per month and $1.5 billion annually due to illicit financial flows and smuggling of minerals like gold and diamond to countries like South Africa and Dubai. The main cause for this trend has been the control of mineral resources by the military which allows the looting of public resources with the aid of security apparatus. In 2020 Henrietta Rushwaya, the head of Zimbabwe Miners Federation tried to smuggle gold worth US366,000 with the aid of security apparatus and government acolytes portraying the red tape and rent seeking activities which are chocking Zimbabwe into the abys of economic turmoil (Muronzi, 2020). This has affected the political economy of Zimbabwe through political instability in the form of violent protests, poor infrastructural development, weak social services, human capital flight and the disabling absolute capital accumulation. In addition, the militarization of the state has also allowed the unchecked abuse of property rights especially by security apparatus. Matimaire (2021) reported that "Anjin Investment, a mining company linked to the military took the most lucrative diamond mine claim in Marange from the Zimbabwe Consolidated Diamond Company." The dilemma of poor people in resource-rich communities argued for by Kativu (2020) within the context of unequal resources exchange assumes a strong institutional rooting difficult to challenge or displace in cases such as this. The abuse of property rights has caused major economic implications in Zimbabwe by warding off potential investors and casting doubts on the promises made by Mnangagwa to ensure economic recovery.

The capture of the judiciary in tandem with a militarized state has developed a corrupt administration system which makes the judiciary system susceptible to political interference. Politicization and militarization of the judiciary system hinders pragmatic efforts to curb endemic corruption. Magaisa (2020) argues that "Chief justice Malaba, by demanding that each judge presents his judgement to a superior before delivering judgment shows the worrisome levels of judiciary capture". This depicts an absolute veneer of extreme political meddling in the judiciary system which breeds systemic bias and bribery for personal interest.

The year 2020 was laden with scandalous corruption cases involving top military and government elites. From the Reserve Bank led Farm Mechanisation scandal which also implicated members of the judiciary system, to the $20 million Covid 19 funds embezzlement scandal which included former health minister Obadiah Moyo a close ally of Mnangagwa. A bizarre feature from these corruption scandals is how instantaneously implicated government officials are released from custody, in what has been publicly dubbed and correctly perceived as "catch and release" in the public eye, albeit a ruse that the wheels of justice are turning within the realm of non-militarised territory and the fight against corruption is bearing fruits. Magaisa (2020) argues that this has set a precedence which allows an amalgam of the selective application of law and perpetuation of systemic corruption because of the biased conduction of courts cases. These cases demonstrated how hard it is to stop corruption in a militarized state. What followed was a sequence of public emotional outrage as protests against the self-aggrandizement activities were banned under guise of Covid 19 restrictions. However, the government went on a rampage arresting government critics including investigative journalist Hopewell Chin'ono who had exposed the fraudulent activities. Gruesome human rights abuses which followed the foiled planned protests affected the image of Zimbabwe.

By continuously thwarting the democratic space and the right to protest through using the military, the government has attracted global criticism which affects the political economy of Zimbabwe as re-engagement efforts with multilateral institution to access financial assistance is hindered. Just as Zimbabwe was isolated from the international community in the era of Mugabe, it still remains to be seen the much-needed integration that the pledges of change by and through the second republic promised. In addition, the militarisation of the state has dissolved the independence of institutions in Zimbabwe. For instance, the Anti-Corruption Commission (ZACC) is headed by justice Loise Matanda Moyo who was appointed by Mnangagwa to fight corruption (Chronicle, 2022). However, she is the wife of the late general Sibusiso Moyo. While herself an accomplished professional in her own right, the hints of nepotism are too hard to ignore. The existence of an element of nepotism casts doubts on the operational independence of the commission as it compromises the fight against systemic corruption.

CONCLUSION AND RECOMMENDATIONS

The new dispensation has failed to create a strong core of state institutions with the capacity to promote economic growth without being captured by personal interest and detached from the influence of powerful rent seeking groups. State fragility in Zimbabwe has been due to the associative relationship between the militarization of the state and systematic corruption. The military has been used to resolve civil disputes and maintain the grip to power. This can be termed as administrative insulation as the military has become the law. Arbitrary arrests, rape, abduction and gross human rights violation have become the governance culture, and this has been targeted at government critics and activists. The political polarization in Zimbabwe has caused instability, threatening the possibilities of integration in the international communities from which perceived support for development including financial resources are to be unlocked.

The liberation struggle, ideologically correct rhetoric and the anti-imperialism stances on which the country's leadership, the most powerful of them being of the military mindset, continues to stand on as being the fundamental problem of Zimbabwe that continues to cripple its economy has lately lost its validity as citizens have continued for years to confront the reality that the militarized state and the corruption that fuels it are more endemic and harmful to the country's socioeconomic and political progress. The militarization of institutions and the centralized power that comes with it is a frustration on many levels and a dissuasion of sustainable development that cannot continue to be ignored.

It is conceivable that the prevailing dehumanizing condition in Zimbabwe requires a compendium of solutions to return the country to normalcy, if at all there is still known a normalcy to return to. International integration through resolving outstanding debts, perpetual international good will, image rebranding and normalization of relations with the western countries and international financial institutions is key in restoring Zimbabwe to bargain on the international grid. Despite the "Zimbabwe is open for business" mantra, open animosity has continued with countries like the US and UK due to the deteriorating human rights situation and endemic corruption. South Africa's relationship with Zimbabwe is on a downward spiral following sequence of diplomatic spats from the ANC against ZANU PF to border disputes. what is left is the political will from the Mnangagwa regime. Critical to this aspect is need for flexible servant and malleable leadership in Zimbabwe which puts public interests ahead of individual interests. With the Southern African Development Committee and the African Union chinning in to help Zimbabwe in the fight against sanctions through the Anti-sanctions' day commemoration on 25 October, however leaders like Paul Kagame and Cyril Ramaphosa need to use the same energy to support Zimbabwe by exerting pressure on the Mnangagwa regime to improve human rights conditions and end systemic corruption for the betterment of the citizens.

- Promoting constitutionalism and improving civil military relations
- A total divorce between the military, ZANU PF the party and the state or government which have lately become indistinguishable as separate entities.
- Revisiting legal statutes that establish independent commissions with an objective of improving independency.
- Promoting legal mechanisms which protect whistle blowers like Hopewell Chin'ono should be prioritized by the government as a way of curbing corruption.
- Independence of the judiciary to proffer uncompromised justice should be ushered through sustainable financial security for judges and magistrates.
- A judiciary that is immune from executive powers of the presidium, which is synonymous with the military state is necessary to remove judicial biases that have been rising in the courts and justice system.
- Serious implementation of mechanisms that safeguard property rights which is a critical aspect to attract foreign direct investment.
- Policy consistency
- Restructuring the prosecution channels with the objective of improving agility.
- An honest practice of commissions such as ZACC with independent, not symbolic power, sufficient to enforce anticorruption laws as its mandate allows and through the courts for which an honest possible indicator would be the removal of ministers involved in corruption cases from office; currently impossible as some officials remain more powerful than institutions.
- Retransferring power back into institutions from the military and individuals who control power.

REFERENCES

Apata, G. O. (2019). Corruption and the postocolonial state: How the west invented African corruption. *Journal of Contemporary African Studies*, *37*(1), 43–56. doi:10.1080/02589001.2018.1497292

Army deals blow to Mugabe rival. (2002, January 9) http://news.bbc.co.uk/2/hi/africa/1749933.stm

Banda, I. (2020). Zimbabwe and US Tensions- DC calls Harare a Foreign Adversary. *Africa Report*.

Bellina, S., Darbon, D., Sundstøl, S., & Sending, O. (2009). *The Legitimacy of the State in Fragile Situations*. Norwegian Agency for Development Cooperation.

Bratton, M. (2015). *Power Politics in Zimbabwe*. Lynne Rienner Publishers.

Brinkerhoff, D. W. (2007). *Capacity Development in Fragile States*. ECDPM Discussion Paper 58d.

Chronicle, T. (2022). *President swears in anti-corruption commissioners. . . 200 cases for Zacc*. The Chronicle. Retrieved 13 January 2022, from https://www.chronicle.co.zw/president-swears-in-anti-corruption-commissioners-200-cases-for-zacc/

Fisher, J. (2014). When it pays to be a 'fragile state': Uganda's use and abuse of a dubious concept. *Third World Quarterly*, *35*(2), 316–332. doi:10.1080/01436597.2014.878493

Fund For Peace. (2019). *Fragile States Index Annual Report*. Author.

Geddes, B., Wright, J., & Frantz, E. (2014). Autocratic Breakdown and Regime Transitions: A New Data Set. *Perspectives on Politics*, *12*(2), 313–331. doi:10.1017/S1537592714000851

Grävingholt, J., Ziaja, S., & Kreibaum, M. (2012). State Fragility: Towards a Multi- Dimensional Empirical Typology. SSRN *Electronic Journal*. doi:10.2139/ssrn.2279407

Greer, S. L., Wismar, M., Figueras, J., & European Observatory on Health Systems and Policies. (Eds.). (2016). *Strengthening health system governance: Better policies, stronger performance*. Open University Press.

Grimm, S., Lemay-Hébert, N., & Nay, O. (2014). 'Fragile States': Introducing a political concept. *Third World Quarterly*, *35*(2), 197–209. doi:10.1080/01436597.2013.878127

Herald, T. (2022). *Just In: VP Chiwenga New Minister of Health*. The Herald. Retrieved 13 January 2022, from https://www.herald.co.zw/just-in-vp-chiwenga-new-minister-of-health/

Hlatywayo, G. K., & Mangongera, C. (2020). *The Challenges for Social Movements in Post-Mugabe Zimbabwe*. https://www.usip.org/publications/2020/01/challenges-social-movements-post-mugabe-zimbabwe

Hoffmann, N., & Hendricks, F. (2018). African perspectives on corruption. *Journal of Contemporary African Studies*, *36*(4), 425–432. doi:10.1080/02589001.2018.1584718

Houngnikpo, M. C. (2016). *Guarding the Guardians: Civil-Military Relations and Democratic Governance in Africa*. Routledge. doi:10.4324/9781315586014

Joslyn, J. (2019). Bribery in Sub-Saharan Africa: The Mediating Effects of Institutional Development and Trust. *Socius: Sociological Research for a Dynamic World*, *5*. doi:10.1177/2378023118824804

Kaplan, S. (2014). Identifying Truly Fragile States. *The Washington Quarterly*, *37*(1), 49–63. doi:10.1080/0163660X.2014.893173

Khan, M. H. (2006). Determinants of Corruption in Developing Countries: The Limits of Conventional Economic Analysis. In *Chapters*. Edward Elgar Publishing. https://ideas.repec.org/h/elg/eechap/3740_8.html doi:10.4337/9781847203106.00015

Levi, M. (1981). The Predatory Theory of Rule. *Politics & Society*, *10*(4), 431–465. doi:10.1177/003232928101000403

Magaisa, A. (2020). *Understanding Judiciary Capture in Zimbabwe*. Big Saturday Read.

Maguchu, P. S., & Maja, I. (2019). The New Zimbabwean Government's War on Corruption: A Lesson for Anti-Corruption and Transitional Justice Scholars and Practitioners? *Journal of Anti-Corruption Law*, *3*, 76.

Masunungure, E. V. (2011). *Zimbabwe's Militarized, Electoral Authoritarianism*. Columbia University.

Mazarr, M. J. (2014, January 15). *The Rise and Fall of the Failed-State Paradigm*. https://www.foreignaffairs.com/articles/2013-12-06/rise-and-fall-failed-state-paradigm

Mubangizi, J. C., & Sewpersadh, P. (2017). A Human Rights-based Approach to Combating Public Procurement Corruption in Africa. *African Journal of Legal Studies*, *10*(1), 66–90. doi:10.1163/17087384-12340015

Muronzi, C. (2020). *3 years after Mugabe overthrow, many Zimbabweans say life's worse*. Retrieved 13 January 2022, from https://www.aljazeera.com/news/2020/11/14/three-years-since-mugabe-overthrow-zimbabweans-say-life-is-worse

Ndlovu-Gatsheni, S. J., & Ruhanya, P. (2020). *The History and Political Transition of Zimbabwe: From Mugabe to Mnangagwa*. Springer Nature. doi:10.1007/978-3-030-47733-2

Nichols, P. M. (2017). What is Organizational Corruption? In M. S. Aßländer & S. Hudson (Eds.), *The Handbook of Business and Corruption* (pp. 3–23). Emerald Publishing Limited. doi:10.1108/978-1-78635-445-720161001

Njini, F., & Marawanyika, G. (2020). *Zimbabwe Gold Smugglers Shipping over $1.5 billion a year*. Bloomberg.

Nyoni, T. (2017). *The Curse of Corruption in Zimbabwe* (*SSRN* Scholarly Paper ID 3085213). Social Science Research Network. https://papers.ssrn.com/abstract=3085213

OECD. (2018). *States of Fragility 2018*. OECD. doi:10.1787/9789264302075-

OECD. (2020). *States of Fragility 2020*. OECD. doi:10.1787/ba7c22e7-

Otaluka, W. O. (2017). *The cultural roots of corruption: An ethical investigation with particular reference to nepotism* [Thesis]. https://researchspace.ukzn.ac.za/handle/10413/14232

Riddell, R. (1984). *The Economy Four Years after Independence*. doi:10.1093/oxfordjournals.afraf.a097644

Rothstein, B., & Varraich, A. (2017). *Making Sense of Corruption*. Cambridge University Press. doi:10.1017/9781316681596

Shah, A., & Schacter, M. (2004). Combating Corruption: Look Before You Leap: A lack of progress in eradicating corruption could be due to misguided strategies. *Finance & Development*, *41*(4). Advance online publication. doi:10.5089/9781451922578.022.A012

Tendi, B.-M. (2013). Ideology, Civilian Authority and the Zimbabwean Military. *Journal of Southern African Studies*, *39*(4), 829–843. doi:10.1080/03057070.2013.858543

Torsello, D., & Venard, B. (2016). The Anthropology of Corruption. *Journal of Management Inquiry*, *25*(1), 34–54. doi:10.1177/1056492615579081

Tweet, Share, & 11:58, 01 Oct 2020. (2020, October 1). *Zimbabwe to make doctors army employees to stop wage strikes*. Zimbabwe News Now. https://www.zimlive.com/2020/10/01/zimbabwe-to-make-doctors-army-employees-to-stop-wage-strikes/

United Nations Economic Commission for Africa (2016-2003). African Governance Report IV 2016: Measuring Corruption in Africa: The International Dimension Matters. Author.

Wellington Garikai, B., Chiminya, J., & Mudzingiri, C. (2015). *An Explanatory Analysis of the Economic and Social Impact of Corruption in Zimbabwe*. Academic Press.

Yamamoto, K. (2014, April 10). Zimbabwe: Mugabe Fighting Corruption? Forget It! *New Zimbabwe*. https://allafrica.com/stories/201404100145.html

Zimbabwe Democratic Institute. (2017). *Zimbabwe Transition in a muddy terrain: Political Economy Under Military Capture*. https://kubatana.net/wp-content/uploads/2017/12/Zimbabwe-Transition-in-A-Muddy-Terrain-Political-Economy-Under-Military-Capture-Terrain.pdf

Chapter 7
International Law in the Field of Human Rights

Valeria Gonitashvili
Ukrainian Youth Organization of Georgia, Georgia

ABSTRACT

A series of international human rights treaties and other instruments adopted since 1945 have conferred legal forms on inherent human rights and developed the body of international human rights. Other instruments have been adopted at the regional level reflecting the particular human rights concerns of the region and providing for specific mechanisms of protection. Most states have also adopted constitutions and other laws which formally protect basic human rights. While international treaties and customary law form the backbone of international human rights law, other instruments, such as declarations, guidelines, and principles adopted at the international level, contribute to its understanding, implementation, and development. Respect for human rights requires the establishment of the rule of law at the national and international levels.

INTRODUCTION

International human rights law is a set of principles and norms governing the international protection of the rights and fundamental freedoms of individuals and representing international human rights standards for national law. International human rights law is a branch of public international law. The basis is the treaties of the UN system, as well as regional organizations (the main ones are in the systems of the Council of Europe, the African Union, and the Organization of American States). International human rights law is closely related to such branches of international law as refugee law and international humanitarian law.

History

Before the First World War, certain issues of human rights (mainly the rights of religious minorities) were included in bilateral and multilateral treaties.

DOI: 10.4018/978-1-6684-4543-3.ch007

Several treaties devoted to certain issues of human rights were adopted with the participation of the League of Nations - the Minority Treaties, as well as the Slavery Convention that is still in force and several conventions of the International Labor Organization (founded under the League).

In June 1945, the UN Charter was signed, the first article of which declared the implementation of international cooperation "in the promotion and development of respect for human rights" one of the goals of the organization. In April 1948, the Organization of American States adopted the American Declaration of the Rights and Duties of Man (Organization of American States, 1948).

Universal Declaration of Human Rights

The Universal Declaration of Human Rights of 1948, although it enshrines the fundamental rights and freedoms of the individual, is not a binding international legal instrument. At the same time, some lawyers consider the provisions of the UDHR as a source of customary norms of international law. The Universal Declaration of Human Rights was adopted at the third session of the UN General Assembly by resolution 217 A (III) (International Covenant on Human Rights) on December 10, 1948. The Declaration defines basic human rights (UN, 1948).

The Declaration has only the status of a recommendation, but on its basis, two binding treaties were adopted: the International Covenant on Civil and Political Rights and the International Covenant on Economic, Social, and Cultural Rights. Certain provisions of the declaration, such as the prohibition of torture and slavery, are mandatory as an imperative norm; in some countries, the Declaration is partially recognized.

Structure and Content

The structure underlying the Universal Declaration was influenced by the Napoleonic Code, including the preamble and introductory general principles. The final structure took shape in a second draft prepared by French jurist René Cassin, working on an initial draft prepared by Canadian legal scholar John Peters Humphrey.

The declaration consists of the following:

- The preamble sets out the historical and social reasons that led to the need for the Declaration.
- Articles 1-2 establish the basic concepts of dignity, freedom, and equality.
- Articles 3-5 establish other rights such as the right to life, and the prohibition of slavery and torture.
- Articles 6-11 deal with the fundamental legitimacy of human rights, with specific remedies for violations.
- Articles 12-17 set out human rights of the community, including freedom of movement, residence, property rights, and the right to citizenship.
- Articles 18-21 sanction the so-called "constitutional freedoms", as well as spiritual, social, political freedoms, such as freedom of thought, opinion, expression, religion and conscience, freedom of association, as well as the receipt and dissemination of information and ideas through any means mass media.
- Articles 22-27 establish economic, social, and cultural human rights. Includes the right to health care, support for the right to an adequate standard of living, provision for additional accommoda-

tions in the event of physical exhaustion or disability, and emphasis on care for those in motherhood or childhood.

- Articles 28-30 set out the general ways in which these rights can be exercised and areas in which individual rights cannot be applied (UN, 2005).

History of the Document - Background

During the Age of Enlightenment, ideas about Natural Law began to flourish. Based on these ideas, the Bill of Rights in Great Britain, the Bill of Rights in the USA, and the Declaration of the Rights of Man and Citizen in France were created and adopted.

The Second World War demonstrated the need for a universal human rights treaty. In 1941, Franklin Roosevelt, in his State of the Union address, called for the support of four essential freedoms: freedom of speech, freedom of conscience, freedom from want, and freedom from fear. This gave a new impetus to the development of human rights as a necessary condition for peace and the end of the war (UN, 2005).

As the public became aware of the atrocities committed by Nazi Germany, it became clear that the UN Charter did not clearly define human rights. A universal contract that would list and describe the rights of the individual was needed.

The first meeting of the UN Commission on Human Rights was held in the town of Lake Success from January 27 to February 10, 1947, where Eleanor Roosevelt was elected chairman of the Commission. The Commission included representatives of such states of the world as Australia, Belgium, Great Britain, China, Cuba, Egypt, India, Iran, Libya, Panama, USSR, USA, Uruguay, Philippines, France, Chile, Yugoslavia. They were to prepare a document that was first supposed to be called the International Bill of Rights. John Humphrey, a Canadian expert in the field of international law, who was invited to this position by the UN Secretary-General in 1946, also participated in the work of the Commission (Karumidze, 2003).

Since the Commission consisted of 18 members and their views differed in many ways, it was very difficult to carry out the work of drafting such an important document as the Declaration. In the end, it was decided that the initial test would be prepared by three representatives so that the Commission could consider it at its second meeting. The subcommittee drafting the Declaration included Eleanor Roosevelt herself, China's representative Zhang Pengchun, and Lebanese diplomat and philosopher Charles Malik. The subcommittee commissioned Humphrey, a highly experienced lawyer, who also had a good team of assistants from his department, to submit an initial draft of the text. This was also influenced by the fact that at first even such a small group of three people could not come to any common view of the document. The draft of the project consists of 48 articles. In the same period, it was decided to expand the composition of the subcommittee to include also representatives of Europe and the Soviet Union.

On June 9, 1947, the expanded composition of the subcommittee began its work. In addition to Roosevelt, Zhang Pengchun, Malik, and Humphrey, they included René Cassin of France, William Hodgson of Australia, Geoffrey Wilson of Great Britain, and Hernan Santa Cruz of Chile, and Vladimir Koretsky of the Soviet Union (Karumidze, 2003). The audience faced the most difficult task of creating a document not yet known to world politics. As Charles Malik wrote, at first everyone was "absolutely lost; we had no idea how to cope with the assigned task." (Karumidze, 2003).

Malik feared that human rights could be reduced to essential basics such as the need to have enough food, a roof over one's head, and the ability to work. At the same time, possibly less urgent, but key ideas, such as the ability to reason, to have one's own opinion, to defend one's political views, which distinguish a person from the rest of the animal world and which also had to be taken into account, could be left aside.

René Cassin was one of the most experienced among his colleagues. A Jew who survived two world wars was sentenced to death by the Nazis, and lost about thirty of his relatives in German concentration camps, Cassin made one of the most significant contributions to the creation of the text of the Declaration.

The preliminary text submitted to Humphrey for consideration was an exhaustive summary of all possible types of human rights. Occupying 400 pages in volume, the document was created based on an analysis of all existing constitutions, and existing norms of human rights law, Humphrey's assistants even considered appeals from individuals containing certain proposals. An extensive work, Humphrey's draft could not have been created from scratch, it was based on such documents as the English Magna Carta, the American Declaration of Independence, and the Bill of Rights, as well as the French Declaration of the Rights of Man and Citizen. It is the breadth of the base used that determined that the document considers such a wide range of rights: social, economic, and cultural. And if representatives of some countries initially did not want this or that circle of rights to be included in the project, then after the creation of the initial draft they could no longer cancel it with a simple desire, they had to reasonably prove why they think so. The most important documents from which Humphrey derived his text were proposal texts submitted for preliminary review by the American Law Institute and the Inter-American Juridical Committee.

After discussing the preliminary version of the Humphrey project, it was decided to again narrow the composition of the development team to speed up the process, which threatened to get bogged down in lengthy discussions. This time the group included Kassen, Malik, Roosevelt, and Wilson. The task of compiling a second version of the draft for consideration first by the group, and then by the Commission, was entrusted to René Cassin, both a specialist in the field of law and an excellent writer. In the same years, Cassin headed the French Council of State and was engaged in the restoration of the post-war French legal system.

Cassin completed his work in two days in June 1947. Cassin's main merit was to give the document a clear and precise structure, from Humphrey's list he formed a logically coherent document. To build this structure, Cassin wrote an introductory preamble where general principles were outlined, six introductory articles were included, 32 articles were grouped into 8 groups, and two final provisions on the application were added. Cassin compared the Declaration to a portico of a Greek temple with a foundation, stairs, four columns, and a pediment.

Articles 1 and 2 lay the foundation by emphasizing the principles of dignity, liberty, equality, and fraternity. The seven paragraphs of the preamble proclaim the reasons for promulgating the "Declaration" and are steps towards it. The main text of the "Declaration" forms four columns. The first column (Vv. 3-11) proclaims the rights of the individual, such as the right to life and the prohibition of slavery. The second column (Vv. 12-17) proclaims the rights of the individual in civil and political society. The third column (Vv. 18-21) proclaims spiritual, social, and political freedoms, such as freedom of religion and association. The fourth column (Vv. 22-27) defines social, economic, and cultural rights.

According to Cassin's model, the last three articles of the Declaration form a pediment that links the entire structure into one. These articles are devoted to the duties of the individual to society and prohibit the abuse of rights to the detriment of the purpose that the United Nations has laid down in them.

For many years, it was Cassin who was considered the creator of the Declaration. Only at the end of the twentieth century did researchers discover a draft document in Humphrey's papers, its first handwritten version. However, even after that, Humphrey refused to consider himself the creator of the Declaration, stating that it was impossible to create a draft alone, and "the final text of the Declaration is the work of hundreds of people."

Although in the future the text of the Declaration was subjected to significant revisions before being approved, it was Humphrey's draft, deeply revised by Cassin, that became the basis of the future document.

The Cassin variant was presented to the group on June 17, 1947. It has been partially revised to be presented to the Commission. In December 1947, the entire Commission on Human Rights of the United Nations met in Geneva. The session was attended by consultants from many organizations (for example, the American Federation of Labor, the Inter-Parliamentary Union, the International Committee of the Red Cross, the International Council of Women, the World Jewish Congress, etc.). The most complicated document had to be considered and approved for further transfer to the UN. Eleanor Roosevelt had a busy schedule that included meetings until late at night. It was thanks to her that it was possible to complete the consideration of the Declaration and come to a common position, despite differences of opinion, by the end of the session on 17 December (Karumidze, 2003).

One of the key issues considered at the session was the issue of including provisions in the Declaration providing tools that would allow monitoring the implementation of the provisions stated in the Declaration. The representative of India, Hansa Jivraj Mehta, as well as the Australian William Hodgson, insisted that without them the text of the document would have no force, and those who violated it would not be punished. They proposed either to introduce provisions on liability for non-observance of rights in the document itself or to establish an international tribunal that would consider such cases.

The positions of young, newly formed nations also came into conflict with the positions of large states. Former colonies and young countries wanted to see in the Declaration a legal precedent for the implementation of human rights, which they could use in building a free society in their own country. Large states, on the contrary, feared that too radical provisions could undermine their integrity.

As a result of heated debate, the third version of the Declaration, the so-called "Geneva draft" (Geneva draft), was created.

The discussion of the document continued in May 1948 at the next meeting of the Commission in New York. She had to work out the final text of the document for submission to further instances. The work was completed on June 18, when the document was adopted by general vote with 12 votes in favor, 0 against, and three abstentions - the countries of the USSR (Russia (RSFSR), Ukraine (Ukrainian SSR), and Belarus (BSSR).

Adoption

The vote for the declaration was carried out gradually. 23 out of 31 articles of the draft declaration were adopted unanimously. As a result of the discussion, article 3 of the draft declaration was merged with article 2. During the discussion and voting point by article, the confrontation between the Western countries and the countries of the Soviet bloc was revealed. The head of the Soviet delegation to the UN, Andrei Yanuarievich Vyshinsky, spoke of the declaration as follows:

Despite some of its merits, this project has several major shortcomings, the main of which is its formal legal nature and the absence in this project of any measures that would be able to promote the implementation of the fundamental freedoms and human rights proclaimed in this project (Karumidze, 2003).
— Birth of the Universal Declaration of Human Rights

The Universal Declaration of Human Rights in its final version was supported by 48 countries (out of 58 then members of the UN) at the 183rd plenary session of the General Assembly of the United Nations in the Palais de Chaillot (Paris) on December 10, 1948. Belorussian SSR, Ukrainian SSR, USSR, Czechoslovakia, Poland, Yugoslavia, South Africa, and Saudi Arabia abstained from the vote, while Honduras and Yemen did not participate in it (Chitadze, 2016). Canada rejected the first version of the Declaration but agreed with it in the final vote.

Status and Distribution

The Declaration has only the status of a recommendation, but on its basis, two binding treaties were adopted: the International Covenant on Civil and Political Rights and the International Covenant on Economic, Social, and Cultural Rights. Many of the declaration's provisions have acquired the status of customary law over many years of practice; in some countries, the Declaration is partially recognized.

This document has been translated into many languages of the world (more than 500 in 2018) and is the most translated document in the world.

Eleanor Roosevelt referred to the Declaration as the "Magna Carta" for all mankind (which is why the Declaration is sometimes referred to as the Charter of Human Rights).

Human Rights Day

In 1950, in honor of the Declaration, the UN established the Human Rights Day holiday, celebrated on December 10th. People, various communities and religious groups, parliaments, governments, and, of course, the United Nations itself take part in the celebration. Campaigns are launched every ten years to promote the Declaration and directly human rights. On December 10, 2007, a campaign called "Human dignity and justice for all of us" was launched, in which all UN member countries took an active part, which lasted exactly one year, until the 60th anniversary (UN, 2005).

Rights Covenants

Both Covenants and the First Optional Protocol to the ICCPR (International Covenant on Civil and Political Rights) was adopted in 1966 and entered into force in 1976.

The ICESCR (International Covenant on Economic, Social and Cultural Rights) is characterized by softer language than the ICCPR, in particular the principle of "progressive realization" of rights. The Second Optional Protocol to the ICCPR, which limits the death penalty, was adopted in 1989 and entered into force in 1992. The Optional Protocol to the ICESCR (establishing a complaints mechanism similar to the First Protocol to the ICCPR) was adopted in 2008 and entered into force in 2013 The Covenants, along with their Optional Protocols and the UDHR, constitute the so-called International Bill of Human Rights (Karumidze, 2003).

International Covenant on Civil and Political Rights

The International Covenant on Civil and Political Rights is a United Nations pact based on the Universal Declaration of Human Rights. Adopted on December 16, 1966, entered into force on March 23, 1976.

The Covenant is an international treaty and is binding on 172 state parties, as of August 2017. In addition to the participating states, the pact was signed by 7 more countries (UN, 2022).

The pact obliges the parties to respect the civil and political rights of people, including the right to life, freedom of religion, freedom of speech, freedom of assembly, voting rights, the right to due process of law, and a fair trial, etc. The pact was ratified by Decree of the Presidium of the USSR Supreme Court on September 18, 1973, of the year (UN, 2022).

Oversight of the implementation of the pact is carried out by the UN Human Rights Committee, considering the reports of the participating countries, publishing comments ("general comments") on the pact, and considering complaints about violations of the pact by the countries participating in the first optional protocol.

Participating states are highlighted in dark green. Signatory but not yet ratified countries are highlighted in light green.

Main Stages of the Document`s Adoption

The Universal Declaration of Human Rights for the first time approved a list of political, socio-economic, and cultural human rights. Since this document was in the form of a resolution of the UN General Assembly, it was advisory and could not be recognized as legally binding. That is why the General Assembly at the same time instructed the Commission on Human Rights through the UN Economic and Social Council to develop a single human rights pact that would cover a wide range of fundamental rights and freedoms.

Based on the Universal Declaration of Human Rights, the UN Commission on Human Rights developed legally binding documents proposed in 1966 for adoption - the International Covenant on Civil and Political Rights and the International Covenant on Economic, Social and Cultural Rights, which most fully determined the list and content of fundamental human rights. Both documents entered into force in 1976 after ratification, as agreed, by 35 countries. The content of the pacts fixed a different level of binding nature of their provisions for the participating states (Karumidze, 2003).

To date, the Pact has been signed and ratified by most (172) countries of the world (among the latest it has entered into force in Fiji, Qatar, the Republic of the Marshall Islands, Sao Tome and Principe, and the State of Palestine). 6 states have signed but not ratified the Pact: China, the Union of Comoros, Cuba, Nauru, Palau, Saint Lucia. Among the countries that have not acceded to the Pact are the Vatican, Taiwan, Myanmar, Malaysia, Bhutan, Singapore, Brunei Darussalam, Saudi Arabia, Oman, UAE, South Sudan, several island states of Oceania (Federated States of Micronesia, Kiribati, Tonga, Solomon Islands, Tuvalu) and the Caribbean (Grenada, Saint Kitts, and Nevis, Antigua and Barbuda) (Chitadze, 2016).

Structure of the Pact

The Covenant follows the structure of the UDHR and the ICESCR, with a preamble and 53 articles divided into six parts.

Preamble

In the Preamble, the participating States, relying on the principles proclaimed by the UN Charter and the Universal Declaration of Human Rights, recognize the dignity of all people and their equal and inalienable rights as the basis of freedom, justice, and peace in the world, recognizing that the idea of a free human person can only be realized in conditions of free enjoyment of their economic, social, cultural, civil and political rights, considering that states are obliged to promote respect for and observance of human rights and freedoms, agreed on the text of the Covenant.

Part I

Article 1 recognizes the right of every people to • self-determination, including the free determination of their political status and the free pursuit of their economic, social and cultural development; • free disposal of their natural wealth and resources; • inadmissibility of depriving him of his means of subsistence.

The right of peoples to self-determination, guaranteed by Article 1.1 of the Covenant, differs from other rights specified in the Covenant in that this right is vested not in individuals, but in "peoples". It is also the only right common to both the International Covenant on Civil and Political Rights and the International Covenant on Economic, Social, and Cultural Rights.

Part II

Articles 2-5 - the procedure for fulfilling the obligations provided for by the Covenant.

Article 2 obliges States to • Respect and ensure to persons within their territories and subject to their jurisdiction the rights recognized in the Covenant, regardless of race, color, sex, language, religion, political or another opinion, national or social origin, property position, birth or other circumstance; • Take the legislative or other measures necessary to give effect to the rights outlined in the Covenant; • provide an effective remedy for persons whose rights and freedoms have been violated; • to ensure that the right to legal protection is established by the competent judicial, administrative, legislative authorities or other competent authorities, to develop the possibilities of judicial protection; • Ensure that legal remedies are applied by the competent authorities when they are granted.

Article 2 is regarded as the most important article of the Covenant, its "cornerstone", given establishing the obligation of States parties to respect and ensure the rights recognized by the Covenant. These rights (except for the right to vote) apply not only to citizens but also to all persons located on the territory of the state. General comment No. 31 on the nature of the general legal obligation incumbent on States parties to the Covenant (CCPR/C/74/CRP.4/Rev.6) provides further information on the obligations arising from article 2 of the Covenant.

Article 3 obliges states to ensure the equal right of men and women to enjoy all the civil and political rights provided for in the Covenant.

Article 3 correlates with article 26 of the Covenant regarding protection against discrimination based on sex.

Article 4 allows states during the period of an officially declared state of emergency (when the life of the nation is under threat) to derogate from their obligations under the Covenant, but only to the extent determined by the severity of the situation, provided: • they do not violate their international legal obligations; • non-discrimination solely on the basis of race, colour, sex, language, religion or social origin; • non-derogation from articles 6 (right to life), 7 (inadmissibility of torture, cruel inhuman, degrading treatment or punishment, experiments without consent), 8 (par. 1 and 2) (inadmissibility of slavery, slave trade, captivity), 11 (inadmissibility of deprivation of liberty due to inability to fulfill a contractual obligation), 15 (inadmissibility of bringing to criminal responsibility for an act that was not a criminal offense at the time of the commission, or imposing a punishment more severe than was subject to application), 16 (the right to recognition of legal personality) and 18 (right to freedom of thought, conscience and religion) of the Covenant; • immediately informing other participating States through the UN Secretary-General of: the provisions from which the derogation has taken place, the reasons for such derogation, the date the derogation ends.

The UN Human Rights Committee, if necessary, may raise the question of whether a state party has officially declared a state of emergency when the life of the nation is threatened, as well as whether other mandatory provisions of article 4 of the Covenant have been observed. Further information on the obligations arising from article 4 of the Covenant is set out in General Comment No. 29 on derogations due to states of emergency (CCPR/C/21/Rev.1/Add.11).

Article 5 provides for the inadmissibility of • any State, group, or individual interpreting any provision of the Covenant as giving him (them) the right to destroy in any way any rights or freedoms recognized by the Covenant or to restrict them more than is provided for in the Covenant;

- Restriction or derogation of any fundamental human rights provided for in the state party by the law, convention, rule or custom, under the pretext of their absence in the Covenant or their recognition by the Covenant to a lesser extent.

Article 5, paragraph 2, deals with cases where the internal law of a State party provides for greater protection of human rights than provided by the Covenant, without allowing them to be limited or restricted by reference to their lesser protection by the Covenant.

Part III

Part III (Articles 6-27) is the basis of the Covenant, which lists the substantive rights and fundamental freedoms guaranteed by the document. These are the articles commonly referred to by individuals who claim violations of their rights under the Covenant.

Article 6 defines that: • the right to life is an inalienable, legally protected right of every person, where no one can be arbitrarily deprived of life; • Countries that have not abolished the death penalty can only impose the death penalty for the most serious crimes following the law in force at the time of the commission of the crime, consistent with the Covenant and the Convention on the Prevention and Punishment of the Crime of Genocide; • When deprivation of life constitutes genocide, States Parties may not derogate from their obligations under the Convention on the Prevention and Punishment of the Crime of Genocide; • those sentenced to death have the right to pardon, commutation (replacement) of the sentence, amnesty; • The imposition of the death penalty for crimes committed by persons under eighteen years of age is unacceptable; • It is unacceptable to carry out the death penalty against pregnant women.

Despite the unambiguity of many of the provisions specified in Article 6 of the Covenant, nevertheless, some provisions relating to the issue of the inalienability of the right to life are debatable, such as, for example, the definition of the age from which the right to life arises.

Article 7 establishes the inadmissibility of • torture; • cruel, inhuman, or degrading treatment or punishment; • conducting medical or scientific experiments without the consent of the person.

Article 8 provides for the inadmissibility of • slavery; • slave trade; • servitude; • Compulsion to forced or compulsory labor (except hard labor and other similar work by a court decision, military and alternative service, compulsory work in emergencies, ordinary civic duties).

Article 9 determines that: • Everyone has the right to liberty and security of person; • Arbitrary arrest and detention are unacceptable; • deprivation of liberty is admissible only on the grounds and according to the procedure established by law; • those who are arrested must be immediately informed of the reasons for the arrest and the charges against them; • Those arrested and detained must be brought before a court immediately and have the right to a trial within a reasonable time or to release; • release from custody may be subject to guarantees to appear: for court, for trial, for the execution of a sentence; • Arrested and imprisoned persons have the right to have their case heard by a court for an immediate decision on the lawfulness or illegality of the detention. • victims of unlawful arrest or imprisonment are entitled to compensation.

Article 10 provides that: • persons deprived of their liberty have the right to humane treatment and respect for human dignity; • in the absence of exceptional circumstances, the accused, with the observance of the status of unconvicted persons, are placed separately from the convicted; • Defendants (and prisoners, subject to the aging regime and legal status) minors are separated from adults and immediately brought to court for a decision; • The penitentiary system should provide for a regime aimed at the correction and social re-education of prisoners.

Article 11 establishes the inadmissibility of deprivation of liberty due to the inability to fulfill any contractual obligation.

Article 12 determines that: • Everyone lawfully within the territory of the State has the right to freedom of movement and choice of residence; • Everyone has the right to leave any country, including their own; • the right to freedom of movement and choice of residence and the right to leave any country may be limited only by law for the protection of state security, public order, health, morals of the population, rights, and freedoms of others; • Arbitrary deprivation of the right to enter one's own country is unacceptable.

Article 13 provides that: • An alien legally present in the territory of a State Party may be expelled only by the lawful decision; • A foreigner who is being expelled has the right to present arguments against expulsion; review the case; present before competent subjects for review by a person or persons.

Article 14 specifies that: • all are equal before the courts and tribunals; • in criminal or civil proceedings, everyone has the right to a fair and public hearing by a competent, independent and impartial tribunal established by law; • Restriction of access of the media and the public to trials is allowed only to protect: morality, public order, national security, privacy of the parties, interests of justice in special circumstances; • judicial decisions must be public, except for the following cases: protecting the interests of minors; matrimonial disputes; child custody cases; • everyone accused of a crime is presumed innocent until proven guilty in the prescribed manner; • Every accused person has the right to: Prompt and detailed notification, in a language he or she understands, of the nature and basis of the accusation; the necessary time and facilities to prepare their defence; interaction with the defender chosen by him; court without delay; court in his presence; defending himself in person or through legal counsel of his choice; notice of the right to have a defense counsel; appointed, including free of charge, a defender; interrogation of witnesses testifying against him; calling and interrogating their witnesses; free assistance of an interpreter; not being forced to testify against oneself or to plead guilty; • the process for juveniles should take into account their age and the desirability of promoting their education; • every convicted person has the right to review the sentence by a higher court; • A person who has been convicted and punished as a result of a miscarriage of justice is entitled to compensation, unless the miscarriage of justice was the fault of that person; • No one can be reconvicted or punished for a crime for which they have already been convicted or acquitted.

The right to a fair trial in both criminal and civil cases, as set out in article 14, is of fundamental importance, especially in conjunction with the right to an effective remedy under article 2 of the Covenant.

Article 15 establishes that: • No one may be found guilty of an offense for an act that was not, at the time it was committed, a criminal offense under domestic law or international law; • no more severe punishment may be imposed than that which was applicable at the time of the commission of the crime; • A mitigating law applies to an offender who committed a crime before the entry into force of such a law; • Any person who commits an act which at the time of its commission was a criminal offense under the general principles of law recognized by the international community may be tried and punished.

Article 16 provides that every person, regardless of location, has the right to recognition of his legal personality.

Article 17 establishes: • the inadmissibility of arbitrary or unlawful interference or encroachment on: private and family life; the inviolability of the home; secrecy of correspondence; honor and reputation; • the right to the protection of the law against such interference or encroachment.

Article 18 determines that: • every person has the right to freedom: thoughts, conscience, religion (freedom to have, adopt, profess religion, beliefs, worship, perform religious and ritual rites and teachings); • infringement of the freedom to have or adopt a religion and beliefs of one's choice is unacceptable; • freedom of religion and belief may be limited only by the law to protect: public safety, order, health, morality, fundamental rights and freedoms of other persons; • the Participating States must respect the freedom of parents and guardians to provide for the religious and moral education of their children following their convictions.

Article 19 provides that: • everyone has the right to: freely hold their opinions; to freely express one's opinion (freely seek, receive, disseminate information and ideas by any means) • free expression of one's opinion may be restricted by law for respect of the rights and reputation of other persons; protection of state security, public order, health and morality of the population.

Article 20 establishes the obligatory prohibition by law: • war propaganda; • propaganda of national, racial, or religious hatred, which constitutes incitement to discrimination, hostility, or violence.

Article 21 guarantees the right to peaceful assembly, which may be restricted by law in the interests of the state or public security, public order, public health, morality, and protection of the rights and freedoms of other persons.

The right to peaceful assembly guaranteed by Article 21 is also enshrined in Article 20 of the Universal Declaration of Human Rights, and Article 11 of the European Convention for the Protection of Human Rights and Fundamental Freedoms.

Article 22 determines that: • everyone has the right to: freedom of association with others; the creation of trade unions; joining trade unions to protect their interests; • the right to freedom of association with others may be restricted by law in the interests of the state or public security, public order, public health, morals, protection of the rights and freedoms of others, as well as for members of the armed forces and the police; • States parties to the International Labor Organization Convention on Freedom of Association and the Protection of the Right to Organize, 1948 (No. 87) may not legislate the right to freedom of association with others.

Article 23 establishes that: • the family is the natural and fundamental unit of society, entitled to protection by society and the state; • men and women of marriageable age have the right to marry and found a family; • marriage can be entered into only with the consent of those who are getting married; • Participating States must ensure the equality of rights and obligations of spouses about entering into marriage, during the marriage, at the dissolution of marriage; • Divorce must ensure the protection of all children.

Article 24 provides that every child: • without being discriminated against based on race, color, sex, language, religion, national or social origin, property or birth, has the right to be protected by his family, society, and state; • must be registered immediately after birth and given a name; • is eligible for citizenship.

Article 25 determines that every citizen, without being discriminated against on the grounds of race, color, sex, language, religion, political or other opinions, national or social origin, property status, birth or another status, must have the right and opportunity to • taking part in public affairs directly and through elected representatives; • voting and election in elections held based on universal equal suffrage by secret ballot, ensuring the free expression of the will of voters; • Equal access in their country to public service.

Article 25 is of particular importance because it enshrined the most important right to participate in political life - to vote and be elected in elections.

Article 26 establishes that: • all persons are equal before the law and are entitled, without being discriminated against, to the equal protection of the law; • any discrimination should be prohibited by law; • The law must guarantee everyone equal and effective protection against discrimination based on: race, color, sex, language, religion, political or other opinions, national, social origin, property status, birth, other circumstances.

Article 26, along with articles 2 and 14 of the Covenant, is fundamental to the Covenant, establishing the right to equality before the law and equal protection of the law, with broad guarantees of non-discrimination. The Human Rights Committee interprets this provision broadly, extending it to all legal provisions, and not just to the rules specified in the Covenant.

Article 27 determines that in countries with existing ethnic, religious, and linguistic minorities, persons from such minorities cannot be denied the right, in common with other members of the same group: to enjoy their culture, profess their religion, practice their religious rites, use their native language.

Although formally the provisions of article 27 are formulated as an individual right, it should be regarded in its essence as a group right that protects the totality of individuals.

Part IV

Articles 28-45 are the rules for the operation of the Human Rights Committee.

Part V

Articles 46-47 are rules for the interpretation of the pact.

Part VI

Articles 48-53 - the procedure for signing and entry into force of the pact.

List of Rights

- Article 1 - the right of peoples to self-determination;
- Article 6 - the right to life;

- Article 7 - prohibition of torture;
- Article 8 - prohibition of slavery and forced labor;
- Article 9 - the right to liberty and security of person;
- Article 10 - the right of persons deprived of their liberty to be treated with humanity and dignity;
- Article 11 - prohibition of imprisonment for debts;
- Article 12 - the right to free movement and freedom to choose one's place of residence;
- Article 13 - restriction of the possibility of the expulsion of aliens;
- Article 14 - equality before the courts, the presumption of innocence, prohibition of reconviction, right to reconviction, and other procedural rights;
- Article 15 - prohibition of criminal punishment for actions that were not recognized as criminal at the time they were committed;
- Article 16 - the right to recognition of legal personality;
- Article 17 - prohibition of interference in private and family life, inviolability of the home, the secrecy of correspondence, and protection against unlawful encroachments on honor and reputation;
- Article 18 - the right to freedom of thought, conscience, and religion;
- Article 19 - freedom of speech;
- Article 20 - prohibition of propaganda for war and speech in favor of national, racial, or religious hatred, which constitutes incitement to discrimination, hostility, or violence;
- Article 21 - freedom of assembly;
- Article 22 - freedom of association;
- Article 23 - the right to marry;
- Article 24 - children's rights;
- Article 25 - the right to take part in the conduct of public affairs, to vote, and to be elected;
- Article 26 - equality before the law, prohibition of discrimination;
- Article 27 - rights of ethnic, religious, and linguistic minorities (Karumidze, 2003).

Optional Protocols

The Optional Protocol to the Covenant on Civil and Political Rights, which provides for a procedure for considering reports of violations by states parties to the pact, was adopted and opened for signature on December 16, 1966, and entered into force on March 23, 1976. For 2016, 115 participating States.

The Second Optional Protocol to the International Covenant on Civil and Political Rights, aimed at the abolition of the death penalty, was adopted on December 15, 1989, by resolution 44/128 of the General Assembly at its 82nd plenary meeting, entered into force in 1991. For 2016 - 82 participating States (Chitadze, 2016).

International Covenant on Economic, Social, and Cultural Rights

The International Covenant on Economic, Social, and Cultural Rights is a pact adopted by the UN General Assembly on December 16, 1966, and entered into force on January 3, 1976.

As of October 2016, 164 states are participating in the pact. The largest state that is not a party to the pact is the United States (signed in 1977, but not ratified). Several countries have joined the pact with reservations, usually relating to labor rights (usually retaining the possibility of restricting the right to strike; but there have been exceptions to the contrary - for example, when New Zealand signed the pact, its legislation included a provision for universal membership in trade unions, which is wider than covenant right to join trade unions).

On December 10, 2008, the UN General Assembly adopted an optional protocol to the pact, providing for the possibility of filing complaints about violations of the pact. For the Protocol to enter into force following its Art. 18 requires its ratification or accession to it by ten countries participating in the Pact (the threshold was reached on February 5, 2013, when Uruguay became a party to the protocol; the protocol entered into force 3 months after this event, that is, on May 5, 2013). As of October 2016, the protocol entered into force for 22 countries out of 45 signatories (Chitadze, 2016).

History of Preparation of the Document

In 1948, the UN General Assembly asked the commission to prepare, as a matter of priority, a draft human rights pact and a draft of measures for their implementation. In 1949, the commission considered the text of the draft pact, and the following year it revised the first 18 articles based on comments received from governments. In 1950, the General Assembly declared in its resolution that "the enjoyment of civil and political liberties and the enjoyment of economic, social and cultural rights are interrelated and mutually dependent." The Assembly then decided to include in the human rights covenant economic, social and cultural rights, as well as some definition of the equality of men and women concerning these rights, as provided for by the statute.

In 1951, the commission drew up 14 articles on economic, social, and cultural rights, based on proposals from governments and opinions from specialized agencies. She also formulated ten articles on measures to implement these rights, according to which state parties to the pact must submit periodic reports.

After a lengthy debate at its session in 1951, the General Assembly instructed the Commission "to draw up a draft of two covenants on human rights, one of which should contain civil and political rights, and the other economic and social rights and cultural rights." The Assembly emphasized that both pacts should include as many similar provisions as possible, as well as an article that provides that "all peoples have the right to self-determination".

The Commission completed the drafting of the two pacts at its ninth and tenth sessions, held in 1953 and 1954 respectively. The General Assembly considered the draft pacts in 1954 and decided to publish the draft pacts as widely as possible so that governments could study them in detail and so that public opinion too could be freely expressed. It recommended that the Third Committee begin an article-by-article discussion of the texts at its session in 1955. Although the article-by-article discussion began on time, the development of the pacts was not completed until 1966.

Thus, in 1966, the development of two International Covenants on Human Rights (instead of one, as initially thought) was completed: the International Covenant on Economic, Social, and Cultural Rights and the International Covenant on Civil and Political Rights. In addition, the Optional Protocol to the International Covenant on Civil and Political Rights provides a mechanism for considering communications from individuals who claim to be victims of a violation of any of the rights outlined in the Covenant (Karumidze, 2003).

Rights Catalog

- Article 1 - the right to self-determination;
- Article 6 - the right to work;

- Article 7 - the right to just and favorable working conditions;
- Article 8 - the right to form trade unions and strike;
- Article 9 - the right to social security;
- Article 10 - protection of the family, motherhood, and children;
- Article 11 - the right to an adequate standard of living (includes the right to housing and food);
- Article 12 - the right to the highest attainable standard of physical and mental health;
- Article 13 - the right of every person to education;
- Article 14 - plan of action for the introduction of compulsory free universal primary education;
- Article 15 - the right to participate in cultural life, enjoy the results of scientific progress and protect the interests associated with one's creativity (Karumidze, 2003).

Compliance Supervision

The observance by state parties of their obligations under the pact and the level of implementation of the corresponding rights and obligations are monitored by the Committee on Economic, Social, and Cultural Rights.

In its activities, the Committee relies on many information sources, including reports submitted by States Parties and information from the specialized agencies of the United Nations: the International Labor Organization, the United Nations Educational, Scientific and Cultural Organization, the World Health Organization, the Food and agricultural organization of the United Nations, as well as from the Office of the United Nations High Commissioner for Refugees, the United Nations Center for Human Settlements and other agencies. In addition, it is provided with information by non-governmental and public organizations operating on the territory of states that have ratified the pact, international human rights organizations, and other non-governmental organizations, as well as other treaty bodies of the United Nations. In addition, the Committee uses publicly available sources (Chitadze, 2016).

International monitoring of the observance of economic, social, and cultural rights is usually not associated with the consideration of individual complaints.

UN Human Rights Treaties

There is the list of main international conventions, treaties, and other documents in the field of Human Rights:

- International Convention on the Elimination of All Forms of Racial Discrimination (1965, in force 1969)
- Convention on the Elimination of All Forms of Discrimination against Women (1979, in force since 1981, there is an optional protocol)
- Convention against Torture and Other Cruel, Inhuman or Degrading Treatment or Punishment (1984, in force since 1987, with optional protocol)
- Convention on the Rights of the Child (1989, in force since 1990, there are three optional protocols)
- International Convention on the Protection of the Rights of All Migrant Workers and Members of Their Families (1990, in force 2003)
- Convention on the Rights of Persons with Disabilities (2006, in force since 2008, with an optional protocol)

- International Convention for the Protection of All Persons from Enforced Disappearance (2006, in force 2010) (UN, 2022).

All of the conventions mentioned have mechanisms for review by the committees overseeing their implementation of allegations of violations of the conventions by those countries that agree to such review by making a special declaration or by joining an optional protocol. The mechanism for considering complaints about violations of the Convention on the Rights of Migrant Workers, as of November 2020, is not yet working - at least 10 states must agree to consider complaints about violations.

Allegations of violations can be filed by both other participating States (for the first time, states used this right in 2018), as well as people who consider themselves victims of violations of conventions.

The adoption of most of these conventions was preceded by the adoption by the UN General Assembly of non-binding declarations on relevant topics: on the rights of the child in 1959, on the elimination of racial discrimination in 1963, on the elimination of discrimination against women in 1967, on protection from torture and rights of persons with disabilities in 1975, on enforced disappearances in 1992 (several conventions and recommendations of the ILO were adopted on the rights of migrants before the UN convention) (UN, 2022).

As of 2020, the UN Human Rights Council is developing another human rights treaty, namely, on the regulation of the activities of transnational corporations and other businesses (UN, 2022).

International Human Rights Institutions

European Court of Human Rights

The European Court of Human Rights (ECHR) (French Cour européenne des droits de l'homme) is an international judicial body whose jurisdiction extends to all member states of the Council of Europe that have ratified the European Convention for the Protection of human rights and fundamental freedoms, which includes all questions relating to the interpretation and application of the convention, including interstate cases and individual complaints (ECHR, 2022).

History of the ECHR

The European Convention for the Protection of Human Rights and Fundamental Freedoms, which entered into force on September 3, 1953, not only proclaimed fundamental human rights but also created a special mechanism for their protection (ECHR, 2022).

Initially, this mechanism included three bodies that were responsible for ensuring compliance with the obligations assumed by the states parties to the convention: the European Commission of Human Rights, the European Court of Human Rights, and the Committee of Ministers of the Council of Europe (ECHR, 2022).

On November 1, 1998, upon the entry into force of Protocol No. 11, the first two of these bodies were replaced by a single, permanent European Court of Human Rights. Its location is the Human Rights Palace in Strasbourg (France), where the Council of Europe itself is located.

Under the original system, all complaints filed by individual applicants or state parties to the convention were subject to prior review by the European Commission of Human Rights. It considered their admissibility and if so, referred the case to the European Court of Human Rights for a final, binding decision. If the case was not referred to the Court, it was decided by the Committee of Ministers. Since 1 October 1994, applicants have been granted the right to refer their cases to the Court on applications declared admissible by the Commission (ECHR, 2022).

The European Court is called upon to ensure strict observance and implementation of the norms of the convention by its member states. It performs this task by examining and resolving specific cases accepted by it for consideration based on individual complaints filed by an individual, a group of individuals, or a non-governmental organization. It is also possible to file a complaint about a violation of the convention by a member state of the Council of Europe by another member state.

Starting its activity in 1959, by the end of 1998 (when it was reformed), the European Court had ruled on the merits in 837 cases, the vast majority of which were based on complaints from citizens. The first decision on the merits of the case was taken by the court in 1960 (Lawless v. Ireland), the first decision on the merits in favor of the applicant in 1968 (Neumeister v. Austria). After the reform of the Court in 1998, its activity increased, and by the beginning of 2010, the court had already issued 12,198 judgments on the merits, of which 10,156 found violations of the convention or its protocols (ECHR, 2022).

ECHR since 2009: changes in the procedure for considering complaints and requirements for them

In 2009-to-2018, several regulations were adopted that changed the procedure for considering complaints, the rules for filing them, introduced the priority of considering complaints, and limited the right to appeal in minor cases.

First, in June 2009, the Rules of the ECHR were amended, establishing a breakdown of all complaints into six categories (complaints of a higher category are considered before complaints of a lower one, although the President of the ECHR or the Grand Chamber of the ECHR has the right to give priority to consideration of any complaint):

1. Urgent complaints (if the applicant's life or health is endangered, the applicant is deprived of liberty due to a violation of rights, there are other circumstances related to the applicant's personal or family life, especially if the well-being of the child is endangered, as well as complaints on which interim measures under Rule 39 of the Rules of the European Court of Human Rights);
2. Complaints that raise issues that could affect the effectiveness of the Convention system (for example, concerning systemic and extremely widespread situations that have not yet been the subject of ECHR consideration, applications for which ECHR pilot judgments are issued) or complaints that raise important issues, affecting general interests (in particular, concerning issues that can have a significant impact on national or European legal systems);
3. Complaints, the main issues of which, according to the preliminary assessment, are violations of articles 2, 3, 4, and paragraph 1 of article 5 of the European Convention for the Protection of Human Rights and Fundamental Freedoms, regardless of whether they are repetitive, as well as complaints about imminent threats the physical integrity and dignity of a person;
4. Substantiated claims of violations of other Articles of the Convention.
5. Complaints about violations that were the subject of proceedings resulting in pilot or most significant judgments of the European Court of Human Rights ("repetitive cases")
6. Complaints, the admissibility of which is questionable.
7. unacceptable complaints (ECHR, 2022).

Secondly, from January 1, 2014, the so-called "preliminary complaints" were canceled (the Rules of the Court were changed). Previously, the applicant filed a free-form complaint with the ECHR, and then, following the instructions of the Court, re-executed it. At the same time, the filed "preliminary complaint" interrupted the six months for appeal. Instead, the court published a form (in the languages of the countries of the Council of Europe), which the applicant must fill out, print out, and send by mail to the ECtHR. The day of filing a complaint with the ECHR was considered the day when a fully completed form with documents was sent by mail.

Thirdly, the Complaint Form began to require the applicant to attach quality copies of documents supporting the arguments of his complaint.

Fourthly, the decision on the admissibility of the complaint began to be taken by a single judge, and not by a troika of judges.

Fifthly, since the entry into force of Protocol No. 10 to the European Convention, the court has received the right to reject complaints if their submitter has not suffered significant damage from the violation of rights.

Since January 2019, the ECHR, on an experimental basis (for 1 year), has introduced a new procedure for considering admissible complaints (except complaints relating to issues of law new to the ECHR):

- Before the start of consideration of the complaint, the complainant and the respondent state are required to conclude a settlement agreement. 12 weeks are allotted for negotiations on the settlement agreement;
- In case of failure to reach a settlement agreement, the ECHR proposes that the respondent state make a unilateral declaration - to recognize the violation of the applicant's rights and offer the applicant compensation (based on the practice of the ECHR);
- If the respondent government refuses to issue a unilateral declaration, the ECHR proceeds to the normal adversarial process. It took 12 weeks.
- Protocol No. 15 to the European Convention makes several changes to the ECHR's work procedure
- Depriving the complained state of the right to object to the cession of the case to the Grand Chamber of the ECHR;
- Reduction of the period for applying to the ECHR for an applicant from 6 months to 4 months;
- Prohibition for the ECtHR to declare admissible an application in which the applicant has not suffered significant harm. Before Protocol No. 15, the ECHR could not refuse to accept such an application if the applicant's case had not been properly examined by the national court. With the entry into force of Protocol No. 15, the ECHR can accept such a complaint only out of respect for the law.

As of May 1, 2017, Protocol No. 15 has been ratified by 34 countries of the Council of Europe.

On April 21, 2021, Italy was the last Council of Europe country to ratify Protocol No. 15, and the date of its entry into force was set as August 1, 2021 (ECHR, 2022).

Territorial Jurisdiction: The Choice of the Respondent State

The ECHR proceeds from the fact that each country that is a member of the Council of Europe is responsible only for violations of the Convention and its Protocols in the territory that it controls. The state may not recognize part of this territory as its own, but this circumstance does not matter. For example, the ECHR considers the Transdniestria Moldavian Republic as a territory controlled by Russia (the Russian authorities deny the existence of control) and recognizes the obligation of Russia to compensate for the harm caused to persons in the territory of Transdniestria by state bodies.

In 2021, the Grand Chamber of the ECHR in case No. 38263/08 recognized that after the end of the Russia-Georgia war in 2008, Russia exercised de facto control over former South Ossetia, Abkhazia, and the "buffer zone" in the period from August 12 to October 10, 2008, when they were officially withdrawn Russian troops, and therefore the events that occurred after the cessation of hostilities fall under the jurisdiction of the Russian Federation (ECHR, 2022).

The loss of de facto control over a territory releases the authorities of the state from the responsibility for human rights violations committed in that territory after the loss of de facto control by the state. In the complaint in the Khlebik v. Ukraine case, the applicant insisted that he had been deprived of the right to a fair trial since the Ukrainian court had been unable to consider his appeal against a court verdict that had not entered into legal force for more than 4 years, filed in the Luhansk region (the territory of the unrecognized LPR) before the outbreak of hostilities (Khlebik himself remained in custody in Starobelsk, in the territory controlled by the Ukrainian authorities). On July 25, 2017, the ECtHR recognized that the Ukrainian authorities had not violated the applicant's right to a fair trial, since the Luhansk Regional Court was evacuated from the territory of the LPR due to the war and lost access to the applicant's case file, which was under the control of the authorities of the unrecognized republic. Thus, Khlebik was kept in custody by the Ukrainian authorities based on a sentence that has not entered into force and will never enter into force, since the Ukrainian court could not consider the appeal against him. At the same time, the ECHR noted that since Khlebik did not simultaneously file a complaint against Russia, the ECHR was limited in its consideration.

In the case of Caesar and Others v. Ukraine, the applicants contested the fact that to receive social benefits they had to sue on the territory of Ukraine at the request of the Ukrainian authorities, and they lived in the territory lost by Ukraine during the war in Donbas. On February 13, 2018, the ECtHR recognized the requirement of the Ukrainian authorities for residents of Donbas to file claims in courts in the territory controlled by the Ukrainian authorities (outside the place of residence of the applicants) to receive social benefits did not violate the rights of the applicants (ECHR, 2022).

Complaint Conditions

Before an application can be lodged with the Court, several indispensable conditions must be strictly observed.

1. Only the rights and freedoms guaranteed by the Convention or its protocols may be the subject of a complaint. The list of these rights is quite wide, but it lacks some of the rights known in the latest constitutional legislation. In particular, the Constitution of many countries, covering all the human rights that the convention speaks of, also names some others, for example, the right to work in conditions that meet safety and hygiene requirements, the right to social security, etc. These rights are enshrined in another convention of the Council Europe - the European Social Charter, but the jurisdiction of the European Court of Justice is based solely on the Convention for the Protection of Human Rights and Fundamental Freedoms.
2. according to Article 34 of the European Convention for the Protection of Human Rights and Fundamental Freedoms, the Court may receive applications from any individual, any non-governmental organization, or any group of individuals who claim to be victims of a violation by states

parties to the convention (they are referred to in convention by high contracting parties) of their rights recognized in the Convention or its protocols.

The applicant doesn't need to be a citizen of a member state of the Council of Europe or, in general, a citizen of the state against which he is filing a complaint.

Most often, when considering complaints, the Court has to deal with the so-called direct (immediate) victims: the applicant himself has already become a direct victim of a violation of his rights.

In addition, there are other concepts of a victim in the practice of the European Court. A person may be recognized as a potential victim if he is exposed to a real risk of application to him of legislation that is contrary to the European Convention, and his rights enshrined in the convention will be violated. In this case, it is very important to indicate why the provisions of the law are applicable to the applicant, and under what circumstances there is a real risk of such application.

Indirect victim: in the case-law of the European Court it is recognized that a person may experience a violation of his rights because the rights of another are violated. Therefore, in certain circumstances, a person may file a complaint about the violation of his rights, even though he did not directly suffer damage. To do this, this person must have a very close relationship (family or otherwise) with the immediate victim. The most common example is the appeal of relatives of a person who has suffered through the fault of state bodies due to their failure to adequately protect the right to life, as a result of which relatives experience moral suffering and incur material losses.

1. The complaint must be filed no later than 6 months after all effective (from the point of view of the ECtHR) means of appeal to the national court have been exhausted;
2. It is possible to complain only about those violations that took place after the date of ratification of the convention by the state. In the case of the Russian Federation, that date would be 5 May 1998.
3. For the complaint to be declared admissible on the merits, the applicant must have exhausted all effective (from the point of view of the ECHR) domestic remedies for the protection of his right, and above all judicial remedies for such protection.
4. Applications submitted to the European Court must relate to events for which the public authorities are responsible. Complaints against individuals and organizations are not accepted by the European Court.
5. The complaint must be filed on the official form approved by the ECHR.

Inadmissibility of abuse of the right to file with the ECHR

Under Article 17 of the European Convention, persons (groups of persons) whose actions are aimed at undermining (destruction) the democratic values protected by the Convention are deprived of its protection. Therefore, the ECHR may be based on Art. 35 of the Convention to reject any complaint if it considers that its submitter has abused the right. There are exceptions to this rule (prescribed in the practice of the ECHR):

- Violations against the applicant under Art. Art. 5 and 6 of the Convention. The ECHR consistently states that no one in a state governed by the rule of law can be deprived of the guarantees of the Convention at the stages of preliminary investigation and trial;

- The very motives of the applicant when applying to the ECHR are not considered an abuse of the right. In Shamayev and 12 Others v. Georgia and Russia, the authorities of the respondent countries argued that by applying to the ECHR, the applicants sought to evade justice. The ECHR rejected these arguments, noting that a complaint can be dismissed based on abuse of right only if the complaint is based on fictitious facts. The applicants' complaints, on the other hand, described real events and the authorities did not prove that the facts were fictitious. In Frizen v. Russia, the applicant complained about the confiscation of her car in connection with a criminal case against her husband. The Russian authorities insisted that the applicant was abusing her right, as she was trying to return the property confiscated by the court from her husband. But the ECHR rejected these arguments. In the case of Zhigalev v. Russia, the authorities included an interview with the applicant, which stated: "When I was just writing the application, 'good people' advised: they say, where have you seen anyone manage to deceive the state?" On this basis, the Russian authorities accused the applicant of applying to the ECHR to deceive the state and, allegedly, thereby abusing the right to file a complaint. The ECHR rejected these arguments of the authorities.

The ECHR noted that the rejection of the complaint due to the applicant's abuse of the right is an exceptional measure ("Mirolubovs and Others v. Latvia").
Examples of abuses of the right (according to the practice of the ECHR:

- Misinformation of the ECHR by the applicant by distorting the facts when filing a complaint ("Varbanov v. Bulgaria");
- Filing a complaint in the name of others (not by proxy) - Drijfhout v. the Netherlands;
- Forgery of documents sent to court ("Jian v. Romania" and others);
- The applicant's initial failure to provide the court with key information in his case (Al-Nashif v. Bulgaria and others);
- The applicant's failure to communicate to the ECHR the important developments that had already taken place in the course of the proceedings on his complaint.

At least one case is known when the ECHR recognized the negative statements of the applicant against the ECtHR as an abuse of the right. Russian LGBT activist Nikolai Alekseev has repeatedly publicly expressed his dissatisfaction with the decisions of the ECHR on his complaints filed against Russia. In July 2019, the ECHR, on the complaint of Nikolai Alekseev, issued a decision in which it recognized the abuse by Alekseev of the right to file a complaint in connection with his offensive statements on social networks addressed to the ECtHR. In connection with these words of Alekseev, the ECHR refused to consider his complaint and noted:

It is unacceptable to seek protection from a court in which (the plaintiff) has lost all confidence

The ECHR sometimes joins the cases of several applicants. The practice of the ECtHR shows that in a consolidated case, the recognition of the complaint of one of the applicants as inadmissible for abuse of the right does not at all entail the recognition of the complaints of other applicants as inadmissible. So, on January 16, 2020, the ECHR delivered a judgment in the case of Alekseev and Others v. Russia. In this case, the ECHR consolidated the complaints of several applicants (including Nikolai Alekseev) who challenged the Russian authorities' ban on gay pride parades. Almost every one of these complaints was filed by several individuals (including Alekseev). During the consideration of the case, Alekseev's complaints were declared inadmissible for insulting remarks against the ECHR. However, the ECHR considered the complaints of other applicants and recognized that the Russian authorities had violated their rights (however, the ECHR did not award any compensation to the applicants) (ECHR, 2022).

Declaring the Applications Inadmissible Because the Complainant Has Not Suffered Significant Harm

The ECHR may declare an application inadmissible if the applicant has not suffered significant damage as a result of the violation of his rights by the respondent state. At the same time, the criteria for what damage to consider insignificant are not defined. On November 19, 2019, the ECHR published the decision in the case of Obote v. Russia, based on the complaint of Andrei Obote, who was fined 500 rubles (22 euros) by a court in Russia. The Russian authorities pointed out that the damage suffered by Obote was insignificant and therefore his complaint should be declared inadmissible. The ECHR recognized that the fine was indeed small and the applicant did not give any arguments that the fine was significant for him. However, the ECHR indicated that Obote, due to the very fact of bringing to administrative responsibility, received such an impact that would affect his further exercise of the right to freedom of assembly. Therefore, the ECHR noted that Obote suffered significant damage as a result of the very fact of initiating an administrative offense case against him. Accordingly, Obote's complaint was declared admissible, a violation of Article 11 of the European Convention for the Protection of Human Rights and Fundamental Freedoms. Obote was awarded compensation for non-pecuniary damage of 4 thousand euros (ECHR, 2022).

Jurisdiction of the European Court of Human Rights

The European Court of Justice is not the highest authority regarding the judicial system of a state party to the convention. Therefore, it cannot reverse a decision made by a public authority or a national court, does not give instructions to the legislator, does not exercise abstract control over national legislation or judicial practice, and does not have the right to order measures that have legal consequences. The court considers only specific complaints to establish whether violations of the requirements of the convention have been committed. However, the Court is entitled to award "just satisfaction" in the form of financial compensation for pecuniary and non-pecuniary damage, as well as reimbursement to the prevailing party of all costs and expenses.

Failure to comply with the decisions of the Court by the member states of the Council of Europe, following the Charter of the Council of Europe, may lead to the suspension of the state's membership and, in the end, following the decision of the Committee of Ministers, the exclusion of the state from the Council of Europe. There are exceptions, for example, the UK refused to comply with the decision of the ECHR in the Hearst case. If the state states that without changing the legislation or judicial practice the situation considered by the European Court can be repeated, it, as a rule, implements the necessary innovations.

Following Art. 46 of the Convention, the Committee of Ministers of the Council of Europe supervises the execution of the decisions of the Court, which, in pursuance of this rule, is called upon to monitor not only the timely payment of monetary compensation but also how the state party to the convention corrects the discrepancies in the rules of its internal rights or positions of judicial practice with the standards of the Council of Europe. Legally, the decision rendered by the Court is binding only on the respondent state in the case. However, often the significance of the decisions of the Court goes beyond national limits, affecting the law and jurisprudence of other States' parties to the convention (ECHR, 2022).

Competence of the European Court of Human Rights

The European Court of Human Rights has the right:

- consider individual and interstate complaints submitted to the European Court of Human Rights against one or more member states of the Council of Europe or the European Union;
- recognize the fact that one or another right of the applicant has been violated;
- award the winning applicant fair compensation;
- interpret the Convention for the Protection of Human Rights and Fundamental Freedoms;
- establish the fact that any violation in a certain state is massive due to a systemic problem, and therefore instruct this state to take measures to correct this deficiency;
- consider the request of the Committee of Ministers of the Council of Europe on whether the respondent State has violated its obligation to comply with the judgments (decisions) of the European Court of Human Rights;
- give interpretation to an earlier judgment at the request of the Committee of Ministers of the Council of Europe;
- issue Advisory opinions on the interpretation of the Convention for the Protection of Human Rights and Fundamental Freedoms on matters not related to the consideration of cases (ECHR, 2022).

Decisions of the European Court of Human Rights

The European Court makes three main types of decisions (there are more than 10 types in total):

- a decision of inadmissibility in the form of a letter addressed to the applicant (more than 95% of complaints filed);
- a decision on the inadmissibility or admissibility of the complaint in the form of a separate motivated document, translated into Russian referred to as the actual decision;

As of February 13, 2014, the European Court of Human Rights issued 16,995 reasoned decisions (judgments and judgments).

Interstate Processes

Any contracting state to the European Convention on Human Rights can sue another contracting state for alleged violations of the Convention, although this is very rare in practice. Until 2020, only four interstate cases were decided by the court:

- Ireland v. Great Britain (no. 5310/71), the judgment of 18 January 1978 concerning the inhuman and degrading treatment in Northern Ireland (art. 3);

- Denmark v. Turkey (no. 34382/97), the judgment of 5 April 2000 ratifying a friendly settlement of DKK 450,000 in respect of a Danish citizen detained in Turkey (art. 3);
- Cyprus v. Turkey (no. 25781/94), the judgment of 10 May 2001 on the treatment of missing persons (arts. 2, 3 and 5), the right to return of Greeks who fled to the south (arts. 8, 13 and P1-1), the rights of the Greeks still living in the north (Articles 3, 8, 9, 10, 13, P1-1, P1-2) and trial by military courts (Article 6). A subsequent judgment of 12 May 2014 awarded €90 million in "just satisfaction" (Article 41);
- Georgia v. Russian Federation (no. 13255/07), the judgment of 3 July 2014 on the collective expulsion of Georgians from Russia (arts. 3, 5, 13, 38, P4-4).

In 2017, the ECHR considered 86,000 complaints, of which 70,400 complaints were declared inadmissible or withdrawn from consideration (including a settlement agreement was concluded on 1,500 complaints, and a unilateral declaration was adopted on 754 complaints).

Deadline for Consideration of a Complaint to the ECHR

The term for considering complaints to the ECHR varies. There are complaints, the consideration of which took the ECHR more than 10 years. On November 19, 2019, the ECHR published a decision in the case of Obote v. Russia (it was about imposing a fine on the applicant of 500 rubles for a street action), which had been considered for more than 10 years. In January 2020, the ECHR published a decision on the complaint filed by journalist Georgy Pirogov in 2008 (the ECHR recognized that Pirogov's rights had been violated and awarded him compensation for violating Article 10 of the European Convention). On February 25, 2020, the ECHR delivered a decision in the case "Dubrovina and Others v. Russia", in which the applicants' complaints were submitted to the ECHR on July 11, 2007 (the decision found a violation of Article 11 of the European Convention, and while the case was being considered, one of the applicants died) (ECHR, 2022).

United Nations Human Rights Committee

The UN Human Rights Committee is an organization that oversees the implementation of the International Covenant on Civil and Political Rights in the countries participating in the pact. Established under Part 4 of the Covenant. Consists of 18 experts elected for a term of 4 years. Concerning countries that have ratified the protocol to the Covenant, the Committee is empowered to receive and consider individual complaints about violations by the authorities of the rights provided for by the International Covenant on Civil and Political Rights and make recommendations on them to the authorities. These recommendations are sometimes implemented by the authorities, sometimes not (UN Human Rights Committee, 2022).

Functions and Country Reports

The Committee evaluates the reports on the implementation of the Covenant submitted by the participating countries, draws up comments on the Covenant ("general comments"), and expresses views on complaints from states and individuals about violations of the Covenant (except for Article 1) by countries that have ratified the First Optional Protocol to the Covenant. Members of the Committee shall have the right to express dissenting opinions attached to the Views.

The Committee is a body of independent experts, and all States parties are required to submit regular reports to the Committee on how the rights are being implemented. The state must submit an initial report one year after accession to the Covenant, and then at the request of the Committee (usually every four years). The Committee examines each report and sets out its views and recommendations to the State party in the form of "concluding observations".

J. Møller and A. de Zayas assess the legal significance of the Views as follows: "Even though the Committee's Views are not formally legally binding, the opinion is gaining strength that the States Parties are obliged to provide the victim of a violation found by the Committee with an effective remedy following Part 3(a) of Article 2 of the Covenant" (UN Human Rights Committee, 2022).

Consideration of Individual Complaints

For countries that have ratified the Optional Protocol to the International Covenant on Civil and Political Rights, the Committee has the right to take into consideration individual complaints of human rights violations. Based on the results of consideration of an individual complaint, the Committee makes recommendations to the authorities. These recommendations may contain requirements for reconsideration of the applicant's case, and payment of any compensation to him (without specifying a specific amount in the decision of the Committee).

For example, on October 31, 2012, the UN Human Rights Committee satisfied Fedotova's complaint against Russia, recognizing the provisions of the law of the Ryazan region on the prohibition of propaganda of homosexuality among minors as contradicting two articles of the International Covenant on Civil and Political Rights.

In practice, the recommendations of the Committee (as well as other UN treaty instruments) are not implemented by individual countries. For example, in April 2017, it was announced that since 2011, 25 decisions had been issued by UN committees in favor of applicants from Kazakhstan, but none of them had been enforced by the authorities of Kazakhstan due to the lack of necessary national legislation.

Despite the protests of the representatives of the Committee, the authorities of Belarus carry out even death sentences, complaints about which are still being considered by the Committee. For example, in 2014, P. Selyun and A. Goryunov were executed in Belarus, even though they filed complaints with the Committee, which asked the Belarusian authorities to postpone the execution of their sentences: 38-39. In October 2015, the Committee ruled that the execution of V. Yuzepchuk (who was shot in 2010) was a violation of his right to life, his confession of guilt in the crime was obtained under torture, and the trial itself, which ended in the imposition of a death sentence on him, did not meet the criteria of independence and impartiality (UN Human Rights Committee, 2022).

Human Rights Council (UN)

The United Nations Human Rights Council, UNHRC is an international human rights body in the UN system that replaced the Commission on Human Rights. It is a subsidiary body of the UN General Assembly. The first meeting of the Council was held on June 19, 2006 (UNHRC, 2022).

Predecessor

The United Nations Commission on Human Rights was established on December 10, 1946. By the mid-2000s, it finally lost its authority, mainly due to the presence of human rights violators in its composition, and also because of its politicization. The last meeting of the Commission was held in Geneva on 27 March 2006 (UNHRC, 2022).

Origins

The Human Rights Council was established by resolution 60/251 adopted by the UN General Assembly on March 15, 2006.

The resolution establishing the UN Human Rights Council states that "the members of the Council shall uphold the highest standards in the promotion and protection of human rights." The General Assembly is authorized, by a two-thirds vote of its members, to suspend the rights and privileges of a member of the Council if he persistently commits gross and systematic violations of human rights (UNHRC, 2022).

Board Structure

The members of the General Assembly elect members who occupy 47 seats. The term of office of each member is three years, and no member may serve more than two consecutive terms. The seats are distributed among the UN Regional Groups as follows: 13 seats for the African States, 13 for the Asian States, 6 seats for Eastern Europe, 8 seats for Latin America and the Caribbean, and 7 seats for Western European and other States (including the United States, Canada, and Israel) (UNHRC, 2022).

Advisory Committee

Acting under the Council since 2008 consists of 18 experts. Replaced the Subcommittee on the Promotion and Protection of Human Rights that existed until 2006 (at the end of its activity it consisted of 26 experts).

Special Procedures

The Human Rights Council, as before the Commission, can establish and abolish the so-called special procedures - the positions of rapporteurs, experts, or working groups on individual human rights problems or human rights in a certain territory (for 2010 - Burundi, Cambodia, DPRK, Haiti, Myanmar, Palestinian territories, Somalia and Sudan. Previously there were also rapporteurs for Cuba and Belarus.

Office of the United Nations High Commissioner for Human Rights

The Office of the United Nations High Commissioner for Human Rights is the agency of the United Nations that monitors the observance and protection of human rights guaranteed by the Universal Declaration of Human Rights.

History of the Office of the High Commissioner for Human Rights

This commissariat was founded by the UN General Assembly in 1993. Michelle Bachelet has been the United Nations High Commissioner for Human Rights since September 1, 2018.

Since the creation of the UN, fundamental human rights and freedoms have been proclaimed and the priority of these rights has been established, and their protection is the main duty of states. The main structural unit of the UN for the protection of human rights is the Office of the United Nations High Commissioner for Human Rights. It is the focal point for United Nations human rights activities. It is headed by the UN High Commissioner for Human Rights. This is the official who bears primary responsibility for the activities of the UN in the field of human rights. The High Commissioner for Human Rights is appointed by the General Assembly for a four-year term and is entrusted with many tasks, including the promotion and protection of the effective enjoyment of all human rights; promotion of international cooperation for the observance of human rights; stimulating and coordinating action in the field of human rights within the UN system.

On July 28, 2008, the General Assembly approved without a vote the proposal of UN Secretary-General Ban Ki-moon to appoint Navanethem Pillay (South Africa) as the new UN High Commissioner for Human Rights. Her four-year term began on September 1, 2008. After the expiration of the term, her mandate was extended for another two years, starting from September 1, 2012.

From July 1, 2004, to June 30, 2008, Louise Arbor (Canada) was the UN High Commissioner for Human Rights. Her predecessor, Sergio Vieira de Mello (Brazil), was killed in the line of duty as head of the UN mission in Iraq in an explosion at the UN office in Baghdad on August 19, 2003 (The Office of the High Commissioner for Human Rights, 2022).

Activity

The legal basis of the Office is the Bulletin of the Secretary-General "Organizational structure of the Office of the United Nations High Commissioner for Human Rights", which also fixes the main functions of the Commissioner, the main sector of activities, etc. of the United Nations High Commissioner for Human Rights, as well as for its management and performs the functions specifically assigned to him or her by the General Assembly in its resolution 48/141 of 20 December 1993 and subsequent legislative resolutions. In its activities, the department is guided by two main documents OHCHR Plan of Action and its Strategic Management Plan 2008-2009.

The main activity of the department is the protection of human rights: assisting in the development of new standards in the field of human rights; promoting the ratification of human rights treaties. The High Commissioner must also take action against serious human rights violations and take preventive action.

In addition, since governments have the primary responsibility for protecting human rights, the High Commissioner supports them. This is expressed as follows: advises the Secretary-General on the policy of the United Nations in the field of human rights; provides substantive and administrative support for the implementation of projects and activities, as well as human rights program bodies; represents the Secretary-General at meetings of human rights bodies and other events dedicated to human rights, and performs special assignments as decided by the Secretary-General.

The areas of activity are very broad: democracy, globalization, business, children, civil and political rights, HIV, AIDS, housing, health, executions, emigration, minorities, terrorism, racism, etc. And in each field of activity, a speaker and a group of specialists are appointed on individual committees.

The High Commissioner for Human Rights is taking concrete actions to institutionalize cooperation and coordination with such UN bodies dealing with human rights issues as the United Nations Children's Fund (UNICEF), the United Nations Educational, Scientific and Cultural Organization (UNESCO), the Development Program United Nations (UNDP), Office of the United Nations High Commissioner for Refugees (UNHCR) and United Nations Volunteers (UNV). Similarly, OHCHR works on peace and security issues in close collaboration with departments of the UN Secretariat. OHCHR also sits on the Inter-Agency Standing Committee that oversees the international response to humanitarian emergencies ((The Office of the High Commissioner for Human Rights, 2022).

OSCE Office for Democratic Institutions and Human Rights

The Office for Democratic Institutions and Human Rights is one of the institutions of the OSCE. Engaged in ensuring respect for human rights and fundamental freedoms, strengthening and protecting democratic institutions. The headquarters is located in Warsaw. The ODIHR Director from July 2008 to June 2014 was Janez Lenarcic (Slovenia). On July 1, 2014, German politician and diplomat Georg Link became director of the ODIHR. Ingibjörg Solrun Gisladottir (Iceland) was appointed to the position in 2017, and Matteo Mecacci (Italy) in 2020.

The activities of the ODIHR cover the entire OSCE region and are financed from the core budget, which is adopted annually by all OSCE participating States, as well as from voluntary contributions from participating States.

The ODIHR was founded in 1990 as the Bureau for Free Elections. The 1992 Helsinki Document gave the ODIHR a mandate to assist OSCE participating States to "ensure full respect for human rights and fundamental freedoms, act based on the rule of law, enforce the principles of democracy and, in this regard, build, strengthen and protect democratic institutions, and to develop the principles of tolerant attitude on the scale of the whole society" (ODIHR, 2022).

CONCLUSION - THE BASIS OF INTERNATIONAL HUMAN RIGHTS STANDARDS

Adopted in 1948, the Declaration became the foundation upon which an impressive number of legally binding international human rights treaties and the development of human rights norms around the world are based. It continues to be a pillar of strength for all of us: when we fight injustice, when conflicts rage, when people are repressed, and when we strive to achieve the human rights of all people.

It enshrines the universal recognition that fundamental rights and fundamental freedoms are inherent in all human beings, inalienable to every human being, and equally applicable to everyone and that every human being is born free and equal in dignity and rights. On December 10, 1948, the international community committed itself to ensure respect for the dignity of every human being and justice for all of us.

The Basis of our Common Future

Over the years, this obligation has been enshrined in law, both in treaties and customary international law and in general principles, regional agreements, and domestic law, which set out and guarantee human rights. Indeed, the provisions of the Universal Declaration of Human Rights have formed the basis of more than 80 international human rights treaties and declarations, a huge number of regional human rights conventions, national human rights laws, and state constitutions, and together they constitute a comprehensive system of norms that have legally binding force and designed to ensure the promotion and protection of human rights.

The successful implementation of the Universal Declaration of Human Rights led to the entry into force in 1976 of the International Covenant on Civil and Political Rights and the International Covenant on Economic, Social, and Cultural Rights. Both Covenants further developed most of the rights already enshrined in the Universal Declaration of Human Rights, with the result that they became, in effect, legally binding on states that ratified them. They enshrine such "everyday" rights, the right to life, the right to equality before the law, the right to freedom of expression, the right to work, the right to social security, and the right to education. Together with the Universal Declaration of Human Rights, these covenants constitute the International Bill of Human Rights.

Over time, international human rights treaties have become more focused and specialized in terms of both the issues they address and the social groups that need to be protected under their provisions. The number of international human rights instruments continues to grow, they continue to improve, and they further develop the fundamental rights and freedoms enshrined in the International Bill of Human Rights, and address issues such as racial discrimination, torture and enforced disappearances, as well as the rights persons with disabilities, women, children, migrants, minorities and indigenous peoples.

Universal Values

The basic principles of human rights first set out in the Universal Declaration of Human Rights, such as universality, interdependence and indivisibility, equality and non-discrimination, and the principle that human rights entail both rights and duties of responsible actors and rights holders were reflected in numerous international conventions, declarations, and resolutions on human rights. To date, all Member States of the United Nations have ratified at least one of the nine core international human rights treaties, and 80 percent of them have ratified four or more, a concrete manifestation of the universality of the Universal Declaration of Human Rights and its rights.

How Does International Law Ensure the Protection of Human Rights?

International human rights standards set out obligations that States must comply with. By becoming a party to international treaties, States assume obligations and obligations under international law to respect, protect and enforce human rights. The obligation to respect human rights implies that states must refrain from infringing upon them or from attempting to infringe on human rights. The obligation to protect human rights imposes on States the responsibility to protect individuals and groups of people from attacks on their human rights. The obligation to ensure respect for human rights means that states are obliged to take appropriate measures to contribute to Conclusion - The basis of international human rights standards

By ratifying international human rights treaties, governments commit themselves to implement measures and enacting legislation at the national level consistent with their treaty obligations and responsibilities. Therefore, the national legal system provides the basic mechanisms for the protection of human rights guaranteed by international law. Where national legal mechanisms do not protect against human rights violations, mechanisms and procedures at the regional and international levels are used to address complaints from individuals and groups of people, which help to ensure that international human rights standards are truly respected, respected, and were applied in practice.

REFERENCES

Chitadze, N. (2016). *Political Science*. International Black Sea University.

European Court of Human Rights. (2022). *General Presentation*. Retrieved from: https://www.echr.coe.int/Pages/home.aspx?p=home

Inter-American Commission on Human Rights. (1948). *American Declaration of the Rights and Duties of Man*. Retrieved from: https://www.cidh.oas.org/basicos/english/basic2.american%20declaration.htm

Karumidze, V. (2003). *International Organizations*. Tbilisi State University.

OSCE Office for Democratic Institutions and Human Rights. (2022). *Institutions and Structures*. Retrieved from: https://www.osce.org/odihr

UN. (2022). *United Nations Treaty Series Online*. Retrieved from: https://treaties.un.org/pages/AdvanceSearch.aspx?tab=UNTS&clang=_en

United Nations. (1948). *Universal Declaration of Human Rights*. Retrieved from: https://www.un.org/en/about-us/universal-declaration-of-human-rights

United Nations. (2005). *Basic facts about the United Nations*. UN Department of Public Information.

United Nations. (2022). *Declaration on principles of international law friendly relations and cooperation among states following the charter of the United Nations.* Retrieved from: https://www.un.org/ruleoflaw/files/3dda1f104.pdf

United Nations Human Rights Committee. (2022). *Human Rights Overview*. Retrieved from: https://www.ohchr.org/en/treaty-bodies/ccpr

United Nations Human rights Office of the Hugh Commissioner. (2022). *Human rights overview*. Retrieved from: https://www.ohchr.org/en/ohchr_homepage

KEY TERMS AND DEFINITIONS

European Convention on Human Rights: The Convention for the Protection of Human Rights and Fundamental Freedoms, better known as the European Convention on Human Rights, was opened for signature in Rome on 4 November 1950 and came into force on 3 September 1953. It was the first instrument to give effect to certain of the rights stated in the Universal Declaration of Human Rights and make them binding. Under the original system, three institutions were responsible for enforcing the obligations undertaken by the Contracting States: the European Commission of Human Rights, the European Court of Human Rights and the Committee of Ministers of the Council of Europe. All applications lodged under the Convention by individual applicants and Contracting States were the subject of a preliminary examination by the Commission, which decided whether they were admissible. If a complaint was declared admissible, and where no friendly settlement was reached, the Commission drew up a report establishing the facts and expressing a nonbinding opinion on the merits of the case. The Commission and/or the Government of the State in question could then decide to refer the case to the Court for a final, binding adjudication. If the case was not brought before the Court, the Committee of Ministers would decide. Since its adoption in 1950 the Convention has been amended a number of times and supplemented with many rights in addition to those set forth in the original text.

Human Rights Committee: The body of independent experts that monitors implementation of the International Covenant on Civil and Political Rights by its state parties. The Committee's work promotes the enjoyment of civil and political rights, resulting in numerous changes of law, policy and practice. As such, it has improved the lives of individuals in all parts of the world. It continues to strive to ensure all the civil and political rights guaranteed by the Covenant can be enjoyed in full and without discrimination, by all people.

OSCE Office for Democratic Institutions and Human Rights: Provides support, assistance, and expertise to participating States and civil society to promote democracy, rule of law, human rights and tolerance and non-discrimination. ODIHR observes elections, reviews legislation, and advises governments on how to develop and sustain democratic institutions. The Office conducts training programmes for government and law-enforcement officials and non-governmental organizations on how to uphold, promote and monitor human rights.

Universal Declaration of Human Rights: A milestone document in the history of human rights. Drafted by representatives with different legal and cultural backgrounds from all regions of the world, the Declaration was proclaimed by the United Nations General Assembly in Paris on 10 December 1948 (General Assembly resolution 217 A) as a common standard of achievements for all peoples and all nations.

Chapter 8
Touching the Untouchables:
Pre-Service Teachers' Views About the Rights of the Child Based on Focus Group Discussions

Merja Paksuniemi
https://orcid.org/0000-0002-5884-1027
University of Lapland, Finland

Minna Körkkö
University of Jyväskylä, Finland

Satu-Maarit Korte
https://orcid.org/0000-0001-9768-3431
University of Lapland, Finland

Tanja Joona
University of Lapland, Finland

Pigga Keskitalo
University of Lapland, Finland

ABSTRACT

This chapter discusses pre-service teachers' views about the United Nations (UN) Convention on the Rights of the Child and how teachers perceive their connection to the educational context and their work. The authors argue that pre-service teachers' perceptions determine how successfully human rights education is implemented in practice. The data were collected from workshops and focus group discussions conducted with 82 primary school pre-service teachers in Northern Finland. The participants noted that children's rights are important and deeply connected to their work. However, they were insufficiently familiar with HRE concepts, and they were uncertain about whether it was acceptable to physically restrain children to protect them or others, as this could undermine a child's rights. To adhere to the principles in the UN Convention on the Rights of the Child, the topic must be included in the pre-service study syllabus, more clearly added to the curriculum, and implemented in teacher practice.

DOI: 10.4018/978-1-6684-4543-3.ch008

INTRODUCTION

World Children's Day is celebrated on 20 November each year, signifying both the date in 1959 when the United Nations (UN) General Assembly adopted the Declaration of the Rights of the Child and the date in 1989 when the Convention on the Rights of the Child (herein, referred to as the Rights of the Child), an international legal framework, was adopted. In Finland, the Convention came into force in 1991. The objective of World Children's Day is to promote awareness of children's rights worldwide among children and adults, improve children's overall welfare and enhance international unity and co-operation. The Rights of the Child can be understood to be part of human rights (Quennerstedt, 2010).

The Universal Declaration of Human Rights was adopted on 10 December 1948 by the UN General Assembly. Although people had advocated for and debated about human rights for centuries, the Declaration brought together, for the first time, the most basic human rights that were considered to belong to every human being, regardless of age, origin, culture or religion. The destruction and events of World War II, including the Holocaust and the detonation of nuclear bombs, as well as the blatant trampling on human rights, informed the preparation of the UN Declaration so that similar atrocities would never occur again. On the basis of these ideas, the UN was founded in 1945, calling for respect for human rights and the safeguarding of world peace. However, moral values vary greatly, so it is relevant to teach children about such values and discuss current topics at school. Moreover, children need to be taught about their rights and how these rights are connected to human rights.

Today, children construct their worldview by combining elements from multiple sources rather than by basing it on the ideologies held by previous generations. With widespread access to the Internet, we are living in a global transition period in which children are developing their interpretations of the world through their own perceptions, their cultural heritage and the media. Society, community and family all influence the development of a child's worldview (Kuusisto & Gearon, 2019). Schools play a particularly important role in supporting the learning of different worldviews and tolerance, while also preventing exclusion and radicalisation. Teachers play a central role in this process of openness, fairness and justice. Furthermore, children and young people need a conversational, harmonious and communal school environment. The teacher is required to create a pedagogical space that supports peer relationships and improves children's social skills, increasing their sense of belonging and inclusion (Syrjämäki, Pihlaja, & Sajaniemi, 2019). However, pre-service teachers may be sorely underprepared for the challenging and diverse educational contexts they may encounter in their future career (Jones, 2019). Moreover, implementation of human rights education (HRE) remains challenging in the context of teacher education (see Olsson, 2020).

The rights of children are perceived to be at a high level in Finland: education is open to everyone, high quality social and health care is accessible for all and paid for by the society. The care provided to children and their level of well-being are high, and the standard of living of families and the rate of employment of parents are relatively good. However, according to the Ministry for Foreign Affairs in Finland (2011) the increase in the level of children's exclusion is concerning; some children and adolescents do not feel well and they face a variety of risk factors in their lives. The concerns include loneliness, violence, mental health problems, substance abuse and family poverty. Harinen and Halme (2012) found that Finnish schools offer an encouraging growth environment for students who are already doing well in life. Pupils who do not do well in school also face challenges outside the classroom and they need more support and guidance. UNICEF Finland commissioned a study on the Rights of the Child (UNICEF, 2006) to determine the extent to which high school students in Finland know about human rights and children's rights. The study found that children have a poor understanding of human rights; nearly half of them would allow mild corporal punishment (UNICEF, 2006). Thus, information about the Rights of the Child and human rights should be more purposefully included in education and must be taught in all grades. This matter was considered when planning the new curriculum in 2014.

In Finland, the core curriculum promotes the principles advocated for in the Rights of the Child. The basic education curriculum (2016) requires that children's rights must be considered in the curriculum and in all school activities, and inclusion must be promoted. Hence, conducting a study in a teacher education context with pre-service teachers is important and interesting. What is their perspective of the principles set out in the Rights of the Child? Since, in general, children's rights are viewed as being important in Finnish society (see Jalonen, 2011; Lastensuojelun keskusliitto, 2020), this article discusses pre-service teachers views of the Declaration and how they can utilise those principles when they instruct children in their classrooms in the future.

Previous studies have mainly focused on pre-service teachers' attitudes towards human rights or the rights of children, or topics related to those rights, such as inclusive education (see e.g. Bilgen, 2019; Goddard & Evans, 2018). To promote the role of HRE in the teacher education curriculum, more research is needed to determine what pre-service teachers actually know about human rights and how they connect those to their daily work.

To fill the research gap, the study discussed in this article addressed the following research questions:

- What kind of knowledge do pre-service teachers demonstrate regarding human rights education?
- How do pre-service teachers perceive human rights education in connection to their work?

These research questions aimed to provide more insight into how pre-service teacher education should be developed based on the study results. Toward that end, the study focused on the need to produce knowledge about pre-service teachers' perceptions of HRE. Every day, teachers work with students with diverse backgrounds. Recently, the student body has become even more diverse because of migration and societal changes, such as urbanisation.

HRE IN TEACHER EDUCATION

As suggested by the UN, HRE is consists of all educational training that seeks to raise awareness and promote respect for human rights. The UN Declaration on Human Rights Education and Training was adopted in 2011 (United Nations General Assembly, 2011). Its fundamental objective is to declare access to HRE and training at all levels and in all types of education. The Declaration pays particular attention to three aspects of HRE: education about human rights, through human rights and for human rights.

The importance of HRE in general education has grown in the last decade; however, its implementation has been very slow (Roth, 2015), calling for familiarisation with and practice of the concept in teacher training and at schools (Olsson, 2020; Robinson, Phillips, & Quennerstedt, 2020). According to previous studies, teaching human rights in teacher education is a sensitive and somewhat difficult topic, as many people have misconceptions about it. In-service teachers and pre-service teachers often find it difficult to teach human rights, and they might not know how to approach the topic with their students (Cassidy, Brunner, & Webster, 2014; Quennerstedt, 2015). Furthermore, the integration of HRE is often unsystematic, as a study in 12 countries revealed (Lundy, Kilkelly, Byrne, & Kang, 2012). Zembylas,

Charalambous, and Charalambous (2016) reported that pre-service teachers found it difficult to talk about and define human rights. This influenced how they prepared and taught the lessons and their pedagogical perspectives. In terms of the participants' teaching practices, Zembylas et al. (2016) reported on the dominance of a "declarational" approach; decontextualization; the trivialization of human rights; and the retreat to familiar discourses and activities. Similarly, Olsson (2020) found that human rights were usually implicitly present in the course plans of teacher education programmes and the syllabi provided little guidance as to what knowledge pre-service teachers would need and what they are expected to learn about children's rights. Teacher educators supported the idea of including children's rights in the teacher education curriculum, but they were uncertain about where that topic should be included in the curriculum. Similarly, Boutros (2018) found that teacher training on the issues of HRE was deficient, resulting in the teachers' inability to connect human rights and children's rights to the students' everyday lives and implement it into their practice. Based on previous studies, it is evident that teachers need more knowledge about and guidance concerning children's rights and how to use this in their teaching.

Although we talk about a multicultural society and tolerating, accepting and rejoicing in otherness, studies have shown that children and adolescents with an immigrant background, who speak a language at home other than the majority language, or who are raised to hold religious values, are more likely to be bullied (Schihalejev, Kuusisto, Vikdahl, & Kallioniemi, 2019). The predisposing factors for radicalisation include discrimination, lack of self-regulation, feelings of superiority and lack or incomprehension of knowledge. The factors that prevent radicalisation include knowledge, worldview, positive self-perception and strong social relationships. Dialogue about empathy and human dignity can be achieved through HRE; in turn, this can enhance intercultural respect and acceptance (Yamniuk, 2017).

Positive social relationships, and strong relationships with immediate family members, relatives, friends and school-related peers are able to combat exclusion, which is a potential cause of radicalisation and violence (Kuusisto & Gearon, 2019; Zambeta, Leontsini, Askouni, Papadakou, & Psochios, 2016). Previous studies (Howe & Covell, 2011; Tibbitts, 2009) also confirmed that, in schools in which HRE has been implemented, empathy skills and understanding were enhanced when they were combined with the application of human rights principles. HRE can be seen as a process towards social change (Kingston, 2018; Tibbitts, 2017).

According to Bilgen (2019), the attitudes of pre-service teachers in Turkey towards children's rights were high; female students had a better attitude than the male students, and the attitudes of the students varied between the different universities. Thus, Bilkin (2019) suggested including the courses related to the Rights of the Child within the framework of compulsory courses and increasing the number of informative education activities for male students regarding the rights of children. Leblebici and Çeliköz (2017) studied the pre-service teachers' attitudes towards children's rights; they found that female pre-service teachers had more positive attitudes than their male counterparts. They also found that the pre-service teachers who had read the Rights of the Child exhibited a more positive attitude toward children's rights in comparison to pre-service teachers who had not. Thus, educating pre-service teachers about children's rights is a starting point for an academic audience interested in developing HRE. In addition to attitudes, it is essential to more closely investigate pre-service teachers' knowledge about and perceptions of human rights.

METHODOLOGY

Primary School Teacher Education Programme as a Context

The primary school teacher education programme of the University of Lapland follows a research-based approach; thus, the study courses are integrated with research and pre-service teachers must independently complete empirical research. The programme lasts five years, and each pre-service teacher completes a master's degree in education studies, which includes both academic studies and practical professional development in a primary school (called the teaching practicum). Pedagogical and methodological studies are interconnected with the teaching practicum both chronologically and by content.

Pre-service teachers are seen as reflective practitioners and researchers; therefore, their identity formation and professional development are promoted throughout the programme (Kaasila & Lauriala, 2010). The ultimate aim is to educate pedagogical and didactic experts that can work creatively and flexibly in changing situations and environments in cooperation within their own profession and as part of an interprofessional team. The programme uses an inclusive approach; thus, this topic is included in the study courses and curriculum as a cross-cutting theme.

Participants, Data Collection and Data Analysis

The study participants were 82 first-year pre-service teachers who attended the *Didactics of History and Social Studies* course as part of their interdisciplinary studies. There were five divided groups of whole approximately 100 pre-service teachers (18–25 students in each group). Each group attended its own sessions. The last session addressed human rights and children's rights. The pre-service teachers were given a pre-assignment for the session with a flipped learning type model, which can be executed in various ways (see Yoshida 2016; Yungweil & Lee, 2016). The pre-service teachers were asked to study the Convention on the Rights of the Child by themselves through specific material given to them as well as with all the online material they could find, so they would have prior knowledge of the topic when participating in the session (see Denscomben, 2003.)

The session began with a short introduction to children's rights led by the university lecturer. Then, the pre-service teachers were given the following instructions: "The workshop will be held using learning café teaching methods. You will be divided into four smaller groups, and each group will attend one of the workshop sessions. The themes in the workshop sessions are linked to the Convention on the Rights of the Child. Read the instructions carefully and write down your own opinions or/and your group's opinions on the sheets of paper. You have 15 minutes to work on this."

The topics of the workshops were: 1) How do Articles 2, 12 and 13 of the Convention on the Rights of the Child challenge the Finnish educational system? 2) What opportunities and challenges do Articles 2, 3, 30 and 31 present to schools and teachers from the point-of-view of minority students? 3) How do Articles 2, 3, 28 and 29 address the inclusivity? What ideas can you suggest for how to improve this? What should be taken into consideration? 4) What topics from the Rights of the Child should teachers consider in their work when educating students to be good citizens?

The pre-service teachers were randomly divided into smaller four person groups. Using the learning café method, the groups sat around four different tables where they discussed certain topics related to the Rights of the Child. The pre-service teachers could write down their thoughts on poster paper. They were guided by the university didactic lecturer of history and social sciences, a researcher with expertise in the supervision of pre-service teachers and a university researcher with expertise in Sámi educational issues, and, in two cases, another university lecturer with expertise in multiculturalism in education. Thus, the workshop leaders represented a group of interdisciplinary experts on HRE.

After compiling their ideas, each group presented one poster and summarised the main topics that were written down. The lecturers and researchers acted as experts and led discussions on the topics. They also supervised the pre-service teachers' group discussions as when needed. The pre-service teachers were actively involved in the process, and they perceived this kind of working method to be motivating. They raised questions for the experts during the workshop so the sessions can be seen as a fruitful learning situation. The discussions in plenary mode after the group work were recorded by the research team and transcribed later for research purposes (see Hennink 2014; Parker & Tritter, 2007). At the end of the lesson, the pre-service teachers were encouraged to bring up other articles from the Convention of the Rights of the Child that they saw as being relevant for teachers' work.

During the workshops, the data were collected using focus group discussions. The focus group participants independently familiarised themselves with the topic beforehand; thus, when the group met, everyone had the same knowledge (Denscomben, 2003). This is relevant because the interactions among members of the group make it possible for the results to develop. The moderator stays in the background and functions as the facilitator of the discussion (Hennink, 2014; Parker & Tritter, 2007).

To effectively facilitate ta focus group, the discussion must be planned in detail prior to the session (Krueger, 1988; Morgan, 1988; Stewart & Shamdasani, 1990). The pre-assignment and material must be determined, key questions about the workshop must be addressed, the number of people needed for a group to be functional must be determined, clear instructions must be given at the end of the workshop and the closing discussion must be thought through, beforehand. It is also important to plan how to collect the data, create a relaxing atmosphere and maintain a neutral attitude and appearance (Krueger, 1988; Morgan,1988; Stewart & Shamdasani, 1990).

The data consist of a recorded discussion that lasted 2 hours and 38 minutes, 41 pages of transcriptions (in a Microsoft Word document) and 20 posters that were developed by the pre-service teachers during the workshop. The data were analysed using qualitative thematic analysis (Castleberry & Nolen, 2018; Mayring, 2014); in this study, this meant frame familiarisation, coding, generating themes, reviewing themes, defining and naming themes and finally writing up the analysis. The first phase, familiarisation, involved reading the data and becoming familiar with it. The second phase, coding the data, included identifying important features of the data that would be relevant when seeking answers to the research questions. The third phase, generating themes, included looking closely at the coding and identifying wider patterns. The fourth phase meant reviewing the themes and double checking that they all were relevant to the research. Before writing the task, a detailed analysis of each theme was developed. The analysis consists of the top themes: pre-service teachers' views and their perceptions about how the Rights of the Child is connected to teachers' daily educational practice, such as understanding the meaning of the principles presented in the Rights of the Child and uncertainty about their practical implications in education.

FINDINGS

Pre-Service Teachers' Views About the Rights of the Child

Firstly, this article presents pre-service teachers' views on the Rights of the Child. The data were gathered from discussions with pre-service teachers based on participation in the learning café workshop. The pre-service teachers learned about the Rights of the Child independently as a flipped learning method before participating in the workshop. In the workshop, one of the tasks was to discuss how various articles of the Rights of the Child were perceived by the pre-service teachers.

According to pre-service teachers, the articles in the Rights of the Child are constructed in a manner that supports children's development. For example, Article 2, which refers to prohibiting discrimination, was seen to ensure that children are accepted as individuals and be seen for who they are, while also guaranteeing that they are treated in a just and equal way. Articles 12–13 refer to allowing children to express their opinions as long as doing so does not hurt others. The pre-service teachers felt that this supports children's ability to develop into adults that are capable of have a positive influence on society. Overall, the Rights of the Child was also seen to support immigrants' social integration and prevent marginalisation in society.

There were several perceived ambiguities in the proclamations included in the Rights of the Child. The pre-service teachers were unsure about the practical implications of some of the articles, especially Article 3, which states that a child's best interest shall be considered in all decision-making concerning the child. The pre-service teachers also found it challenging to define in practice the situations in which teachers could undermine a child's right to not be touched against their will. For example, some of the pre-service teachers were uncertain whether they were allowed to physically restrain children engaged in a fight, or protect themselves in case a child was attacking them. Overall, they felt that the child's subjective experience was the best way to determine the difference between acceptable and unacceptable touch. They also noted that, in certain cases, for instance protecting a child from physical danger, touching could not be avoided regardless of the child's feelings. It was also pointed out that sometimes children are not aware of their right not to be touched, or of what constitutes inappropriate touching or abuse. Conversely, the pre-service teachers in another group felt that children are very aware of their rights with regards to being touched. This is a good reminder that teacher education instructors must consider the up-to-date regulations and ethics concerning the teachers' rights to work with children. In response the issue of touch, two of the pre-service teachers noted:

Some situations are very clear, I've been in a situation where I had to physically separate two children from one another, because one attacked the other. In that case, the situation is clear; you can't just sit and watch what's going to happen. (Pre-service student no. 26.)

Is there a law that says you're not allowed to touch? Are there some limits? (Pre-service student no. 58.)

The pre-service teachers perceived Article 3, which states the importance of considering the best interest of a child, to be the most important, generally, as well as in an educational context. It was also seen to be closely linked to all the other articles. However, Article 3 was seen to pose practical challenges, as considering the best interest of one child can lead to undermining the rights of another child. This was perceived to be a risk, especially in the context of education, where a teacher must consider the best interests of multiple children with various backgrounds and needs. Pre-service teachers also noted that a child's own needs or wishes do not necessarily constitute the best interests of that child, nor should they be considered as such. A child's best interest is also determined by his/her unique situation and needs, which requires careful consideration from adults. One of the pre-service teachers noted:

Then, we were also thinking about what is in the best interest of the child. If we think about for example, that children should be with their parents or they should get to spend a lot of time with their parents, but is it in every child's best interests. (Pre-service teacher no. 8.)

Freedom to express one's opinion and the right to one's own culture and language were also perceived as ambiguous from a practical perspective. The pre-service teachers found it difficult to define the difference between what constitutes a simple expression of one's opinion and what constitutes speech that violates the rights of others. Defining the difference was considered to be increasingly challenging because people are often easily offended. Pre-service teachers also felt this lack of clarity could have practical implications on their work. One of the pre-service teachers noted:

As for Articles 12 and 13, we were thinking about, that we have freedom of speech in Finland and that's often used as justification for offending other people, but then the question is where is the line. (Pre-service-teacher no. 11.)

The right to one's own culture and language was brought up several times by the pre-service teachers, and its importance in ensuring fair and equal treatment of all children was also highlighted. However, the pre-service teachers identified a possible conflict between a child's right to his/her own culture and language, and wider societal interests, especially in cases where a child's cultural background and the values and norms attached to it clash with the values and norms generally accepted by the mainstream society. This can also cause anxiety in the child, who is forced to balance between two conflicting sets of norms. One of the pre-service teachers noted:

How about if you come from a different culture and there are different rules regarding touching and so on, that physical punishment is allowed there or something like that. And the children learn that at home, and then when they come here, the family doesn't necessarily change their behaviour. So, what if the child is taught completely different values at home and at school? (Pre-service teacher no. 87.)

Excerpts from the collaborative discussions illustrated above, as well as information provided on the posters produced by the pre-service teachers, indicate that the pre-service teachers held multiple ideas of children's rights, and that they found many challenges in applying those rights in practice. However, the pre-service teachers' views about the components of human rights, such as cultural diversity and inclusive education, were quite narrow. Culturally diversity was perceived through every student's right to maintain his/her language and culture and be provided with an inclusive educational environment. It is understandable that, as first-year pre-service teachers, the participants lacked specific knowledge about and concepts of those themes, which affected the way they understood human rights.

The Rights of the Child's Connection to the Educational Context and the Teachers' Work

Overall, pre-service teachers felt that, in general, the principles in the Rights of the Child were effectively upheld in the Finnish school system. The pre-service teachers felt that many factors supported the realisation of the Rights of the Child in the educational context: comprehensive school in Finland is free, which ensures all children have access to education, and teachers and other personnel at school are highly educated and most are competent in their jobs. Equality is also an important value of the Finnish school system.

However, most of the pre-service teachers saw a clear link between the realisation of the Rights of the Child and the resources available in a specific municipality or school. Lack of resources, such as an adequate number of competent personnel, appropriate premises or teaching materials, was perceived as a risk and a challenge that can lead to children's rights not being respected, especially when it comes to issues related to inclusion and minorities. Several pre-service teachers felt that the lack of assistants in the classroom makes it difficult or even impossible for the teacher to provide good quality education to all students, especially in cases where there are several children with special needs in the classroom. The lack of qualified teachers and teaching materials was perceived as posing a possible risk to children's rights to learn about their own language, culture and religion at school. Language barriers can also hinder the cooperation between the teacher and the child's family, thus preventing them from working together to ensure the best interests of the child. Two of the pre-service teachers noted:

Children must have a right to their own language and to be taught in their own language, which unfortunately is not realised everywhere and is difficult to implement. (Pre-service teacher no. 45.)

The challenge is to find competent teachers and teaching material, and it also mentions challenges posed by a language barrier et cetera; so, if we're, for example, talking about a language minority, it can be challenging to find a teacher who speaks that particular language. (Pre-service teacher no. 4.)

Lack of support for the teachers was also seen to pose a challenge to their ability to provide good quality education to their students. Teachers' high workload due to large classroom sizes and students with special needs can lead to stress and even burnout, which prevents them from providing the best possible education to children. One of the pre-service teachers noted:

Connected to this is also teachers' burnout and, whether good quality education can be realised from that perspective, that how much of a strain is the teacher under if there are those children with special needs in the class. (Pre-service teacher no. 79.)

While pre-service teachers thought it was sometimes challenging to uphold the principles in the Rights of the Child due to a lack of resources, they also saw it as an opportunity to improve and enrich their teaching. For example, one group brought up the possibility of incorporating religious and cultural studies of ethnic minority students into the lesson plan for the whole class, thus allowing the everyone to learn about different cultures while respecting minority students' rights to receive education concerning their own religion and culture. The participants also felt this could provide them with an opportunity to gain new perspectives as teachers. One of the pre-service teachers noted:

Treating everyone equally, and then you have immigrants and other minorities and that is also a possibility, in the sense that it gives you new perspectives for teaching. (Pre-service teacher no. 68).

Other groups saw that upholding the principles presented in the Rights of the Child could also provide clear guideline for decision-making. This was especially seen to be the case with Article 3, which states that the best interest of the child should be considered at all times. Several of the preservice teachers noted:

The best interest of the child, and we think that should always be a priority when it comes to teaching (Pre-service teacher no. 38).

The best interest of the child must be the starting point for everything (Pre-service teacher no. 2).

It's basically connected to all these others, all activities should be thought about from that perspective, that it's in the best interest of the child. Not in the best interest of the teacher or the parents, but in the best interest of the child on all those level.s (Pre-service teacher no. 10.)

When it comes to considering the best interest of the child, we thought about it as an opportunity, that when a teacher knows that now they have to think about the best interest of the child, perhaps it helps them make consistent decisions in their teaching when there is a clear line. (Pre-service teacher no. 12.)

The pre-service teachers highlighted that teachers should ensure that the principles in the Rights of the Child are respected in the educational system, and that children understand their own rights and learn to respect each other's rights. According to the participants, teachers can support the realisation of the Rights of the Child by teaching children about their right to not be touched against their will or their right to express their own opinion. This was seen as especially important for rights that can be ambiguous; for example, not all children know the difference between appropriate and inappropriate touching, or the difference between expressing one's opinion and offending someone. Thus, teachers can support students by creating a safe and open atmosphere to explore the topic. The pre-service teachers also noted that teachers act as an example for students:

You need to respect a child's right to privacy, and teach the others to respect each other's right to privacy as well (Pre-service teacher no. 6).

When you have children from different cultures in the classroom, it's important that you teach them about the boundaries everyone is allowed to have. In a way we as teachers are spreading the knowledge about what is right and what is wrong. (Pre-service teacher no. 11.)

As a teacher, you need to teach where the line is between offending someone and expressing your own opinion; children need to be taught that (Pre-service teacher no. 77).

Teachers' expertise was seen as vital in ensuring that the principles of the Rights of the Child are successfully realised in education. The pre-service teachers emphasised that teachers need to know their students well to avoid situations where they might offend or hurt them, and to know when they might need help or support. This was seen as especially challenging in matters that are not straightforward, such as being able to recognise when students are alone by choice and when they are being discriminated against, or when they are fine with being touched and when they are not. Some pre-service teachers noted that the large number of students in one classroom often means that teachers have difficulties noticing and getting to know each individual. Sometimes, they might be forced to make decisions under a lot of pressure. For example, one pre-service teacher expressed their concern about having to notify child welfare in suspected cases of child abuse, because it can be challenging to recognise the difference between a child telling a story to gain attention and a child being actually abused, like some of the pre-service teachers noted:

As a teacher, you really need to know your pupils, so you'll be able to know that you're not offending that pupil (Pre-service teacher no. 12).

Knowing your pupils is important because some pupils are just fine with you guiding them a bit by hand, whereas others don't like being touched (Pre-service teacher no. 44).

You need to have your feelers constantly up; there is a certain kind of emotional intelligence in this job (Pre-service teacher no. 18).

According to the pre-service teachers, the concept of inclusion has both positive and negative implications. It was seen as being positive because it prevents discrimination by providing all children with an equal chance to learn regardless of any special needs they may have. Inclusion also guarantees that all children can belong to the same group as their peers. However, some pre-service teachers felt that the practice of inclusion can lead to not all children's rights being fully realised. One of the issues emerging from the data was the fact that the practice of inclusion can sometimes lead to discrimination, for instance in cases where a child with special needs is labelled as a troublemaker by other students. One group also pointed out that sometimes measures introduced with the intention of supporting students with special needs in an integrated classroom, such as sequestering them from the rest of the class, can feel discriminatory to the pupil in question. Another group also brought up the fact that sometimes inclusion is practiced in a municipality to save money rather than because it is in the best interest of the child. However, this is against the spirit of Article 3, which states that a child's best interest shall be the most important factor in decision-making. Two of the pre-service teachers noted:

Does that pupil feel that they are being discriminated against, if you put that folding screen there, and they are not able to see? (Pre-service teacher no. 76).

It should decrease discrimination, but on the other hand it can also increase discrimination from the perspective of a pupil with special needs, because that pupil may be labelled as a troublemaker and it might also highlight his/her constant need for additional support. (Pre-service teacher no. 68.)

Previous studies found that pre-service teachers' attitudes towards inclusion are mainly positive and become even more so as they progress in their programme; however, pre-service teachers may have many concerns about the implications of inclusion and their attitudes vary depending on the child, the teacher and the environment-related variables (see Goddard & Evans, 2018; Sharma, Forlin, & Loreman, 2008; Woodcock, Hemmings, & Kay, 2012). Pre-service teachers' attitudes are shaped by their personal experience and personality traits as well as demographics (e.g. age and gender) and socio-cultural beliefs, values and practices (Florez & Smith, 2009; Goddard & Evans, 2018). It is encouraging to see that the pre-service teachers seemed to be willing to take responsibility for linguistically and culturally diverse students (cf. Florez & Smith, 2009).

All children should have the right to be members of the school community without having to lose their own culture and identity; moreover, their cultural, ethnic and religious background should be respected at school. According to the pre-service teachers, this can be challenging if the values a child receives at home contradict the values of the school. The pre-service teachers felt uncertain about what they are supposed to do if a child's cultural background results in him/her behaving in a manner that is against the rules of the school or wider societal norms. For example, pre-service teachers noted:

The challenge is that you are supposed to meet people as people, but at the same time take into consideration the cultural differences (Pre-service teacher no. 89).

There's no way we can ignore the differences in values et cetera, because there are always differences (Pre-service teacher no. 19).

[According to the child's family values], you don't have to listen to women and women are inferior to men, so the child in question didn't listen to her at all and also told the other students that I'm not listening to [that woman]. How do you root out that kind of behaviour in the classroom? (Pre-service teacher no. 78.)

Overall, according to the collaborative discussions and the posters, the pre-service teachers identified a strong connection between the Rights of the Child and the educational context and teacher's work. A child's rights were seen to be placing different, at times even conflicting, demands on teachers and posing various challenges to their day-to-day work. Most of these challenges are connected to a lack of resources. The participants were concerned that they would be unable to act according to what is in the best interest of every child due to a lack of resources, such as time, required support, adequate number of assistants or appropriate teaching materials. Previous studies also reported similar pre-service teachers' concerns about inclusion (Goddard & Evans, 2018; McCray & McHatton, 2011). The pre-service teachers seemed to be fairly aware of the inequalities in Finnish education concerning the linguistic and cultural rights of students. However, the principles in the Rights of the Child were seen as something that can enrich the curriculum and support teachers in their work by providing a clear framework upon which to make decisions. Overall, the pre-service teachers identified adequate support and resources, the development of teaching practices and teacher education and multi-professional cooperation as prerequisites for fully realising the principles of the Rights of the Child in schools. The pre-service teachers identified their responsibility to act in the best interests of the child; however, they struggled with suggesting solutions to the challenges that posed and acting as active members of society to overcome the barriers.

CONCLUSION AND DIRECTIONS OF FUTURE RESEARCH

This article discussed HRE in relation to pre-service teacher education from two points of view. It discussed how pre-service teachers perceive the Rights of the Child and identified the kinds of impact it has on their daily life as teachers, namely how understandable specific articles are and what kinds of challenges they see in them. They held different views on the meaning of children's rights and human rights in education and they were unsure about the practical implications of some of the articles in terms of supporting children's development by securing their ability to face their life circumstances. The pre-service teachers also saw that these international conventions are a way to prevent marginalisation of children in societies.

The pre-service teachers felt some of the content of the Rights of the Child was ambiguous. They were also unsure about the practical implications of certain articles, such as a child's right not to be touched against his/her will, even if it is for his/her own good or to protect his/her classmates. The results also indicate that the pre-service teachers felt that the Rights of the Child lacked detailed information about not touching children in a harmful manner, so they were unsure when it was permissible to touch young children in their classrooms. In the workshop, the participants discussed the different aspects to touching or not touching children due to changes in the rules in Finland on how teachers should behave in a situation when they need to protect themselves or when working with aggressive children or those with emotional problems. The pre-service teachers also discussed how providing equal support might be challenging, for example, if one focuses on working with one child at the exclusion of others. The workshop functioned as an ethical supervision session for pre-service teachers, enabling them to consider a second opinion during the discussion. One's opinion and one's right to one's own culture and language were also perceived as ambiguous from a practical perspective. According to the results, it seems that linguistically and culturally responsive education perspectives were challenging for the pre-service teachers. Some of the participants perceived the teacher's job to be complicated, and challenging in that their task consisted of ensuring the general well-being of children and understanding the future effects on their learning.

In terms of the Rights of the Child's connection to teachers' work, the effects on teacher education are clear; every pre-service teacher needs a safe place to construct their concepts and ideas concerning HRE. The functional café model used in this study is based on the idea of producing knowledge in focus group discussions. These discussions provide a supervised context where pre-service teachers can learn more about diverse themes in teacher education programmes.

Based on our results, the opinions of first-year pre-service teachers were fairly narrow when analysing the posters they made during the workshops. While they were able to identify the challenges, they approached human rights from a limited point of view. They found the development and content of teacher education programmes to be essential to addressing those challenges and increasing their knowledge about inclusion and cultural and linguistic diversity. For example, teacher education should include more topics on discrimination and how to prevent bullying at school. However, while seeing that a teacher plays an essential role in promoting the enhancement of children's rights, the pre-service teachers were unable to state how they could promote the realisation of those rights, such as inclusivity, in their teaching practices. This issue is where pre-service teachers need more guidance and help from teacher educators.

Corroborating the findings reported by Boutros (2018), our results indicate that the learning café method was a practical way to introduce the pre-service teachers to human rights, but it was insufficient in helping them know how to apply this knowledge in teaching. In the future, it is important to consider how pre-service teachers could be better guided to think about how to apply their knowledge of human rights with their students. Pre-service teachers need theoretical and practical knowledge about human rights and related topics, such as inclusion. When pre-service teachers acquire more knowledge and apply those skills in practice during the teacher education programme, they gain confidence and their concerns and fears might disappear over time. It is important to remember that the pre-service teachers were first-year students in the teacher education programme. In this phase of the programme, pre-service teachers' reflections tend to be descriptive and narrow when they are only practicing more analytic thinking.

Future research should focus more on different aspects of pre-service teachers' knowledge of human rights to obtain more in-depth information about their views. It would be essential to also study the perceptions and ideas of the teacher educators that are responsible for designing teacher education curriculum.

REFERENCES

Bilgen, K. (2019). The investigation of the attitudes of preservice teachers regarding the Rights of the Child. *Journal of Education and Training Studies*, *7*(2), 148–156. doi:10.11114/jets.v7i2.3882

Boutros, A. (2018). The right to rights: Education as the problem and solution to the lack of enforcement of international human rights law. *International Journal of Progressive Education*, *14*(2), 161–175. doi:10.29329/ijpe.2018.139.12

Cassidy, C., Brunner, R., & Webster, E. (2014). Teaching human rights? 'All hell will break loose!'. *Education, Citizenship and Social Justice*, *9*(1), 19–33. doi:10.1177/1746197913475768

Castleberry, A., & Nolen, A. (2018). Thematic analysis of qualitative research data: Is it as easy as it sounds? *Currents in Pharmacy Teaching & Learning*, *10*(6), 807–815. doi:10.1016/j.cptl.2018.03.019 PMID:30025784

Denscomben, M. (2003). *The good research guide*. Open University Press.

Flores, B. B., & Smith, H. L. (2009). Teachers' characteristics and attitudinal beliefs about linguistic and cultural diversity. *Bilingual Research Journal*, *31*(1), 323–358. doi:10.1080/15235880802640789

Goddard, C., & Evans, D. (2018). Primary pre-service teachers' attitudes towards inclusion across the training years. *The Australian Journal of Teacher Education*, *43*(6), 122–142. Advance online publication. doi:10.14221/ajte.2018v43n6.8

Harinen, P., & Halme, J. (2012). *Hyvä, paha koulu. Kouluhyvinvointia hakemassa* [Good, bad school. Seeking school well-being]. Verkkojulkaisuja 56. Helsinki: Suomen UNICEF Nuorisotutkimusverkosto/Nuorisotutkimusseura. Retrieved from https://unicef.studio.crasman.fi/pub/public/pdf/hyva_paha_koulu-1.pdf

Hennink, M. (2014). *Focus group discussions. Understanding qualitative research*. Oxford University Press. doi:10.1093/acprof:osobl/9780199856169.001.0001

Howe, R. B., & Covell, K. (2011). Countering disadvantage, promoting health: The value of children's human rights education. *The Journal of Educational Thought*, *45*(1), 59–85.

Jalonen, R. (2011). *Lapsen oikeuksien sopimuksen ja sen näkökulmien sisältyminen korkeakouluopintoihin Suomessa*. Sarja B. Projektiraportit ja selvitykset 21, 2011. Humanistinen ammattikorkeakoulu. Retrieved from https://www.theseus.fi/bitstream/handle/10024/34714/978-952-456-113-6.pdf?sequence=1

Jones, T. (2019). A global human rights approach to pre-service teacher education on LGBTIs. *Asia-Pacific Journal of Teacher Education*, *47*(3), 286–308. doi:10.1080/1359866X.2018.1555793

Kaasila, R., & Lauriala, A. (2010). Towards a collaborative, interactionist model of teacher change. *Teaching and Teacher Education, 26*(4), 854–862. doi:10.1016/j.tate.2009.10.023

Kingston, L. N. (2018). *Human rights in higher education: Institutional, classroom, and community approaches to teaching social justice.* Palgrave McMillan. doi:10.1007/978-3-319-91421-3

Krueger, R. A. (1988). *Focus groups: A practical guide for applied research.* Sage.

Kuusisto, A., & Gearon, L. (2019). Why teach about religions? Perspectives from Finnish professionals. *Religions, 10*(6), 347. doi:10.3390/rel10060347

Lastensuojelun keskusliitto. (2020). *Children's rights.* Helsinki. Retrieved from https://www.lskl.fi/english/childrens-rights/

Leblebici, H., & Çeliköz, N. (2017). Öğretmen adaylarının çocuk haklarına yönelik tutumları [Prospective teachers' attitudes towards children rights]. *International Journal of Social Sciences and Education Research, 3*(1), 307–318. doi:10.24289/ijsser.270584

Lundy, L., Kilkelly, U., Byrne, B., & Kang, J. (2012). *The UN Convention on the Rights of the Child: A study of legal implementation in 12 countries.* Centre for Children's Rights, Queens University.

Mayring, P. (2014). *Qualitative content analysis: Theoretical foundation, basic procedures and software solution.* GESIS Leibniz Institute for the Social Sciences. Retrieved from http://nbn-resolving.de/urn:nbn:de:0168-ssoar-395173

McCray, E. D., & McHatton, P. A. (2011). "Less afraid to have them in my classroom": Understanding pre-service general educators' perceptions about inclusion. *Teacher Education Quarterly, 38*(4), 135–155.

Ministry for Foreign Affairs in Finland. (2011*). Lasten oikeudet paremmin esiin Euroopan unionissa* [Children's rights better highlighted in the European Union]. Eurooppatiedotus. Valtioneuvosto. https://eurooppatiedotus.fi/2011/08/26/lasten-oikeudet-paremmin-esiin-euroopan-unionissa/

Morgan, D. L. (1988). *Focus group as qualitative research.* Sage.

Olsson, Å. (2020). Children's rights in Swedish teacher education. *Human Rights Education Review, 3*(2), 49–67. doi:10.7577/hrer.3925

Parker, A., & Tritter, J. (2007). Focus group method and methodology: Current practice and recent debate. *International Journal of Research & Method in Education, 29*(1), 23–37. doi:10.1080/01406720500537304

Quennerstedt, A. (2010). Children, but not really humans? Critical reflections on the hampering effect of the '3 p's'. *International Journal of Children's Rights, 18*(4), 619–635. doi:10.1163/157181810X490384

Quennerstedt, A. (2015). Mänskliga rättigheter som värdefundament, kunskapsobjekt och inflytande: En läroplansanalys [Human rights as value base, object of knowledge and influence: A curriculum analysis]. *Utbildning & Demokrati: Tidskrift för Didaktik och Utbildningspolitik, 24*(1), 5–27. Retrieved from https://www.oru.se/globalassets/oru-sv/forskning/forskningsmiljoer/hs/humus/utbildning-och-demokrati/2015/nr-1/ann-quennerstedt---manskliga-rattigheter-som-vardefundament-kunskapsobjekt-coh-inflytande--en-laroplansanalys.pdf

Robinson, C., Phillips, L., & Quennerstedt, A. (2020). Human rights education: Developing a theoretical understanding of teachers' responsibilities. *Educational Review*, *72*(2), 220–241. doi:10.1080/00131911.2018.1495182

Roth, H. I. (2015). Det sena genombrottet för mänskliga rättighetsutbildningar [The late breakthrough for human rights education]. *Utbildning & Demokrati: Tidskrift för Didaktik och Utbildningspolitik*, *24*(1), 29–49. Retrieved from https://www.oru.se/globalassets/orusv/forskning/forskningsmiljoer/hs/humus/utbildning-ochdemokrati/2015/nr-1/hans-ingvar-roth---det-sena-genombrottet-formanskliga-rattighetsutbildningar.pdf

Schihalejev, O., Kuusisto, A., Vikdahl, L., & Kallioniemi, A. (2019). Religion and children's perceptions of bullying in multicultural schools in Estonia, Finland and Sweden. *Journal of Beliefs & Values*. Advance online publication. doi:10.1080/13617672.2019.1686732

Sharma, U., Forlin, C., & Loreman, T. (2008). Impact of training on pre-service teachers' attitudes and concerns about inclusive education and sentiments about persons with disabilities. *Disability & Society*, *23*(7), 773–785. doi:10.1080/09687590802469271

Stewart, D. W., & Shamdasani, P. N. (1990). *Focus groups: Theory and practices*. Sage Publications, Inc.

Syrjämäki, M., Pihlaja, P., & Sajaniemi, N. K. (2019). Enhancing peer interaction in early childhood special education: Chains of children's initiatives, adults' responses and their consequences in play. *Early Childhood Education Journal*, *47*(5), 559–570. doi:10.100710643-019-00952-6

Tibbitts, F. (2009). *Impact assessment of Rights Education Leading to Action Programme (REAP)*. Amnesty International.

Tibbitts, F. (2017). Evolution of human rights education models. In M. Bajaj (Ed.), *Human rights education. Theory, research, praxis* (pp. 69–95). University of Pennsylvania Press. doi:10.9783/9780812293890-005

UNICEF. (2006). *Tutkimus asenteista. Yli puolet yläkoululaisista ei tiedä, että lapsilla on erityisoikeudet* [A study of attitudes. More than half of high school students do not know that children have special rights]. Retrieved from https://www.unicef.fi/unicef/tyomme-suomessa/tutkimukset-suomessa/tutkimus-asenteista/

United Nations General Assembly. (2011). United Nations Declaration on Human Rights Education and Training. GA 66/127, Art.2 paras. 1-2. Geneva: United Nations.

Woodcock, S., Hemmings, B., & Kay, R. (2012). Does study of an inclusive education subject influence pre-service teachers' concerns and self-efficacy about inclusion? *The Australian Journal of Teacher Education*, *37*(6), 1–11. doi:10.14221/ajte.2012v37n6.5

Yamniuk, S. (2017). The importance of including human rights education in primary and secondary schools: A focus on empathy and respect. In J. Zajda & S. Ozdowski (Eds.), Globalisation, human rights education and reforms. Globalisation, Comparative Education and Policy Research, vol. 17. Springer. doi:10.1007/978-94-024-0871-3_9

Yoshida, H. (2016). Perceived usefulness of "flipped learning" on instructional design for elementary and secondary education: With focus on pre-service teacher education. *International Journal of Information and Education Technology*, *6*(6), 430–434. doi:10.7763/IJIET.2016.V6.727

Yungweil, H., & Lee, K. S. (2016). Teaching in flipped classrooms: Exploring pre-service-teachers concerns. *Computers in Human Behavior*, *57*, 250–260. doi:10.1016/j.chb.2015.12.022

Zambeta, E., Leontsini, M., Askouni, N., Papadakou, Y., & Psochios, N. (2016). *Addressing violence in schools through education for democratic citizenship and human rights education*. Human Rights and Democracy in Action. Pilot Projects on the Council of Europe Charter on Education for Democratic Citizenship and Human Rights Education.

Zembylas, M., Charalambous, C., & Charalambous, P. (2016). Teachers' pedagogical perspectives and teaching practices on human rights in Cyprus: An empirical exploration and implications for human rights education. *Pedagogies*, *11*(3), 197–217. doi:10.1080/1554480X.2016.1182436

Chapter 9
The Relation Between Digital Technology and Democracy

Arun Teja Polcumpally
Jindal School of International Affairs, O. P. Jindal Global University, India

ABSTRACT

This chapter provides a conceptual understanding of the impact of advanced digital technologies on democracy with a special focus on artificial intelligence (AI). The explanation of the impact of the internet and allied technologies is themed into 1) power at the hands of the state or 2) diffuses from the state. In the current global politics, almost all the major powers of the world are vying for an upper hand in developing advanced digital technologies, especially AI. Among these, AI is the major technological development that brings the dichotomy in state's behaviour pitching surveillance against freedom. Anchored to AI, this chapter provides a good understanding of technology impact on the sustenance of democracy. The chapter concludes by providing a co-protectionist approach in formulating a new conceptual framework for digital democracy.

1. INTRODUCTION

When the debates were rising on the usage of digital surveillance to meet political and business ends, the pandemic has legitimated the usage of invasive surveillance technologies. During the period of pandemic, the debate on surveillance and democracy took the road not taken. The debate is now no more on whether to use surveillance or note, but to develop frameworks to use it in such a way that the values of democracy are maintained. With the pandemic, these technologies have become a part of the socio-economic systems. Heuristically, it is easy to argue that the public health is increasingly seen to be wedded to digital technologies in the post-pandemic world (Jobie Budd 2020). One example that strengthens the above argument is that of contact tracing applications. Contact tracing applications have become rampant across the world and, also seen as the only solution to combat the spread of the Coronavirus (Hallam Stevens 2020). There is no doubt that data-based technologies and products have become invasive in society. These technologies have also become the fundamental functionaries of the

DOI: 10.4018/978-1-6684-4543-3.ch009

economy. Work From home and the hybrid model of education has become the new normal in the post-pandemic world.

It is true that these technologies helped to contain the spread of COVID and given a new way of life for the societies across the world. In addition, pandemic forced states across the world adopt restrictive measures on public freedom. However, invasive surveillance and media restrictions violate the international democratic norms unconditionally. According to the V-Dem report 2021, the level of democracy enjoyed by the average global citizen in 2020 is down to levels last found around 1990 (Nazifa Alizada 2021, 6). The report identifies the downfall of democracy in the regions of middle-east, Eastern – Europe, Latin America, Central Asia and Asian – Pacific region. However, the NSA whistleblower Edward Snowden in his auto-biography reveals that the USA has violated its constitution by snooping onto the private lives of American citizens (Snowden 2019, 230). This provides a rough qualitative estimation that across the world, democracy is under threat with the latest surveillance technologies.

Not all the moves by the governments are deemed to curb internet freedom are anti-democratic. To some extent, governments are acting as protectors of the democratic laws by regulating the private companies that exploit private data. However, the government's intervention by creating data legislation is also seen as an expansion of its scope to control the private information of the public (Shahbaz and Allie 2021).

If state deems that a particular technology would benefit the nation economically. If it enhances the governance efficiency, them any resistance in tis adoption would be futile. For any technology to be adopted, there are incidents of resistance that are often futile. The state finds its way to implement the technology in one or another way (Itty Abraham 2015). States which fail to make the public accept these technologies try to learn from the mistakes and put effort to bring back the required technologies (Itty Abraham 2015, 74). The case with digital technologies is the same. Again, heuristically, it can be concluded that these technologies and the internet are here to stay for a long time. The question is how do they impact the state and democratic values.

With digital technologies becoming a disposable part of an individual lives across the world, for any academician, analyst, or political science student working on democracy, a critical understanding of the impact of ICT on democracy becomes imperative. Deutsche Bank research report reiterates that evaluating the risk and opportunities of ICT in advancing democratic institutions is the major hurdle in the 21st century (Körner 2019). A report published by Pew research centre (Anderson and Rainie 2020) further reiterates this point. It poses questions on whether to regulate the digital technologies or to let the information flow free? Statements like "Free internet will favor competition over collaboration," and other such statements in the pew report reiterate the damage caused by the misinformation campaigns, surveillance of the state, and unregulated digital companies (Anderson and Rainie 2020). Heuristics are enough to say that all future studies on democracy will have ICT as one of the core attributes.

2. DATA SHOWS THAT DIGITAL TECHNOLOGIES ASSIST AUTHORITARIANISM AND NOT DEMOCRACY

Here is a quantitative analysis showing a negative correlation between digital technologies adoption and democracy. The initial fascination of the public and scholars regarding the positive relationship between the internet and democracy appears to be false. This validates the above-claimed need for a conceptual understanding of the impact of ICT on Democracy.

For this quantitative measure, Cisco's digital readiness score 2021 is correlated with the democracy scores of 'The Economist,' 2021. This peripherally shows how democracy indices are correlated with digital technology adoption. The Spearman correlation heatmap for the indices from the economist's Democracy index and Cisco's technology adoption index is shown below.

Figure 1. Heat map - Economist's democracy index and Cisco's technology adoption index

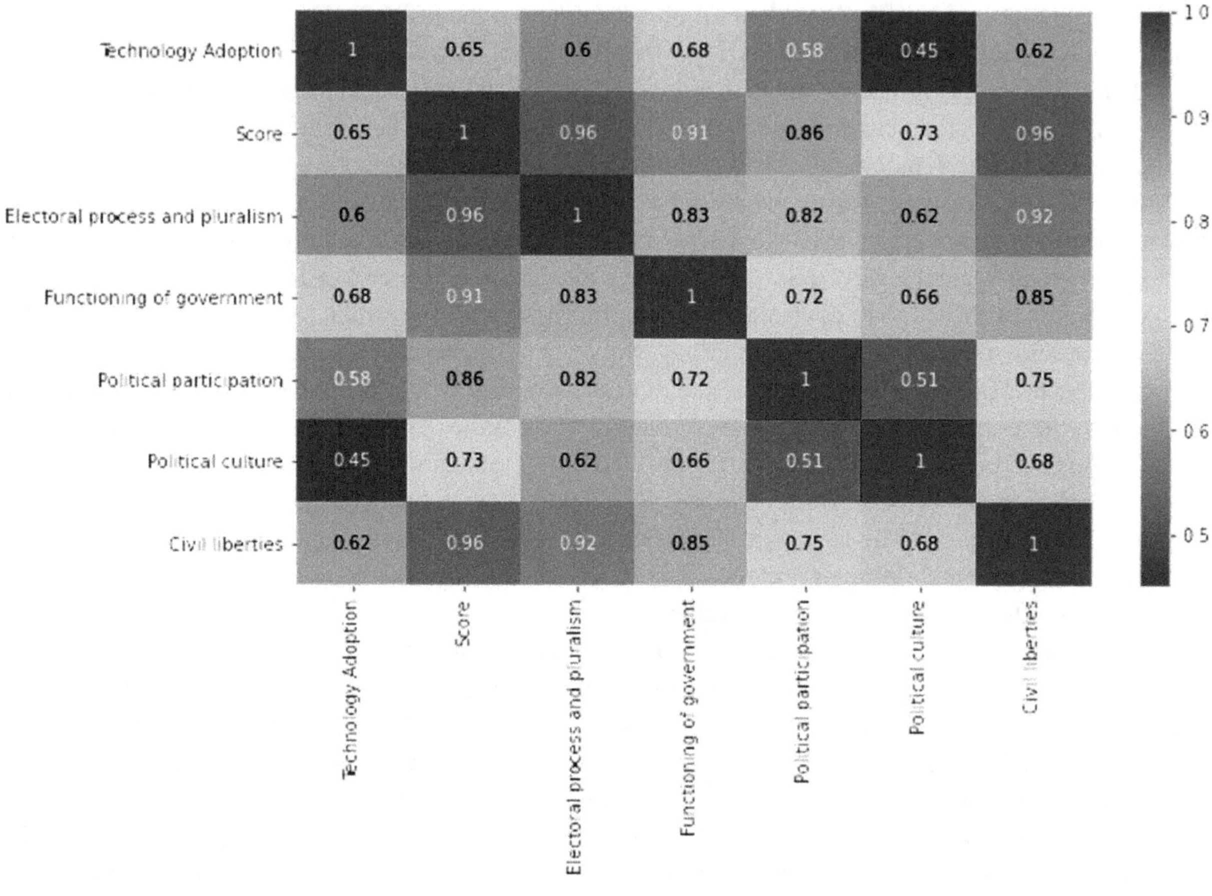

The figure provides a peripheral correlation heat map to show that there is not a significant linear correlation between the Technology adoption and the overall democracy score. Even with the other parameters, the correlations stand weak. This shows that the technology adoption is not directly encouraging the democratic attributes like civil liberties, political participation, electoral process & pluralism. To understand whether the technology adoption is enhancing democracy or encouraging authoritarianism, the following is tabulated. As per the categories made by 'The Economist' index dataset, the following results.

Table 1. Categorical correlation between technology adoption and Democracy Score

Correlation Between Technology Adoption and Democracy Score	Spearman Correlation Score
Full democracy	0.45
Flawed Democracy	0.56
Hybrid Regimes	0.28
Authoritarian	0.07

The correlation data shows that authoritarian countries do not have a linear correlation between technology adoption and their democracy scores. That means that with the increase of technology, democracy will not increase in these countries. Similar can be the conclusion between the correlation of technology adoption of Full democracies and digital technology adoption. Already, the V- Dem democracy report of 2020 and 2021 shows that digital technologies are dragging the democracies to become authoritarian (Anna Lührmann 2020; Nazifa Alizada 2021). These correlation matrices provide further impetus to have more conceptual understanding of the nexus between digital technologies and democracy.

The next sections of this chapter detail the impact of digital technology on the current understanding and practice of democracy. This analysis takes a deterministic approach and deals with the digital technologies as if they are artefacts. These artefacts are ontological realities that externally impact society.

3. POWER CONCENTRATION WITH STATE

In the previous section of this chapter, it is established that digital technologies are more assisting the authoritarian regimes. The April 6 movement of Egypt, when it was on the swing was considered an example to show how social media will bring down the authoritarian regimes and assist democracy (Snider and David 2011, 57). But soon, it faded away and the country fell back into the authoritarian rule of president Al – Sisi (A. T. Polcumpally 2018). There are other examples like the failure of the Umbrella movement of Hong Kong (Francis L. F. Lee 2019, 5), false narratives of Twitter being used to mobilise the public during the Green revolution of Iran (Etling, Robert and John 2010, 45), shows that the digital technologies are not assisting in public empowerment and promotion of democracy.

Today, surveillance has become a necessary trait of a state with the capacity to tap every human action (Susskind, 2018). States also engage in perception control (behaviour control) of the entire nation using advanced-digital technologies such as ML and AI algorithms (Susskind 2018). The public in the digital world becoming data providers that are ready to be exploited (Calzada 2019). It is found that states covertly tap undersea fibre optics of internet servers connecting across continents (Smith and Carol 2019.). Politics of data is also seen as a means to secure power over the nation (Fejerskov 2017). This has gone to such an extent that technologies such as AI are bringing a new cold war between the US and the People's Republic of China (PRC) (Bindra 2019; Susskind 2018). A research paper titled "*Geopolitics of Cyberspace After Snowden*" establishes that states which do not have capabilities are getting surveillance technologies from private firms. Citizen's lab researchers found that 25 states have brought such spyware from private firms (Deibert 2015). It appears as if Stasi, East Germany's intelligence agency has returned but in a more sophisticated way. Anchored on advanced digital technologies, nation-states' defining attributes such as sovereignty, citizenship is being questioned for their relevance.

3.1 Literature Says That Digital Technology Assists Authoritarianism

No matter how globalised the current world is, it has to be accepted that the state is still powerful and considered legitimate. In authoritarian countries, legitimacy is imposed and in democracies, the state's legitimacy is accepted without any option. This research does not bring any negative connotations for the state being the most powerful political entity. It is just establishing the fact so that further discussion is put into context.

To scientifically argue the impacts of ICT on democracy, the analysis is made from the Project Muse platform. Keyword search has been conducted using "Democracy" + "Digital technologies" + "authoritarianism." It returned 29 search results with the filters

- Only journal I have access to
- Articles option within the journals

This activity has been carried out on 23 November 2021. There was no data mentioned as this is a conceptual understanding exercise.

Liberal theories emphasize that modernization can be endogenous or exogenous (Przeworski and Fernando 1997), and the fundamentals on which it happens are anchored to the communication channels. This was the theory espoused when the internet or social media were conceptual. Going with this explanation, with the internet and hindrance free online communications, democracy should have been at the full fledge percolation into the societies across the world.

There is literature which argues that an increase in public participation and empowerment of civil society organisations will eventually remove authoritarianism.

...although there is variation in each democratic transition, a substantial combination of civil society actors—including trade unions, student organizations, churches, professional associations, women's groups, human rights organizations, ethnic associations, underground media, and various groups of intellectuals, journalists, merchants, and peasants—aim to coerce or force the exit of authoritarian leaders. (Etling, Robert and John 2010)

There are studies published recently that accept that the communication from the north or propaganda initiatives would not be effective in propagating democracy (GSDRC Applied Knowledge Services 2011). It is also agreed that today's theories are inadequate to assess the impact of digital technologies (Itty Abraham 2015) on democracy or to provide a simplistic program in promoting democracy with digital technologies (Katharine and Peter 2021).

The internet and aligned digital technologies indeed encourage the public to come together against unfavourable practices of an authoritarian state. However, the trend of the sustenance of democracy shows a contradiction. An excerpt from the research shows that there is an increase in the rate of democratic failure.

If we break the period since 1976 into four equal segments of eleven years each, we find that the rate of democratic failure declined from 14 percent in the first period (1976–86) to under 11 percent in the next two segments. In the most recent period (2009–19), however, this figure has increased to 18 percent, with democracy failing in key states including Bangladesh, Thailand, and Turkey, and for the first time in an EU member state, Hungary. (Diamond 2020)

One example to reiterate this point is the failure of the infamous Umbrella protests of Hong Kong (Francis L. F. Lee 2019, 2). They lasted for 79 days and could effectively achieve their demands. Why? They had no political elite backing their demands, not all public go with the popular opinion, and more importantly, the state can adopt the attrition strategy but the public cannot (Francis L. F. Lee 2019). This shows that no matter how digital technology assists the public movements and gathers popular consent, there is a high possibility that they are not sustained.

3.2 Is Social Media and Internet Curbing Democracy?

Media, the internet, and social media platforms are seen to be falsely encouraging public movements and the emergence of civil society organisations. However, they are mostly used to deceive the public or to gain a political advantage by taping the emotional inclinations of the public. There is a term called 'febrile environment' that reiterates that the usage of the internet sides with emotions rather than facts (Tomsa 2020, 3). Advanced digital technologies like AI are used to swim through the vast amounts of data being generated by internet users and tap into the patterns of individual behaviour.

There is a good number of patents whose techniques are used to determine the behaviour of groups or individuals from the given set of discriminate and meaningless data. These uncomfortable patents are literally against the moralistic principles of these companies that are shown to the public. The intentional usage of the user base for their profits is hiding in the anodyne terms *(R. J. Deibert 2019, 28)*. For example, Facebook uses the term 'community' so that they can exploit it. It becomes nothing but a consumer base. They gather people and allow them to interact to secretly gain insights into their lives. With all this information, all they do is sell goods and services for a profit. Who is gained from this? Not the workers who are assisting in building this technology but the one who owns it. Even the state does not have access to these technologies are they are patented and not even a single data protection legislature points these patents. This shows how uneducated the governments are, (or) maybe they are not worried about the surveillance capitalism of the private companies as long as they help the political leaders to win power.

This is not only with the digital companies which want to capture the market. It is increasingly the case with the political agencies across the democracies. Political leaders are more prone to sustain their influence using propaganda techniques and produce biased online information (Frantz, et al. 2021, 106).

The digitization exercise of India - Unique Identification number (AADHAR), revealed its own set of problems. The intended problems might have been solved to an extent but there emerged other significant problems like the increase in the cost for the marginalised to avail the Aadhar linked benefits, exploitation by private companies, and also an un-due disadvantage of informal lending, and transactions. This leads to a situation where digital technologies create a permanent economic divide. This argument does not discourage the digitization process. It shows the ignorance of the governance on the impact assessments. The digitization processes are being rolled out without giving a decent consideration on the holistic implementation and public acceptance.

These attitudes make the ICT artefacts to be tools for the political elites, business firms to make their profit. They are easing the governance. There is no argument against it. However, the relative increase in the economic benefits for the capital owners of digital technology is huge.

3.3 The State Is Getting Strong

As observed in the initial sections, authoritarian states are more prone to use these digital surveillance technologies. They are enhancing their control over the public and disincentivising democratic transition. Not only that they are using these technologies to be more repressive, but they are using technologies to be responsive. China is increasingly seen to use digital engagements of the public to have a watch over the efficiency of the provincial governance. However, being a bit responsive is nothing but a façade to increase the state's surveillance of the citizens. Earlier, the Chinese state has hired more than 2 million micro-bloggers to report the posts which go against the party and the state *(Qiang 2019, 58)*. With the advent of AI and its NLP techniques, even these micro-bloggers would become redundant and the online content will be filtered automatically, in real-time. Three painful truths about social media that enhance the state power are *(R. J. Deibert 2019, 28)* -

1. The social media business is modelled on the deep and relentless surveillance
2. People permit this level of surveillance willingly, if not altogether wittingly
3. Social media is the most effective enabler of authoritarian regimes.

This is true when we look back at how we install the smartphone applications without reading the terms and conditions. Though we know that they are tracking the metadata of phones and accessing contacts, email information, IMEI numbers, browsing history, data from other applications on the phones, we are forced to accept them because they are necessary conditions to use the service. Most of the applications mandate user consent even though it is not necessary for the functioning o the services. GDPR strictly prohibits such consents and considers them to be invalid (Information Commissioners Office n.d.). However, such provisions are not present in most of the data protection laws across the world. This shows that the users give away their precious data willingly or one can say they are forced to give consent.

When these social media giants share the data with the state unconditionally, they empower them with an unparallel power in history. China has something called meetings with authorities 'Yuetan,' which reports the social media companies on the violations of regulations (Qiang 2019, 57). The social media companies should immediately remove the content deemed false, inciting mass movements, and appear to defame the nation. To adhere to these laws, companies should hire a dedicated team and perform filtering operations. There are no specific rules or instances to show what exactly should be removed and this vague rule forces the companies to censor as much as information for them to be safe (Vatsala Mishra 2021). Apart from China, even the countries like Russia, Saudi Arabia, Egypt are opined to raise their repressive capacities using digital technologies (Diamond 2020, 39).

It can be concluded that unregulated social media is assisting the authoritarian forces which fund these digital companies to manipulate the thoughts of the public. Usage of biased and false information tactics results in the polarization of the societies (Tomsa 2020, 3). If the free internet is encouraged, there is a danger that in democracies power-hungry political leaders might use it to their advantage. If the internet and social media communications are controlled by the state, it gives away individual liberty to the state.

The current existing laws are not evolved to tackle digital technologies. A new normal for society has to be constructed to respect digital privacy or internet privacy (The Center for Internet and Society n.d.).

4. ANOTHER SIDE OF THE DIGITAL TECHNOLOGY'S IMPACT ON DEMOCRACY

Another side for the impact of digital technologies has a positive discourse. It opines these digital technologies, especially internet-based borderless communications will enhance politics of individuation and give away for deliberative democracy. Data accessibility provided by the internet and allied tools will empower citizen's media and data activists (Gutierrez and Stefania 2017). Devolution policies of states and cities are developed because of these technologies to achieve citizen-centric governance (Calzada 2017).

Such empowerment would bring new political stakeholders through politics of individuation and has the potential to bring the proletariat public sphere (Caballero and Francisco 2018). In a situation where the domestic social contract is not respected and adhered to by the state, the available mass information will show the inefficiency of the government. This will result in public rebellion against the state. This rebellion can be in many forms. It can take a violent form, or mass protests like that of Hong Kong, or people would just wash away their respect and responsibility towards the state. If states do not act with the public requests, there would be a decent probability of the public making state-less social contracts (Sassen 1996).

In some cases, authoritarian regimes have become more responsive because of internet-based technologies and communications. As the information generated on social media can strike the chords of the public and become viral, regimes will be careful not to attract opposition from the public (Etling, Robert and John 2010, 41). The adoption of digitization in the governance system has received more support from the public in China. It eased the licensing process, reduced corruption, and increased the accountability of the provincial governments (Gao and Jie 2020).

However, it is clear from the earlier section that the state is trying hard to adopt these digital technologies to enhance its control. At the same time, people are finding these technologies to empower themselves. Jamie Susskind argues that new forms of democracy, such as Wiki Democracy, AI democracy, and Data democracy, are entirely hinged upon open data and algorithms (Susskind 2018). How exactly does technology assist the growth of democracy? Maybe one needs to change the lens through which they look at the relation between surveillance and democracy.

4.2 Surveillance and Transparency Are Closely Related to Accountability

Surveillance and transparency are an aspect of accountability (Johnson and Kent, Surveillance and Transparency as Sociotechnical Systems of Accountability 2010). They are deemed to be a part of the same socio-technical systems. It is argued that in democracies, transparency in political systems and their operations provide a way for the public to watch the government, and the government to watch the public. In the authoritarian setting, surveillance is used for the same reasons of accountability. Unlike democracies, there wouldn't be any power in the hands of the public. It becomes a top-down approach to being watched. These two systems are seen to exist parallelly in democracies. Johnson and Kent proposed in 2010 that the public in democracies can use the same surveillance technologies to bring the government or the watchers to the table of negotiation (Johnson and Kent, Surveillance and Transparency as Sociotechnical Systems of Accountability 2010, 29). Collective approaches like protests, elections might also be used to make a mutually agreed stage of surveillance. However, during 2010, the technologies like AI were not vigorously discussed. Deep neural networks were still developing. Authors might not have taken the possibility of behavioural hacking (what I call it) using information and communication technologies. Though the argument made is made before the surge of AI technologies, it provides a reasonable change in the perspective of looking at the relation between the digital technologies and democracy.

5. CONCLUSION

Rather than sceptically eying the digital technologies as something that takes away liberty from the public and make the state power, it is to be accepted that this technology has empowered the public with information. Social media, the internet is used for various daily needs. News, shopping, investments, education, jobs, entertainment, social interaction, and name it. It has become a go-to platform for every daily usage. Further, it provides a platform to cover the social anxieties, fear and let out the inner thoughts of an individual. Anonymity, escape from the reality, ease of communication, companionship, are found to be some of the major reasons (Caplan, Elizabeth and Janice 2011, 45) for the public to increasingly use the internet. The usage of the internet is a conscious choice of the public.

This conscious choice is also a tool is that it provides information. Lack of information is a major attribute of the economic and knowledge divide among societies (Jeffres 2011, 135). Internet-based communication is one of the major sources to bridge the knowledge gap.

To arrive at a solution, one needs to theoretically understand the increasingly invasive surveillance and democracy together. It is majorly being accepted that technology and societies are co-constructed (Johnson and Kent 2010, 19). Be it Democracy or authoritarian systems, technology is not an objective influencer that is present outside the society. It is constructed by society and the process it takes during its course of development is a result of political decisions of people who work on these technologies or those who fund the research and development. This discussion till now is conducted from the perspective of determinism. A shift towards co-production will provide a different lens. Perhaps one may not start their theoretical understanding with the question – 'what are the impacts of the digital technologies on democracy?" They would rather start by defining the newly emerged digital society by not considering digital technology as an artefact. They also might consider refining the definition of liberty, privacy, public sphere and finally the democracy itself.

Contradicting technological determinism, Mark Poster, in his work interestingly shows how the internet should be understood. Here is an excerpt that makes his point clearer.

"The effect of Germany on its people is to make them feel Germans .... the effect of hammers to .. force metal spikes into woods. As long as we understand internet as a hammer we will fail to discern the way it is like Germany." (Poster 1997, 205)

Written in 1997, this article refers internet to provide a new platform in the history of communications. A platform that moves away from the gender bias, identity, restrictions, and pave a path towards new power relations between the individuals and materials and also materials and other non – tangible aspects of society. However, the extent of control a company or a state can have on this internet was not conceived. The reason most would be the non-existence of AI technology products that can make meaning out of the voluminous data. The reiteration of co-adoption of technology and society, according to me is one of the best options to reinvent the age-old concepts like privacy, public, democracy, liberty.

REFERENCES

Abraham, I., & Rajadhyaksha, A. (2015). State Power and Technological Citizenship in India: From the Postcolonial to the Digital Age. *East Asian Science, Technology and Society*, *9*(1), 65–85. doi:10.1215/18752160-2863200

Alizada, N., Cole, R., Gastaldi, L., Grahn, S., Hellmeier, S., Kolvani, P., Lachapelle, J., Lührmann, A., Maerz, S. F., Pillai, S., & Lindberg, S. I. (2021). *Autocratization Turns Viral: Democracy Report 2021. University of Gothenburg*. V-Dem Institute.

Anderson, J., & Rainie, L. (2020). *Broader thoughts from key experts on the future of democracy at a time of digital disruption.* Pew Research Center. https://www.pewresearch.org/internet/2020/02/21/broader-thoughts-from-key-experts-on-the-future-of-democracy-at-a-time-of-digital-disruption/

Arun, teja, polcumpally. (2018). Challenges to Egypt under Al-Sisi Rule. In *India and its Emerging Foreign Policy Challenges*. New Delhi: Vji Publications.

Brancati, D. (2019). *Hong Kong protests have taken the globe by storm. Now the world must stand up to China.* https://www.scmp.com/comment/opinion/article/3037678/hong-kong-protests-have-taken-globe-storm-now-world-

Budd, J., Miller, B. S., Manning, E. M., Lampos, V., Zhuang, M., Edelstein, M., Rees, G., Emery, V. C., Stevens, M. M., Keegan, N., Short, M. J., Pillay, D., Manley, E., Cox, I. J., Heymann, D., Johnson, A. M., & McKendry, R. A. (2020). Digital technologies in the public-health response to COVID-19. *Nature Medicine*, *26*(8), 1183–1192. doi:10.103841591-020-1011-4 PMID:32770165

Caballero, Sierra, & Francisco. (2018). Cyberactivism and social movements. The Oppositional Public Space in contemporary technopolitics. *Revista Latina de Comunicación Social*, *73*, 980–990.

Calzada, I. (2017). The techno-politics of data and smart devolution in city-regions: Comparing Glasgow, Bristol, Barcelona, and Bilbao. *Systems*, *5*(1), 1–18. doi:10.3390ystems5010018

Calzada, I. (2019). Deciphering Smart City Citizenship: The Techno-Politics of Data and Urban Co-operative Platforms. *IEV (Revista Internacional de Estudios Vascos/International Journal on Basque Studies), 63*(1), 42-81.

Caplan, E., Scott, M., Perse, E., & Gennaria, J. (2011). Computer Mediated Technology and Social Interaction. In Communication Technology and Social Change. Routledge.

Carter, A. (2012). *People Power and Political Change*. Routledge.

Deibert, R. (2015). The geopolitics of cyberspace after Snowden. *Current History (New York, N.Y.)*, *114*(768), 9–15. doi:10.1525/curh.2015.114.768.9

Deibert, R. (2019). The Road to Digital Unfreedom: Three Painful Truths About Social Media. *Journal of Democracy, 30*(1), 25–39. doi:10.1353/jod.2019.0002

Diamond, L. (2020). Breaking Out of the Democratic Slump. *Journal of Democracy, 31*(1), 36–50. doi:10.1353/jod.2020.0003

Etling, B., Robert, F., & John, P. (2010). Political Change in the Digital Age: The Fragility and Promise of Online Organizing. *SAIS Review (Paul H. Nitze School of Advanced International Studies), 30*(2), 37–49. doi:10.1353ais.2010.0016

Fejerskov, A. M. (2017). The new technopolitics of development and the global south as a laboratory of technological experimentation. *Science, Technology & Human Values, 42*(5), 947–968. doi:10.1177/0162243917709934

Frantz, E., Kendall, T. A., Carisa, N., & Joseph, W. (2021). How Personalist Politics Is Changing Democracies. *Journal of Democracy, 32*(3), 94–108. doi:10.1353/jod.2021.0036

Gao, X., & Jie, T. (2020). From Web to Weber: Understanding the Case of "One-Go at Most" as ICT-Driven Government Reform in Contemporary China. *China Review, 20*(3), 71–97. https://muse.jhu.edu/article/764071

GSDRC Applied Knowledge Services. (2011). *The role of communication in governance and development.* GSDRC Applied Knowledge Services. Accessed December 2, 2021. https://gsdrc.org/topic-guides/communication-and-governance/the-role-of-communication/

Gutierrez, M., & Stefania, M. (2017). Technopolitics in the Age of Big Data. In Networks, Movements & Technopolitics in Latin America: Critical Analysis and Current Challenges. Oxford University Press.

Harari, Y. N. (2018). Why Technology Favors Tyranny. *The Atlantic.* Accessed November 22, 2021. https://www.theatlantic.com/magazine/archive/2018/10/yuval-noah-harari-technology-tyranny/568330/

Information Commissioners Office. (n.d.). *What is Valid Consent?* Accessed December 7, 2021. https://ico.org.uk/for-organisations/guide-to-data-protection/guide-to-the-general-data-protection-regulation-gdpr/consent/what-is-valid-consent/

Jeffres, W. L. (2011). Media Technology and Civic Life. In Communication Technology and Social Change: Theory and Implications. Routledge.

Johnson, G. D., & Wayland, K. (2010). Surveillance and Transparency as Sociotechnical Systems of Accountability. In Surveillance and Democracy. Routledge Cavendish.

Katharine, D., & Verovšek, P. (2021). Promoting Democracy in the Digital Public Sphere: Applying Theoretical Ideals to Online Political Communication. *Javnost - The Public, 28*(4), 358-374. . doi:10.1080/13183222.2021.1955206

Körner, K. (2019). *Digital politics AI, big data and the future of democracy.* Deutsche Bank. https://www.dbresearch.com/PROD/RPS_EN-PROD/PROD0000000000497768/Digital_politics%3A_AI%2C_big_data_and_the_future_of_d.pdf?undefined&realload=w0PW0FfqzELp4Jz0nI9xGDZpOR5hNc22qYDSsr/0tY40ogr0mdY9qlOqtoLr2WXo

Lee, F. L. F., Yuen, S., Tang, G., & Cheng, E. W. (2019). Hong Kong's Summer of Uprising: From Anti-Extradition to Anti-Authoritarian Protests. *China Review*, *19*(4), 1–32. https://muse.jhu.edu/article/743118

Mishra, V., & Arun, T. P. (2021). Understanding Chinese media censorship: From Ming to Jinping. *ORF*. https://www.orfonline.org/expert-speak/understanding-chinese-media-censorship-from-ming-to-jinping/

Polcumpally, A. T. (2018). Egypt's Uncertain Future under Al-Sisi's Rule. In India and its Foreign Policy Challenges. Vji Publications.

Polcumpally, A. T. (2021). Artificial intelligence and global power structure: Understanding through Luhmann's systems theory. *AI & Society*. Advance online publication. doi:10.100700146-021-01219-8

Poster, M. (1997). Cyberdemocracy: Internet and the Public Sphere. In Internet Culture. Routledge.

Przeworski, A., & Fernando, L. (1997). Modernization: Theories and Facts. *World Politics*, *49*(2), 55–183. doi:10.1353/wp.1997.0004

Qiang, X. (2019). The Road to Digital Unfreedom: President Xi's Surveillance State. *Journal of Democracy*, *30*(1), 53–67. doi:10.1353/jod.2019.0004

Sassen, S. (1996). *Losing control?: sovereignty in the age of globalization*. Columbia University Press.

Shahbaz, A., & Allie, F. (2021). *The Global Drive to Control Big Tech*. Freedom House. https://freedomhouse.org/sites/default/files/2021-09/FOTN_2021_Complete_Booklet_09162021_FINAL_UPDATED.pdf

Smith, B., & Ann, B. C. (2019). *Tools and Weapons: The Promise and the Peril of the Digital Age*. Penguin Press.

Snider, E. A., & Faris, D. (2011). The Arab Spring: U.S. Democracy Promotion in Egypt. *Middle East Policy*, 49-62. https://d1wqtxts1xzle7.cloudfront.net/46753903/j.1475-4967.2011.00497.x20160624-4760-yc6wg7-with-cover-page-v2.pdf?Expires=1637610095&Signature=cmurVotOyOhf--BJVvX-DxgyoysIIa5qR8HvlWjUvD7f0bSKVgcc1UuOLaWi6cI9vdsNsHN~34ztNgGYkJ~HJ9y4zQnfoJYBZYZXGNiuIr~R1kS6

Snowden, E. (2019). *The Permanent Record*. Macmillian.

Stevens, H., & Haines, M. B. (2020). TraceTogether: Pandemic Response, Democracy, and Technology. *East Asian Science, Technology and Society*, *14*(3), 523–531. doi:10.1215/18752160-8698301

Susskind, J. (2018). *Future Politics: Living Together in a world transformed by tech*. Oxford University Press.

The Center for Internet and Society. (n.d.). *Internet Privacy in India*. Accessed December 7, 2021. https://cis-india.org/telecom/knowledge-repository-on-internet-access/internet-privacy-in-india

Tomsa, D. (2020). Public Opinion Polling and Post-truth Politics in Indonesia. *Contemporary Southeast Asia: A Journal of International and Strategic Affairs*, *42*(1), 1-27. https://muse.jhu.edu/article/754333

Chapter 10
Profiling the Citizens Based on Their Offline and Online Political Participation Level

Süphan Nasır
https://orcid.org/0000-0002-2302-334X
Istanbul University, Turkey

Onur Şahin
Club Muskebi Hotel, Turkey

Merve Kır
Istanbul University, Turkey

ABSTRACT

Political participation is an important component of democracy. The aim of this study is to reveal the tendency of citizens' offline and online political participation. As a result of factor analysis, active participation, civic participation, and passive participation are determined as the dimensions of offline political participation. Political participation on social media is determined as two dimensions which are slacktivism and following up. Cluster analysis was used to identify political participation typologies based on the dimensions of offline and online political participation. Four clusters were identified, namely politicized citizens, politically mindful citizens, politically concerned followers, and apolitical citizens. Politicized citizens explicitly express their political tendencies without any hesitation. Politically mindful citizens are aware of the manipulative power of social media so that they do not actively participate politics on social media. Politically concerned citizens only follow political issues passively, and finally, apolitical citizens do not have an interest in politics.

DOI: 10.4018/978-1-6684-4543-3.ch010

INTRODUCTION

Political participation has recently become an important topic all over the world because low rates of participation means that only the freewill of a small group is reflected within the political system and the rest of the citizens' thoughts are ignored. Thus, political participation is at the heart of democracy and democracy is unthinkable without the ability of citizens to participate freely in politics. Democracy provides the opportunity to citizens participate in decision making process (Van Deth, 2016, p. 2).

The public's ability to select those who govern them and to influence the decisions taken are considered essential component of democracy. Although using the right to vote and selecting the politicians who govern the public is seen as essential for democracy, but it is not sufficient to maintain democracy. Thus, from this perspective representative democracy has been criticized. For well-established democracy, people have to be included in the decision making process of governors. The concept of participatory democracy gains importance, which emphasized the significance of establishing different ways for inclusion of people into governance processes.

Participative democracy model allows citizens to influence political decision making processes and it puts greater emphasis on citizen participation compares to representative democracy. Participatory democracy is primarily concerned with ensuring that citizens are given the opportunity to be involved in decision making on matters that affect their lives (De Vos et al., 2014). Participative democracy defined as "process of collective decision making that combines elements from both direct and representative democracy and citizens have the power to decide on policy proposals and politicians assume the role of policy implementation" and the main advantage of participation democracy is that it has more reasonable policy implementation mechanism than direct democracy (Aragones & Sanchez-Pages, 2008). Considering the democratic deficiency in representative democracy model, participatory democracy is seen between direct and representative democracy. It encourages greater citizen involvement, social empowerment, and egalitarian social relations.

Political participation is one of the most influential mechanism by which individuals influence the decisions that may affect their lives. Since individuals possess equal worth in democracies, the preferences and interests of all citizens, who are subject to the decision, have to be equally considered while making collective decisions. It is assumed that individuals know best their own interests, so these preferences must be communicated to the political system through participation in politics (Dahl, 1989; Best & Kruger, 2005). Ensuring the political participation is crucial for participative democracy. As Parry et al. (1992) indicated that any book about political participation is also a book about democracy. In other words, the level of citizen participation is a signal for understanding how a democracy operates in a country.

The aim of this study is to reveal the tendency of Turkish citizens offline political participation as well as their political participation on social media, and segmenting the citizens based on their offline and online political participation level.

Political Participation

Political participation is considered as important criteria for assessing the quality of democracy. If few citizens' take part in decision-making in a country, this means that there is less democracy; likewise, if more citizens participate in decision-making, this signal for well-established democracy in that country.

Although political participation is defined as the act of taking part in political action, there is no consensus on what can be considered as political actions. Verba and Nie (1972) define the political participation as "activities by private citizens that are more or less directly aimed at influencing the selection of governmental personnel and/or the actions they take" (Verba & Nie, 1972, p. 2). Verba and Nie's definition is considered as narrow and it is criticized since this definition excludes some forms of participation such as passive political participation. In the literature, there are many attempts to define and broader conceptualization of the political participation (Conge, 1988; Parry et al., 1992: Van Deth, 2014; Van Deth, 2016, Verba et al., 1995). The concept of political participation covers different modes, intensities, and qualities of participation from voting to directly influencing the implementation of public policies (Parry & Anderson, 1972).

Van Deth (2001, 2014, 2016) lists the main features of political participation and tries to conceptualize the political participation as an activity or action which is voluntary, nonprofessional activity (excluding the activities of politicians, civil servants, or lobbyists) concerning government, politics, or the state (not restricted to specific phases such as parliamentary decision-making processes or executing laws). Based on these listed features any voluntary, nonprofessional activity concerning government, politics, or the state is a specimen of political participation (Van Deth, 2001, 2014, 2016).

Political participation literature has witnessed continuously expansion of political participation concept and inclusion of new political participation activities. Obviously, this development leads to blurring of the distinction between political and non-political activities between the private and public spheres. Van Deth (2001) outlines the expansion of the political action repertoire on the timeline. Based on this timeline, in 1940s and 1950s political participation was mainly restricted to casting a vote and campaign activities; by the early 1960s conventional political participation was covered the activities such as campaigning and contacting with public officials. On the other hand, remarkable extension of the scope of political participation was seen in the late 1960s and early 1970s. Within this period, the concept of political participation was no more seen restricted with proper (or conventional) activities), its scope has expanded and covered protest actions and social movements. This form of unconventional participation accepted as clear expressions of citizens' interests and opinions. Another expansion of political participation took place in the 1990s, political participation covered the civil participation and social engagement. This expansion caused to the disappearing borderline between political and non-political spheres of society. As a result of this stepwise expansion the domain of political participation grew from the act of voting in the 1940s to almost every conceivable form of non-private activity by the end of the century (Van Deth, 2001, pp.5-6).

The scope political participation has been expanded significantly in the last few decades. Casting vote (Verba & Nie, 1972; Barnes & Kaase, 1979; Parry et al., 1992; Verba et al., 1995; Van Deth, 2014), party membership (Verba & Nie, 1972; Barnes & Kaase, 1979; Parry et al., 1992); contacting with politicians and public officials (Verba et al. 1995), persuade others how to vote (Verba & Nie, 1972; Barnes & Kaase, 1979), wearing campaign badge or sticker (CID Survey), reading politics in newspapers (Barnes & Kaase, 1979), discussing politics (CID Survey), donating money (Verba et al. 1995), attending political meetings (Verba & Nie, 1972; Barnes & Kaase, 1979; Parry et al., 1992), attending protest meeting (Parry et al., 1992; Verba et al., 1995) and lawful demonstrations (Barnes & Kaase, 1979; Parry et al., 1992; Verba et al., 1995), signing petition (Barnes & Kaase, 1979; Parry et al., 1992), boycotting products (CID Survey), social engagement or work for social-welfare organization (Verba et al. 1995) are considered as examples of political participation forms.

In the literature the concept of political participation was handled as multi-dimensional. Similar to the study of Verba and Nie (1972), Verba et al. (1995) categorized political participation forms into four that are voting, campaign activity, communal activity, and contacting. Barnes and Kaase (1979) made the distinction between conventional and unconventional political participation forms. On the other hand, Parry et al. (1992) identified six types of political participation, which are voting, party campaigning, collective action, contacting, direct action, and political violence. In the light of literature, generally voting, campaign activities, contacting with officials or politicians, protest activities and social engagement are handled as major type of political participation (Van Deth, 2001). In some of the studies political participation taken as three dimensional that are active, passive and civic participation (Tola, 2007; Pakhuylu 2013; Çakan, 2017).

Being member of a political party or non-governmental organization related to politics, work for campaign of a political party or candidate, spread the thoughts of a political party, attendig meetings and demonstrations organized by a political party, persuade people to vote in a certain direction are considered as acts of active political participation. On the other hand, following political affairs from mass media, thinking and speculating on political issues and discussign on politics are among the examples of passive political participation. Civic participation refers to participating in activities such as participating in a boycott action on a social issue, signing on petition about social issues, boycotting certain brands for political reasons, communicating with the politicians, government officials to solve local problems (Tola, 2007; Pakhuylu 2013; Çakan, 2017).

Previous studies on political participation have analyzed the factors that affect citizens' political participation from different perspectives. The influence of gender (Henn & Foard, 2014; Kassa, 2015), age (Quintelier, 2007; Holt et al., 2013; Melo & Stockemer, 2014; Sloam, 2016), generational differences (Grasso, 2014; Grasso et al., 2019), education level (Kuenzi, 2006; Kam & Palmer, 2008; Henn & Foard, 2014; Persson, 2015), ethnic group (Jugert et al., 2013), social class (Ødegård & Berglund, 2008; Henn & Foard, 2014), sense of community (Davidson & Coffe, 1989), psychological traits (Dawes et al., 2014), socio-economics (Cohen et al., 2001; Quaranta, 2018) are among the factors that are studied in the political participation literature.

Reasons for low political participation (Bratton, 1999), participatory democracy (Zittel, 2006), women's political participation (Lowndes, 2004; Kassa, 2015; Mlambo & Kapingura, 2019), youth political engagement (Delli, 2000; Jugert et al., 2013; Pakhuylu, 2013; Keating & Melis, 2017; Pontes et al., 2019), civic engagement (Ekman & Amnå, 2012; Loader et al., 2014; Boulianne, 2020; Kwon, 2021), motivating political participation (Levy & Akiva, 2019; Mann et al., 2020), the relationship between life satisfaction and political participation (Pacheco & Lange, 2010; Flavin & Keane, 2012; Cheng et al., 2021), and comparison of online and offline political participation (Jugert et al., 2013; Vissers & Stolle, 2014; Oser et al., 2013; Skoric & Zhu, 2016) are topics that are studied in the political participation literature.

Online Political Participation

As the wide spread use of social media in the recent decade, investigation the influence of social media on offline political participation becomes the trendiest research topic. The impact of social media use on citizens offline political participation was investigated in the literature and the findings of these studies clearly indicated that use of social media has positive effect on offline political participation and increases the likelihood of offline political participation (Kim & Chen, 2016; Holt et al., 2013; Skoric & Zhu, 2016; Halpern & Katz, 2017; Wang; 2007; Kruikemeier et al., 2014; Boulianne & Theocharis, 2020; Boulianne 2020).

Best and Kruger (2005) analyzed the representativeness of online political participation and compared it to traditional offline forms of political participation. Their results suggested that the factors predicting online participation often differ from the factors that predict offline participation. They investigated whether online participators' opinions reflect the general population's opinion. They found that online participation tends to relate with liberal preferences; however offline participation relates to political attitudes similarly. Thus online participation only favors the political voice of liberals (Best & Kruger, 2005).

Similarly, Oser et al. (2013) conducted a study for understanding if online political participation is distinct from offline political participation. They found that online political participation is distinct from offline political participation. They concluded that online activism is indeed a distinctive type of political participation (Oser et al., 2013). Jugert et al. (2013) analyzed offline and online civic engagement among adolescents and young adults from three ethnic groups. This study investigated differences and similarities in young people's offline and online civic engagement with Ajzen's theory of planned behavior (TPB). The findings of this study indicated that TPB showed good fit for a model relating intention for offline and online civic engagement to motivation for civic engagement, peer and parental norms, and collective efficacy (Jugert et al., 2013).

The role of internet and social media in relation to young citizens' political participation has attracted a great deal of scholarly attention (Ahmad et al., 2019; Kahne & Bowyer, 2018; Bakker & Vreese, 2011). Bakker and Vreese (2011) studied political participation of young people. Finding of this study revealed that Internet use is a stronger predictor for newer forms of political participation and interactive online communication is positively related to political participation. Ahmad et al. (2019) examined how online political activities impact political efficacy and real-life political participation among university students. The results revealed that the majority of the students use social media for political awareness and information. They also concluded that social media is a significant platform for netizens to participate in real-life political activities. Morevover, Boulianne and Theocharis, (2020) found a very strong relationship between online political activities, such as joining political groups and signing petitions, with offline political activities, which undermine claims of slacktivism among youth.

Political expression and participation on social media was measured in a variety of ways, including "posting or sharing political thoughts", " post a political comment", "posting or sharing photos, or videos about politics", "forwarding someone else's political comments", "communicated with a politician,", "discuss a political issue online"; "support a campaign" "signed up to volunteer for a political campaign," (Gil de Zúñiga et al., 2014; Velasquez & LaRose, 2015; Yoo et al., 2017; Noland, 2020; Waeterloos et al.,2021).

Şener et al. (2015) considered political participation on social media two dimensional. Those dimensions are active participation and passive participation. Active participation on social media refers activities such as posting news or posts about political issues, making comment on posts about political issues, signing internet campaigns related to political problems and sharing them on social media, communicating with politicians through social media. Passive participation on social media refers activities such as following pages, blogs or groups about political issues, liking posts about political issues, keeping up with political parties and politicians through social media (Şener et al., 2015).

Waeterloos et al. (2021) developed a new instrument for measuring the social media political participation. This scale aims to cover both active, expressive forms of political action (sharing posts) through social media as well as cognitive political social media use (information seeking). The analyses revealed four constructs measured with 21 items, that are latent engagement (e.g., reading posts, comments, news), follower engagement (e.g., signing and sharing a petition, being a group member), expressive engagement (e.g., posting, sharing, commenting) and counter engagement (e.g., breaking into someone's account to post something or get information) (Waeterloos et al., 2021).

In the light of the literature, social media political action is considered as a valuable addition to citizens' political repertoires and it is clear that there is need to study online and social media political action as independent forms of participation (Bennett, 2012; Gibson & Cantijoch, 2013; Loader et al., 2014; Waeterloos et al., 2021).

Research Methodology

The aim of this study is to find out the tendency of citizens' offline political participation as well as their political participation on social media, and segmenting the citizens based on their offline and online political participation level. To reach this aim, an online survey was conducted with 548 people. The data collection took place over eight weeks from December 2020 to January 2021. An online questionnaire was administered via Google Forms (https://forms.gle/dYYMpSjXZQz61e8v6). The link to the survey was distributed through e-mails, messaging applications, and social media, particularly on LinkedIn and Facebook groups. Demographic profile of the respondents can be seen from Table 1.

Attitude toward offline political participation was measured with a fourteen-item scale (reliability (α) = 0.93), adapted from Cohen et al. (2001), Tola (2007), Pakhuylu (2013), Çakan (2017). Political participation on social media was measured with ten-item scale (reliability (α) = 0.911), adapted from Pew Research (2012), Holt et al. (2013), Yamamoto et al. (2013) Şener et al. (2015) Keating and Melis (2017). Lastly, five-item scale (α=.81) adapted by Arklan (2016) was used to measure barriers for social media political participation. All the items were measured on a ten-point Likert scale with the endpoints "Strongly Disagree" and "Strongly Agree".

Among the 548 respondents, 230 are female and 318 are male. 50.5% of the respondents are between the ages of 26-45 and 36.9% of them between the ages of 46-65. Most of the respondents (62%) have bachelor or graduate degree. On the other hand, 24.3% of the respondents have less than high school degree or have a high school degree.

Table 1. Demographic profile of respondents

		N	%			N	%
Gender	Female	230	42,0	**Age**	18-25	41	7,5
	Male	318	58,0		26-35	124	22,6
Education	High School	133	24,3		36-45	153	27,9
	Associate Degree	75	13,7		46-55	128	23,4
	Graduate	221	40,3		56-65	74	13.5
	Master's Degree	76	13,9		65 +	28	5,1
	Ph.D.	43	7,8				

Finding of the Study

Offline Political Participation

Political participation was measured with 14 items and its mean value is 6.97 (see Table 2). Within the context of Turkey, citizens are reluctant to become a member of a political party (μ = 5,80) and a member of a non-governmental organization related to politics (μ = 5,94). They are also far from the idea of attending political parties' meetings and demonstrations (μ = 5,51) and working in the election campaign of a political party (μ = 5,91). Although citizens are afraid to attend meetings and demonstrations organized by political parties; they are moderate towards the idea of participating in demonstrations for a social issue that is important to them (μ = 7,27). Moreover, Turkish citizens have a strong tendency to participate a boycott action on a social issue which is important for them (μ = 8,36). Respondents follow current political affairs from mass media (μ = 8,49) and like to think ((μ = 8,01) and discuss on politics (μ = 7,90).

Table 2. Descriptive statistics for offline political participation

Scale Items	Mean	SD
Political Participation [reliability (α) = 0,931]	**6,97**	**2,4**
I follow current political affairs from television and newspapers.	8,49	2,50
I participate in a boycott action on a social issue which is important for me.	8,36	2,56
I like to think and speculate on political issues.	8,01	2,68
I like to discuss on politics.	7,90	2,79
I try to communicate with the politicians, government officials to solve local problems.	7,39	3,06
I would like to participate demonstrations for a social issue.	7,27	3,37
I sign on petition about social issues.	7,09	3,28
I boycott and/or do not buy certain brands or brands for political reasons.	7,00	3,44
I try to persuade people to vote in a certain direction.	6,68	3,39
I would like to spread the thoughts of a political party.	6,23	3,62
I would like to be a member of a non-governmental organization related to politics.	5,94	3,73
I would like to work in the election campaign of a political party or candidate.	5,91	3,74
I would like to be a member of a political party.	5,80	3,80
I attend events such as meetings and demonstrations organized by a political party.	5,51	3,76

Exploratory Factor Analysis (EFA) was used to determine the dimensions of offline political participation. The Kaiser-Meyer-Olkin measure of sampling adequacy value was 0,927. It can be said that the data set is suitable for factor analysis. The Bartlett test results indicate a significant relationship between the variables, with a significance level of 0,000. Principal component analysis was chosen as the method in explanatory factor analysis and the Promax factor rotation was applied. The EFA results indicated that the three factors with eigenvalues were above 1. According to the factor analysis, 69,78% of the total variance was explained by the three factors representing the fourteen variables and are named: active, passive, and civic participation. Results of factor analysis are presented in Table 3.

Table 3. Factor analysis of offline political participation

	Component		
	1	2	3
Active political participation [reliability (α) = 0,927] (μ = 6,01)			
I would like to be a member of a political party.	1,020		
I would like to be a member of a non-governmental organization related to politics.	0,896		
I would like to work in the election campaign of a political party or candidate.	0,871		
I would like to spread the thoughts of a political party.	0,818		
I attend events such as meetings/demonstrations organized by a political party.	0,778		
I try to persuade people to vote in a certain direction.	0,487		
Civic participation [reliability (α) = 0,807] (μ =7,42)			
I participate in a boycott action on a social issue which is important for me.		0,924	
I sign on petition about social issues.		0,871	
I would like to participate demonstrations for a social issue.		0,674	
I boycott and/or do not buy certain brands or brands for political reasons.		0,600	
I try to communicate with the politicians, government officials to solve local problems.		0,556	
Passive politcal participation [reliability (α) = 0,838] (μ = 8,13)			
I follow current political affairs from television and newspapers.			0,972
I like to think and speculate on political issues.			0,722
I like to discuss on politics.			0,715
Extraction Method: Principal Component Analysis. Rotation Method: Promax with Kaiser Normalization.			
a. Rotation converged in 5 iterations.			

Considering the offline political participation forms, citizens are more prone to the passive political participation (μ = 8,13) compare to active political participation (μ = 6,01) activities. Besides, Turkish citizens are sensitive to social issues and if it is necessary they do not hesitate to take part in social movements that are important for them (μ =7,42).

Online Political Participation

As indicated in Table 4, political participation on social media was measured with ten items and its mean value is 5,83. Compare to citizens' offline political participation level (μ = 6,97), citizens' online political participation level is low (μ = 5,83). Within the context of Turkey, tolerance to expression of freedom is limited. On the social media there is risk of distortion of political posts; thus they may fear facing with legal sanctions because of their posts. Since they do not want to reveal their political thoughts and be perceived as overly political person, people also pay attention to their posts on political issues. Because of these reasons, it is not surprising that overall online political participation is low. As a result, citizens do not have tendency to share their opinion on political issues (μ = 4,48) and post & share news about political issues (μ = 4,60) through their social media account. Moreover, they are reluctant to share the posts of politicians (μ = 5,01) and comment on political posts (μ = 5,12). But they are moderate about liking posts about political issues (μ = 6,26) and signing and sharing social campaigns about political or social issues on social media (μ = 6,33). As it can be seen in Table 2, citizens are open to communicate with the politicians, government officials to solve local problems (μ = 7,39); however, they are distant the idea of communicating with politician on social media (μ = 3,89).

Table 4. Descriptive statistics for online political participation

Scale Items	Mean	SD
Political Participation on Social Media [reliability (α) = 0,911]	**5,83**	**2,4**
I stay informed about political parties and politicians through social media.	7,91	2,70
I follow politicians and political parties on social media.	7,48	3,09
I follow online blogs or groups about politics and current affairs.	7,19	3,05
I sign and share social campaigns about political or social issues on social media.	6,33	3,38
I like posts about political issues on social media.	6,26	3,29
I comment on posts about political issues.	5,12	3,28
I share the posts of politicians and political parties.	5,01	3,56
I post and share news about political issues.	4,60	3,30
I share my personal opinion on current political issues on my social media account.	4,48	3,24
I communicate with politicians on social media.	3,89	3,23

To identify the factors of online political participation, EFA was used. The Kaiser-Meyer-Olkin measure of sampling adequacy value was 0,892. It can be said that the data set is suitable for factor analysis. The Bartlett test results indicate a significant relationship between the variables, with a significance level of 0.000. Principal component analysis was chosen as the method in explanatory factor analysis and the Promax factor rotation was applied. The EFA results indicated that the two factors with eigenvalues were above 1. According to the EFA results, 68,43% of the total variance was explained by the two factors representing the ten variables are named: slacktivism and following up (staying informed). Results of factor analysis are presented in Table 5.

Table 5. Factor analysis of political participation on social media

	Component	
	1	**2**
Slacktivism [(α) = 0,89] (μ = 5,09)		
I share my personal opinion on current political issues on my social media account.	0,952	
I post and share news about political issues.	0,946	
I comment on posts about political issues.	0,811	
I share the posts of politicians and political parties.	0,697	
I sign and share social campaigns about political or social issues on social media.	0,598	
I like posts about political issues on social media.	0,587	
I communicate with politicians on social media. .	0,580	
Following up [reliability (α) = 0,86] (μ = 7,52)		
I stay informed about political parties and politicians through social media.		0,975
I follow politicians and political parties on social media.		0,939
I follow online blogs or groups about politics and current affairs.		0,697
Extraction Method: Principal Component Analysis. Rotation Method: Promax with Kaiser Normalization.		
a. Rotation converged in 3 iterations.		

As aforementioned reasons, Turkish citizens do not have tendency to actively participate and support a political or social cause on social media which is called slacktivism (μ = 5,09); however, they passively participate politics on social media through following and staying informed (μ = 7,52).

Profiling the Citizens Based on Their Offline and Online Political Participation Level

Cluster analysis was used to develop typology of political participation based on the dimensions of offline and online political participation. K-means cluster analysis was used on the extracted factors. Four groups were determined and classified into "politized citizens", "politically mindful citizens", "politically concerned followers", and "apolitic citizens". To determine whether there were group differences among clusters in terms of political participation forms that are active political participation, civic participation, passive political participation, slacktivism and online following up (staying informed), One Way Analysis of Variance (ANOVA) was used. Results revealed that all of the mentioned political participation forms were significantly different from each other. When the F values in the ANOVA test are examined (Table 6) to reveal the clarity of the differences between the clusters, it is seen that all F values are above 200, and the average of the "active political participation" scale has the highest F value and is the strongest discriminating factor. These results confirm the validity of cluster analysis.

Table 6. Differentiation power of each factor in cluster analysis

Factors	*F*	Sig.
Active Political Participation	700,734	0,001
Passive Political Participation	284,763	0,001
Civic Participation	220,261	0,001
Slacktivism	379,582	0,001
Online Following Up Politics	326,925	0,001

Clustering consisting of four separate profiles revealed the most statistically and conceptually significant results. The resulting four clusters are shown in Table 7. When the characteristics of these four clusters are analyzed, four different profile of citizens have been revealed, which differ from each other in terms of attitude toward political participation. The results clearly show that the political participation levels of the citizens differ. The cluster that has a share of 36% in the total is politized citizens.

Table 7. Final cluster center analysis

Cluster Factor	Cluster1	Cluster 2	Cluster 3	Cluster 4
	Politized Citizens	Politically Mindful Citizens	Politically Concerned Followers	Apolitic Citizens
	n = 200	n = 137	n = 97	n = 114
	36%	25%	18%	21%
Cluster Mean	8,97	7,13	5,91	3,53
Active Political Participation	8,93	7,57	3,32	2,27
Passive Political Participation	9,61	9,03	8,09	4,83
Civic Participation	9,25	8,16	6,51	4,62
Slacktivism	8,00	4,45	4,17	2,35
Online Following Up Politics	9,47	8,04	7,74	3,73

Cluster 1-Politized Citizens: Politicized citizens involve in political issues through all channels (both offline and online channels) and explicitly express their political tendencies without any hesitation. Unlike the other three clusters, they are willing to participate and support political and social issues on social media. This is known as slacktivism; however, they also actively participate and support social issues in the real life; so that they can be considered as activist. This cluster has the biggest share in total (36%).

Cluster 2-Politically Mindful Citizens: These citizens staying informed political issues both mass media and social media. They like to follow political affairs and discuss on politics. Their social engagement level is high, they are social responsible citizens and they are willing to take part in social movements that are important for them. Although they actively participate in politics; they are aware of the manipulative power of social media so that they do not actively participate politics on social media. They are politically mindful and aware of the risk of distortion of political posts on social media. Thus, they are reluctant to actively participate and support political and social issues on social media.

Cluster 3- Politically Concerned Followers: Politically concerned citizens do not actively participate politics but they only follow political issues passively, especially they follow political developments on social media. Since they do not want to reveal their political thoughts and be perceived as overly political person, they pay attention to their posts on political issues. Their concerns about facing with legal sanctions, keep them away from slacktivism. However, they are somewhat moderate towards the idea of participating in demonstrations for a social issue that is important to them.

Cluster 4- Apolitical Citizens: They are unwilling to show active political participation; even they do not follow political issues since they do not interest in politics. %21 of the citizens are apolitical.

CONCLUSION

The public's ability to influence the decisions taken are considered essential component of democracy. Participative democracy model allows citizens to influence political decision making processes and it puts greater emphasis on citizen participation. The level of citizen participation is an important indicator for understanding how a democracy operates in a country. This study revealed the tendency of Turkish citizens' offline political participation as well as their political participation on social media. Besides, this study identified Turkish citizens' typology of political participation based on the dimensions of offline and online political participation.

The findings of this study indicated that active, passive, and civic participation are the forms of offline political participation. In the context of Turkey, citizens are more prone to the passive political participation compare to active political participation. Besides, Turkish citizens are sensitive to social issues and if it is necessary they do not hesitate to take part in social movements that are important for them. Considering the active political participation activities, Turkish citizens are reluctant to become a member of a political party, attend political parties' meetings and demonstrations and work in the election campaign of a political party.

In this study, slacktivism and following up (staying informed) were found as the two dimensions of online political participation. Turkish citizens do not have tendency to actively participate and support a political or social cause on social media which is called slacktivism; however, they passively participate politics on social media through following and staying informed. They do not want to reveal their political thoughts and be perceived as overly political person, and their concerns about facing with legal sanctions, keep them away from slacktivism. Slacktivism is the least preferred form of political participation.

Result of cluster analysis identified four types of political participation typologies based on the dimensions of offline and online political participation. Four groups were determined and named as "politized citizens", "politically mindful citizens", "politically concerned followers", and "apolitic citizens". Politicized citizens involve in political issues through all channels and explicitly express their political tendencies without any hesitation. Apolitical citizens do not interest in politics. Politically mindful citizens actively participate in politics; they are aware of the manipulative power of social media so that they do not actively participate politics on social media. Finally, politically concerned citizens do not actively participate politics but they only follow political issues passively, especially they follow political developments on social media.

REFERENCES

Ahmad, T., Alvi, A., & Ittefaq, M. (2019). The use of social media on political participation among university students: An analysis of survey results from rural Pakistan. *SAGE Open*, *9*(3), 2158244019864484. doi:10.1177/2158244019864484

Arklan, Ü. (2016). Sosyal medyanın siyasal amaçlı kullanımı: Ağ kuşağının kullanım alışkanlıkları üzerine bir araştırma. *Gümüşhane Üniversitesi İletişim Fakültesi Elektronik Dergisi, 4*(2).

Bakker, T. P., & De Vreese, C. H. (2011). Good news for the future? Young people, Internet use, and political participation. *Communication Research, 38*(4), 451–470. doi:10.1177/0093650210381738

Bennett, W. L. (2012). The personalization of politics: Political identity, social media, and changing patterns of participation. *The Annals of the American Academy of Political and Social Science*, *644*(1), 20–39. doi:10.1177/0002716212451428

Best, S. J., & Krueger, B. S. (2005). Analyzing the representativeness of Internet political participation. *Political Behavior*, *27*(2), 183–216. doi:10.100711109-005-3242-y

Boulianne, S. (2020). Twenty years of digital media effects on civic and political participation. *Communication Research*, *47*(7), 947–966. doi:10.1177/0093650218808186

Boulianne, S., & Theocharis, Y. (2020). Young people, digital media, and engagement: A meta-analysis of research. *Social Science Computer Review*, *38*(2), 111–127. doi:10.1177/0894439318814190

Bratton, M. (1999). Political participation in a new democracy: Institutional considerations from Zambia. *Comparative Political Studies*, *32*(5), 549–588. doi:10.1177/0010414099032005002

Cheng, E. W., Chung, H. F., & Cheng, A. (2021). Life satisfaction and the conventionality of political participation: The moderation effect of post-materialist value orientation. *International Political Science Review*, 01925121211006567. doi:10.1177/01925121211006567

Cohen, A., Vigoda, E., & Samorly, A. (2001). Analysis of the mediating effect of personal-psychological variables on the relationship between socioeconomic status and political participation: A structural equations framework. *Political Psychology*, *22*(4), 727–757. doi:10.1111/0162-895X.00260

Conge, P. J., Barnes, S. H., Kaase, M., Nelson, J. M., Booth, J. H., Seligson, M. A., Seligson, M. A., & Booth, J. H. (1988). The Concept of Political Participation: Toward a Definition. *Comparative Politics*, *20*(2), 241–249. doi:10.2307/421669

Dahl, R. (1989). *Democracy and its Critics*. Yale University Press.

Davidson, W. B., & Cotte, P. R. (1989). Sense of community and political participation. *Journal of Community Psychology*, *17*(2), 119–125. doi:10.1002/1520-6629(198904)17:2<119::AID-JCOP2290170203>3.0.CO;2-C

Dawes, C., Cesarini, D., Fowler, J. H., Johannesson, M., Magnusson, P. K., & Oskarsson, S. (2014). The relationship between genes, psychological traits, and political participation. *American Journal of Political Science*, *58*(4), 888–903. doi:10.1111/ajps.12100

De Vos, P., Freedman, W., & Brand, D. (Eds.). (2014). *South African constitutional law in context.* Oxford University Press.

Delli Carpini, M. X. (2000). Gen. com: Youth, civic engagement, and the new information environment. *Political Communication, 17*(4), 341–349. doi:10.1080/10584600050178942

Ekman, J., & Amnå, E. (2012). Political participation and civic engagement: Towards a new typology. *Human Affairs, 22*(3), 283–300. doi:10.247813374-012-0024-1

Flavin, P., & Keane, M. J. (2012). Life satisfaction and political participation: Evidence from the United States. *Journal of Happiness Studies, 13*(1), 63–78. doi:10.100710902-011-9250-1

Gibson, R., & Cantijoch, M. (2013). Conceptualizing and measuring participation in the age of the internet: Is online political engagement really different to offline? *The Journal of Politics, 75*(3), 701–716. doi:10.1017/S0022381613000431

Gil de Zúñiga, H., Jung, N., & Valenzuela, S. (2012). Social media use for news and individuals' social capital, civic engagement and political participation. *Journal of Computer-Mediated Communication, 17*(3), 319–336. doi:10.1111/j.1083-6101.2012.01574.x

Gil de Zúñiga, H., Molyneux, L., & Zheng, P. (2014). Social media, political expression, and political participation: Panel analysis of lagged and concurrent relationships. *Journal of Communication, 64*(4), 612–634. doi:10.1111/jcom.12103

Grasso, M. T. (2014). Age, period and cohort analysis in a comparative context: Political generations and political participation repertoires in Western Europe. *Electoral Studies, 33*, 63–76. doi:10.1016/j.electstud.2013.06.003

Grasso, M. T., Farrall, S., Gray, E., Hay, C., & Jennings, W. (2019). Socialization and generational political trajectories: An age, period and cohort analysis of political participation in Britain. *Journal of Elections, Public Opinion, and Parties, 29*(2), 199–221. doi:10.1080/17457289.2018.1476359

Halpern, D., Valenzuela, S., & Katz, J. E. (2017). We face, I tweet: How different social media influence political participation through collective and internal efficacy. *Journal of Computer-Mediated Communication, 22*(6), 320–336. doi:10.1111/jcc4.12198

Henn, M., & Foard, N. (2014). Social differentiation in young people's political participation: The impact of social and educational factors on youth political engagement in Britain. *Journal of Youth Studies, 17*(3), 360–380. doi:10.1080/13676261.2013.830704

Holt, K., Shehata, A., Strömbäck, J., & Ljungberg, E. (2013). Age and the effects of news media attention and social media use on political interest and participation: Do social media function as leveller? *European Journal of Communication, 28*(1), 19–34. doi:10.1177/0267323112465369

Jugert, P., Eckstein, K., Noack, P., Kuhn, A., & Benbow, A. (2013). Offline and online civic engagement among adolescents and young adults from three ethnic groups. *Journal of Youth and Adolescence, 42*(1), 123–135. doi:10.100710964-012-9805-4 PMID:22903193

Kahne, J., & Bowyer, B. (2018). The political significance of social media activity and social networks. *Political Communication, 35*(3), 470–493. doi:10.1080/10584609.2018.1426662

Kam, C. D., & Palmer, C. L. (2008). Reconsidering the effects of education on political participation. *The Journal of Politics*, *70*(3), 612–631. doi:10.1017/S0022381608080651

Kassa, S. (2015). Challenges and opportunities of women political participation in Ethiopia. *Journal of Global Economics*, *3*(4), 1–7. doi:10.4172/2375-4389.1000162

Keating, A., & Melis, G. (2017). Social media and youth political engagement: Preaching to the converted or providing a new voice for youth? *British Journal of Politics and International Relations*, *19*(4), 877–894. doi:10.1177/1369148117718461

Kim, Y., & Chen, H. T. (2016). Social media and online political participation: The mediating role of exposure to cross-cutting and like-minded perspectives. *Telematics and Informatics*, *33*(2), 320–330. doi:10.1016/j.tele.2015.08.008

Krueger, B. S. (2002). Assessing the potential of Internet political participation in the United States: A resource approach. *American Politics Research*, *30*(5), 476–498. doi:10.1177/1532673X02030005002

Kruikemeier, S., Van Noort, G., Vliegenthart, R., & de Vreese, C. H. (2014). Unraveling the effects of active and passive forms of political Internet use: Does it affect citizens' political involvement? *New Media & Society*, *16*(6), 903–920. doi:10.1177/1461444813495163

Kuenzi, M. T. (2006). Nonformal education, political participation, and democracy: Findings from Senegal. *Political Behavior*, *28*(1), 1–31. doi:10.100711109-005-9000-3

Kwon, S. (2021). Do Populist Parties Increase Civic Political Participation? Empirical analysis of 30 countries in Europe. *Journal of International and Area Studies*, *28*(1), 73–98.

Levy, B. L., & Akiva, T. (2019). Motivating political participation among youth: An analysis of factors related to adolescents' political engagement. *Political Psychology*, *40*(5), 1039–1055. doi:10.1111/pops.12578

Loader, B. D., Vromen, A., & Xenos, M. A. (2014). The networked young citizen: Social media, political participation and civic engagement. *Information Communication and Society*, *17*(2), 143–150. doi: 10.1080/1369118X.2013.871571

Lowndes, V. (2004). Getting on or getting by? Women, social capital and political participation. *British Journal of Politics and International Relations*, *6*(1), 45–64. doi:10.1111/j.1467-856X.2004.00126.x

Mann, C. B., Arceneaux, K., & Nickerson, D. W. (2020). Do negatively framed messages motivate political participation? Evidence from four field experiments. *American Politics Research*, *48*(1), 3–21. doi:10.1177/1532673X19840732

Melo, D. F., & Stockemer, D. (2014). Age and political participation in Germany, France and the UK: A comparative analysis. *Comparative European Politics*, *12*(1), 33–53. doi:10.1057/cep.2012.31

Mlambo, C., & Kapingura, F. (2019). Factors influencing women political participation: The case of the SADC region. *Cogent Social Sciences*, *5*(1), 1681048. doi:10.1080/23311886.2019.1681048

Noland, A. (2020). Like, share, retweet: Testing competing models of the theory of planned behavior to predict slacktivism engagement. *Journal of Nonprofit & Public Sector Marketing*, *32*(3), 264–285. doi:10.1080/10495142.2019.1589626

Ødegård, G., & Berglund, F. (2008). Political participation in late modernity among Norwegian youth: An individual choice or a statement of social class? *Journal of Youth Studies*, *11*(6), 593–610. doi:10.1080/13676260802247573

Oser, J., Hooghe, M., & Marien, S. (2013). Is online participation distinct from offline participation? A latent class analysis of participation types and their stratification. *Political Research Quarterly*, *66*(1), 91–101. doi:10.1177/1065912912436695

Pakhuylu, S. (2013). *Social psychological variables affecting political participation of youth in Turkey* (Master's thesis). Middle East Technical University.

Parry, G., & Anderson, B. (1972). *Participation in politics: By Bryce Anderson and others-edited by Geraint Parry*. Manchester University Press.

Parry, G., Moyser, G., & Day, N. (1992). *Political participation and democracy in Britain*. Cambridge University Press. doi:10.1017/CBO9780511558726

Persson, M. (2015). Education and political participation. *British Journal of Political Science*, *45*(3), 689–703. doi:10.1017/S0007123413000409

Pew Research. (2012). *Survey questions: Civic engagement tracking survey 2012*. Available at: https://www.pewinternet.org/files/oldmedia/Files/Questionnaire/2012/SurveyQuestions_PoliticalEngagement.pdf

Pontes, A. I., Henn, M., & Griffiths, M. D. (2019). Youth political (dis) engagement and the need for citizenship education: Encouraging young people's civic and political participation through the curriculum. *Education, Citizenship and Social Justice*, *14*(1), 3–21. doi:10.1177/1746197917734542

Quaranta, M. (2018). Repertoires of political participation: Macroeconomic conditions, socioeconomic resources, and participation gaps in Europe. *International Journal of Comparative Sociology*, *59*(4), 319–342. doi:10.1177/0020715218800526

Quintelier, E. (2007). Differences in political participation between young and old people. *Contemporary Politics*, *13*(2), 165–180. doi:10.1080/13569770701562658

Şener, G., Emre, P. Ö., & Akyıldız, F. (2015). Türkiye'de sosyal medyanın siyasi katılıma etkileri. *folklor/edebiyat, 21*(83), 75-98.

Skoric, M. M., & Zhu, Q. (2016). Social media and offline political participation: Uncovering the paths from digital to physical. *International Journal of Public Opinion Research*, *28*(3), 415–427. doi:10.1093/ijpor/edv027

Sloam, J. (2016). Diversity and voice: The political participation of young people in the European Union. *British Journal of Politics and International Relations*, *18*(3), 521–537. doi:10.1177/1369148116647176

Teorell, J. (2006). Political participation and three theories of democracy: A research inventory and agenda. *European Journal of Political Research, 45*(5), 787–810. doi:10.1111/j.1475-6765.2006.00636.x

Tola, Ö. (2007). *Türkiye'de üniversite öğrencilerinin siyasal katılım düzeylerinin incelenmesi.* Yayımlanmamış Yüksek Lisans Tezi, Ankara Üniversitesi Sosyal Bilimler Enstitüsü.

Van Deth, J. W. (2001, April). Studying political participation: Towards a theory of everything. Joint Sessions of Workshops of the European Consortium for Political Research, 6-11.

Van Deth, J. W. (2014). A conceptual map of political participation. *Acta Politica, 49*(3), 349–367. doi:10.1057/ap.2014.6

Van Deth, J. W. (2016). What is political participation? In Oxford research encyclopedia of politics. doi:10.1093/acrefore/9780190228637.013.68

Velasquez, A., & LaRose, R. (2015). Youth collective activism through social media: The role of collective efficacy. *New Media & Society, 17*(6), 899–918. doi:10.1177/1461444813518391

Verba, S., & Nie, N. H. (1972). *Participation in America: Social equality and political democracy.* Academic Press.

Verba, S., Schlozman, K. L., & Brady, H. E. (1995). *Voice and equality: Civic voluntarism in American politics.* Harvard University Press. doi:10.2307/j.ctv1pnc1k7

Vissers, S., & Stolle, D. (2014). The Internet and new modes of political participation: Online versus offline participation. *Information Communication and Society, 17*(8), 937–955. doi:10.1080/1369118X.2013.867356

Waeterloos, C., Walrave, M., & Ponnet, K. (2021). Designing and validating the Social Media Political Participation Scale: An instrument to measure political participation on social media. *Technology in Society, 64*, 101493. doi:10.1016/j.techsoc.2020.101493

Wang, S. I. (2007). Political use of the Internet, political attitudes and political participation. *Asian Journal of Communication, 17*(4), 381–395. doi:10.1080/01292980701636993

Yamamoto, M., Kushin, M. J., & Dalisay, F. (2015). Social media and mobiles as political mobilization forces for young adults: Examining the moderating role of online political expression in political participation. *New Media & Society, 17*(6), 880–898. doi:10.1177/1461444813518390

Yoo, S. W., Kim, J. W., & Gil de Zúñiga, H. (2017). Cognitive benefits for senders: Antecedents and effects of political expression on social media. *Journalism & Mass Communication Quarterly, 94*(1), 17–37. doi:10.1177/1077699016654438

Zittel, T. (2006). *Participatory democracy and political participation.* Routledge. doi:10.4324/9780203969311

Chapter 11
The Role of the Constitution in Establishing Legality in the State

Valeria Gonitashvili
Ukrainian Youth Organization of Georgia, Georgia

ABSTRACT

Constitution (from lat. constitutio – "device, establishment, addition") is the basic law of the state, a special normative legal act that has the highest legal force. The constitution defines the foundations of the political, legal, and economic systems of the state. The constitution is the founding document of the state, which sets out the main goals of the creation of the state. In the vast majority of countries, the constitution is adopted by a constituent assembly or by referendum. The constitution is given the following legal designation: a normative legal act of the highest legal force of the state (or state-territorial commonwealth in interstate associations), fixing the foundations of the political, economic, and legal systems of this state or commonwealth, the foundations of the legal status of the state and the individual, their rights and obligations.

INTRODUCTION

Constitution (from lat. constitutio - "device, establishment, addition") - the basic law of the state, a special normative legal act that has the highest legal force.

The Constitution defines the foundations of the political, legal, and economic systems of the state. The constitution is the founding document of the state, which sets out the main goals of the creation of the state. In the vast majority of countries, the Constitution is adopted by a constituent assembly or by referendum. The Constitution is given the following legal designation: a normative legal act of the highest legal force of the state (or state-territorial commonwealth in interstate associations), fixing the foundations of the political, economic, and legal systems of this state or commonwealth, the foundations of the legal status of the state and the individual, their rights and obligations. The constitution in the material sense is a set of legal norms that determine the highest bodies of the state, the order of their formation

DOI: 10.4018/978-1-6684-4543-3.ch011

and functioning, their mutual relations and competence, as well as the fundamental position of the individual about state power. The theory of the social contract defines the Constitution as an agreement between the population and the state, which determines the procedure for the formation of the state and the relationship of the parties. In law, a legal and factual concept of the constitution is distinguished. A legal constitution is a system of legal norms that regulate a certain range of social relations. The actual constitution consists of real-life relations (McKean, 2005).

CLASSIFICATION

According to the form of the constitution, they are divided into two groups:

- Written
- Unwritten.

Written constitutions (constitutions in the formal sense) are either a single normative act (exist in the vast majority of countries), or a combination of several constitutional or organic laws (for example, the Constitution of Sweden, and the Constitution of Spain).

Unwritten constitutions consist of norms of a constitutional nature, "scattered" over a large number of acts, as well as those contained in constitutional customs (typical for the countries of the Anglo-Saxon legal family (except the USA), the British Constitution).

In turn, written constitutions are divided into:

- Codified (consisting of a single piece of legislation called the Constitution). An example is the constitutions of France, Russia, and the USA.
- Non-codified (consisting of laws, judicial precedents, legal customs, doctrines, and having a collective name "constitution" that is not fixed anywhere). These include the constitutions of New Zealand and Great Britain.
- Constitutions are drawn up and adopted:
- extremely convened parliament (constituent assembly) (e.g. French Constitution, 1947 Italian Constitution, 1948 Czechoslovak Constitution, 1946 Yugoslav Constitution, Romanian Constitution, 1946 Albanian Constitution, 1919 German Constitution, Greek Constitution, Bulgarian Constitution, Constitution Poland 1920 and 1952, Constitution of Norway;
- a regular parliament (for example, the Danish Constitution, the 1978 RSFSR Constitution, the 1968 Constitution of the GDR, the 1949 and 2011 Hungarian constitutions, and the 1997 Polish Constitution)
- Congress of Councils of Deputies (Constitution of the RSFSR of 1918, 1925, 1937)
- provisional parliament (Constitution of Czechoslovakia 1919, Constitution of the Federal Republic of Germany 1949, Constitution of the GDR 1949)
- by the people, bypassing elected bodies (French Constitution of 1958, Russian Constitution of 1993)
- the head of state (German Constitution of 1871, French Constitution of 1814, Italian Constitution of 1861, Fundamental Laws of the Russian Empire of 1906);

Also, the constitution usually establishes the procedure for adopting amendments and additions. According to the order of adoption of amendments and additions, flexible, rigid, and combined constitutions are distinguished:

- Modification of flexible constitutions is achieved through customary law. Each subsequent law containing constitutional norms changes or replaces the previous one or establishes provisions that were not previously regulated or regulated by customary law. An example of a flexible constitution in Russian history was the Constitution of the RSFSR of 1978, amendments to which in 1989-1992 changed the state system of the country (for example, the separation of powers was introduced)
- Changing rigid constitutions is either impossible or very difficult.
- Changes to the combined constitution are possible, but there are several chapters where changes are prohibited (Constitution of the Russian Federation).

In addition, constitutions are divided according to their duration into permanent and temporary.

Difference Between the Constitution From Other Normative Legal Acts

The Constitution has several differences from other legislative acts:

- It has a constituent character (fixes the state system, basic duties and rights (freedoms), determines the form of the state and the system of higher bodies of state power);
- Has the highest legal force (the action of the constitution extends throughout the state. All laws and other legal acts of state bodies are issued based on the constitution and following it);
- Differs in relative stability;
- Is the basis for current legislation;
- Differs in a special order of adoption and change;
- It is a normative act of direct action (constitutional norms are valid without approval by any state authorities or officials);
- Has supremacy throughout the state (Aleksidze, 2016).

Contents of the Constitutions

As a rule, all constitutional acts are similar in their content. They include the following provisions:

- Determination of the organization of state power, the rights and powers of the authorities, and its relationship to citizens.
- Duties and basic rights of citizens - civil liberties.

These include the following civil rights and obligations:

1. The right of personal integrity, that is, the control of the court over arrests, searches, and the secrecy of private correspondence.
2. Freedom of work and movement, that is, the abolition of the police passport system.

3. Freedom of conscience.
4. Freedom of speech and press.
5. Civil equality - the destruction of class privileges and religious restrictions.
6. Freedom of assembly and association.
7. The right to petition.
8. The right of citizens to take part in national and local regional representation, in control over the activities of the authorities, in the political and social activities of the country (Chitadze, 2016).

The totality of these provisions is called constitutional law, and their system is called constitutionalism.

Functions of the Constitution

Regardless of the social system of the state, each constitution has certain functions:

- Constituent function.

According to this function, the constitution, which appears as a result of significant changes in public life, becomes the political and legal basis for its further development. Thus, the Constitution either consolidates already existing human deeds or creates prerequisites for the creation of new social relations that have matured in society but have not arisen due to the lack of a legal basis for them, which is established with the adoption of the Constitution. Also, the constituent principles are manifested in the political (social) system of the state as a whole, to specific state-legal institutions that exist in this country.

- The organizational function not only consolidates the results achieved, but at the same time sets new tasks for society and the state. It also increases political activity, directs state bodies and public associations, and all citizens to carry out activities in the spirit and within the framework of the new fundamental law. Thus, the Constitution not only reflects the role of relevant factors but at the same time contains certain mechanisms that are necessary to achieve them.
- The foreign policy function is addressed not only to political life but at the same time is the foundation of the state's foreign policy activities.
- The ideological function is to enshrine in the Constitution the provisions of a certain political doctrine as dominant. An example of the implementation of this function can serve as the Constitution of the USSR.
- Humanistic function. The Constitution embodies universal human values, enshrines the rights and freedoms characteristic of a civilized society, and declares universally recognized principles and norms of international law as an integral part of the legal system of the state.
- Legal function.

The essence of the legal function lies in the fact that it becomes the basis of a new legal system and legal order in the country, and also regulates public relations and, as a document of direct action, is the basis for their emergence. In addition, it gives impetus to the development of legislation and the adoption of a large number of new legal acts that embody the general ideas and certain provisions of the Constitution.

To control the compliance with the constitution of the decisions taken, there may be a special body of judicial power - the Constitutional Court. In some countries, its functions are performed by another authority, such as the Supreme Court (Demetrashvili, 2010).

The Constitution as the Main Normative Legal Act

Each constitution has features (legal properties) that define it as the main normative legal act of the state. These include:

- The Constitution is one of the legal acts and has all its features. It has both legal supremacy over all other normative acts, and political supremacy - the state's top management bodies cannot act contrary to its provisions.

An example of such a single supreme act is the Constitution of the Russian Federation. In constitutional law, such a document is commonly referred to as a "written constitution". In the absence of a single document, acts of different years, the so-called. "unwritten constitutions".

In some countries, one or more normative acts, which are usually referred to as constitutional laws, may be tied to the main normative legal act. Sometimes sacred texts act as the main normative legal act, the norms of which cannot be contradicted by-laws adopted in the state.

- The supremacy of the Constitution means that it has the highest legal force over other normative documents. This applies not only to federal laws but also to federal constitutional laws. They must fully comply with the provisions enshrined in the Constitution and cannot contradict them under any circumstances.
- Constitution - the legal framework that determines the nature and content of existing legislation in the country.

Legislation develops the provisions of the Constitution. It proceeds from its provisions in the regulation of various social relations. Constitutions often provide for the need to adopt regulations that develop their provisions (Shubitidze, 2010).

History of the Constitution

Basic Laws of the Ancient World

The constituent laws established in ancient Greek policies, as a rule, by special legislators, of which the laws of Solon and Cleisthenes in Athens, can be considered the prototypes of modern constitutions. In Rome, King Servius Tullius acted as such a legislator. The Spartan unwritten constitution was attributed to the legendary Lycurgus. The constitutional character in Sparta was orally transmitted "Big Retra" (decree), which read: Let the people be divided into phyla and obs, let 30 people enter the Gerousia together with the kings, and the people from time to time gather at the river Eurotas for meetings. There, let the people offer decisions that they can accept or reject. Let the people have supreme power and strength.

Medieval Codes of Laws

The forerunners of modern constitutions were medieval codes of laws.

In particular, the Law Rule (nomocanon) of St. Sava was the first charter of Serbia since 1219, a collection of civil law based on Roman law and the canon law of the Ecumenical Councils, and its main goal was to organize the functioning of the young Serbian kingdom and the Serbian Church. Saint Sava began work on the Serbian Nomocanon in 1208, while on Mount Athos, using the Nomocanon in fourteen titles, the Synopsis of Stephen the Ephesian, the Nomocanon of John Scholasticus, the documents of the Ecumenical Councils, which he modified with the canonical commentaries of Aristinos and John Zonar, local church assemblies, canons of the holy fathers, the Law of Moses, the translation of Prochiron, and the short stories of the Byzantine emperors (most of them were taken from the short stories of Justinian and Corpus iuris civilis). The Nomocanon was a new set of civil and canonical rules taken from Byzantine sources and adapted to Serbian conditions. Legal transplants[en] of Roman-Byzantine law became the basis of medieval Serbian law.

Stefan Dušan, emperor of the Serbs and Greeks, received the Zavodnik in Serbia at two-state congresses: in 1349 in Skopje and 1354 in Sera. This code of laws regulated all social spheres. The code was based on Roman-Byzantine law. Legal transplantation is notable for articles 171 and 172 of the Dušan Code, which govern legal independence. They were taken from the Byzantine codex Vasiliki (book VII, 1, 16-17) (Maria Kruk-Larosz, 2007).

In 1529, the Statute of the Grand Duchy of Lithuania was adopted, consisting of 13 sections (283 articles). Already at the Berestey Sejm of 1544, the statute was revised, and the final version was published in 1588 and remained in effect until it was completely abolished in 1840.

One of the oldest and current constitutions in the world is the Basic Law of San Marino, which was adopted back in 1600, even though this law was based on the city charter, adopted back in 1300. However, it should be taken into account that it was supplemented only in 1974 with the Declaration of the Rights of Citizens and the Basic Principles of the State System (Shubitidze, 2010).

Constitutions of the New Age

The first constitution in the modern sense of the term - that is, a document describing and establishing the separation of powers and the competence of each of them - is the US Constitution (adopted September 17, 1787), ratified by the State of Delaware on December 7, 1787. The first written constitutions on the European continent also include the Constitution of the Commonwealth (adopted on May 3, 1791) and the Constitution of France (adopted on September 3, 1791). Both constitutions did not last long, in the Commonwealth - because of the final division of the country, and in France - because of the development of revolutionary events (Demetrashvili, 2010).

Significance of the Text of the Constitution

Even though in the last half of the twentieth century there was a qualitative leap in the adoption of national constitutions by states around the world, there is a problem of losing the significance of the text of the constitution itself. For example, surveys of the population of the United States revealed that the majority of Americans recognize the importance of the US constitution, but few could say what the content of the text of the constitution is, what it says. The well-known weakness of constitutions, when the principles laid down in them can be trampled on with sufficient ease by the authorities, also does not contribute to the assertion of their importance.

The tendency for the text of the constitution to lose its significance can also be traced to the scientific community. There are several reasons behind this. One of them is the frequent consideration of the basic law exclusively in its legal meaning. Often, laws and institutions based on the constitution are subjected to a comprehensive analysis, and the legal application of the basic law in the courts and its influence on the formation of legislative and executive power is considered. Attempts to get closer to the text itself often end up with one interpretation or another of the text, and not with an answer to the question of the necessity of the text as such. The other side of the coin is the approach when constitutions are considered in strict relation to specific conditions, which means the significance of the document only for a limited territory, a limited number of people, and for a limited time. When a text begins to acquire meaning only based on the vastness and depth of the analysis of the conditions for its appearance or interpretations of its application, this means a decrease in the significance of the text itself.

The text of the basic law itself is directly significant, which is created for specific purposes and has an important symbolic meaning. Constitutions can shape the civil character of the country, and help in the self-identification of the nation. The texts of the best constitutions have such a strong spirit that they serve as a source of pride and reverence for the people. The worst ones can emphasize the entire disunity of the population.

Despite the vast differences, most constitutions are similar in their functions, which means the importance of the text itself, and not just the political and legal institutions it generated. The primary and most important function is to limit the power of the ruling person. This is the answer to the main questions of the creators: what is the text of the constitution for and what should it do. Other functions include: the destruction of the old political regime and the formation of a new one; creating an image of the political future that will be a source of inspiration for the population; designation of the structure of political institutions; resolution of the conflict of institutions in the country; ensuring the rights of minorities and their inclusion in the political dialogue, etc. Different constitutions may or may not have certain functions in their text, they may remain only words on paper, but the creation of the text of the constitution as such serves quite specific purposes (Chitadze, 2016).

The texts of constitutions, from the very first to our times, have changed significantly. They have become longer, and if earlier they only fixed basic principles, now they are more detailed, which, perhaps, means a decrease in their effectiveness. Especially detailed are the constitutions of the countries of Eastern Europe, when all the most complex economic and political features of the transition from socialism to new social orders were built into the texts.

CONCLUSION

The Constitution is the basic law of a state with the highest legal force adopted especially. The Constitution regulates the legal status of the individual in the society, and the relations related to the organization and functioning of the public authority. The Constitution is a complex multifunctional public institution. It is often interpreted as the supreme law of the state, the catalog of rules, the guarantee of the individual about the state, and so on.

Adherents of the Liberal-Democratic School see in the Constitution the essence of the public agreement is mainly conditioned by the nature of things (Scientific School of Natural Law), the highest expression of a legal idea (normative), and the set of rules determining the status of state and nation (institutionalists).

The Marxist-Leninist doctrine viewed the Constitution as an instrument through which different social classes strengthened their political domination.

The slightly different social purpose of the Constitution is also noted by modern scholars who are far removed from Marxism. According to Professor Andras Shayo, most of the constitutions were created to crown and complete the social revolution; The purpose of creating other constitutions, in his opinion, is to prevent a revolution and restore the pre-revolutionary state (Chitadze, 2016).

Almost all modern scholars, when defining the meaning of the Constitution, focusing on its founding nature and regulatory function. The norms of the Constitution legitimize public institutions, determine the scope of their power and the basic rights of citizens, and regulate relations between the state and the people.

REFERENCES

Aleksidze, L. (2016). *International Law. Handbook.* Tbilisi State University.

Chitadze, N. (2016). *Political Sciences.* International Black Sea University.

Demetrashvili, A. (2010). *Constitutional Law.* Tbilisi State University.

Kruk-Larosz. (2007). *La Constitition europeenne et le constitutionnalisme contemporain.* VII-e Congres international de droit constitutionnel.

McKean, E. (2005). *The New Oxford American Dictionary* (2nd ed.). Oxford University Press.

Robbers, E. (2006). *Encyclopedia of World Constitutions.* Retrieved from: https://books.google.ge/books?id=M3A-xgf1yM4C&pg=PA626&redir_esc=y

Shubitidze, V. (2010). *Political Sciences.* Georgian Technical University.

Wormuth, F. (1949). *The Origins of Modern Constitutionalism.* Harper & Brothers.

KEY TERMS AND DEFINITIONS

Constitution: An aggregate of fundamental principles or established precedents that constitute the legal basis of a polity, organization, or another type of entity and commonly determine how that entity is to be governed.

Constitutional Democracy: Government processes that allow people, through their elected representatives, to exercise power and influence the state's policies.

Democracy: Is a form of government in which the people have the authority to deliberate and decide legislation ("direct democracy"), or to choose governing officials to do so ("representative democracy"). Who is considered part of "the people" and how authority is shared among or delegated by the people has changed over time and at different rates in different countries, but over time more and more of a democratic country's inhabitants have generally been included. Cornerstones of democracy include freedom of assembly, association and speech, inclusiveness and equality, citizenship, consent of the governed, voting rights, freedom from unwarranted governmental deprivation of the right to life and liberty, and minority rights.

Unwritten (or Uncodified) Constitution: Would be defined, as Lord Bolingbrooke once put it, as "the whole assemblage of laws, institutions, traditions, customs, and practices that embody how we are governed". Parts of that 'unwritten constitution' are of course written down, but that is immaterial: what they lack, and what makes the term 'unwritten constitution' as self–contradictory as an 'unfloating boat' or 'inedible food', is supreme and fundamental law status. Form and function can't be separated.

Written Constitution: A supreme and fundamental law. It is supreme in the sense that it is harder to change than ordinary law and prevails over ordinary law in case of incompatibility. It occupies a place at the apex of the hierarchy of legal norms, as the lex superior from which other laws derive their authority. It defines the state, proclaims its basic principles, protects the rights of citizens, establishes governing institutions, and regulates the relationship between them.

Chapter 12
Rule of Law as a Basis for the Establishment of a Constitutional State

Irakli Kervalishvili
Georgian Technical University, Georgia

ABSTRACT

The term rule of law is closely related to both constitutionalism and the rule of law, and it refers to the political situation and not to any particular legal law. According to the rule of law, all people are subject to the law, including legislators, law enforcement, and judges. In this sense, it opposes tyranny or oligarchy, where rulers stand above the law. Lack of the rule of law can be found in both democracies and monarchies where laws are not taken into account. The rule of law is at stake where the government does not have the appropriate corrective mechanism to restore it.

INTRODUCTION

The rule of law is a legal doctrine according to which no one can be above the law, everyone is equal before the law, no one can be punished except in the manner prescribed by law and only for its violation. The rule of law implies that all by-laws and enforcement acts are subject to and do not contradict the law. According to natural law theory, the rule of law requires that all normative legal acts (including the constitution and legislation) and all activities of state power be subordinated to the protection of dignity, freedom, and human rights. A state in which the rule of law is implemented is called a legal state.

The concept of the rule of law has been known since ancient times when the ancient Greek philosopher Aristotle wrote: “The law must rule” (Aristotle).

Main Principles

In modern philosophy of law, the rule of law is opposed to the idea that individual officials or authorities can be above the law or have excessive powers and thus exercise arbitrariness. Rule of law doctrine

DOI: 10.4018/978-1-6684-4543-3.ch012

requires rules to be published, stable, and predictable in their application. It requires the accessibility of the justice system and its independence from the executive and legislative branches of government so that judges make decisions only based on facts and laws. Modern versions of the doctrine also hold that members of society should be able to participate in the creation and modification of the laws that govern their behavior.

Two main concepts of the rule of law can be distinguished: formal and substantive ("thin" and "thick" in the English tradition; associated with the theories of legal positivism and natural law, respectively) (Chitadze, 2016). The formal interpretation of the rule of law does not make judgments about the fairness of the rules themselves but defines the procedural attributes that a legal system should have. This approach seeks to isolate the efficiency and predictability of the system from ethical questions about its responsibility for the result. Meaningful interpretations of the rule of law make demands on the content of laws and explicitly include fundamental human rights, which, as these concepts argue, follow from the highest unwritten principles of legality, morality, and justice. Such interpretations were greatly strengthened after the Nuremberg trials, which recognized the leadership of Nazi Germany as criminals despite their formal observance of the law, as well as after the human rights work of Mahatma Gandhi and Martin Luther King. In order not to confuse a formal interpretation with a substantive one, the Parliamentary Assembly of the Council of Europe recommends using the term "rule of law" for the former, and "rule of right" for the latter (Jurgens, 2013).

As defined in the 2004 UN Secretary-General's report The Rule of Law and Transitional Justice in Conflict and Post-Conflict Societies, "The rule of law is a concept at the very heart of the UN's mission. It is a principle of governance in which all persons, institutions, and entities, public and private, including the State itself, function under laws that have been publicly enacted, are equally enforced and independently enforced by the judiciary, and are compatible with international human rights norms and standards" (UN, 2004).

The Ukrainian legal scholar A. N. Kostenko, based on the theory of social naturalism, proposed to interpret the principle of the rule of law as "the principle of the rule of laws of natural law" (Aleksidze, 2016).

History

The term has been used since the beginning of the 17th century (a petition to James I from the House of Commons in 1610; a little earlier this idea was voiced in the decision of the Court of Common Claims presided over by Edward Coke, although the king himself considered such a view of his power "treason") (England and Wales High Court, 1610).

It should be noted that the concept itself is much older and is far from always connected with ideas about democracy in the modern sense. For example, Aristotle insisted that "the law must govern" (Aristotle). Similar views were held by Cicero, who said: "We are all slaves of the laws" (Cicero). The law was absolutized by the ancient Chinese "legists" - adherents of the Fajita school, who during the period of being in power established in the state, as a rule, very severe punishments for numerous misconducts (Zhang). However, from the point of view of the Legalists, the law was not to be a means for the people to restrain the rulers, but rather a means for the rulers to govern the people. In contrast, in the thirteenth century, Thomas Aquinas argued that it was the rule of law that constituted God's "natural order" (Aquinas).

The idea that the freedom of action of persons in power should have legal restrictions is characteristic primarily of the Anglo-Saxon legal tradition (in the 18th century - John Locke, Samuel Johnson,

Thomas Paine, John Adams). In many respects, despite some differences in emphasis, the rule of law is close to the concept of "Rule of law" (German Rechtsstaat, French État de Droit) that developed in Romano-Germanic legal philosophy (Heuschling, 2002). The use of this or that terminology is mainly due to differences in legal customs and their history.

The most ancient source in which the idea of subordinating power to the law is affirmed is the Torah (part of the Holy Scripture) of Moses, who, according to the traditional point of view, lived in the 13th century. BC (Electronic Jewish Encyclopedia, 2015).

When he (the king) sits on the throne of his kingdom, he must copy for himself a list of this law from the book that is with the priests of the Levites, and let it be with him, and let him read it all the days of his life, so that he learns to fear the Lord, God his own, and tried to do all the words of this law and these ordinances; lest his heart is puffed up before his brethren, and lest he deviates from the law either to the right or to the left, so that he and his sons may dwell in his kingdom for long days amid Israel.

In the Middle Ages, this idea received the power of state law in the non-Jewish world, when the Holy Scripture also became the highest source of truth in it. According to this source, "the law (of God) is the truth." This law was the common basis for all political and legal doctrines of the Middle Ages. But even earlier, during the Christianization of the Roman Empire, in 390, the Christian emperor Theodosius I was already forced to obey the law and bring public repentance (Kazakov, 2016).

In 1215, the English king, recognizing the supremacy of Christ over himself, signed the Magna Carta, which established the principle of subordination of power to the law (Krasheninnikova, 2002). In the same century, court judge Henry de Bracton (d. 1268) first codified the basic rules of English law. His work De legibus et consuetudinibus Anglia ("On the Laws and Customs of England") played a major role in the formation of medieval England. He argued that "the king should not be under man, but under God and law, because the law makes the king the king" (Brachon, 2016).

And in the future, the legislative acts of medieval Europe regulated the power of monarchs, based on the primacy of Christ and the supremacy of Holy Scripture. So in 1221-1225. Judge Eike von Repkow compiled the Saxon Mirror, the oldest legal collection in Germany, which served as the basis for the Swabian Mirror and the law of the city of Magdeburg (see Magdeburg city law), from where it spread to Holland, Livonia, and Poland (Dembo, 1985).

In 1525, the Twelve Articles manifesto of the Reformation was adopted by the peasants of Swabia (Chitadze, 2016).

In 1571, 39 articles were approved by an Act of Parliament in England (see Art. 37) (Shubitidze, 2009).

The Bill of Rights of 1689 further limited the power of English monarchs and declared the rights and freedoms of subjects (Bill of Rights, 1689).

Thus, relying on the name of Christ and the height of his law, the idea of the rule of law received the force of state law in medieval Europe, and the absolute monarchy, inherited from Roman law, turned into a monarchy limited by laws.

Subsequently, the normative legal acts of democratic states ceased to recognize the supremacy of Christ and the supremacy of Holy Scripture. However, these states did not stop building their legislation on the principle of the rule of law, but continued to develop this principle in their lawmaking, making it the basis of the modern world order.

Legality

Legality is a political and legal regime or the principle of the real operation of law in the state, in which state bodies, officials, and citizens strictly observe legal norms and, first of all, laws.
In political science, the synonymous term legality is used: for example, the legality of power.

Principles of Legality

The principles of legality are the initial provisions determined by the nature of the formation and functioning of the legal system, which underlie the implementation of legal prescriptions and the basis of the requirements for the behavior of subjects of legal relations.

1. The rule of law (ensures the hierarchical harmony of the system of normative acts, when the subordinate legal act does not contradict the law)
2. The unity of legality (assumes its operation throughout the state);
3. The universality of legality (implies its effect on all persons);
4. The expediency of legality (contributes to the achievement of the goals of the state and society, which are expressed in law, in the law);
5. Equality before the law (granting the same rights and presenting uniform requirements for all citizens);
6. Guaranteeing the fundamental rights and freedoms of citizens (universal protection of the individual and the need to ensure the priority of general humanitarian values);
7. The inevitability of punishment for the committed offense (a characteristic of the legal nature of legality);
8. The relationship between legality and culture (characterizes the moral nature of legality; without reaching a certain level of legal culture by all subjects of law, the population of the country as a whole, it is impossible to ensure the proper level of legality).

Guarantees of Legality

Guarantees of legality are objective conditions, subjective factors, as well as special means that ensure the regime of legality.

General Guarantees of Legality

General guarantees of legality are opportunities that develop in the life of society, which, to one degree or another, ensure the implementation of legal prescriptions. Among them are considered:

1. Economic guarantees. They form the basis for all other warranties. The crisis in the economy leads to a weakening of the rule of law. Economic freedom is not always conducive to strengthening the rule of law. The level of law-abiding is declining as a result of the state's failure to fulfill its social obligations to citizens (there is no support for vulnerable segments of the population, massive non-payment of salaries, the collapse of the system of free medical care, education, etc.). Unemployment is also a "reserve" for the crime.

2. Political guarantees. This is the functioning of the political system of society. Democracy, separation of powers, political pluralism, freedom of the press are the political preconditions for legitimacy. But the most important thing is that political rights and freedoms should not be declarative, but implemented.
3. Spiritual guarantees. This is a worldview, legal awareness, a high level of general and legal culture of the population, morality, deep respect for the requirements of the law, and the development of legal science.
4. Public guarantees. These are measures taken by the public to combat violations of the law, to maintain and strengthen it (commissions, committees, voluntary people's teams, the media).

Special Guarantees of Legality

Special guarantees of legality are legal and organizational means designed solely to ensure the rule of law.

Legal guarantees (methods and means fixed in the current legislation, as well as organizational and legal activities for their application, directly aimed at ensuring the rule of law, the unhindered exercise of rights and freedoms, and their protection). This may be the further development, improvement, and increase in the effectiveness of legislation as the normative basis of legality, the improvement of the law-making activities of the state. Legislation must also meet the requirements of the times. Intradepartmental and interdepartmental control over legality. Intradepartmental consists in the control of a higher body over the observance of the rule of law in the activities of subordinate lower bodies, that is, it is carried out vertically (the control of the prosecutor's office over the police). Judicial control over the activities of all state authorities and officials. Complaints and statements of citizens, their timely and correct consideration. The legal profession also plays an important role in strengthening the rule of law.

Forms of Legality

- Embodiment in the legislation of the best legal ideas, the priority of human rights and freedoms, the justice of the Constitution and laws, their compliance with real social relations.
- The supremacy of the main law - the hierarchy of normative legal acts (the subordination of all by-laws to the laws, and the laws of the constitution).
- Strict observance of laws, other regulations, and court decisions by all members of society, state bodies, and officials who are obliged to implement the law (principle of the rule of law in the rule of law).
- Effective state and public protection of the operation of the constitution and laws.

To apply the principle of legality in practice, it must be possible for citizens to effectively appeal against the actions of the state and its structures in court.

Many scientists emphasize the versatility of legality. On the one hand, it is a principle that obliges all subjects of law to comply with the current legislation. On the other hand, it is a requirement that the methods of public administration be legal, use legal means, and have a legal form. At the same time, the meaningful interpretation of legality considers non-legal such normative acts expressing the will of the authorities, which in their content contradict the fundamental concepts of justice, freedom, and equality.

Constitutional State

The rule of law (German: Rechtsstaat) is a state whose entire activity is subject to the rule of law, as well as fundamental legal principles aimed at protecting dignity, freedom, and human rights. The subordination of the activities of the supreme authorities to stable laws or judicial decisions is a hallmark of constitutional political regimes. The principle of compliance with the prescriptions of law by all its subjects, including persons or bodies with power, is called legality in the jurisprudence of many states and the rule of law in common law countries. It should be borne in mind that in some countries jurisprudence there is also the term rule of law, which means the subordination to the law of all by-laws and acts of law enforcement. The rule of law is one of the main components of the rule of law.

The idea of a rule of law state, first of all, is opposed to arbitrariness in all its varieties: the dictatorship of the majority, despotism, a police state, as well as the absence of the rule of law.
This idea has several goals:

1. Limitation and direction of the process of exercising power. The rule of law does not seek to belittle the importance of competence, authority, personal will, and other qualities of leaders, but sets the standard for the legitimacy of leadership methods.
2. Formation of a sense of certainty and legitimate expectations regarding the behavior of all subjects of law.
3. Protection of established public ideas about morality, justice, freedom, and equality, as well as protection of the dignity and rights of citizens following these ideas. Some jurists believe that this function is inseparable from ensuring a more complete implementation of the listed values.

The rule of law requires the following institutions:

- Sentencing offenses solely following published and clearly defined procedures and standards.
- Equality before the law, so that all citizens receive equal protection under the law, and offenders of the law are punished proportionately, regardless of their political, social, or economic status.
- The existence of independent, efficient, impartial, and accessible courts, police, and other law enforcement agencies.
- Performance of the function of normative regulation of the actions of the state by a legislative body separated from the executive branch.

An important role is played by agreement among the ruling classes regarding the norms of political behavior, the principles of conflict resolution, and basic cultural values, including the rule of law.

There are two main concepts of the rule of law. The formal interpretation is related to the theory of legal positivism and focuses on the efficiency and predictability of legal procedures. The meaningful interpretation is connected with the theory of natural law and raises the question of the justice of the laws themselves while proclaiming fundamental human rights as the highest value.

Principles

The ideal of the rule of law is not tied to any national experience, and among the most important principles, jurists usually single out the rule of law, equality, the feasibility of the requirements of the law, and the protection of civil liberties. At the same time, the implementation of this ideal in each country had many individual characteristics, due to different customs and history. The institutions of the rule of law also depend on the current tasks facing society. The most successful models of the legal order were those in which:

- courts are separated from other branches of government (executive and legislative) and isolated from external pressure;
- judgments are based on a reasonable interpretation of existing laws;
- Fair trial guarantees exist. Rule by Law. Law is lord over rulers and they are his servants (Plato).

Where there is no rule of law, no state structure (Aristotle).

The rule of law means that the law has the highest legal force, and all other legal acts and law enforcement acts must comply with it. It follows that no official or authority, including the government, parliament, and (in a democracy) the people as a whole, can act outside the limits established by law. Legal norms can be issued and changed only following the existing legal or pre-agreed procedures. There must be legal and effective ways to force the government and any officials to comply with the rule of law.

Rule by law is also the antithesis of lawlessness and lynching. One of the main tasks of the state is to ensure security, in particular, the state should be the only source of the legitimate use of force. Legal processes must be sufficiently strong and accessible, and the activities of law enforcement agencies effective.

Equality

Laws apply equally to everyone without exception, including those who make laws. Justice should not take into account the origin, power, wealth, or social position of the persons standing before it. The jurisdiction of the courts that rule in the cases of ordinary citizens should extend to all citizens (Held, 2000).

Deviations from this norm in modern times have been called "selective justice".

Generalization of Legal Norms. Laws should formulate the conditions for their applicability in general terms, without pointing to specific individuals, organizations, or small social groups. They should not be issued to solve specific problems if under other circumstances similar actions of the authorities would be illegal. However, in some cases, the generalization requirement runs into difficulties. For example, in welfare states, some norms apply to persons of a clearly defined socio-economic status, and since part of society does not consider these laws justified, from the point of view of critics, they represent a form of legal discrimination.

Equal Access to the Legal System. Due to social inequality, some people have better access to resources to protect their interests and, therefore, a better chance of winning a lawsuit[9]. Correction of such trends is often associated with objective difficulties, which are complicated by the above requirement for the generalization of legal norms and procedures.

Feasibility

Laws must be such that people can follow them. At a minimum, they must exist, be available for review, and contain clear (at least for a lawyer) requirements. The creation of unpublished or retroactive laws, the internal inconsistency, or frequent variability of legislation makes it unenforceable at the system level and leaves the possibility of only selective application. In particular, no one can be punished for acts that did not violate the law at the time they were committed. Laws should clearly and consistently formulate the criteria for punishability to minimize arbitrariness in their application.

Laws should also not conflict with established public ideas about justice. To do this, constitutional democracies have several institutions, including parliaments, competitive and periodic elections, and freedom of the media.

Independence of the Judiciary

The independence of the court from other branches of government and their isolation from external pressure play a significant role in the rule of law. If the court is dependent on the executive, it may not be able to protect the defendant from the illegitimate use of force. If the judiciary merges with the legislature, the freedom of the defendant may become subject to arbitrary regulation.

The separation of powers is also closely related to the requirement that in a state governed by the rule of law it should be possible in principle to enumerate all forms of expression of state power. Violation of this requirement would lead to the restriction of the freedom of citizens of the state.

Justice

On the procedural side, justice is ensured because the legal system contains a complete set of previously known procedures and decision-making rules, the application process of which is fair, consistent, and transparent. The principles of the system should allow ordinary people to predict what actions will be regarded as legal and what will not. Justice becomes unpredictable, for example, if corruption allows known perpetrators to escape punishment or deprive owners of their rightful property, or if executive-dependent courts legitimize its arbitrariness.

According to New York University professor Jeremy Waldron, criminal penalties should be imposed under the following conditions:

- adjudication of the case in a court that decides impartially based on facts, laws, and the arguments presented in connection with them;
- judges who are competent and independent from other branches of state power;
- collection of evidence according to established procedures;
- the right to be present at all significant stages of the process;
- the right to prepare for defense and to be assisted by a lawyer;
- the right to personally challenge the evidence in favor of the prosecution;
- the right to provide evidence and arguments in their favor;
- the right to know the motivation of the court that served as the basis for the sentencing;
- some possibilities of appeal to the highest court (Aleksidze, 2016).

For example, if the investigation used means of inquiry prohibited by law (torture), to ensure procedural justice, the court must exclude from the case any evidence of the defendant's guilt obtained through such means. That the perpetrator may be acquitted as a result should not be taken into account.

At the same time, government officials may impose a fine for minor administrative offenses if their actions can be challenged in court, subject to the above requirements. The listed rights and freedoms are positive, that is, they formulate active obligations of the state, rather than protect the individual from its interference.

The justice system must also operate without undue delay, otherwise, it creates loopholes for arbitrariness.

Protection of Human Rights

Supporters of natural law theories argue that no laws should encroach on the universal rights and freedoms of man and citizen. However, in fact, in different countries, the understanding of human rights differs: in the United States, the death penalty is not considered a deprivation of the right to life, in Scandinavia high taxes are not considered a violation of the right to private property, in many countries of Eastern Europe and Latin America people do not see a contradiction between the persecution of homosexuals and the principles of equality. Some legal scholars believe that legislative protection of human rights is only effective if these rights are valued in the local culture.

Other Components of the Rule of Law

The stability of the rule of law depends on the perception of legality as a cultural value. Typically, a legal culture finds its expression in the use of laws to protect one's interests, the demand for new laws, the periodic issuance of such laws, and daily law abidance.

Several jurists believe that the rule of law implies not only the responsibility of citizens to the state but the responsibility of the authorities to the population and its subordination to the interests of society.

According to some experts, the rule of law state is also characterized by the presence of a developed civil society and the decentralization of power, so that it is not concentrated in any institution or the hands of a narrow group of people. Other theorists believe that the rule of law should protect the market from measures to redistribute resources.

The Nature of Law

The interpretation of the rule of law largely depends on the understanding of the nature of law. The idea of a rule of law state is fundamentally incompatible with the early theories of legal positivism, where the law is seen as just one of the instruments of political power to implement the will of the leadership.

However, in later versions of positivism, generally accepted rules and established legal customs are considered the basis of the law, and the task of the rule of law is to protect them. In such a state, normative acts reflect the ideas of morality, justice, freedom, and equality recognized in the environment that constitutes the social base of the regime. At the same time, legal positivism separates the content of legal norms from ethical assessments of the result of their application, arguing that the justice system is not responsible for the imperfection of society. Theorists come to a similar conclusion, who see the main function of the rule of law in the formal observance of legal procedures, regardless of their outcome.

According to meaningful interpretations, the rule of law state has not only a protective function but also a constructive one. It sets the standard for legal methods of leadership and ensures a fuller realization of universal values. The general principles that stand at the top of the hierarchy of legal norms are developed in the process of analyzing laws and judicial decisions in terms of morality and political consequences. As a result, the actual content of any laws is inseparable from the question of what these laws should be. This approach is a development of the theory of natural law, according to which the moral content of laws is the basis for their legitimacy, so lat. lex iniusta non est lex - "an unjust law is not a law" (Blessed Augustine). It is reflected in the constitutions of many countries. For example, according to the Swiss Constitution, the actions of the state must respect the fundamental freedoms of citizens, proceed from the public interest and be proportionate to the goals pursued.

Constitutional Regime

Although the rule of law can significantly limit the arbitrariness of power, the containment of certain types of arbitrariness requires additional institutions. A heterogeneous society is characterized by division into interest groups, which carries the risk of creating laws that secure the privileges of the stronger at the expense of the weaker. The purpose of the constitutional regime is such a state structure in which no single body or narrow group of persons has supreme power, and everyone is forced to take into account the interests and rights of others. Along with the rule of law, such a device usually includes the following components:

- System of checks and balances. Partial functional separation of powers prevents the concentration of power in any one of the branches: executive, legislative or judicial. At the same time, some officials can restrain the arbitrariness of others.
- Government accountability and openness to other authorities (parliament, courts, ombudsmen, auditors general), media, and citizens.
- Distribution of power so that no ruling group can ignore the interests of the ruled. Rules of law are the product of compromise and common property.
- Political equality of citizens as participants in the process of creating laws. This process should also allow citizens to be informed about the preferences of others so that they can work out common rules together.
- A court-enforced constitution or another supreme statute that guarantees human rights (Gudushauri, 2010).

History

The oldest known code governing the state is the Babylonian law code of Hammurabi (circa 1750 BC). This code is notable in that it is based on published rules, that officials were required to abide by these rules, and that the privilege of interpreting these rules rested with judges (History, 2009).

In ancient Athens, laws served as one of the tools to combat tyranny. To avoid the concentration of power in the hands of one person, the assembly of full-fledged citizens (ekklesia) issued normative acts that were binding on everyone. The judges were chosen by lot. All citizens had an equal right to have their cases heard in court. The supreme body of justice was the people's jury (dicastery). According to the rules, conflicts in trade were to be resolved not by force, but based on commercial law and taking into account concluded contracts. At the same time, the power of popular assemblies was formally unlimited, so Athenian democracy was subject to the arbitrariness of the mob, a famous example of which was the death sentence of Socrates. At the same time, the ancient Greek philosopher Aristotle consistently defended the idea that the state should be "the rule of laws, and not of people" (Aristotle):

Correct legislation should be the supreme authority, and officials - whether one or more - should be decided only in cases where the laws are not able to give an exact answer (Aristotle).

Roman law was created primarily to protect the interests of landowners, however, compared with Athenian democracy, the idea of limiting the arbitrariness of the executive and legislative powers were more pronounced. During the period of the republic, a strong and independent judiciary was created and the equality of citizens before the law was ensured, although legal guarantees did not extend to slaves and non-citizens. Information about laws and judicial procedures was made available to the public. Laws changed according to the evolution of customs. After the transition from a republic to an empire, the emperor became the head of state with virtually unlimited power. At the same time, the Code of Justinian, containing many procedures and rules, reflected the view that it was the right and not the arbitrary will of the emperor, that was the proper way to resolve conflicts (Gudushauri, 2010).

After the fall of Byzantium, Roman law was received and partially included in the legislation of the Holy Roman Empire. In the Middle Ages, economic and social relationships, as a rule, took the form of written laws or contracts. Along with secular legal customs, religious law played a significant role in limiting the arbitrariness of power. According to Christianity (as well as other monotheistic religions), God is the sole ruler of the universe, and His laws are equally binding on every person. From this, Thomas Aquinas concluded that legality is a natural order (Mkurnalidze, 2000). The Roman Catholic Church took an active part in determining the duties, functions, and jurisdictions of power. The legitimacy of the state structure depended on how it was perceived as consistent with religious prescriptions and local traditions. A significant role in the development of the law was played by the unification and codification of legal institutions carried out by the popes in the 11th-13th centuries, as well as the proclamation by Pope Gregory VII of the supremacy of canon law over royal power and his order on the teaching of law in universities. Papal reforms gave rise to the first model of the Western state of modern times, the peculiarity of which was that it was governed by law (Mkurnalizde, 2000).

Similar processes took place in other regions. Thus, in the Arab Caliphate, legal norms based on the requirements of Islam became part of Sharia, and in several Muslim countries, Sharia courts still coexist with secular ones. However, according to many modern jurists, church courts are not effective enough in ensuring the rule of law and protecting citizens from arbitrary power. Their dependence on the interpretation of religious texts and the political interests of the church leads to abuses when courts punish disloyalty to the authorities, do not ensure equality before the law, legitimize discrimination against religious minorities, and do not give defendants an adequate opportunity to defend themselves in court (Chitadze, 2016).

An example of successful legal regulation of the supreme power was the English Magna Carta of 1215. This law for the first time established the limits of the power of the king over his subjects, forbidding the introduction of new taxes without the consent of Parliament and obliging to impose penalties related to the restriction of civil rights, exclusively by jury. Four centuries later, the 1610 petition of the House of Commons to King James I referred to the rule of law as a traditional right of English subjects (De Bracton, 2016).

Separate principles of the rule of law (separation of powers, the rule of law) took place in the Statute of the Grand Duchy of Lithuania (1588). The author and active participant in the publication of the Statute, Chancellor Lev Sapieha, believed that not people, but laws should rule in the state. The statute also divided state power into legislative, executive, and judicial (Papashvili, 2010).

During the period of absolutism, legal methods prevailed in the state administration of the countries of Western Europe. In this, the Western absolute monarchies differed significantly from the feudal regimes in other countries, in particular, from the Russian autocracy.

After the Renaissance and the Reformation, the role of the church declined, and the importance of rational justifications for the principles of state organization increased. An important historical role was played by the arguments that laid the foundations of natural law.

According to Thomas Hobbes, people's fear of other people makes them seek the protection of the state, whose laws they agree to obey. When everyone is equal before the law, the basis for fear of fellow citizens disappears (Heywood, 2021). However, as John Locke pointed out, the state itself can also cause fear. Therefore, it is necessary that the state not only has power but keeps it within certain limits to prevent arbitrariness. The solution to this problem known to Locke was the requirement that rulers govern utilizing enforceable laws and themselves observe them (Khamkhadze, 2000). According to this argument, in the absence of the rule of law, citizens are not protected from gun violence, and rivals within the ruling class have no leverage of mutual control. Locke also believed that just laws should recognize the natural rights of man and that they should not restrict, but protect freedom.

Reflecting on the ways of implementing legality, Montesquieu, in his book On the Spirit of Laws, concluded that it is necessary to separate powers, without which it is impossible to guarantee the impartiality of the courts, and there is a high risk of legitimizing tyranny (Heywood, 2002).

Immanuel Kant believed that the goal of the state should be to ensure a peaceful happy life for its citizens, subject to guarantees of their property rights. Therefore, it should not make laws that are contrary to public ideas about morality, and these ideas should form the basis of the constitution. According to the categorical imperative, any moral principle can be given the form of a universal law that obliges all people to certain decisions, regardless of the expected result. Therefore, for the policy pursued to be moral, the state must obey the relevant legal laws and should not adjust them to its policy. Kant believed that the only stable state system is one in which the law is "autocratic" and does not depend on any individual. If the legislative power belongs to the people, the executive power is subordinate to the legislative, and the judicial power is appointed by the executive, then the balance of powers is ensured, and not just their separation (Chitadze, 2011).

Developing Kant's theory, in 1832-1833 Robert von Mol popularized the term "rule of law" (German: Rechtsstaat). Among other prominent representatives of this trend were Karl Welker, Otto Baer, Friedrich Stahl, Rudolf Gneist, Christoph von Siegwart, Lorenz von Stein, Georg Jellinek (Chitadze, 2016).

These ideas are reflected in regulatory documents that guarantee the protection of personal freedoms of citizens or subjects from arbitrary power, among which are the British Bill of Rights of 1689, the US Declaration of Independence and the US Bill of Rights, the French Declaration of the Rights of Man and Citizen deserve mention. These documents not only forbade the state to encroach on inalienable freedoms but also recognized the obligation of the state to ensure several positive freedoms, including the right to have a case heard and to be defended against charges in court. They also contributed to increasing the independence of the courts from the executive and legislative branches of government. As a result, the first constitutional regimes appeared in modern times, in which the activities of the supreme authorities were regulated by higher laws (such as the constitution or statutes) or by decisions of the supreme courts. By the middle of the 19th century, legality was included in the list of the most important political values of most Western countries (Chitadze, 2016).

An essential feature of constitutional regimes in comparison with previous forms of government is the presence of a rational standard for the legitimacy of the actions of power. The standard covers the legal procedures for the formation of power, the rules for the exercise of power, and the process of changing these rules.

In many implementations, one of the highest courts is involved in assessing the legitimacy of legislation, government decisions, and decisions made in referendums, as well as interpreting higher laws. Such an instance is endowed with a high degree of independence, although the process of its formation leaves the possibility for other authorities or direct citizens to exert some influence on it. Failure to comply with the rulings of the supreme or constitutional court may indicate insufficient measures to ensure the rule of law.

The existence of written constitutions in itself did not always allow regimes to be characterized as constitutional. Although Hitler never formally repealed the constitution of the Weimar Republic, he took advantage of the country's state of emergency to suspend guarantees of civil liberties, rule in the absence of parliament, and further arbitrarily change the procedures and institutions of power. Written constitutions also formally existed in the USSR, but they were not laws of direct action, and therefore did not reflect the real rules of decision-making in the state, many of the rights proclaimed in the constitution were not enshrined in laws issued in pursuance of the constitution, were not supported by state and social institutions, resolutions of the Plenum of the Supreme Court of the USSR, which served as a guideline for judicial practice. This, in particular, concerns civil and political rights and freedoms not related to socio-economic rights. By the principle of party membership in the activities of the judicial and law enforcement agencies of the USSR, in the selection and placement of leading personnel in the system of judicial and law enforcement agencies, and all other state bodies, under the control of the Department of Administrative Bodies of the Central Committee of the CPSU of law enforcement and judicial agencies, starting with the Supreme Court of the USSR, the highest authority in practice, they did not have laws, but decisions of higher party instances. The USSR was not a legal state (Papashvili, 2010).

On the other hand, the absence of a written constitution and a constitutional court in Great Britain did not prevent the construction of a rule of law state in it. As the 17th-century English jurist Edward Cock noted, when a normative act of Parliament is contrary to common sense or impracticable, the court has the right to refuse to see the grounds for its application. A high degree of agreement among rivals within the ruling classes regarding the norms of political behavior played an essential role (Shubitidze, 2010). This allowed the Parliament to only gradually make changes in the principles of government and stop their rare violations.

In post-war Japan, one of the foundations of the rule of law was effective informal mechanisms for resolving civil law conflicts, in the creation of which the state took an active part. Efficiency owed much to professionalism and low levels of corruption in the bureaucracy. The most qualified officials and judges developed clear principles and procedures. Government agencies, police, insurance companies, and community organizations provided free consultations (Heywood, 2021). This allowed the parties to the conflict to predict the potential outcome of the case in court and even calculate the amount of compensation. For this reason, civil lawsuits were extremely rare.

In the second half of the 20th century, the importance of international, labor, and other branches of law increased. The concept of the welfare state was reflected in the post-war constitutions of many countries. Adopted in 1948, the Universal Declaration of Human Rights and the Convention on the Prevention and Punishment of the Crime of Genocide for the first time formulated the international principles of the rule of law, which include the obligation of governments to observe the norms common to the whole world and the right of the international community to intervene in the internal affairs of a state to prevent genocide (UN, 2005). Subsequently, several international courts have been established to provide justice in this area, such as the International Criminal Court and the European Court of Human Rights (UN, 2005).

Conceptual Difficulties

The task of protecting public ideas about justice (for the implementation of which separate institutions can even be established, for example, a jury trial) is complicated by the vagueness and diversity of these ideas. Making a judgment based on common sense contradicts the requirement of clear normative certainty in a state governed by the rule of law.

In a state governed by the rule of law, courts should not allow arbitrariness in the interpretation of laws and make decisions according to personal views. Some legal scholars believe that any judicial decisions inevitably reflect the personal inclinations of judges. Other jurists argue that most laws can be interpreted neutrally, even if different judges offer different interpretations. Judges must always be prepared to impartially examine alternative readings of legal principles.

According to the standards of the rule of law, it must respect the subjects of law as carriers of their understanding of the norms that society must follow. This leads to disagreement in court, when one side insists on a literal reading of the law, while the other considers its interpretation to be better aligned with the system of law as a whole, with the spirit of the law. Such disagreements can adversely affect the certainty of legal norms. The contradictions between various social ideals are also reflected in the system of law. The resolution of these contradictions leads to the predominance of some values or a compromise, but in any case to some discrepancy between the preferences of some citizens and the requirements of the law.

Ensuring the independence of the law enforcement system is a difficult task. For example, in the United States, the appointment of federal judges is one of the main functions of the upper house of the US Congress, while in many states regional judges are elected by popular vote. The positions of state attorneys and heads of district law enforcement agencies (sheriffs) are also elected.

However, the ideological views of all these officials play a role at one stage or another in the selection of candidates.

Although the complete absence of legal restrictions on arbitrary power jeopardizes the ability of society to protect its values, the optimal degree of severity of such restrictions is the subject of debate. In several situations, a decision based on personal knowledge and experience, or a decision taking into account specific circumstances, may be more effective or fairer than a decision made in strict accordance with legal norms and procedures. In addition, the judiciary is also characterized by arbitrariness, which can manifest itself in the manipulation of rules, incompetent decisions, ignoring the spirit of the law.

Strict adherence to statutory decision-making procedures sometimes contributes to the uncertainty of the outcome. In some cases, this can play a positive role, such as in the process of democratic elections. In other cases, this may negatively affect the sense of predictability regarding the actions of others and therefore lead to excessive self-limitation of personal freedom.

Excessive detail and rigidity of the basic laws, combined with the difficulty of changing these laws, can lead to political stagnation, and further a crisis. Rule-of-law states experience the least of these difficulties, either without written constitutions or with relatively short constitutions that focus on the procedure (rather than content), whose substantive prescriptions are general, and whose rules are consistent with the political experience of the population. In such States, consistency of procedure is combined with the flexibility of administration.

Some constitutions not only describe the structure of the state but also formulate social ideals. The discrepancy between the formal prescriptions of the constitution and the practical possibilities of the government may call into question the authority of the supreme laws of the land.

Criticism and Value of the Rule of Law

One of the common arguments against the rule of law was the assertion that if the power belongs to the "right" people, then there is no need to limit or oblige them to do anything. This point of view was held, in particular, by one of the founders of utilitarianism, Jeremy Bentham. Anarchists deny the ability of any state institution to significantly limit the power of those who wield it (Heywood, 2013).

According to Karl Marx and other leftist ideologues, in a capitalist society, laws serve exclusively the interests of the bourgeoisie, therefore the rule of law is necessary as a guarantor of these interests (trade, industry, banking, etc.). Some modern Marxists do not agree with such assessments. The main focus of legality is legal procedures, and therefore it can be the foundation for development both in the direction of a market economy and in the direction of a welfare state (Heywood, 2021).

At the same time, the lower classes often have limited access to legal institutions, which leads to deviations from the ideal of equality.

Supporters of technocracy, beginning with Saint-Simonism, believe that government should be carried out by the most competent specialists in their field, who do not dictate their will or obey a higher will but are guided by scientific principles. With the disappearance of the arbitrariness of power, the need for the rule of law, which is replaced by the rule of knowledge, also disappears.

Procedural justice is the subject of criticism when courts acquit rather obvious criminal offenders due to violation of formal requirements by the investigation. On the other hand, non-compliance with established procedures opens up wide opportunities for arbitrariness, so it becomes fundamentally impossible to guarantee the fairness of the trial. This, in turn, hurts the predictability of the legal consequences of one's own and others' actions, which affects all aspects of socio-economic life.

John Rawls, Friedrich von Hayek, and other philosophers believed that the rule of law provided important information to people who did not know each other about mutual obligations, ways of cooperation, a basis for legitimate expectations, and a sense of certainty (Chitadze, 2016). This facilitates the adoption of important decisions for them and long-term planning, which significantly increases the efficiency of economic activity. On the other hand, the fact that laws can guide people's actions increases the demands on their moral content.

The perception of law as a public good that promotes mutually beneficial cooperation links the rule of law to the concepts of citizenship and equality. Therefore, those political regimes in which these categories have value are best combined with the rule of law.

Legitimacy not only limits the arbitrariness of power but also stimulates the government to pursue a more rational, balanced, fair, and predictable policy. This contributes to the stability of the state and the authority of the authorities.

The existence of universally binding rules simplifies the process of decision-making, allows the weaker to make demands on the stronger without the risk of being accused of personal hostility, softens the feeling of humiliation when submitting to the demands of others.

In liberalism, the rule of law is one of the main values, since it ensures the protection of civil liberties, in particular the right to life, the right to private property, freedom of religion, and freedom of speech.

According to a wide range of jurists, historians, and political scientists, the predominance of legal methods in public administration played a significant role in the development of Western civilization. Many of them see the rule of law as the foundation of democracy, providing political rights, civil liberties, government accountability mechanisms, and, ultimately, political equality and a low level of abuse of power. One of the main differences between imitation democracy is the weakness of the rule of law so that individual authorities can repeal or circumvent the laws that regulate the powers of these bodies. This, in particular, opens up opportunities for manipulation of the justice system and the media to reward those loyal to the regime and punish the opposition without regard to legal procedures. Unlimited direct democracy also carries the risk of making emotional decisions at the expense of long-term interests.

Law and Order

The legal order is a state of social relations in which compliance with the law and other legal norms is ensured, one of the components of public order. This is the state of the actual regulation of social ties, a qualitative expression of legality.

The rule of law is characterized by the level of legality in the state and the degree of realization of the rights and freedoms of man and citizen, as well as the fulfillment by them and state bodies of the duties assigned by law.

The main features of the rule of law are:

- it's regulated by legal norms
- the real embodiment of the content of these norms in life, the settlement of social relations on their basis
- guaranteed by the state.

The main principles of law and order are:

- legitimacy
- constitutionality
- integrity
- structural
- hierarchy
- normativity
- Justice
- accountability
- simplicity
- warranty (Chitadze, 2016).

Structure

The structure of the rule of law is:

- legal organization of society (laws and state bodies legitimized by them, as well as non-state entities and citizens);

- legal relations and connections in society;
- as well as a certain (normative) orderliness of these legal relations and connections (a clear definition of the status of participants in legal relations, their subjective rights, and legal obligations, powers).

Law and order can be classified by territorial scope (law and order in a state, city, etc.), as well as by branches of law and legal scope (constitutional, administrative, financial, etc.).

Signs

The following signs of law and order are distinguished:

- Certainty. The rule of law is based on formally defined legal prescriptions.
- Consistency. The rule of law is a system of relations based on a single essence of law, a dominant form of ownership, a system of economic relations and is provided by the power of single state power.
- Organization. The rule of law arises from the organizing activities of the state and its bodies.
- State guarantee. The existing legal order is provided by the state, protected by it from violations.
- Sustainability. Arising based on law and ensured by the state, the rule of law is quite stable and sustainable.
- Unity. Based on unified political and legal principles, ensured by the unity of the state will and legality, the rule of law is one throughout the country. All its components are equally guaranteed by the state, any violations of it are considered offenses and are suppressed by state coercion.

In 1979, the UN General Assembly adopted the Code of Conduct for Law Enforcement Officials (Karumidze, 2003).

Legitimacy

Legitimacy (from lat. legitimus “consistent with the laws, legal, lawful”) - the consent of the people with the government, its voluntary recognition of its right to make binding decisions. The lower the level of legitimacy, the more often the authorities will rely on coercion.

In-game theory, a legitimate action is an action that is not disputed by any of the “players” who have the right and opportunity to challenge this action. An action ceases to be legitimate when the subject of the action has to make special efforts to protect his right to act as he did.

In political science, legitimacy is a political and legal concept that means a positive attitude of the inhabitants of a country or state, large groups, public opinion (including foreign) to the institutions of power operating in a particular state or country, recognition of their legitimacy.

The process of legitimation is the process of public recognition of the actions of the authorities or a political leader.

With the loss of people’s trust, there is a delegitimation of power, the extreme form of which is a crisis of legitimacy. This situation can be caused by the conflict of interests of the people and the political elite, conflicts between the branches of government, the growing threat of nationalism, etc.

Political Legitimacy

Regarding political legitimacy, the well-known English political scientist David Beetham developed a "normative structure of political legitimacy" outlined in the work "Legitimation of Power":

1. power corresponds to the rules accepted or established in society;
2. these rules are justified by reference to the faith shared by the ruled and the rulers;
3. there is evidence of an agreement to existing power relationships (Beetham, 2017).

Legitimacy is originally the same as legality. In political science, legitimacy is the recognition of power by the population, and legality is legality, compliance with legal norms (law or by-laws).

Relationship Between Legitimacy and Legality

The term "legitimacy" arose at the beginning of the 19th century and expressed the desire to restore the power of the king in France as the only legal one, in contrast to the power of the usurper. At the same time, this word acquired another meaning - the recognition of this state's power and territory of the state at the international level. The demand for the legitimacy of power arose as a reaction against the violent change of power and the redrawing of state borders, against arbitrariness and ochlocracy (Aleksidze, 2016).

Legitimacy means the recognition by the population of this power, its right to govern. Legitimate power is accepted by the masses, not just imposed on them. The masses agree to submit to such power, considering it fair, authoritative, and the existing order is the best for the country. Of course, in society, there are always citizens who violate the laws, who do not agree with a given political course, who do not support the authorities. The legitimacy of power means that it is supported by the majority, that the laws are implemented by the main part of society.

The legitimacy of power should not be confused with the concept of the legality of power, which also exists in political science.

The legality of power is its legal justification, legality, its compliance with the legal norms existing in the state. Legitimacy, unlike legality, is not a legal fact, but a socio-psychological phenomenon. Any government that issues laws, even unpopular ones, but ensures their implementation, is legal, but it may be illegitimate, that is, not recognized by the people.

In society, there may also be illegal power, for example, the mafia, which can be perceived by the people (or part of it) as legitimate or illegitimate.

Legitimacy is the trust and acceptance of power by the public consciousness, the justification of its actions, it is associated with a moral assessment. Citizens approve of the government based on their moral criteria, ideas about goodness, justice, decency, conscience. Legitimacy is designed to ensure obedience, consent without coercion, and if it is not achieved, then justify coercion, the use of force. Legitimate power and politics are authoritative and effective.

To win and retain legitimacy, the trust of the people, the government resorts to arguing its actions (legitimation), referring to the highest values (justice, truth), to history, feelings and emotions, moods, the real or fictitious will of the people, the dictates of the times, scientific and technical progress, the requirements of production, the historical tasks of the country, etc. Violence and repression are often justified by dividing people into "us" and "them".

Principles of legitimacy (belief) may have their origins in ancient traditions, revolutionary charisma, or current legislation. The corresponding typology of legitimacy, which is widely accepted, was introduced by Max Weber. According to him, the three types of legitimacy correspond to the three sources of legitimacy of political power: tradition, charisma, and rational-legal basis. Weber emphasized that we are not talking about attributing any real regime to one of the types, but about abstractions (the so-called "ideal types") that are combined in specific political systems in one proportion or another (Rondeli, 2003).

Depending on which of the listed motives for supporting the political normative order by the population prevails in society, it is customary to distinguish the following types of legitimacy: traditional, charismatic, and rational.

- traditional legitimacy, is formed based on people's belief in the necessity and inevitability of submission to power, which in society (group) receives the status of tradition, custom, the habit of obedience to certain individuals or political institutions. This kind of legitimacy is especially common in the hereditary type of government, in particular, in monarchical states. A long habit of justifying this or that form of government creates the effect of its justice and legitimacy, which gives power high stability and stability;
- rational (democratic) legitimacy arising from people's recognition of the justice of those rational and democratic procedures based on which the system of power is formed. This type of support is formed due to a person's understanding of the presence of third-party interests, which implies the need to develop rules of general behavior, which creates an opportunity for the realization of his own goals. In other words, the rational type of legitimacy has, in fact, a normative basis characteristic of the organization of power in complexly organized societies.
- charismatic legitimacy, emerging as a result of people's belief in the outstanding qualities of a political leader they recognize. This image of an infallible person endowed with exceptional qualities (charisma) is transferred by public opinion to the entire system of power. Unconditionally believing in all the actions and plans of a charismatic leader, people uncritically perceive the style and methods of his rule. The emotional enthusiasm of the population, which forms this highest authority, most often occurs during a period of revolutionary change, when the social orders and ideals familiar to a person are collapsing and people cannot rely either on former norms and values or on the still-emerging rules of the political game. Therefore, the leader's charisma embodies the faith and hope of people for a better future in troubled times. But such unconditional support of the ruler by the population often turns into Caesarism and a cult of personality.

Measuring the Level of the Rule of Law

The World Justice Project publishes an annual index of the countries of the world, which includes 8 indicators: limiting the power of the state, the absence of corruption, order and security, fundamental rights, open government, law enforcement, civil justice, and criminal justice. In 2012, the Scandinavian countries, Finland, the Netherlands, and New Zealand took the top positions in the ranking in almost all indicators (Sweden scored 7.12 out of 8 possible points) (Chitadze, 2016).

Economic Role

The rule of law is a necessary condition for sustainable economic growth. According to the American economist, Nobel laureate Joseph Stiglitz, every American company benefits from the rule of law, infrastructure, and technologies that have been created for centuries. Stiglitz writes (addressing US citizens): "Try asking yourself: what would I achieve if my parents lived in a remote village in Papua New Guinea or the Congo?" (Chitadze, 2017).

CONCLUSION

Based on the above-mentioned concepts in the text, in general, the Rule of Law according to the Oxford English Dictionary is defined as "the power and influence of law in society, especially when it is considered a restriction on individual or institutional action; According to this principle, all members of society (including the government) are considered equal subjects of the legal code and processes. "The term rule of law is closely related to both constitutionalism and the rule of law, and it refers to the political situation and not to any particular legal law (Aleksidze, 2016).

The term was already used in 16th-century Britain, and in the same century Scottish theologian, Samuel Rutherford used it to argue against the divine rights of kings. John Locke wrote that freedom in society means obedience only to the laws which the legislature makes and to which all obey. On the other hand, the individual is free from both state and private restrictions. The "Rule of Law" was later propagated in the 19th century by the British lawyer Albert Van Dyce (Aleksidze, 2016).

According to the rule of law, all people are subject to the law, including legislators, law enforcement, and judges. In this sense, he opposes tyranny or oligarchy, where rulers stand above the law. Lack of the rule of law can be found in both democracies and monarchies where laws are not taken into account. The rule of law is at stake where the government does not have the appropriate corrective mechanism to restore it.

REFERENCES

Aleksidze. (2016). *Dictionary of International Law*. Tbilisi State University.

Annan, K. (2004). *Creation of a common conceptual apparatus in the field of justice for the United Nations. The rule of law and transitional justice in conflict and post-conflict societies*. Report of the Secretary General. United Nations. Retrieved from: https://historyofeconomicthought.mcmaster.ca/aristotle/Politics.pdf

Aquinas, T. (2010). *The Theology Sum. Part II-I. Questions 90-114. K.* Nika-Center.

Baili. (2020). *England and Wales High Court (King's Bench Division) Decisions*. Retrieved from: http://www.bailii.org/ew/cases/EWHC/KB/1607/J23.html

Bevir, M. (2014). *The Encyclopedia of Political Theory*. Wayback Machine.

Bieliński, J. (2017). *Political Legitimacy and Normative Disorientation in European Liberal Democracies.* Retrieved from: https://www.jstor.org/stable/26383075

Bracton. (2016). *On the Laws and Customs of England.* Wayback Machine.

Chitadze. (2011). *Geopolitics.* Universali.

Chitadze. (2016). *Political Sciences.* International Black Sea University.

Chitadze. (2017). *World Geography. Political, Economic and Demographic Dimensions.* Scholars Press.

Cicero, M. T. (n.d.). *Speech in defense of Aulus Cluentius Gabit.* LIII, 146. Archived July 26, 2014 at the Wayback Machine

Constitutions Rights Foundation. (2010). *Plato and Aristotle on Tyranny and the Rule of Law.* Retrieved from: https://www.crf-usa.org/bill-of-rights-in-action/bria-26-1-plato-and-aristotle-on-tyranny-and-the-rule-of-law.html

Grote, R. (1999). Rule of Law, Rechtsstaat and "Etat de droit". In Constitutionalism, Universalism and Democracy: A Comparative Analysis. Nomos Publishers.

Guo, X. (2014). *The Ideal Chinese Political Leader: A Historical and Cultural Perspective.* Wayback Machine.

Held, D. (2000). *Models of Democracy.* Polity Press.

Heuschling, L. (2002). *État de droit, Rechtsstaat. Rule of Law.* Dalloz.

Heywood. (2013). *Politics.* Palgrave Foundations.

Heywood. (2021). *Political ideologies. An introduction.* Bloomsbury.

History. (2009). *Code of Hammurabi.* Retrieved from: https://www.history.com/topics/ancient-history/hammurabi#:~:text=The%20Hammurabi%20code%20of%20laws,and%20finally%20rediscovered%20in%201901

Institute of History and International Relations. (2013). *Arab Spring.* Retrieved from: http://history.kemsu.ru/oldversion/ISV/Vasutin/POZD/source/361.htm

Jewish Encyclopedia. (n.d.). *Moses.* Retrieved from: https://www.jewishencyclopedia.com/articles/11049-moses

Jurgens, E. (2013). *The principle of the Rule of Law.* Wayback Machine / Council of Europe Parliamentary Assembly.

Kazakov, M. (2016). *The Christian Church and the Roman Empire in the 4th century.* Wayback Machine.

Krasheninnikova, N.A. (2002). *Magna Carta of 1215 (modern interpretation).* Moscow University.

Munro, D. (2014). *The Concept of Man in Early China.* Wayback Machine.

Rondeli, A. (2003). *International Relations.* Nekeri.

Shubitidze, V., Papashvili, M., Gudushauri, N., & Kveseleva, I. (2010). *Political Sciences*. Georgian Technical University.

UK Parliament. (2022). *Bill of rights 1689*. Retrieved from: https://www.parliament.uk/about/living-heritage/evolutionofparliament/parliamentaryauthority/revolution/collections1/collections-glorious-revolution/billofrights/

Xiangming, Z. (2017). *On Two Ancient Chinese Administrative Ideas: Rule of Virtue and Rule by Law*. Wayback Machine.

KEY TERMS AND DEFINITIONS

Civil Society: A community that embraces shared norms and ethical standards to collectively manage problems without coercion and through peaceful and democratic procedures for decision making aimed at improving human welfare.

Constitutional Democracy: Government processes that allow people, through their elected representatives, to exercise power and influence the state's policies.

Democracy: A form of government in which the people have the authority to deliberate and decide legislation ("direct democracy"), or to choose governing officials to do so ("representative democracy"). Who is considered part of "the people" and how authority is shared among or delegated by the people has changed over time and at different rates in different countries, but over time more and more of a democratic country's inhabitants have generally been included. Cornerstones of democracy include freedom of assembly, association and speech, inclusiveness and equality, citizenship, consent of the governed, voting rights, freedom from unwarranted governmental deprivation of the right to life and liberty, and minority rights.

Equality Before the Law: Also known as equality under the law, equality in the eyes of the law, legal equality, or legal egalitarianism, is the principle that all people must be equally protected by the law.

European Convention on Human Rights (ECHR; Formally the Convention for the Protection of Human Rights and Fundamental Freedoms): An international convention to protect human rights and political freedoms in Europe.

Human Rights: The political rights and civil liberties recognized by the international community as inalienable and valid for individuals in all countries by virtue of their humanity.

International Human Rights Law (IHRL): The body of international law designed to promote human rights on social, regional, and domestic levels.

Legal Rights: Those rights bestowed onto a person by a given legal system (they can be modified, repealed, and restrained by human laws). The concept of positive law is related to the concept of legal rights.

Legality: In respect of an act, agreement, or contract is the state of being consistent with the law or of being lawful or unlawful in a given jurisdiction, and the construct of power. According to the Merriam-Webster Dictionary, legality is 1: attachment to or observance of law. 2: the quality or state of being legal.

Legitimacy: Conformity to the law or to rules; ability to be defended with logic or justification; validity.

Natural Rights: Those rights that are not dependent on the laws or customs of any particular culture or government, and so are *universal*, *fundamental* and *inalienable* (they cannot be repealed by human laws, though one can forfeit their enjoyment through one's actions, such as by violating someone else's rights). Natural law is the law of natural rights.

Office of the United Nations High Commissioner for Human Rights: Commonly known as the Office of the High Commissioner for Human Rights (OHCHR) or the United Nations Human Rights Office, is a department of the Secretariat of the United Nations that works to promote and protect human rights that are guaranteed under international law and stipulated in the Universal Declaration of Human Rights of 1948. The office was established by the United Nations General Assembly on 20 December 1993[3] in the wake of the 1993 World Conference on Human Rights.

Political Tolerance: Means accepting and respecting the basic rights and civil liberties of persons and groups whose viewpoints differ from one's own. All citizens, including political leaders, have a responsibility to practise political tolerance in their words and actions. As a clear rejection of "might makes right," political tolerance is a key principle of democracy.

Rule of Law: The political philosophy that all citizens and institutions within a country, state, or community are accountable to the same laws.

UN Human Rights Council: Created in 2005, has a mandate to investigate alleged human rights violations.

Universal Declaration of Human Rights (UDHR): An international document adopted by the United Nations General Assembly that enshrines the rights and freedoms of all human beings. Drafted by a UN committee chaired by Eleanor Roosevelt, it was accepted by the General Assembly as Resolution 217 during its third session on 10 December 1948 at the Palais de Chaillot in Paris, France.

Chapter 13
International Humanitarian Law:
Protection of Human Rights During Armed Conflicts

Mary Tseruashvili
The Center for International Studies, Georgia

ABSTRACT

The purpose of this chapter is to analyze the international humanitarian law and its effectiveness in contemporary conflicts. In particular, it focuses on the analysis of the challenges that international humanitarian law faces in contemporary international or non-international armed hostilities. While the ongoing progress in the modern world offers new challenges, the issue of the effectiveness of humanitarian law becomes controversial. Therefore, the chapter presents an academic paper, and it is based on the analysis of the various articles, reports, analytical papers, and case studies, depending on which it became possible to answer the main research question and to demonstrate the effectiveness of international humanitarian law enforcement mechanisms in modern conflicts.

INTRODUCTION

Despite the changes of time, the current progressive events in the modern world, and the increase in interstate cooperation, war, and armed conflicts are still used as one of the main means of achieving the goal and pursuing personal interests by states. Unfortunately, the consequences of the war affect most of the innocent population. Even in today's world, the rate of deaths of civilians as a result of armed hostilities, the number of people forced to leave their homes, and the need for humanitarian assistance are constantly growing. It is evident that, based on the perception of the seriousness of the damage caused by the war, the foundation was laid for the creation of international humanitarian law. Nevertheless, the current technological or other changes in the modern world create new challenges and even give armed conflicts a different direction.

Changes like armed conflicts, terrorism, and the protection of the principles of international humanitarian law by states are the main topics on which this chapter is based and aims to answer the main research question: How effective is International Humanitarian Law in modern conflicts. The chapter

DOI: 10.4018/978-1-6684-4543-3.ch013

offers qualitative research and it is based on the analysis of various articles, reports, analytical papers, and case studies.

To answer the research question, this chapter begins by analyzing the reasons for the establishment of international humanitarian law and discusses all the conventions on which it was founded. It then focuses on its sources, principles, and actors, and to better understand the essence and specificity of international humanitarian law, it is compared to international human rights. The chapter also focuses on the mechanisms of enforcement of international humanitarian law and at the same time discusses the challenges that may become a precondition for its ineffectiveness. Moreover, to determine its resilience to modern challenges, terrorism and the effectiveness of international humanitarian law concerning terrorist acts are also discussed. Finally, to outline how the principles of international humanitarian law are being neglected and modified by specific states, the Nagorno-Karabakh war 2020 and the relations of the Russian Federation with Georgia and Ukraine have been discussed as case studies.

The Emergence of International Humanitarian Law: Conventions

It is well known that the war between states and the threat of war, in general, presents a prohibited act according to the Charter of the United Nations, although the interstate differences and the conflict of interests still create grounds for tension and confrontation. While the war is considered forbidden and states continue to use it as a means of pursuing personal interests, the idea of the creation and existence of International Humanitarian Law is called in being questioned (Gasser, 1993).

International humanitarian law is a set of legal laws, the main purpose of which is to set the minimum standards in armed conflict that all parties to the war must comply with. At the same time, international humanitarian law focuses on protecting the rights of people who are not directly involved in armed conflict (Melzer, 2016). The idea of its creation is linked to the name of Henry Dunant. More specifically, the creation of international humanitarian law was preceded by the foundation of the International Committee of the Red Cross thus initiated by Henry Dunant, whose primary purpose was to help soldiers wounded in the war. Subsequently, based on Dunant's second initiative, international humanitarian law was created, the main purpose of which was to bring about positive changes by joint efforts, which could not be implemented by individual states or international organizations separately (Gasser, 1993).

Everything started with the first treaty on the protection of military victims of warfare which was signed in 1864 in Geneva by Henry Dunant and all states of that time. Later in 1899, in Hague, changes were made in terms of expanding international protection. Based on this decision, international protection also affected naval combatants wounded in the war. Moreover, the practice of captive protection was introduced when 129 prisoners were brought under the protection of Geneva law (Gasser, 1993).

The next and most important stage in the development of international humanitarian law was the 4 Geneva Conventions, adopted in 1949, which categorized the protection of specific categories of persons. The sum of these conventions is represented as the "Geneva Rule", but it is still in force and accepted by all states in the world.

- First Convention: on the care of the wounded and sick members of armed forces in the field;
- Second Convention: on the care of the wounded, sick and shipwrecked members of armed forces at sea;
- Third Convention: on the treatment of prisoners of war;
- Fourth Convention: on the protection of civilian persons in time of war (Gasser, 1993).

- Although the Geneva Conventions have played a pivotal role in shaping international humanitarian law, their effectiveness in protecting human rights in the course of non-international conflicts has been criticized and it became clear that the implementation of international humanitarian law in civil wars seemed impossible based on existing conventions (Melzer, 2016). The following factor, challenges in combat equipment caused by technological development and the new needs related to it in terms of protection of civilians have contributed to new changes in International Humanitarian Law. Therefore, Protocols Additional to Geneva Conventions was adopted on 8 June 1977 (Gasser, 1993).

Sources, Principles, and Actors: International Human Rights Law vs. International Humanitarian Law

It is crucial to outline the sources, principles, and actors of International Humanitarian Law to determine its effectiveness, especially in contemporary conflicts. At the same time, it is interesting to see what distinguishes it from International Human Rights Law.

When it comes to analyzing the sources of International Humanitarian Law, it is essential to underline the similarities between International Human Rights Law and International Humanitarian Law. The legal basis for both comes from international treaties, but while the first envisions the protection of human rights in both peace and war, the second is entirely focused on the protection of human rights in armed conflicts (UN, 2011). Although the International Humanitarian Law by its very nature implies the protection of Human Rights during warfare, it is important to consider two main areas.

In international armed conflicts, International Humanitarian Law enters into force under the 1949 Geneva Conventions, their Additional Protocol 1, and weapon treaties as its main legal sources. However, when it comes to non-international conflicts, International Humanitarian Law still has less improved legal sources, as it is entirely dependent on Article 3, and Protocol II in some cases (Melzer, 2016). Given this information and the fact that most modern conflicts are non-international, the effectiveness of international humanitarian law seems to be in question.

Another distinction is made between International Human Rights Law and International Humanitarian Law when analyzing their principles. While the first focuses on the protection of universal human rights, regardless of gender, religion, or orientation, the second draws a line between the combatants and the civilians in armed conflicts (UN, 2011).

Even though International Humanitarian Law is based on the six major treaties with 600 articles and customary law rules, it is evident that its essence is expressed in only four major principles. The first principle is entirely focused on protecting the rights of people who are no longer involved in hostilities, and it emphasizes the need for humane treatment of them. The next principle focuses on the need for the humane treatment of captives. It highlights the necessity of a fair trial and the non-acceptance of all forms of violence. The third principle concerns the limitation of the use of armed methods by the parties involved in the war, and the last principle indicates the importance to separate the warring parties from the civilian population (Gasser, 1993).

Although the principles of international humanitarian law are universally accepted and recognized by all states, shortcomings in its concretization should not be overlooked. Since the creation of International Humanitarian Law, there have been several cases in which states have disregarded its principles. Consequently, these developments have once again raised the question of the effectiveness of international humanitarian law. Case studies and analysis have shown that the flexibility of the principles of international Humanitarian Law allows states to interpret it, often leading to their complete disregard (ICRC, 2007).

As International Human Rights Law, International Humanitarian Law is presented by two types of actors: primary and secondary actors. While the primary actors include states, the secondary implies all other non-state actors. Although international human rights law and international humanitarian law have differing views on the distribution of responsibilities to actors, both are mainly focused on the positive and negative obligations of so-called duty-bearers. "While the positive obligation implies to do something, negative obligation means to refrain from doing something" (UN, 2011).

As it was mentioned above, International Human Rights Law focuses on the protection of Human Rights regardless of gender, religion, orientation, or other characteristics. Therefore, any kind of obligation, positive or negative, falls directly on the states as the main subjects of the law. In the case of international humanitarian law, states are represented as major actors only if they represent the parties to the conflict (UN, 2011). It is clear that this situation makes states the main actors in international humanitarian law only in certain cases and therefore allows them to maneuver and interpret.

The practice of imposing obligations under international humanitarian law towards non-state actors was established after the development of two Additional Protocols in 1977 when the specificity of the enforcement of international humanitarian law in terms of involvement in non-international conflicts became apparent. International human rights law and international humanitarian law are generally similar to non-state actors. International humanitarian law explicitly shares the practice of punishing the perpetrators of genocide or crimes against humanity; however, despite the establishment of Customary International Law, there is still the main challenge related to International Humanitarian Law applicability in non-international conflicts (ICRC, 2007). While there is no official definition of non-international conflicts and non-state actors according to those mentioned in Additional Protocols and Common Article 3, the existence and effectiveness of an international humanitarian law enforcement mechanism are becoming controversial (UN, 2011).

As the non-state actors can be the group of individuals who are actively involved in armed conflicts and can deny or interpret the International Humanitarian Law principles, there is no effective mechanism that might be used to address this situation. Given the fact that the practice of International Humanitarian Law enforcement during non-international conflicts is less developed, it is evident that the observance of universally recognized and legally recognized principles is still based on the goodwill of the parties involved in the war (ICRC, 2007).

Implementation of International Humanitarian Law

An analysis of International Humanitarian Law revealed that it is a set of laws, which the main goal is to reduce the consequences of armed conflicts, protect the rights of the combatants directly involved in the warfare and the civilians most affected by the results of hostilities (Melzer, 2016). Despite the mentioned, it is interesting how these rules are transformed into actions.

Every state has an unequivocal obligation to adopt and implement measures for the implementation of humanitarian law. These measures can be taken by one or more state ministries, legislatures, courts, the armed forces, or other state bodies. Moreover, professional or educational bodies or other volunteer organizations may also be involved. Measures have also been taken at the international level to address violations of humanitarian law since the International fact-finding commission has been set up and nowadays, it is recommended that states use its service (ICRC, 2019).

Despite all of this, to promote the effectiveness of enforcement, taking appropriate measures not only at the international but also at the national level presents an inevitable solution. These actions are mainly related to raising public awareness of international humanitarian law, ensuring access to a fair trial, preventing war crimes, and so on (ICRC, 2019).

Moreover, it should be mentioned that the majority of the necessary measures require fundamental changes on the national level, which presents the main challenge in the application process of International Humanitarian Law. Based on the recommendations of the International Committee of the Red Cross, the solution in this situation is related to the constant communication between the states, for the promotion of which humanitarian law committees and similar bodies have been established (ICRC, 2019).

These above-mentioned measures of implementation are relevant when it comes to conflicts where the primary actors are the states. Accordingly, International Humanitarian Law enforcement mechanisms have a different dimension where the main actors are the non-state actors. All of this is directly related to the effectiveness of International Humanitarian Law in non-International conflicts.

Challenges in Implementation of International Humanitarian Law

While an international armed conflict manifests itself between the armed forces of two or more states, an international armed conflict implies a confrontation between organized armed groups. As a result, it becomes clear why the problem of modifying the legal norms of international humanitarian law arises in the course of non-international armed conflicts (Anand, 2017). Therefore, when it comes to analyzing the challenges in the implementation of International Humanitarian Law, it becomes evident that they are mainly related to non-international conflicts and the actors involved in them.

One of the main problems that may arise during the enforcement of International Humanitarian Law in non-international conflicts is related to the denial of the legal rule by the parties involved in the hostilities. While there is a chance that states may present civilian armed confrontation as merely a tension, international humanitarian law loses its effectiveness. Moreover, even in the event of an interstate conflict, one state may refuse to comply with laws that are also recognized by its rival state (ICRC, 2007).

This situation is directly related to the further problem that manifests itself in the lack of political will on the part of states to respect and implement the principles established by international humanitarian law at the national level. Even though legal laws are universally recognized and accepted by all nations, when it comes to following them, in most cases states prefer to interpret, modify or sometimes ignore them. The latter has become a special practice in non-international conflicts when the parties to the conflict grossly violate and ignore the obligations imposed by law. Even though the analysis and research of specific examples provide opportunities to increase the effectiveness of international humanitarian law, it is unfortunate that no groundbreaking changes have taken place in this direction (ICRC, 2007).

Due to technological development and the modern changes in methods of confrontation, the process of effective enforcement of International Humanitarian Law is significantly hampered, especially when it comes to non-international conflicts. Recent studies reveal that 80-90 percent of the victims in modern internal conflicts are civilians. While these hostilities are being waged by certain individuals, and group leaders, there is a need to further promote the principles of international humanitarian law. Despite the need for the obvious necessary changes in terms of increasing information about the International Humanitarian Law principles in society, the main problem is the specificity of the behavior of the group leaders, who recognize the violent solution of the conflict as the only and correct solution. Given the fact that there is no specific mechanism that would be appropriate and effective in this kind of situation, the value of International Humanitarian Law is becoming controversial (Klenner, 1999).

Although the role of the International Committee of the Red Cross and its support for training in International Humanitarian Law should not be left out of the spotlight. Over the years, there have been positive changes in the training of state army commanders. While the Red Cross recognizes the need to raise the awareness of warring parties in the protection of the innocent population, great resources and attention are paid to the training of soldiers and their involvement in sharing the importance of the principles of humanitarian law (Klenner, 1999).

The means of disseminating information are also increasing. Various educational tools are used to raise the awareness of soldiers, including seminars, as well as different audio, text, or video materials. There is no doubt that those developments give the illusion of further positive results, however, the slow pace of the process and the small number of "educated" soldiers leave the overall situation stable in terms of International Humanitarian Law effectiveness (Klenner, 1999). In addition, it is obvious that the modern world and current events create new challenges for International Humanitarian Law and rises the need for its systematic modification.

International Humanitarian Law and Terrorism

In discussing the effectiveness of international humanitarian law and the new challenges of the modern world, it is necessary to pay attention to terrorism and the approach of international humanitarian law to this. It is interesting to analyze which group of actors in international humanitarian law belong to terrorist groups and what mechanisms are in place to prevent their actions or to mitigate the consequences caused by terrorist acts.

Since the first group of actors in international humanitarian law unites the states, therefore terrorist groups should be non-state actors. Nevertheless, international humanitarian law focuses on armed groups, while the term "terrorist organizations" is used to refer to terrorism. Given this fact, it should be mentioned that when there is a discussion about armed forces as a warring party, it refers to all fighters who are directly involved in combat operations and therefore targeted. Meanwhile, the analysis of terrorist organizations offers a much different picture. While international humanitarian law focuses on the parties to the conflict, to whom it imposes sanctions if necessary, there is no specific explanation for the attitude towards members of these terrorist organizations. Members of terrorist organizations can be considered not only those who are directly involved in violent acts but also the sponsors of these organizations and other members who are not directly targeted during the confrontation. Given all this, there is no definition given by international humanitarian law that presents members of terrorist organizations as subject to the law and imposes an obligation on them to uphold the principles of law (Bartels, 2016).

At the same time, the geographical scope of the implementation of international humanitarian law in the fight against terrorism should not be overlooked. While terrorist groups do not have a single specific location and conflict can start in different places simultaneously, the issue of enforcing the principles of international law becomes controversial. Terrorist groups can be located in the territory of any one country and attack another state from that location. In this particular case, an attack by a state on a terrorist group is directly linked to an attack on the country in whose territory the terrorist group is located. This situation raises questions about the extent to which the rights of a third state are being violated, whether it is considered a party to the conflict, and whether international humanitarian law sanctions will be imposed on it in terms of the territorial provision of terrorist groups. The fact of the matter is that international humanitarian law fails to specify the conflict and the parties involved (Lubell, 2016).

While the conflict is fragmented and we are dealing with a multitude of conflict zones, it is difficult to apply the appropriate mechanisms and enforce international humanitarian law in general. When one state digs into the territory of another state without its consent, even in response to and suppression of violent actions by independent terrorist groups there, the situation is classified as an armed confrontation between the two states (Lubell, 2016). There is no doubt that this circumstance obscures the principles of international humanitarian law, especially in a force majeure situation, and as a result, makes its effectiveness even more controversial. Therefore, there is a need to modify the mechanisms of operation of international humanitarian law, the need for concretization, and the ability to constantly adapt to the types of modern conflict in non-international conflicts.

Another problem arising from the ambiguous relationship between international humanitarian law and terrorism is that states interpret the actions and justify their involvement in non-international conflicts. An example of this is the statements of the Supreme Court of the United States and the Supreme Court of Israel regarding the relations between these states and the terrorist group Al-Qaeda. It is a well-known fact that America's confrontation with Al Qaeda has always been viewed by the US government as a country involved in an international conflict. Nevertheless, the US Supreme Court has focused on the definition of non-international conflict and underlined the fact that international conflict is only an inter-state confrontation. Consequently, America's confrontation with a terrorist organization could not be perceived as an example of a confrontation between states (Milanovic, 2007).

On the other hand, a radically different position was taken by the Supreme Court of Israel. It was mentioned that, in some cases, even non-international conflicts may turn into international conflicts. Therefore, the Israeli Supreme Court shared the government's position that the country's confrontation with the terrorist organization Al-Qaeda was Israel's involvement in the international conflict (Milanovic, 2007). Based on these examples, it becomes clear that terrorism and its peculiarities pose a major challenge to the effectiveness of international law. When there are no written recommendations and means of action, states are allowed to interpret, which is often based on their interests.

Protection of Human Rights During the Nagorno-Karabakh War 2020

The conflict between Armenia and Azerbaijan can be considered as an example to illustrate how grossly International Humanitarian Law is violated by states. More specifically, to identify the effectiveness of International Humanitarian Law in modern times, it is important to consider recent developments and humanitarian law enforcement mechanisms in support of the war-affected population.

The basis of political tensions between Azerbaijan and Armenia dates back to 1991. The case concerns Nagorno-Karabakh and the interest of the parties in gaining full control over the region. The main cause of political tensions in the South Caucasus region was also the break-up of the Soviet Union, which became a precondition for the countries of the region to gain independence. The escalation of tensions between Armenia and Azerbaijan was also facilitated by Turkey's full support for Azerbaijan, which was also in its interest to promote the only Muslim state in the region. The aggravation of the situation and its escalation into the war led to the loss of more than 20,000 lives. At the same time, 750,000 Azerbaijanis and 300,000 Armenians were forced to flee their homes (Carney, 2020).

Although there were several confrontations between the national groups of Armenia and Azerbaijan, from 1994 to 2016 the situation in the region was under control. Officially the situation between the countries has worsened again since 2016, which was eventually followed by the 2020 war (Carney, 2020). Despite the urgency of the conflict, the question of which side is to blame, who started the war, and which has more grossly violated the principles of international humanitarian law should be ignored at this stage. It is essential to pay attention to the role of international humanitarian law in the course of the conflict and its mechanisms of action during the period of the end of the conflict.

The conflict in Nagorno-Karabakh began on September 27, 2020. Several weeks of armed conflict have claimed the lives of numerous people, including 140 innocent civilians and thousands of soldiers. It is important to mention that although the center of the conflict was the region, both sides also carried out military airstrikes against each other in various cities. At the same time, local infrastructure and homes were destroyed during the ongoing hostilities, forcing thousands of locals to flee their homes. The confrontation finally ended on November 9, when Russia intervened in the conflict as a mediator, and the parties signed a peace agreement based on which the conflict region would come under the control of Azerbaijan (IPHR, 2021).

Due to tensions in the region, even before the escalation of the conflict into war, the Red Cross was the only organization that could enter and moves directly into the area, although it should be noted that it has a limited representation. It is also worth noting that the Red Cross delegation had to leave Nagorno-Karabakh after the start of the war, and the effectiveness of its actions is a vague issue (caps, 2020). Based on these facts, there is no doubt that the principles of international humanitarian law have been grossly violated, manifested not only in the killing of innocent people or other indirect means of violence but also in the torture of numerous soldiers and the loss of their lives on both sides. Given all this, the dynamics of international humanitarian law are unclear and its direct or indirect effectiveness is becoming controversial.

The result of the war posed even greater challenges to International Humanitarian Law, one of which is the information gaps. There is currently no detailed information on the needs of the population remaining in Nagorno-Karabakh, and at the same time, there is no information on the whereabouts of people who have been forced to move and leave their homes. In addition to that, there is no specific information on whether ethnic Armenians can be returned to their homes in the Nagorno-Karabakh region (caps, 2020).

Despite the lack of information, the extreme hardships of the population trapped in the region are well known and need international attention. There are several problems related to the safety of the remaining population in the region, including lack of education, and social and economic well-being. Civilians struggle to get a proper education while the schools are not operating properly and they have to overcome the problems related to food security and livelihoods. At the same time, the threat of landmines left behind by the war makes their daily lives more unbearable. Based on the given facts, the question arises as to what steps have been taken within the framework of humanitarian law to protect the rights of the victims of the war. According to Red Cross, the current pandemic situation and related border problems further complicate the involvement of delegation members in the protection of war victims (caps, 2020). Consequently, it is not surprising why the potential of international humanitarian law to act effectively in contemporary conflicts is being questioned in the wake of contemporary challenges.

Another event that can be considered with the tendency of countries to grossly violate international humanitarian law is Baku's Military Trophies Park established by Azerbaijan. While the principles of International Humanitarian Law are recognized and accepted by all nations, including Azerbaijan, the Military Trophies Park and the humiliating sculptures of Armenian soldiers on display represent a direct example of how the general principles of humanitarian law can be ignored. Moreover, the fact that the Government of Azerbaijan defines this event as the establishment of a war museum, which is not contrary to the principles of law and presents a practice adopted by all states, illustrates the tendency and danger of interpreting the principles of international law by countries (Hauer, 2021).

International Humanitarian Law and Russia

To provide a more detailed analysis of how states violate international humanitarian law, it is appropriate to consider the foreign policy steps of the Russian Federation. Russia's recent actions against Ukraine and Georgia are specific cases that directly show the tendency of states to violate and interpret the principles of international humanitarian law.

First of all, it should be noted that Russia recognizes the four Geneva Conventions of 1949, as well as the 1977 protocols. Nevertheless, Russia grossly violates the principles of international law. The Georgian-Russian war of 2008 and the occupation of Crimea in 2014 are clear examples of this, which are of concern to the international community. Given that these actions are a direct violation of the principles of humanitarian law, Russia still manages to offer its version, interpret the law and confirm the legitimacy of its foreign policy steps. The Kremlin sees its political moves toward Ukraine and Georgia as legitimate actions under international humanitarian law, such as Kosovo's declaration of independence, the 2003 invasion of Iraq, or the 2011 NATO intervention in Libya. Therefore, Russia not only violates the principles of international humanitarian law but also seeks to modify them based on its interests (Hetherington & Noble, 2018).

Given the political moves of modern Russia, it is perhaps hard to imagine that Russia played a very large role in shaping the international legal order in its time. It is well known that the Soviet Union was significantly involved in the Nuremberg Trials after World War II, based on which Nazi Germany's actions were declared an unacceptable practice. At the same time, the Soviet Union also played a major role in the implementation of various treaties introduced by the UN (Hetherington & Noble, 2018).

The practice of interpreting international humanitarian law dates back to the Cold War. Opposing parties often accused each other of violating the principles of humanitarian law and called on each other to act within the law. It was during this period that the Soviet Union modified international humanitarian law while putting state interests above the importance of individuals established by the principles of humanitarian law. Although international humanitarian law should have a privileged place in the 1993 Constitution of the Russian Federation, modern events show that it has long since lost this privileged place (Hetherington & Noble, 2018).

Russia-Georgia War 2008 and Kremlin's "Humanitarian Aid" in Conflict Regions

The main basis of the confrontation between Russia and Georgia is the regions of Abkhazia and South Ossetia. The separatist-motivated confrontation between Abkhazians and Georgians, and Ossetians and Georgians, is, in fact, a visible expression of Russia's interests in the region. The Kremlin's interest in blocking all access to NATO forces in the South Caucasus is becoming a source of internal unrest and human suffering in Georgia (Hamilton, 2008). Despite the urgency of this issue, at this stage, it is necessary to highlight the role of international humanitarian law in protecting human rights during the Russia-Georgia war of 2008 and the way it is used by the Russian Federation.

The 5-day war between Russia and Georgia and the aggressive policy of official Moscow resulted in the death of many soldiers, and the forcing of innocent people - to flee their homes. Based on the involvement of the Red Cross and humanitarian aid, the war-affected population was provided with food and medical assistance. At the same time, during the conflict, the immediate placement of wounded soldiers in medical facilities and the supply of medicines necessary for their lives were facilitated. It is also worth mentioning the role of the Red Cross in finding suitable assistance for the Russian pilots and handing them over to the Russian side. The city of Gori has been the seat of the Red Cross delegation in Georgia since 2008 and its main mission is to provide for the various needs of the population stranded in the conflict villages around the city (ICRC, 2008). Nevertheless, the fact that international humanitarian law is effective in this situation presents a controversial topic.

Based on the fact that Russia justifies its invasion of Georgia and the 2008 war in terms of protecting the rights of civilians there, we are dealing with a direct case of interpretation of humanitarian law. Russia has been providing "humanitarian assistance" to the regions of Abkhazia and South Ossetia since 1990, helping to increase its ties with those regions and, as a result, the ineffectiveness of the Georgian side's dialogue to facilitate the integration of conflict regions into Georgian politics. The Kremlin's "humanitarian missions" are not just about providing general assistance. The passportization policy implemented over the years for these regions and the constant assistance to increase military armaments pose many challenges for Georgia (Pamment & Sazonov, 2019).

One of the main challenges is the inability of the Georgian government to end the long-standing conflict with the regions. While Russia has played a major role in resolving the conflict with Abkhazia and South Ossetia since the collapse of the Soviet Union, Georgia has become dependent on the Kremlin. While Russia has been a "key mediator" in resolving the conflict with Abkhazia and South Ossetia since the collapse of the Soviet Union, Georgia has become dependent on the Kremlin. Therefore, at present, any attempt by the Georgian government to resolve the conflict with the regions independently and to facilitate dialogue seems impossible. In addition to this, the danger that taking radical measures in Georgia to resolve the conflict quickly could even lead to a new war with Russia (Pamment & Sazonov, 2019).

When it comes to analyzing the threats posed by this situation, it is necessary to highlight the enormous danger of Russian interference in Georgia's internal affairs. The fact that Russian humanitarian aid is increasing ties between the conflict regions and the Kremlin and forcing the Georgian government to be as careful as possible about its foreign policy presents a policy of indirect Russian interference in the country's domestic and foreign affairs (Pamment & Sazonov, 2019).

While Russian "humanitarian aid" reflects the Kremlin's greater political interests than simply protecting the civilians in the regions, Russia's international position remains firmly unchanged. The Kremlin always tries to justify its actions against Georgia with dubious legal arguments and in compliance with the principles of humanitarian law and presents itself as a mediator in resolving the conflict between the regions and the government of Georgia (Pamment & Sazonov, 2019). There is no doubt that Russia is not only violating international humanitarian law but also interpreting it to pursue its personal goals. While the international community can see how rudely the principles of humanitarian law are being modified in the interests of a particular country, there is no specific mechanism that can prevent this process. Therefore, the issue goes back to the effectiveness of international humanitarian law and the problem related to the possibility of its easy interpretation by states.

Russia, Ukraine, and International Humanitarian Law

Developments in Ukraine since 2014 and Russia's political moves are other good example for discussing the effectiveness of international humanitarian law. While the Kremlin has often resorted to gross violations and interpretations of humanitarian law to promote foreign policy interests, it is interesting to see what its political steps are in terms of its relations with Ukraine.

The classification of the conflict in Ukraine under international humanitarian law since 2014 is associated with certain challenges. First of all, we are dealing with several different events that took place in 2014-2015 and, consequently, gave a different look to the conflict. There is an international political opinion that the so-called crisis in Ukraine is similar in development dynamics to the practice of the Cold War when Russia and NATO were presented as opposing sides. While there is a geographical diversity of the conflict, which is manifested in the existence of different centers of conflict, it seems difficult to identify the type of conflict and, consequently, the effectiveness of mechanisms for the enforcement of international humanitarian law (Heinsch, 2015).

The escalation of the situation began in February 2014, when pro-Russian forces gradually began to take control of the Crimean Peninsula. It is noteworthy that Russian armaments were actively engulfed at this stage of the conflict, despite the visibility of state symbols on the soldiers' uniforms. The fact that Russian soldiers without state symbols were represented in the early stages of the conflict allows Russia to deny its involvement and role in the early stages of the escalation of the conflict. Nevertheless, Putin's statement in April 2014 about the involvement of Russian troops was another justification for the Kremlin's aggressive policy in the context of assistance to the defense forces in Crimea. The escalation of the conflict after the occupation of Crimea was facilitated by the events in the Donetsk region, where there were clear traces of the action of pro-Russian forces. Despite the Russian side's denial of involvement in the conflict and the use of aggressive military action, many facts show examples of violations of the principles of international humanitarian law based on the Kremlin's foreign policy interests. The Kremlin's supply of weapons to the rebels and the covert involvement of Russian military personnel in the escalation of the conflict illustrates the Kremlin's gross involvement in the Ukraine crisis and makes it even more difficult to determine the qualifications of the conflict (Heinsch, 2015).

The main problem is related to the question of whether the events in Ukraine in 2014 should be given the status of an international conflict. While these developments formally take the form of a non-international armed conflict, Russia's direct or indirect involvement in the confrontation calls into question the legitimacy of this status. Although the opinion of international experts on this issue is divided, one explanation can finally be reached: The 2014 Ukraine crisis is, in essence, a non-international armed conflict that has turned into an international conflict based on Russian intervention (Heinsch, 2015). Based on this analysis, there is no doubt that the question of the effectiveness of international humanitarian law will arise again, how quickly it can determine the type of conflict and act accordingly.

The consequences of the current conflict in Ukraine from 2014 to the present affect most civilians. Even at the beginning of the conflict, the confrontation between the parties claimed the lives of countless people, forcing residents to flee their homes, which in some cases caused the greatest damage to the elderly population trapped in the conflict region. The war-affected civilians need humanitarian assistance expressed through medical or other livelihoods. Despite the urgent need for humanitarian assistance, it is noteworthy that the financial assistance allocated to help the population is much less than it was for example in Afghanistan. Moreover, recent developments and rising tensions are further endangering the innocent population and putting them at great risk of harm (Kurtzer, Lohsen, Nzuki, & Yayboke, 02).

With up to 100,000 Russian troops standing near the Ukrainian border, it is expected that the Kremlin will not stop using violence to further its interests this time too. Although Russia does not directly address the idea of an attack on Ukraine, it notes that inappropriate steps taken by Kyiv to move closer to the West may necessitate its intervention. It is clear that the events in Ukraine are another example of a confrontation between the West and Russia, but this confrontation is accompanied by violence against countless civilians. While the Ukrainian people are still suffering from the consequences of the 2014 war, the prospect of a new confrontation threatens to put them in an unbearable position (Kirby, 2022). Given these events, it is unclear what steps are being taken within the framework of international humanitarian law. As long as Russia can interpret the principles of international humanitarian law in the pursuit of personal interests and disguise its acts of violence in the name of a peacekeeping operation, the question of the effectiveness of universally recognized principles will remain controversial.

CONCLUSION

The main purpose of the chapter was to determine the effectiveness of International Humanitarian Law in contemporary conflicts. The study identified the challenges facing international law today, and based on them, its effectiveness becomes controversial. The weakness of humanitarian law enforcement mechanisms in non-international armed conflicts, the modern challenges of the modern world, and the ability to modify and interpret its principles are among the major shortcomings that call into question the effectiveness of international Humanitarian Law. At the same time, the fact that the implementation of its officially recognized principles still depends on the goodwill of the parties to the armed conflict poses even greater challenges to the effectiveness of International Humanitarian Law.

The arguments were based on the analysis of various articles, reports, analytical papers, and Case Studies as a result of the use of a qualitative research method. A review of the history of the creation of international humanitarian law has identified the preconditions for its creation, arising from the need to mitigate the damage caused by the war and to protect the combatants involved in the war or the civilians. Nevertheless, it should be noted that since the need to create international humanitarian law stemmed from the needs of that time, the necessity to study its effectiveness in today's world became once again significant.

An analysis of the sources, actors, and principles of international humanitarian law, as well as a review of the challenges of its enforcement mechanisms, revealed two types of armed conflict: International and non-international armed conflicts. At the same time, revealed the ineffectiveness of international humanitarian law in identifying non-international armed conflicts and the ambiguity of the mechanisms of action during them. While humanitarian law has less developed mechanisms for engaging in non-international armed conflict, and at the same time most of the current conflicts are presented in the form of non-international confrontations, the issue of the ineffectiveness of international humanitarian law has once again emerged. The main challenge related to non-international armed conflicts is the neglect of legal rules by the parties. At the same time, the possibility that armed conflict within the country may be interpreted by the representation of that country as a minor tension further complicates the involvement of international law and the implementation of its principles.

The analysis also highlighted the role of the Red Cross in training soldiers and raising awareness of international humanitarian law. However, this training process is slow and the current changes in the modern world require immediate modification and concretization of international humanitarian law.

The challenges of the modern world have been analyzed in terms of terrorism and the effectiveness of international humanitarian law in identifying terrorist acts. First of all, the issue of identifying terrorist acts is complicated, it should be considered an international or non-international armed confrontation. This misunderstanding arises from the existence of international terrorist organizations when international humanitarian law is challenged whether to consider the members of these organizations and the sponsors as the same parties to war as ordinary combatants. Moreover, the issue of the geographical diversity of terrorist acts highlights the ineffectiveness of maneuvering international humanitarian law in force majeure situations. Besides, when there are no specific mechanisms under international humanitarian law in this situation, states are allowed to interpret and engage in conflicts in terms of pursuing their interests.

Examples of the interpretation and modification of generally accepted principles by states were revealed in the analysis of different cases. The events in Nagorno-Karabakh and the precedent set by Azerbaijan for the establishment of the Military Trophies Park demonstrated the simplicity of interpretation of international humanitarian law. At the same time, revealed the inability of the Red Cross to protect the victims of the war, which has become an even greater challenge in the modern coronavirus situation. Finally, the Kremlin's foreign policy towards Georgia and Ukraine has shown how it is possible to violate the principles of international humanitarian law, interpret it and justify the actions with unsubstantiated arguments. Until the principles of international law are concretized, formally modified to meet modern challenges, and concrete action mechanisms developed, the question of its effectiveness will remain controversial.

REFERENCES

ACAPS. (2020, November 20). *Azerbaijan and Armenia: Conflict in Nagorno-Karabakh.* Retrieved from reliefweb: https://reliefweb.int/sites/reliefweb.int/files/resources/20201120_acaps_short_note_update_nagorno-karabakh_0.pdf

Anand, P. L. (2017). *International and non-International Armed Conflicts And Application of International Humanitarian Law as Lex Specials.* Academic Press.

Bartels, R. (2016). Terrorist groups as parties to an armed conflict. In *Terrorism, Counter-Terrorism and International Humanitarian Law* (pp. 56–67). College of Europe.

Carney, T. (2020, January 22). *Applying International Law to the Nagorno-Karabakh Conflict.* Retrieved from OpinioJuris: http://opiniojuris.org/2020/01/22/applying-international-law-to-the-nagorno-karabakh-conflict/

Gasser, H.-P. (1993). *International Humanitarian Law: an Introduction.* Paul Haupt Publishers.

Hamilton, R. E. (2008). *August 2008 and Everything After A Ten-Year Retrospective on the Russia-Georgia War.* Foreign Policy Research Institute.

Hauer, N. (2021, April 22). *Azerbaijan's 'Ethnic Hatred' Theme Park Draws Ire, Imperils Reconciliation.* Retrieved from RadioFreeEurope | RadioLiberty: https://www.rferl.org/a/azerbaijan-karabakh-theme-park-armenia-ethnic-hatred-aliyev/31217971.html

Heinsch, R. (2015). Conflict Classification in Ukraine: The Return of the "Proxy War"? *International Law Studies*, 324-360.

Hetherington, P., & Noble, B. (2018, March 23). *Russia doesn't just violate international law – it follows and shapes it too.* Retrieved from the conversation: https://theconversation.com/russia-doesnt-just-violate-international-law-it-follows-and-shapes-it-too-92700

ICRC. (2007). *International humanitarian law and the challenges of contemporary armed conflicts*. ICRC.

ICRC. (2008, August 20). *Georgia/Russian Federation: ICRC arrives in South Ossetia as the humanitarian operation expands*. Retrieved from International Committee of the Red Cross: https://www.icrc.org/en/doc/resources/documents/press-briefing/georgia-briefing-200808.htm

ICRC. (2019). *Implementing International Humanitarian Law: From Law to Action*. International Committee of the Red Cross.

IPHR. (2021). *When Embers Burst Into Flames: International Humanitarian Law and Human Rights Law Violations During the 2020 Nagorno-Karabakh War*. Global Diligence.

Kirby, P. (2022, February 3). *Is Russia preparing to invade Ukraine and what does Putin want?* Retrieved from BBC News: https://www.bbc.com/news/world-europe-56720589

Klenner, D. (1999, August 1). *Does international humanitarian law still stand a chance?* Retrieved from International Committee of the Red Cross: https://www.icrc.org/en/doc/resources/documents/misc/57jq6v.htm?fbclid=IwAR0fmqWubtzMBeupK68QVSxO6Rc0ueK7QW8fPifVJblkfOk_IK-Tkx2dels

Kurtzer, J., Lohsen, A., Nzuki, C., & Yayboke, E. (2022). *The Civilian Impacts of a Possible Russian Invasion of Ukraine*. Retrieved from The Center for Strategic and International Studies: https://www.csis.org/analysis/civilian-impacts-possible-russian-invasion-ukraine

Lubell, N. (2016). Limits of the geographical scope of application of IHL in combating terrorism. In Terrorism, Counter-Terrorism and International Humanitarian Law (pp. 67-72). CICR: College of Europe.

Melzer, N. (2016). *International Humanitarian Law: A Comprehensive Introduction*. ICRC.

Milanovic, M. (2007). Lessons for human rights and humanitarian law in the war on terror: Comparing Hamdan and the Israeli Targeted Killings case. *International Review of the Red Cross*, *89*(866), 373–393. doi:10.1017/S181638310700104X

Pamment, J., & Sazonov, V. (2019, June 6). *Hybrid Threats: Humanitarian aid in the Russo-Georgian conflict.* Retrieved from NATO Strategic Communications Center of Excellence: https://stratcomcoe.org/publications/hybrid-threats-humanitarian-aid-in-the-russo-georgian-conflict/83

Sachariew, K. (1989). States' entitlement to take action to enforce international humanitarian law. *International Review of the Red Cross*, *N270*(270), 177–195. doi:10.1017/S0020860400073058

UN. (2011). *International Legal Protection of Human Rights in Armed Conflicts.* United Nations Publication.

KEY TERMS AND DEFINITIONS

Combatant: The legal status of an individual who has the right to engage in hostilities during an armed conflict. The legal definition of "combatant" is found in article 43(2) of Additional Protocol I (AP1) to the Geneva Conventions of 1949. It states that "Members of the armed forces of a Party to a conflict (other than medical personnel and chaplains covered by Article 33 of the Third Convention) are combatants, that is to say, they have the right to participate directly in hostilities.

Geneva Convention 1949: The Third Geneva Convention, relative to the treatment of prisoners of war, is one of the four treaties of the Geneva Conventions. The Geneva Convention relative to the Treatment of Prisoners of War was first adopted in 1929 but significantly revised at the 1949 conference. It defines humanitarian protections for prisoners of war. There are 196 state parties to the Convention.

Geneva Conventions: Four treaties, and three additional protocols, that establish international legal standards for humanitarian treatment in war. The singular term Geneva Convention usually denotes the agreements of 1949, negotiated in the aftermath of the Second World War (1939–1945), which updated the terms of the two 1929 treaties and added two new conventions. The Geneva Conventions extensively define the basic rights of wartime prisoners (civilians and military personnel), established protections for the wounded and sick, and provided protections for the civilians in and around a war zone; moreover, the Geneva Convention also defines the rights and protections afforded to non-combatants. The treaties of 1949 were ratified, in their entirety or with reservations, by 196 countries. The Geneva Conventions concern only prisoners and non-combatants in war; they do not address the use of weapons of war, which are instead addressed by the Hague Conventions of 1899 and 1907, which concern conventional weapons, and the Geneva Protocol, which concerns biological and chemical warfare.

Hague Conventions of 1899 and 1907: A series of international treaties and declarations negotiated at two international peace conferences at The Hague in the Netherlands. Along with the Geneva Conventions, the Hague Conventions were among the first formal statements of the laws of war and war crimes in the body of secular international law. A third conference was planned for 1914 and later rescheduled for 1915, but it did not take place because of the start of World War I.

International Committee of the Red Cross: The ICRC is the only institution explicitly named under international humanitarian law as a controlling authority. The legal mandate of the ICRC stems from the four Geneva Conventions of 1949, as well as from its Statutes. The International Committee of the Red Cross (ICRC) is an impartial, neutral, and independent organization whose exclusively humanitarian mission is to protect the lives and dignity of victims of war and internal violence and to provide them with assistance.

International Human Rights Law (IHRL): Is the body of international law designed to promote human rights on social, regional, and domestic levels. As a form of international law, international human rights laws are primarily made up of treaties, agreements between sovereign states intended to have binding legal effect between the parties that have agreed to them; and customary international law. Other international human rights instruments, while not legally binding, contribute to the implementation, understanding, and development of international human rights law and have been recognized as a source of political obligation.

International Humanitarian Law: The law that regulates the conduct of war (Jus in Bello). It is a branch of international law that seeks to limit the effects of armed conflict by protecting persons who are not participating in hostilities and by restricting and regulating the means and methods of warfare available to combatants.

Law of War: Is the component of international law that regulates the conditions for initiating war (jus ad Bellum) and the conduct of warring parties (Jus in Bello). Laws of war define sovereignty and nationhood, states and territories, occupation, and other critical terms of the law.

War Crime: Is a violation of the laws of war that gives rise to individual criminal responsibility for actions by the combatants, such as intentionally killing civilians or intentionally killing prisoners of war, torture, taking hostages, unnecessarily destroying civilian property, deception by perfidy, wartime sexual violence, pillaging, the conscription of children in the military, committing genocide or ethnic cleansing, the granting of no quarter despite surrender, and flouting the legal distinctions of proportionality and military necessity.

Chapter 14
The International Importance of Civil and Political Rights

Natalia Beruashvili
Independent Researcher, Georgia

ABSTRACT

Civil and political rights are a class of rights that protect individuals' freedoms from infringement by governments, social organizations, and private individuals. They ensure one's entitlement to participate in the civil and political life of society and the state without discrimination or repression. Civil rights include the ensuring of peoples' physical and mental integrity, life, and safety; protection from discrimination on grounds such as race, gender, national origin, color, sexual orientation, ethnicity, religion, or disability; and individual rights such as privacy, the freedoms of thought and conscience, speech and expression, religion, the press, assembly, and movement. Political rights include natural justice (procedural fairness) in law, such as the rights of the accused, including the right to a fair trial, due process, the right to seek redress or a legal remedy, and rights of participation in civil society and politics such as freedom of association, the right to assemble, the right to petition, the right of self-defense, and the right to vote.

INTRODUCTION

Civil and political rights are two general types of internationally recognized human rights. They provide for the protection of the state (e.g. the right to a fair trial, the presumption of innocence, freedom of speech) and require the state to provide certain legal and political options (e.g. the right to vote, the right to a fair trial by jury). These rights are set out in the International Covenant on Civil and Political Rights and articles 1-21 of the Universal Declaration of Human Rights.

- Civil rights are the possibility of the existence of people in the state, characterizing their physical and biological existence, and satisfaction of material and spiritual needs.

Civil rights can be different in different societies and different eras. It could be:

DOI: 10.4018/978-1-6684-4543-3.ch014

- The right to the proper application of the law (the right to a fair trial),
- The right to be protected from political and social discrimination (based on gender, religion, race, etc.),
- Political freedoms: freedom of thought, freedom of religion, freedom of speech, freedom of the press, as well as the right to participate in public organizations, the right to vote in elections or seek election (the right to vote), and others.

The idea of civil rights grows from the traditional recognition of human rights (such as equality before the law, freedom of speech, and conscience) to the assertion of political (such as the right to vote in elections) and social (health care, pensions, etc.).

Any restrictions on civil rights based on gender, race, class, or religion are regarded as a violation of the status of a citizen, which is contrary to the norms of democracy.

The personal resolution of disputes arising in connection with the issue of civil rights is the prerogative of the court and is carried out on the principles of constitutional legality (International Covenant on Civil and Political Rights, 1966).

These rights are natural and personal. Natural, civil, and personal rights are one group of rights, which include such rights as the right to life, the right to liberty, personal integrity, and so on. \\Civil rights are natural and personal, or are they different groups of rights? It is impossible to focus on this paragraph in this matter since the first sentence inclines us to believe that this is the same thing, the second delimit them.

History

The expression "civil rights" is a translation of the Latin jus civic (rights of a citizen). Roman citizens could be either free (Libertas) or slaves (servitus), but they all had legal rights. After the Edict of Milan in 313, these rights included freedom of religion; however, in 380, the Edict of Thessaloniki obliged all subjects of the Roman Empire to profess Christianity. The Roman legal doctrine was lost in the Middle Ages, but claims to universal rights could still be made based on Christian doctrine. According to the leaders of the Ketta rebellion (1549), "all bound people can become free, for God has made everyone free with his precious bloodshed" (Chitadze, 2016).

Age of Enlightenment

The Age of Enlightenment is one of the key eras in the history of European culture, associated with the development of scientific, philosophical, and social thought. This intellectual movement was based on rationalism and freethinking.

Starting in England under the influence of the scientific revolution of the 17th century, this movement spread to France, and Germany and covered other European countries. Especially influential were the French Enlightenment, who became the "rulers of thoughts." The principles of the Enlightenment were the basis of the American Declaration of Independence and the French Declaration of the Rights of Man and Citizen.

The intellectual movement of this era had a great influence on the subsequent changes in the ethics and social life of Europe and America, the struggle for the national independence of the American colonies of European countries, the abolition of slavery, and the formulation of human rights. In addition, it shook the authority of the aristocracy and the influence of the church on social, intellectual, and cultural life.

The term enlightenment itself came into the English (The Enlightenment) and German (Zeitalter der Aufklärung) from French (siècle des lumières) and mainly refers to the philosophical trend of the 18th century. At the same time, it is not the name of a certain philosophical school, since the views of the philosophers of the Enlightenment often differed significantly from each other and contradicted each other. Therefore, enlightenment is considered not so much a complex of ideas as a certain direction of philosophical thought. The philosophy of the Enlightenment was based on criticism of the traditional institutions, customs, and morals that existed at that time.

There is no consensus regarding the dating of this worldview era. Some historians attribute its beginning to the end of the 17th century, others to the middle of the 18th century. In the 17th century, the foundations of rationalism were laid by Descartes in his Discourse on Method (1637). The end of the Enlightenment is often associated with the death of Voltaire (1778) (Jean Jacques Rousseau died the same year) or with the start of the Napoleonic Wars (1800-1815). At the same time, there is an opinion that the borders of the Enlightenment are tied to two revolutions: the Glorious Revolution in England (1688) and the Great French Revolution (1789) (Heywood, 2019).

Essence

In the Age of Enlightenment, there was a rejection of the religious worldview and an appeal to reason as the only criterion for the knowledge of man and society. For the first time in history, the question of the practical use of the achievements of science in the interests of social development was raised.

Scientists of a new type sought to disseminate knowledge, to popularize it. Knowledge should no longer be the exclusive possession of a few dedicated and privileged but should be available to all and be of practical use. It becomes the subject of public communication and public discussions. Even those who were traditionally excluded from studies - women - could now take part in them. There were even special editions designed for them, for example, in 1737, the book “Newtonianism for Ladies” by the author Francesco Algarotti (Shubitidze, 2010). Characteristically, David Hume begins his Essay on History (1741):

There is nothing that I would recommend to my readers more seriously than the study of history, for this occupation is better suited to both their gender and education than others - much more instructive than their usual books for entertainment, and more interesting than those serious works that can be found. they have in their closet. - “Essay of the study of history” (1741) (Hume, 1741).

The culmination of this desire to popularize knowledge was the publication of Diderot et al. “Encyclopedia” (1751-1780) in 35 volumes. It was the most successful and significant “project” of the century. This work brought together all the knowledge accumulated by mankind up to that time. It clearly explained all aspects of the world, life, society, sciences, crafts, and technology, everyday things. And this encyclopedia was not the only one of its kind. Others preceded it, but only the French became so famous. So, in England, Ephraim Chambers 1728 published the two-volume Cyclopedia (in Greek, “circular education”, the words “-pedia” and “pedagogy” are the same root). In Germany, from 1731- to 1754, Johan Zedler[en] published the Great Universal-Lexicon (Großes Universal-Lexicon) in 68 volumes. It was the largest encyclopedia of the 18th century. It had 284,000 keywords. For comparison:

in the French "Encyclopedia" there were 70,000 of them (Chitadze, 2016). But, firstly, it became more famous, and already among contemporaries, because it was written by the most famous people of their time, and this was known to everyone, while over the German many unknown authors worked as a lexicon. Secondly: her articles were more controversial, polemical, open to the spirit of the time, and partly revolutionary; they were crossed out by censorship, and there were persecutions. Thirdly: at that time, the international scientific language was already French, not German.

Simultaneously with general encyclopedias, special encyclopedias appeared, and for various individual sciences, which then grew into a separate genre of literature.

Latin ceased to be a scientific language. French takes its place. Ordinary literature, non-scientific, was written in national languages. At that time, a great dispute broke out among scientists about languages: whether modern languages can supplant Latin. On this subject, and indeed on the issue of superiority between antiquity and modernity, Jonathan Swift, the famous educator and author of Gulliver's Travels, wrote, for example, the satirical story "The Battle of the books" (The Battle of the books), published in 1704. In the parable of the spider and the bee, contained in this story, he beautifully and wittily expressed the essence of the dispute between the supporters of ancient and modern literature.

The main aspiration of the era was to find, through the activity of the human mind, the natural principles of human life (natural religion, natural law, the natural order of the physiocrats' economic life, etc.). From the point of view of such reasonable and natural beginnings, all historically formed and existing forms and relations (positive religion, positive law, etc.) were criticized.

G. May Periodization

There are many contradictions in the views of thinkers of this era. The American historian Henry May singled out four phases in the development of the philosophy of this period, each of which, to some extent, denied the previous one.

The first was the moderate or rational Enlightenment phase, associated with the influence of Newton and Locke. It is characterized by religious compromise and the perception of the universe as an ordered and balanced structure. This phase of the Enlightenment is a natural continuation of the humanism of the 14th-15th centuries as a purely secular cultural direction, characterized, moreover, by individualism and a critical attitude towards traditions. But the Age of Enlightenment is separated from the era of humanism by a period of religious reformation and Catholic reaction when theological and ecclesiastical principles again took precedence in the life of Western Europe. Enlightenment is a continuation of the traditions not only of humanism but also of advanced Protestantism and rationalist sectarianism of the 16th and 17th centuries, from which he inherited the ideas of political freedom and freedom of conscience. Like humanism and Protestantism, the Enlightenment took on a local and national character in different countries. With the greatest convenience, the transition from the ideas of the Reformation era to the ideas of the Enlightenment is observed in England at the end of the 17th and beginning of the 18th centuries, when deism developed, which, to a certain extent, was the end of the religious revolution of the Reformation era and the beginning of the so-called "natural religion", which was preached by the enlighteners of the 18th century. v. There was a perception of God as the Great Architect, who died from his labors on the seventh day. He gave people two books - the Bible and the book of nature. Thus, along with the cast of priests, the caste of scholars comes to the fore.

The parallelism of spiritual and secular culture in France gradually led to the discrediting of the former for hypocrisy and fanaticism. This phase of the Enlightenment is called the skeptical and is associated with the names of Voltaire, Holbach, and Hume. For them, the only source of our knowledge is an unprejudiced mind. In connection with this term, there are others, which are: enlighteners, enlightening literature, and enlightened (or enlightening) absolutism. As a synonym for this phase of the Enlightenment, the expression "philosophy of the eighteenth century" is used (Gudushauri, 2010).

The skepticism was followed by a revolutionary phase, associated in France with the name Rousseau, and in America with Payne and Jefferson. Characteristic representatives of the last phase of the Enlightenment, which became widespread in the 19th century, are such philosophers as Thomas Reed and Francis Hutcheson, who returned to moderate views, and respect for morality, law, and order. This phase is called didactic.

Religion and Morality

A characteristic enlightening idea is the denial of any divine revelation, especially in Christianity, which was considered the primary source of errors and superstitions. As a result, the choice fell on deism (God exists, but he only created the World and then does not interfere in anything) as a natural religion, identified with morality. Not taking into account the materialistic and atheistic beliefs of some thinkers of this era, such as Diderot, most of the enlighteners were followers of deism, who, through scientific arguments, tried to prove the existence of God and the creation of the universe by Him.

During the Age of Enlightenment, the universe was seen as an amazing machine that is an efficient cause, not a final one. God, after the creation of the universe, does not interfere in its further development and world history, and a person at the end of the path will neither be judged nor rewarded by Him for his deeds. The guide for people in their moral behavior is laicism, the transformation of religion into natural morality, the commandments of which are the same for everyone. The new concept of tolerance does not exclude the possibility of professing other religions only in private life, and not in public.

Dissolution of the Society of Jesus

The attitude of the Enlightenment towards the Christian religion and its connection with civil power was not the same everywhere. If in England the struggle against the absolute monarchy was already partially resolved thanks to the act of the "Bill of Rights" of 1689, which officially put an end to religious persecution and pushed faith into the subjective-individual sphere, then in continental Europe the Enlightenment retained a strong hostility to the Catholic Church. The states began to take a position of independence of domestic politics from the influence of the papacy, as well as increasingly restricting the autonomy of the curia in ecclesiastical matters.

The Jesuits, implacable defenders of papal authority, against the backdrop of growing conflict between church and state, as well as public opinion calling for the destruction of the order, were expelled from almost all European countries. In 1759 they were forced out of Portugal, followed by France (1762) and Spain (1769). In 1773, Pope Clement XIV published the bull Dominus ac Redemptor, which ordered the dissolution of the Society of Jesus (Chitadze, 2011). All the property of the order was confiscated and, for the most part, directed to the creation of public places controlled by the state. However, the Jesuits did not completely disappear from Europe, since in Russia Catherine the Great, although she was very close to the idea of the Enlightenment, refused to publish the papal dissolution report.

Historical Meaning

Pan-European significance in the XVIII century received French enlightenment literature in the person of Voltaire, Montesquieu, Rousseau, Diderot, and other writers. Their common feature is the dominance of rationalism, which directed its criticism in France to questions of a political and social nature, while the German enlighteners of this era were more busy resolving religious and moral issues.

Under the influence of the ideas of the Enlightenment, reforms were undertaken that were supposed to restructure the entire social life (enlightened absolutism). But the most significant consequence of the ideas of the Enlightenment was the American Revolution and the French Revolution.

At the beginning of the 19th century, enlightenment provoked a reaction against itself, which, on the one hand, was a return to the old theological worldview, on the other hand, an appeal to the study of historical activity, which was greatly neglected by the ideologists of the 18th century. Already in the 18th century, attempts were made to determine the basic nature of enlightenment. Of these attempts, the most remarkable belongs to Kant (Answer to the Question: What is Enlightenment? 1784). Enlightenment is not the replacement of some dogmatic ideas with other dogmatic ideas, but independent thinking. In this sense, Kant contrasted enlightenment with enlightenment and declared that it was simply the freedom to use one's intellect (Mkurnalidze, 2000).

Modern European philosophical and political thought, for example, liberalism, largely takes its foundations from the Enlightenment (John Locke is considered the founder of economic liberalism). Philosophers of our day consider the strict geometric order of thought, reductionism, and rationalism to be the main virtues of the Enlightenment, opposing them to emotionality and irrationalism. In this respect, liberalism owes the Enlightenment its philosophical basis and critical attitude towards intolerance and prejudice. Famous philosophers who hold such views include Berlin and Habermas.

The ideas of the Enlightenment also underlie political freedoms and democracy as the basic values of modern society, as well as the organization of the state as a self-governing republic, religious tolerance, market mechanisms, capitalism, and the scientific method. Since the Age of Enlightenment, thinkers have insisted on their right to seek the truth, whatever it may be and whatever it may threaten social foundations, without being subjected to threats of being punished "for the Truth."

After World War II, with the birth of postmodernism, some features of modern philosophy and science began to be seen as shortcomings: over-specialization, neglect of tradition, unpredictability, the danger of unforeseen consequences, and unrealistic assessment and romanticization of Enlightenment figures. Max Horkheimer and Theodor Adorno even considered the ideology of the Enlightenment to be a "totalitarian system" that led, among other things, to fascism and the Holocaust (Khamkhadze, 2000).

Main Principles of Political Freedom

Political freedom is a natural quality that is inalienable from a person and social communities, expressed in the absence of interference in the sovereignty of a person to interact with the political system through coercion or aggression. Political Rights and freedoms are fundamentally different from personal, social, economic, and other rights and freedoms in that, as a rule, they are closely related to belonging to the citizenship of a given state.

Political freedoms are one of the groups of fundamental constitutional rights and freedoms of citizens, as they determine their participation in the public and political life of the country. They are usually enshrined in the constitution, other laws, and regulations of countries.

Classification

As a rule, the following rights and freedoms are classified as political rights (in alphabetical order):

- equality before the law - the absence of estates;
- freedom of religion - the right to profess any religion or not to profess any;
- freedom of conscience - the right to form one's convictions;
- freedom of speech and mass media - prohibition of censorship;
- freedom of assembly - the right to hold meetings both indoors and outdoors;
- freedom of association - the right to form unions without asking permission;
- freedom to strike;
- the right to petition (Karumidze, 2003).

Overview

Although political freedoms are usually enshrined in the legal acts of the highest legal force of the state, between the proclamation of rights and freedoms and their conscious implementation there can be a "great distance".

The person himself must be ready for the conscious exercise of these rights and freedoms. Therefore, an important role is played by the political culture of a person, that is, the ability to make a political choice, find a compromise, reach consensus, and understand the possibility and legitimacy of conscious actions in each specific situation.

In a legal society, unlike a totalitarian one, only legal freedom can exist. However, freedom, not supported by law and practice of implementation, can turn into its opposite - arbitrariness, tyranny, and violence.

There are two aspects to the definition of political freedom. The first - is negative - freedom from coercion and pressure of the state on a person, and the second - is positive - the goal of providing freedom (for what? for what?). In the latter sense, political freedom is presented as an opportunity to reveal the potential of the individual in the relationship between the individual, the strata of society, and the state.

History of Political Freedom

We find the first reasoning about political freedoms in Aristotle's "Politics", where he talks about the contradictions between the category of "freedom" and the democratic form of government.

The first partial reflection in the legislation of political freedoms is found (although without the use of this term) in the English Magna Carta in 1215.

Subsequently, important milestones on the way of formalizing this concept and its classification were the English Bill of Rights, adopted in 1689, the French "Declaration of the Rights of Man and Citizen" of 1789, and the American Bill of Rights of 1791 (Chitadze, 2016).

In the 19th century and at the beginning of the 20th century, the situation with political freedoms in different states develops differently. The original liberal set of civil and political rights (freedom and equality, suffrage, etc.) is still, in the modern sense, very limited (property electoral qualifications, political prohibitions, inequality of men and women, racial restrictions, etc.).

Only after the Second World War, there was a qualitative leap in the development of the institution of human and civil rights, the leading role in the development of which is acquired by international law. On December 10, 1948, the UN General Assembly adopted the "Universal Declaration of Human Rights". In 1950, the European Convention for the Protection of Human Rights and Fundamental Freedoms was signed in Europe, creating a real mechanism for protecting declared rights - the European Court of Human Rights. In 1966, under the auspices of the UN, the International Covenant on Civil and Political Rights and the International Covenant on Economic, Social, and Cultural Rights were adopted (Karumidze, 2003). These and subsequent documents approved the international standard of human and civil rights and guarantees for the provision of these rights with the aim of incorporation (reflection) in the constitutional system of the participating states.

The Difference in Interpretations

There is a significant difference in the understanding of "true" political freedoms by different philosophical schools and political currents.

The left ranks as such freedom from poverty, hunger, incurable diseases, etc., but right-liberal politicians, in particular Friedrich August von Hayek and Milton Friedman, object to such an abuse of the concept. Anarchists have their view on this, calling the freedom supported by the capitalists "selfish".

Some people see political freedoms as synonymous with democracy, while others find significant differences between the two concepts.

Ecologists argue that political freedoms should include restrictions on the use of ecosystems.

There is much philosophical discussion about the nature of political freedom, the different types of freedoms, and the degree to which freedom is desirable. For example, determinists argue that all human actions are predetermined and, therefore, freedom is an illusion, and Isaiah Berlin distinguished between the negative and positive sides of political freedom.

To date, discussions continue, and the meaning of the term, its nature, and its components are continuously refined.

Positive Freedom

Positive freedom in political philosophy is characterized as the possibility and availability of resources to realize one's own potential (this can also mean freedom from internal barriers) and is used as a contrast to negative freedom, which is freedom from external restrictions and the violent interference of other people.

The positive concept of freedom is the central idea of social liberalism (in the US they also use the abbreviation liberalism), which distinguishes it from classical liberalism and libertarianism. Also, ideas about positive freedom influenced the political philosophy of social democracy.

Overview

Isaiah Berlin identified two main types of freedom. Such a statement as "I am not a slave to anyone" Berlin described as characteristic of negative freedom, that is, freedom from direct interference from another individual. As a counterpoint, Berlin used the affirmation inherent in positive freedom, "I am my boss," a statement about the freedom to choose one's path in life (Berlin, 1969).

Charles Taylor explains that negative freedom is the idea of "opportunity" ("opportunity-concept") when an individual acquires negative freedom if he is not enslaved by external forces and has equal access to public resources (regardless of how he decides to spend his time). Positive freedom, Taylor argues, is based on the idea of "exercise-concept": the possession of positive freedom can mean that the individual is internally free and should be able to act prudently following his "I". Suppose a rich and powerful person is also a drug addict. He may have a lot of negative freedom, but very little positive freedom, according to Taylor. Positive freedom entails being in the position of an adult, mature person, able to make decisions, and free from internal constraints (weakness, fear, ignorance, etc.) (UKEssays, 2015).

Negative Freedom

Negative freedom is characterized as freedom from the violent interference of other people and is used as a contrast to positive freedom, which is defined as the individual's freedom from the constraints of the social system within society, such as classism, sexism, or racism.

The negative concept of freedom is a central idea of libertarianism and classical liberalism, which distinguishes it from social liberalism (in the US they also use the abbreviation liberalism) and social democracy.

The difference between negative and positive freedoms is described by Isaiah Berlin in his lecture "Two Concepts of Freedom". According to Berlin, this difference is closely related to political tradition. The concept of negative freedom is associated with British philosophers such as Locke, Hobbes, Adam Smith, and Jeremy Bentham, and the concept of positive freedom with continental thinkers such as Hegel, Rousseau, Herder, and Marx (Mkurnalidze, 2000).

According to Berlin,

... the meaning [of freedom in the negative sense] is implied in the answer to the question: "What is the area within which the subject - whether a person or a group of people - is allowed or should be allowed to do what he can do or be what he can be without being interfered with by other people?" (Berlin, 1969).

The limitations of negative freedom are imposed by people and are not due to natural causes or the inability of the individual himself.

Helvetius expresses this point clearly:

A free man is a man who is not shackled, not imprisoned, not terrified like a slave by the fear of punishment... the inability to fly like an eagle or swim like a whale is not a lack of freedom.

Marxists and socialists considered the distinction between negative and positive freedom to be erroneous, arguing that positive and negative freedom are in practice indistinguishable or cannot exist one without the other (Khamkhadze, 2000).

Overview

Isaiah Berlin identified two main types of freedom. Such a statement as "I am not a slave to anyone" Berlin described as characteristic of negative freedom, that is, freedom from direct interference from another individual. As a counterpoint, Berlin used the affirmation inherent in positive freedom, "I am my boss," a statement about the freedom to choose one's path in life (Berlin, 1969).

Charles Taylor explains that negative freedom is the idea of "opportunity" ("opportunity-concept") when an individual acquires negative freedom if he is not enslaved by external forces and has equal access to public resources (regardless of how he decides to spend his time). Positive freedom, Taylor argues, is based on the idea of "exercise-concept": the possession of positive freedom can mean that the individual is internally free and should be able to act prudently following his "I". Suppose a rich and powerful person is also a drug addict. He may have a lot of negative freedom, but very little positive freedom, according to Taylor. Positive freedom entails being in the position of an adult, mature person, able to make decisions, and free from internal constraints (weakness, fear, ignorance, etc.) (US Essays, 2015).

The Frankfurt School psychoanalyst and humanist philosopher Erich Fromm, in his 1941 work Escape from Freedom, draws a line between positive and negative freedom, anticipating the work of Isaiah Berlin by more than a decade. Fromm believes that the difference between the two types of freedom appeared in the process of human evolution and the emergence of higher nervous activity, which is not characteristic of other living beings. Fromm defines "freedom from doing something" as, among other things, freedom from the instinctive predetermination of human activity (Fromm, 1994). Thus, the acquisition of negative freedom by a person for Fromm means the formation of him as a rational species, free from the basic instinct.

Libertarianism

Libertarianism (from Latin libertas - "freedom") is a set of political philosophies and movements that support freedom as a basic principle (Mkurnalidze, 2000). Libertarians seek to maximize political freedom and autonomy by emphasizing freedom of choice, voluntary association, and individual judgment (Chitadze, 2016). They share a skepticism about state power but differ on the extent of their opposition to existing economic and political systems. Different schools of libertarian thought offer different views on the legitimate functions of public and private power, often calling for the restriction or dissolution of coercive social institutions.

Within libertarianism, several currents have their specifics. In particular, these are right and left-libertarianism, anarcho-capitalism, minarchism, geolibertarianism (Georgism), left market anarchism, and libertarian socialism. Right libertarians place the right of private property at the forefront. Left libertarians believe that the absolutization of private property can violate the freedom of the individual.

Etymology

Nolan Diagram

The concept of libertarian first appeared in the essay "On Liberty and Necessity" (1789) by the American Unitarian philosopher William Belsham. The term was derived from "freedom" (English liberty) by analogy with the formation of the word unitarian from unity) in English and devoted supporters of the philosophical doctrine of "free will". In his essay, Belsham denounced the ideas he attributed to libertarianism and countered them with religious determinism (Belsham, 1798).

In the second half of the 19th century, the term "libertarian" (fr. la libertaire) in the meaning of "anarchist" was adopted by representatives of French anarchism. In 1858, Joseph Dejac began publishing

Le Libertaire, Journal du Mouvement Social in the United States. In 1880, at a congress in Le Havre, anarcho-communists also used this term. Its popularity was boosted in the late 19th century by the imposition of anti-anarchist restrictions on the freedom of the press in France after the terrorist attack carried out by Auguste Vaillant in 1893. As a result, anarchists began to widely use fr. libertaire as a euphemism for the word fr. anarchiste, in particular, in 1895, the newspaper Le Libertaire was established. Subsequently, "libertarianism" and "anarchism" became synonymous, also giving rise to the term "libertarian socialism" (Shubitidze, 2010).

In its modern meaning, the term "libertarianism" was first used by the American politician and founder of the Foundation for Economic Education, Leonard Reed, who declared himself a libertarian in the 1940s. Following him, many supporters of personal and economic freedom also began to call themselves libertarians to distinguish themselves from "liberals", which in the United States and some other countries since the 20th century have been understood as supporters of personal freedom and state redistribution of resources (in particular, the "New Deal Roosevelt), including social democrats and moderate communists. However, many proponents of libertarian ideas do not call themselves libertarians, insisting on the traditional designation of their ideology ("liberalism") or defining themselves as "classical liberals" (Khamkhadze, 2000). Others consider such adherence to the old terms to be erroneous, introducing confusion into the political picture of the modern world, which hinders the spread and understanding of libertarian ideas.

The Nolan Diagram, proposed by the American libertarian David Nolan in 1970, serves to illustrate his claim that libertarianism promotes both economic and personal freedom by limiting government intervention in society. According to Nolan, this contrasts with left-wing "liberalism" that advocates only "personal freedoms", right-wing "conservatism" that advocates only "economic freedoms", as well as with populist "authoritarianism", whose supporters seek tight state control over the life of society. and redistribution of income from the rich to the poor (Mkurnalidze, 2000).

According to the American libertarian socialist Murray Bookchin, the name "libertarianism" was stolen by the right, and right-wing libertarians, who are not interested in freedom, but private property, would be more correctly called proletarians (Chitadze, 2016).

Philosophy

There is debate among libertarians about whether the state is legitimate. Some libertarians (anarcho-capitalists) see the ban on "aggressive violence" as absolute and without exception, even for civil servants. In their opinion, such forms of state intervention as taxation and antitrust regulation are examples of theft and robbery and therefore should be abolished. Protecting citizens from violence should be carried out by private security agencies, and helping the poor should be a charitable task.

Another section of libertarians (minarchists) accepts the prohibition of "aggressive violence" as an important principle, but considers it necessary or inevitable that there should be coercive taxation of the state, whose only task would be to protect the life, health, and private property of citizens.

The difference between this and the previous approach to libertarianism is that in the first case, the prohibition is absolute and applies to each specific action, while in the second, the task of minimizing violence in society is set, for the solution of which the state is considered as a lesser evil.

The libertarian philosopher Moshe Kroy believed that the disagreement over whether the state is immoral is between anarcho-capitalists, who hold views on human consciousness and the nature of Murray Rothbard's values, and monarchists, who hold views on human consciousness and the nature of

Ain values. Rand does not arise from different interpretations of a common moral position (Gudushauri, 2010). He argued that the disagreement between these two currents is the result of different ideas about the nature of human consciousness and that each of the currents draws the correct conclusions from its premises. Thus, these currents do not make mistakes when deriving the correct interpretation of any ethical position, since they do not have a common ethical position.

Schools

Anarcho-Capitalism

Anarcho-capitalism (also called free-market anarchism, market anarchism, and private property anarchism) is a political philosophy that advocates the elimination of the state in favor of individual sovereignty within a free market. In an anarcho-capitalist society, law enforcement, courts, and all other security services would be provided by privately funded competitors rather than through taxation, and money would be provided privately and on a competitive open market. Therefore, personal and economic activity under anarcho-capitalism is governed by private law, not politics.

The philosophy of anarcho-capitalism was formulated in the mid-twentieth century by the Austrian School economist and libertarian Murray Rothbard. Rothbard coined the term and is considered the founder of the movement. He combined the free-market approach of the Austrian school (classical liberalism) with a human rights perspective and abandoned the state, as did 19th-century American individualist anarchists such as Lysander Spooner and Benjamin Tucker (although Rothbard rejected anarchism and anti-capitalism, along with the labor theory of value) (Shubitidze, 2020). Rothbardian anarcho-capitalism will first implement a mutually agreed-upon libertarian "legal code that is universally accepted and that the courts are bound to follow" (Shubitidze, 2010). This legal code will have to recognize the sovereignty of the individual and the principle of non-aggression.

Minarchism

The "night watchman state," or minarchism, is a model state whose only function is to provide citizens with military, police, and judicial services to protect them from external aggression, theft, breach of contract, fraud, and to enforce property laws.

Britain in the 19th century has been described by the historian Charles Townshend as a classic example of this form of state (Chitadze, 2016).

Robert Nozick won the National Book Award in the Philosophy and Religion category for his book Anarchy, State, and Utopia. In it, Nozick argued that only a minimal state limited to narrow functions of protection against "aggression, fraud, theft" can be justified as not violating the rights of the people (Nozick, 1975).

Georgism

Georgism is an economic and philosophical doctrine founded by Henry George, which is based on the idea that everyone owns the product he created, however, all-natural goods, and above all land, belong equally to all mankind. The philosophy of Georgism is usually associated with the idea of a single tax on land use (Chitadze, 2016).

Libertarian Socialism

Libertarian socialism (also called anarchist socialism or socialist libertarianism) is a group of anti-authoritarian political philosophies within the socialist movement that rejects socialism based on state ownership and centralized management of the economy, and sometimes the state itself. Libertarian socialists criticize the employment relationship, suggesting instead worker self-management and decentralized structures of political organization. They argue that a society based on freedom and justice can be achieved by abolishing authoritarian institutions that control the basic means of production and subjugate the majority of the people to the wealthy, economic and political elites. Libertarian socialists advocate decentralized structures based on direct democracy and federal or confederal organization, such as libertarian municipalism, citizen assemblies, trade unions, and workers' councils. They call for the establishment of free and voluntary human relations through the identification, criticism, and practical dismantling of illegitimate power in all aspects of human life (Shubitidze, 2010).

Political philosophies of the past and present that are characterized as libertarian socialist include social anarchism (including anarcho-communism, anarcho-collectivism, anarcho-syndicalism, and mutualism) as well as autonomism, communalism, guild socialism, revolutionary syndicalism, libertarian Marxism (including workers' council communism and Luxembourgianism) and some versions of utopian socialism and individualist anarchism (Heywood, 2020).

Libertarianism and the Austrian School of Economic Thought

Libertarianism is sometimes confused with the Austrian school of economic thought, which concludes the ineffectiveness and destructive effects of government intervention in the economy. Although most libertarians in the field of economics adhere to the approaches of the Austrian school, this identification is erroneous. Libertarianism is a political and legal doctrine containing recipes for the reorganization of society, primarily in the field of legislation. This is the doctrine of due, prescribing to people, and especially to civil servants, certain norms of behavior. Austrian economic theory, on the contrary, does not have a normative character, being a tool for understanding cause-and-effect relationships in the economy. Drawing, for example, the conclusion that the protectionist customs regime reduces the number of benefits available to the population of the country where it is applied, it remains a value-neutral science and does not make calls for changes in legislation and policies.

Political Views of Contemporary Libertarians

- Libertarians believe that people have only the right to freedom from infringement of their person or property, and laws should only ensure such freedom, as well as the enforcement of freely concluded contracts.
- Libertarians advocate free speech.
- Libertarians believe that taxation is immoral, essentially no different from robbery, and therefore taxation should be replaced by voluntary methods of financing the services currently provided by the state to the population. Such services may be provided by private businesses, charities, and other organizations. They oppose any government subsidies, for example, to agricultural producers. Libertarians oppose customs duties and other types of foreign trade barriers.

- Libertarians oppose government oversight of drug safety and efficacy, all or most urban zoning regulations.
- Libertarians oppose legal minimum wages.
- Libertarians are staunch opponents of universal conscription. They oppose military intervention in the affairs of other countries and recognize only protection against aggression.
- Libertarians oppose any government control of the media.
- Some libertarians oppose restrictions on immigration.
- Some libertarians oppose compulsory school laws.
- Libertarians oppose gun bans.
- One of the easily recognizable demands of libertarians - ambiguously perceived by society, but quite naturally arising from the general concept - is the requirement for the full legalization of all or most drugs.
- Some right-wing libertarians support the idea of "voluntary" (contract) slavery, which is criticized by representatives of social movements of the left-libertarian (social-anarchist) persuasion.

Publicist Tom Hartmann notes that, according to a study by Pew Research, only 11% of people who claim to be libertarian understand the essence of libertarianism, in particular, that it advocates increased personal freedom and reduced state control. Thus, 41% of such people believe that the state should regulate business, 38% support social benefits for low-income people, and 42% believe that the police should have the right to stop "suspicious people" (Chitadze, 2016).

Classical liberalism

Classical liberalism is a political ideology, a branch of liberalism that affirms the rights and freedoms of man and citizen, political freedom, and political pluralism. Classical liberalism emphasizes the need for economic freedom.

Classical liberalism was developed in the 19th century in Europe and the USA. Even though classical liberalism was built on ideas known as far back as the 18th century, it is focused on a new type of society, state, power, government, and public relations that appeared in response to the industrial revolution and urbanization. Among the people whose ideas influenced classical liberalism are John Locke, Jean-Baptiste Say, Thomas Malthus, and David Ricardo. Their ideas drew on Adam Smith's economics and belief in natural law, utilitarianism, and progress (Heywood, 2000).

In the 20th century, there was a revival of interest in classical liberalism, led by the economists Friedrich Hayek and Milton Friedman. Some refer to the modern development of classical liberalism as "neoclassical liberalism", which emphasizes the need to minimize the role of the state and focus it on issues of security and justice (Heywood, 2000).

Use of the Term

The term classical liberalism was introduced to distinguish early nineteenth-century liberalism from modern social liberalism.

Differences From Libertarianism

Libertarianism and classical liberalism are related political currents that have the same goal: the establishment of a society based on the principles of a free market and the maximum possible non-interference of the state in people's lives. The difference is that classical liberals perceive the state as a guarantor of the natural or utilitarian ensuing rights and freedoms of citizens, and not as a compromise and a necessary evil, that is, they can advocate those powers of the state that they see as utilitarianly necessary or ethically justified. In addition to the position on the powers of state power, libertarians and classical liberals (especially of a utilitarian orientation) often also differ in their views on the genesis of law, democracy, and the judicial and law enforcement system (Heywood, 2000).

Classical liberals are in favor of control of the army, the judiciary, and the collection of taxes, naturally, at a low level (in turn, some monarchists advocate voluntary taxes or the replacement of taxes with alternative donations to private companies in the same industry). Some of the classical liberals are also in favor of intellectual property, the existence of a central bank, and state licensing of products, and in very rare cases, supporters of this ideology are in favor of public education.

Classical liberalism proceeds from the concept of inalienable natural rights or utilitarianism to justify their existence. From the position of liberals and liberal logic, a state is a social contract that guarantees and helps people to observe and exercise their rights, and also (later variations of liberalism after the second half of the 19th century) carry liberal ideology around the world, because from the point of view of liberals, all people (regardless of their race, citizenship, nationality or religion) are endowed with equal rights, and the task of the state is to protect and enforce these rights.

Libertarianism sees the state as a compromise. Therefore, libertarians continue to have a negative attitude towards the state, even in the form of a "night watchman". Libertarianism has no foreign policy agenda other than the principle that any state activity in this regard can only be directed at protecting its citizens from external threats, and no ideological basis can justify wasting taxpayer money on something that goes beyond the limits of the powers of the state - the "night watchman".

Issues arising from both the general development of economics and the general development of mankind lead to profound differences between classical liberalism and libertarianism.

Civil Society

Civil society - a set of citizens who are not close to the levers of state power; the totality of social relations outside the framework of government-state and commercial structures; the sphere of self-manifestation of free citizens and voluntarily formed non-profit directed associations and organizations, protected from direct interference and arbitrary regulation by the state authorities, as well as other external differences.

A developed civil society is the most important prerequisite for building the rule of law and the rule of law and its equal partner. According to David Easton's classical scheme, civil society acts as a filter for the demands and support of society for the political system.

Conditions for the Existence of Civil Society

- autonomy of society, the transformation of a person into an individual, freed from all bonds that bind him to his neighbors;

- the presence in society of private ownership of the means of production: "The first one who cleared a piece of land and said: "This is mine "became the true founder of civil society" (Jean-Jacques Rousseau, 1762);
- the presence of a confrontation between the haves and the have-nots in the form of a constantly ongoing "cold civil war", "predation of the rich, robbery of the poor" (Rousseau, 1762);
- presence of democracy in the social sphere;
- legal protection of citizens;
- a certain level of civic culture;
- high educational level and high civil activity of the population;
- the most complete provision of human rights and freedoms;
- self-management;
- competition between its constituent structures and different groups of people;
- free-forming public opinion and pluralism;
- mixed economy;
- a large share in the middle-class society.

The Concept of Civil Society

In the social sciences, the following main approaches to defining the essence of civil society are distinguished: as opposed to anarchy; as opposed to the work of the church; as a complex of social relations opposed to the state; as a concrete phenomenon of Western civilization. The history of the development of its concept in Western social and political thought testifies to the difficulties of the formation of civil society.

Thomas Hobbes, English philosopher:

Civil society is a union of individuals, a collective in which all its members acquire the highest human qualities. The state prevails over civil society (Hobbes).

John Locke, English philosopher:

Civil society is a political society, that is, a public sphere in which the state has its interests (Locke).

Charles Montesquieu, French philosopher:

Civil society is a society of enmity of people with each other, which, to stop it, is transformed into a state (Montesquieu).

Thomas Paine, American educator:

Civil society is a blessing, and the state is a necessary evil. The more perfect civil society, the less it needs regulation by the state (Paine).

Georg Hegel, German philosopher:

Civil society is a sphere for the realization of especially the private goals and interests of an individual. There is no true freedom in civil society since there is always a contradiction between private interests and power, which is universal (Hegel).

Karl Marx and Friedrich Engels, German economists, and sociologists:

Civil society is a sphere of material, economic life, and activity of people. It is it that is primarily about the state, civil life as the sum of various interests holds the state together (Marx, Engels).

Stages of Formation of Civil Society

Conventionally, three stages of the formation of civil society can be distinguished:

1. In the first stage, the city and state spheres of society are separated. The interaction of civil society and the apparatus of state power begins through modern democratic mechanisms (elections, referendums, rallies, petitions, etc.). A predominantly private sphere of public life is developing, and various institutions and organizations are emerging that serve the private interests of people. In this period, the system of classical capitalism prevails - with private property, a market economy, and free competition. The main classes at this stage are entrepreneurs and workers. To continue the formation of civil society, the rule of law and the rule of law with a market economic system are necessary.
2. Further, not only the private but also the public sphere of life begins to develop. Civil society, which was forced to independently protect the economic interests of various social strata, transfers these responsibilities to the state, which, thanks to this, becomes not only legal but also social. At this stage, the conflict between the interests of capitalists and wage workers is smoothed out, society seeks a compromise between the interests of various social groups. The main place is occupied by the middle class, and the position of the service class is also being strengthened - these are managers, businessmen, and analysts.
3. At the final stage of the formation of civil society, its globalization and pluralization take place. The class struggle tends to zero, and the polarization of society (the enmity between its classes) practically disappears. Different social groups have different interests only because of their cultural characteristics, and not because of enmity with other groups. Various subjects of civil society develop their strategies and ways of development, and in society itself, tolerance is practiced, tolerance towards the entire spectrum of social groups, classes, ethnic groups, etc.

Philosophical Postulates

- Civil society is a non-state-type society. In the modern sense, civil society is a society with developed economic, political, legal, and cultural relations between people, independent of the state, but interacting with it.
- Civil society is a horizontally structured network of non-profit organizations that operates for the sake of public interests, but without the goal of achieving political or commercial gain, and unites volunteer citizens participating in public life without the goal of material gain.

- Civil society is based on relations of social solidarity, in contrast to the state, built based on power relations and business, functioning within the framework of selfish morality and competitive relations.
- Civil society - a society of people of high social, cultural, moral, and economic status, creating developed legal relations with the state.
- Civil society has a complex structure, which includes: economic, ethnic, religious, and legal relations. Civil ties are relations of competition and solidarity between legally equal partners.
- The condition for the emergence of civil society is the emergence of citizens of the society of economic independence based on private property, as well as civil liberties. Civil society is a society of civilized market relations.
- An important characteristic of civil society is the achievement of a high level of self-organization and self-regulation of society.
- Civil society is organized after the division of spheres of influence between the state and the citizen. The narrowing of the total power of the state is carried out through the introduction of inalienable human rights in certain non-political categories. The categories of inalienable rights are the right to work (economy), national cultural values (culture), to perform religious rites, freedom of information exchange, and freedom of self-realization. All disputes between citizens are resolved by an independent court.
- Civil society is becoming a global phenomenon (Mkurnalidze, 2000).

Functions of Civil Society

- Protecting private areas of people's lives;
- Restraining political power from absolute dominance by monitoring compliance with the constitutional principles of the rule of law and the separation of powers;
- Stabilization of public relations and processes, ensuring a balance between the state and commercial spheres of society;
- Protection and promotion of public interests;
- Constant peaceful struggle for the implementation of the constitutional principle of the rule of law.
- Continuous monitoring of legislation for corruption risks (Khamkhadze, 2000).

Structure of Civil Society

Civil society is a horizontally structured set of independent public organizations and associations that have distanced themselves from state and commercial structures and function by following their goals and objectives for the sake of public interests.

Public organizations unite following their goals and objectives, as well as within the framework of ongoing projects. For example, environmental protection within the framework of a regional problem. Many educational organizations, such as universities and libraries, are organized as non-profit organizations, which allows them to receive grants from various charitable foundations and receive tax benefits from the state.

These organizations are financed within the framework of announced projects on a competitive basis by many different governmental and non-governmental national and international charitable foundations, which also have their specialization: protecting the environment, promoting democracy in a particular country, protecting human rights, etc. For example, the Rockefeller Foundation supports various educational projects around the world, projects in the field of health, etc., or the world's largest charitable foundation, Bill and Melinda Gates, supports projects in the field of health and poverty alleviation.

Charitable foundations, through their grant policy, largely govern the activities of non-profit organizations by monitoring and overseeing the implementation of projects, as well as determining the humanitarian technologies used in projects.

Historical Role - A Positive Evaluation

- Civil society is the most important element in the system of checks and balances of modern society, which allows controlling and restricting the activities of government institutions and businesses, preventing violations of the law and their excessive interference in the private life of citizens.
- Civil society makes it possible to effectively promote the interests of various social groups and protect their rights, including through the promotion of legislative initiatives.
- Institutions of civil society, functioning based on cooperation and cooperation of various social groups, smooth out social contradictions and harmonize social relations.

Negative Evaluation

- The financial policy of charitable foundations often changes, and their support for public organizations is limited to a short period, which often leads to imitation of solving social problems and the collapse of truly independent public organizations.
- The low level of civic engagement and legal illiteracy of the population makes it difficult to build a civil society in such countries.
- S. G. Kara-Murza: "The fundamental meaning of the concept of civil society is based on two concepts: anthropological (man as an individual, atom) and political and economic (private property). Consequently, this concept in its main sense is inapplicable to non-Western cultures, standing on other anthropological and polit-economic ideas" (Chitadze, 2016).
- Herbert Marcuse in the book "Reason and Revolution" states: "Under fascism, civil society dominates the state" (Chitadze, 2016).
- A significant shortcoming in the work of public organizations and associations at this stage is that there is still no stable, systemic, and organized connection between civil formations, which is necessary to create a force capable of influencing the authorities in cases of violations of human and civil rights and freedoms (Chitadze, 2016).

CONCLUSION

Civil law is a civil right that is described in detail in the International Covenant on Civil and Political Rights and the European Convention for the Protection of Human Rights and Fundamental Freedoms. For Western society, this right is considered to be one of the true rights of a person, a citizen, which is a means of participation in public life.

It is necessary to say a few words about what political freedom means and what the guarantee of its real value includes. This will allow us to evaluate the arguments of Rawls and others by which they attached special importance to the right to political freedom.

Political freedom encompasses several more specific freedoms and rights. It includes freedom of expression on political issues and the right to unite in political organizations; It also includes the right to vote and to hold public office. Each of the above freedoms must be restricted and clarified to ensure the basic idea that "every citizen has fair and approximately equal access to the political process." The latter expresses a guarantee of real values. But what exactly does this mean? Rawls explains the guarantee of values in terms of fair opportunities. he says:

"This guarantee means that political freedom should be approximately equal for all citizens, regardless of their social and economic status, in the sense that everyone has a fair opportunity to hold public office and influence the outcome of political decisions."

A fair opportunity to achieve certain goodness is realized when all people who are equally talented and motivated have an equal chance of acquiring it.

Rawls argues that the fair value of political freedom "ensures that such talented and motivated citizens have equal influence over government policy." Citizens must have equal resources to exert political influence. But equality of political influence is not enough to guarantee real value. This can be achieved by giving citizens different political freedoms and opportunities. From the above section, it is clear that Rawls perceives a fair value guarantee that excludes such possibilities. Thus, the description of a goodwill guarantee must relate to public services as well as political influence. Citizens should not only have a fair opportunity to exercise equal political influence, but they should also have a fair opportunity to hold any position of political power in their society. Positions of political power include the positions of the electorate, as well as the executive, legislative, judicial, and administrative public services.

This interpretation of the principle of equitable equality of opportunity provides only a weak definition of the effect of the distinguishing principle. It also explains why the guarantee of the real value of political freedom is not exaggerated. In keeping with this principle, Rawls considers the guarantee of the fair value of political freedom, as he believes that ensuring fair equality of opportunities for political groups alone is not sufficient to eliminate inequality against political influence. Accordingly, it allocates political freedoms and attaches special importance to them. Every citizen should have equal resources to exert political influence.

As it was mentioned above, to ensure the fair value of political freedoms, a democratic society will need to regulate a variety of basic freedoms, such as freedoms related to freedom of speech. These are the inequalities that will improve the material prospects of the worst situation. Since these are serious demands, the special definition that Rawls gives us about political freedoms needs to be justified.

REFERENCES

Belsham, W. (1789). *On Liberty and Necessity. Essays Philosophical and Moral, Historical and Literary, Volume I, Book I, Essay I.* Retrieved from: https://www.informationphilosopher.com/solutions/philosophers/belsham/on_liberty_and_necessity.html

Berlin, I. (1969). *Two Concepts of Liberty*. Retrieved from: https://cactus.dixie.edu/green/B_Readings/I_Berlin%20Two%20Concpets%20of%20Liberty.pdf

Chitadze, N. (2016). *Political Sciences*. International Black Sea University.

Chitadze, N. (2017). *World Geography. Political, Economic, and Social Dimensions*. Scholars Press.

Essays, U. K. (2015). *Analyzing Charles Taylors Critique Of Negative Freedom Philosophy Essay*. https://www.ukessays.com/essays/philosophy/analysing-charles-taylors-critique-of-negative-freedom-philosophy-essay.php#:~:text=These%20inarticulate%20ideas%20have%20their,resources%2C%20regardless%20of%20the%20time

Fromm, E. (1994). *Escape from Freedom*. Retrieved from: https://www.amazon.com/Escape-Freedom-Erich-Fromm/dp/0805031499

Hegel, G. (1798). *Social and Political Thought*. Retrieved from: https://iep.utm.edu/hegelsoc/

Heywood, A. (2013). *Politics* (4th Revised edition). Red Globe Press. doi:10.1007/978-1-137-27244-7

Heywood, A. (2021). *Political Ideologies*. Bloomsbury Publishing.

HobbesT. (2002). *Moral and Political Philosophy*. Retrieved: https://plato.stanford.edu/entries/hobbes-moral/

Hume, D. (2022). *Essays, Moral and Political*. Retrieved from: https://books.google.ge/books?id=IHQPAAAAQAAJ&pg=PR1&redir_esc=y#v=onepage&q&f=false

Jean-Jacques, R. (1762). *Social Contract*. Retrieved from: https://www.britannica.com/topic/The-Social-Contract

Locke, J. (2020). *Social Contract*. Retrieved from: https://www.britannica.com/biography/John-Locke

Marx, K. (1992). *Capital Vol. 1: Volume 1: a Critique of Political Economy by Karl Marx*. Retrieved from: https://www.ebay.com/p/38925?mkevt=1&siteid=1&mkcid=2&mkrid=711-153320-877673

Montesquieu, C. (1732). *Spirit of the Laws*. Retrieved from: https://plato.stanford.edu/entries/montesquieu/

Nozick, R. (1975). *Anarchy, State, and Utopia*. Retrieved from: https://www.nationalbook.org/books/anarchy-state-and-utopia/

Paine, T. (1791). *The Age of Reason*. Retrieved from: https://www.biography.com/scholar/thomas-paine

Shubitidze, V., Gudushauri, N., Papashvili, M., & Kveselava, I. (2010). *Political Science*. Georgian Technical University.

United Nations Human Rights Office of the High Commissioner. (2022). *International Covenant on Civil and Political Rights*. Retrieved from: https://www.ohchr.org/en/instruments-mechanisms/instruments/international-covenant-civil-and-political-rights

KEY TERMS AND DEFINITIONS

Civil Rights: Guarantee equal social opportunities and equal protection under the law, regardless of race, religion, or other personal characteristics. Examples of civil rights include the right to vote, the right to a fair trial, the right to government services, the right to public education, and the right to use public facilities. Civil rights are an essential component of democracy; when individuals are being denied opportunities to participate in political society, they are being denied their civil rights. In contrast to civil liberties, which are freedoms that are secured by placing restraints on government, civil rights are secured by positive government action, often in the form of legislation. Civil rights laws attempt to guarantee full and equal citizenship for people who have traditionally been discriminated against based on some group characteristic. When the enforcement of civil rights is found by many to be inadequate, a civil rights movement may emerge to call for equal application of the laws without discrimination.

Civil Society: A community that embraces shared norms and ethical standards to collectively manage problems without coercion and through peaceful and democratic procedures for decision-making aimed at improving human welfare.

Human Rights: The political rights and civil liberties recognized by the international community as inalienable and valid for individuals in all countries under their humanity.

Legal Rights: Those rights bestowed onto a person by a given legal system (they can be modified, repealed, and restrained by human laws). The concept of positive law is related to the concept of legal rights.

Natural Rights: Those rights that are not dependent on the laws or customs of any particular culture or government, and so are *universal*, *fundamental*, and *inalienable* (they cannot be repealed by human laws, though one can forfeit their enjoyment through one's actions, such as by violating someone else's rights). Natural law is the law of natural rights.

Political Rights: The rights that involve participation in the establishment or administration of a government and are usually held to entitle the adult citizen to exercise of the franchise, the holding of public office, and other political activities.

Universal Declaration of Human Rights (UDHR): Is an international document adopted by the United Nations General Assembly that enshrines the rights and freedoms of all human beings. Drafted by a UN committee chaired by Eleanor Roosevelt, it was accepted by the General Assembly as Resolution 217 during its third session on 10 December 1948 at the Palais de Chaillot in Paris, France.

Chapter 15
The Free Market Economy as the Main Guarantee of the State's Socio-Economic Development and Promoting International Cooperation

Irakli Kervalishvili
Georgian Technical University, Georgia

ABSTRACT

The free market economy is a market system in which the prices of goods and services are the result of an agreement reached freely between sellers and consumers, without the intervention of outside forces. The laws and forces of supply and demand in such a market are free from the influence of government, price-fixing monopolies, or any other power. A free market is a controlled market or a regulated market in which the government intervenes in the regulation of supply and demand through non-market methods, such as laws that prohibit market entry or that directly regulate prices. A free-market economy (market economy) is a market-based economy where the prices of goods and services are freely formed by the forces of supply and demand, and they are able to reach equilibrium without government policy interference.

INTRODUCTION – MAIN PRINCIPLES OF THE FREE MARKET

A free market is a market free from any outside interference (including government economic intervention and government regulation of the economy).

At the same time, the function of the state in the free market is reduced to the protection of property rights and the maintenance of contractual obligations. Also, a free market is defined as a market in which prices are set freely without outside interference and other external factors, solely based on supply and demand. The declared basis of the free market is the right of any manufacturer to create any product or

DOI: 10.4018/978-1-6684-4543-3.ch015

service and offer it to consumers and the consumer's right to purchase any offered product or service from any manufacturer. The price is determined as a result of an agreement between the seller and the buyer.

The History of the Emergence and Development of the Concept

The Spanish and Peruvian jurist and economist Juan de Matienso was the first to develop a detailed development of the free market in the second third of the 16th century. His theory of subjective value leads to a distinction between supply and demand elements within a market. Matienzo uses the term "competition" to describe the rivalry within the free market. In turn, it defines the concept of public auction and rivalry between buyers and sellers. But there are also other factors (described in his treatise "Commentaria Ioannis Matienzo Regii senatoris in cancellaria Argentina Regni Peru in librum quintum recollectionis legum Hispaniae. - Mantuae Carpentanae: Excudebat Franciscus Sanctius, 1580", published posthumously), besides supply and demand, affecting to determine a fair price, and describing such a variable market morphology, namely:

- abundance or shortage of goods
- abundance of buyers and sellers
- the need for some product
- work and production costs
- transformation of raw materials
- transport and wear costs
- abundance or lack of money
- geographical and weather factors
- subjective opinion of market participants
- presence or absence of monopoly structures
- expectation of the future state of all the above factors (Jolia, 2015)

The scholar Oreste Popescu observes of this whole list, extracted from the writings of Matienzo, that "Europe was not even ready to fruitfully use such a treasure of knowledge" in the 16th century (Popescu, 1997).

The representative of the same Salamanca economic school as Matienso, Juan de Lugo in 1643, in his work De Justitia et Jure, finalized the theory of Matienso. Thus, an element of any rational evaluation of a commodity, he suggested, was its usefulness. But, he noted, this was determined according to the collective subjective assessment of people, both prudent and unreasonable. The subjective overall value of a product, de Lugo argued, was thus different from its objective user value. This was further complicated by factors such as the relative scarcity of the good in question and the magnitude of the demand. These observations led de Lugo to conclude that the fair price was the market price. Never considering himself an economist, Cardinal de Lugo produced works that were the culmination of the contribution of the Salaman school to free-market theory. His research exemplifies how a serious theological study of human choice and action helped discover economic laws.

Exchange Principles

According to the representative of the Austrian School of Economics Murray Rothbard, there are only two opposite ways of interaction between people: either voluntary market exchange or coercion.

In a free market, property rights are voluntarily exchanged at a price set solely by mutual agreement between sellers and buyers. Market participants acquire property without the use of physical force, threats, fraud, and coercion through a third party (for example, with the help of the government through transfer payments). Also, in a free market, coercion is not used for unfair competition (so-called free competition). The price of goods in such a market is determined spontaneously following the law of supply and demand.

A free market is contrasted with a regulated market, in which the government directly or indirectly regulates prices or supplies, which, according to free-market theory, is why these markets are less efficient (Rotbard, 2009).

In a free market, price is an information signal that allows one to conclude where resources should be directed so that they are used with maximum efficiency. Intervention in the functioning of the free market leads to the distortion of price signals and a decrease in the efficiency of the use of resources.

The free market model should not be confused with the ideal market model, where subjects have complete information and there is perfect competition. For a free market, these conditions are not mandatory (Barrons, 1995).

Free Market and Politics

The idea of a free market is closely related to the laissez-faire economic policy, according to which government economic intervention should be minimal. The role of the government is to protect the rights, as well as to create and maintain a tax system that ensures the existence of the state. Some free marketers also object to taxation. In particular, anarcho-capitalists propose to replace taxation with arbitration and private security agencies.

Some economists view the free market as a means to social ends, others consider the free market to be a fundamental norm and argue that interference with the functioning of the free market is harmful to society, even if this intervention is believed to bring some short-term social benefits. Ronald Coase wrote that these alternatives are far inferior to the free market system.

In terms of political economy, the extreme opposite of a free market economy is a planned or command economy, where decisions regarding production, distribution, and pricing are the prerogative of the state. A mixed economy is an intermediate option between a planned economy and a free market.

In social philosophy, the free market economy is a system for the distribution of goods within society: it is purchasing power that serves as a link between supply and demand, and not the state or someone's subjective opinion, which determines what exactly will be produced and who will consume what. The first proponents of free-market economics in 18th century Europe contrasted it with medieval economics and mercantilism (Journal of Law and Economics, 1960).

Supply and Demand

In a situation where the demand for a product matches the supply, a transaction occurs. This can happen automatically, which is typical, for example, for the stock exchange. But in reality, most shops and markets are not like the stock exchange, and there are significant transaction costs.

When demand exceeds supply, suppliers may raise their prices. Consumers who can afford higher prices will continue to maintain demand at this level, but others will refrain from buying or demand a better price. They can also buy a substitute product, or look for the same product elsewhere. Once prices rise, suppliers have an opportunity to increase production. It also lowers the barrier to entry for new manufacturers by increasing potential profitability.

In the opposite situation, when supply is higher than demand, some suppliers start to lower the price to have an advantage in the sale. In this situation, profitability and incentives for the production of this product are reduced.

"The invisible hand of the market". Adam Smith

For the first time, the concept of the "invisible hand of the market" was proposed by the Scottish philosopher of the 17th century, Adam Smith, in his work "A Study on the Nature and Causes of the Wealth of Nations". Smith described the operation of the "invisible hand" as follows:

"[Whoever] intends to pursue only his gain is being led by an invisible hand towards a goal that was not part of his original intention. The worst and worst for society are not always represented by structures that are outside this society. By pursuing his interest or benefit, [the individual] contributes to the benefit of society much more effectively than if he intended to promote it" (Smith, 1776).

Smith pointed out that no one has yet received their dinner by appealing to the brotherly love of a butcher, farmer, or baker. Rather, each turns to his benefit and receives it for his work. Smith wrote:

It is not because of the benevolence and generosity of the butcher, brewer, or baker that we look forward to our dinner, but only because of their selfish benefit. We appeal not to their humanism, but their selfish love for themselves, and we never tell them about our needs, but only about their benefit.

Spontaneous Order

Friedrich August von Hayek

The theory of classical liberalism of A. Smith in the middle of the 20th century was developed by representatives of the Austrian economic school. So F. A. von Hayek points out that the free market provides the so-called. "spontaneous order" in which, naturally and without the involvement of regulators, "a more efficient allocation of public resources is achieved than could be achieved with any other solution." According to this view, market economies form complex business networks that produce and distribute goods and services throughout the economy. This network emerges as a result of decentralized individual economic decisions (Hayek, 2001).

Proponents of this view believe that the spontaneous order is superior to any other order, which does not allow individuals to exercise their own choice of what to produce, what to buy, what to sell, and at what prices, due to the multitude and complexity involved in this process factors. They also believe that any attempt to apply central planning will result in more chaos and disorder and less efficient production and distribution of goods and services.

Economic Balance

The law of supply and demand prevails in an ideal free market. It influences prices by maintaining a balance that balances the demand for products. At these equilibrium prices, the market allocates products to buyers according to their preference (or utility) for each product, and within the interrelated limits of purchasing power for each buyer.

This balancing behavior of free markets makes certain commitments to their agents, such as that they act independently. Some models in econophysics have shown that when agents are allowed to interact locally in a free market (that is, their decisions depend not only on utility and purchasing power but also on the decisions of their circle of people), then prices become unstable and deviate from equilibrium quite often., and in a very blunt manner. The behavior of such a free market would thus be non-linear (a pair of agents negotiating with each other would agree on a different price than 100 identical pairs of agents negotiating the same transaction). Speculative bubbles and the type of herd behavior often seen in stock markets are cited as real-life examples of non-linear price trends. Free market advocates, especially those of the Austrian School, often dismiss this endogenous theory as external influences such as the weather, the prices of everyday commodities, the latest technological developments, and government intervention, which they believe lead to unbalanced prices (Ball, 2015). Market equilibrium is determined by a combination of sellers and buyers and is usually not the result of a unique pricing policy.

Wealth Distribution

On a theoretical level, free-market advocates do not care about the distribution of wealth, however, in practical political terms, this issue is very important. The distribution of purchasing power in an economy depends, to a large extent, on the nature of government intervention, social classes, the labor market, and the financial market, as well as on other, less significant factors, such as family relations, the institution of inheritance, gifts, and the like. Many free-market theories focus primarily on consumer product markets, and their descriptions of the labor market or financial markets tend to be complex and controversial. In a free market, buying a product is equivalent to voting for the manufacturer, where the buyer is in favor of continuing to produce that product (COLE, 2007).

The impact of economic freedom on the wealth of society and the individual remains a matter of debate. Kenneth Arrow and Gérard Debreux have shown that, under certain idealized conditions, a free trade system leads to Pareto efficiency, and the traditional Arrow-Debreux paradigm within the economy is now being replaced by the new Greenwald-Stiglitz paradigm. Many advocates of free markets, most notably Milton Friedman, have also argued that there is a direct correlation between economic growth and economic freedom, although this claim is much more difficult to prove empirically. And the ongoing debate among scholars on the methodological aspects of empirical research on the relationship between economic freedom and economic growth points to this: "Several attempts have been made to study the relationship between economic growth and economic freedom. They were helpful but used incomplete or subjective variables (AYAL, 1998)."

Joshua Epstein and Robert Axtell attempted to predict the properties of free markets empirically in a multivariate computer simulation called Sugar Stick. They again concluded that, under ideal conditions, free markets lead to a Pareto distribution of wealth.

On the other hand, recent studies, one of which was conducted by Joseph Stiglitz, contradict Friedman's conclusions. According to Boettke:

If incomplete or imperfect information is entered, then the advocates of the Chicago School market system cannot hold onto descriptive Pareto efficiency formulas for the real world. Thus, Stiglitz's use of rational expectations balance assumptions to achieve a more realistic understanding of capitalism than is usually the case among rational expectations theorists leads to the paradoxical conclusion that capitalism deviates from a model to a certain extent that justifies the act of state intervention - socialism - as a remedy (Boettke, 2011).

Laissez-Faire Economics

Mandatory components of the functioning of an idealized free market include the complete absence of artificial price pressures derived from taxes, subsidies, tariffs, or government regulations and the absence of state-protected monopolies (commonly classified by free-market advocates as coercive monopolies), such as the United States Postal States, Amtrak, patent office and so on.

Deregulation

In an ideal free-market economy, all capital, goods, services, and money flows are not regulated by the government, except in cases of secret agreements or fraud that may occur among market participants. Since this protection must be supported by material funds, it is necessary to have government taxes necessary to perform this important function. Free markets are defended by economic liberals. Since the 1970s, the acceleration of the global free-market economy, deregulation, and privatization has often been described as neo-libertarianism. The term "free market economy" is sometimes used to describe some of the economies that exist today (such as the Hong Kong economy), but free-market advocates would only accept this description if the government practiced a hands-off policy rather than state intervention in the economy. An economy that contains a significant element of economic government intervention while at the same time retaining some of the characteristics found in a free market economy is often referred to as a mixed economy.

Low Barriers to Entry

A free market does not require the existence of competition, however, it requires that there are no barriers for new entrants to the market. From this, it is concluded that the absence of compulsory barriers in a free market leads to the flourishing of competition. Incentives for profit are often assumed, although neither these incentives nor profit itself are necessary for a free market. It is understood that all modern free markets include entrepreneurs, both individual and united on a corporate or cooperative basis. The modern free-market economy includes such sectors of the economy as the stock exchange and the financial services sector, but they are not decisive.

Legal Tender and Taxes

In a completely free market economy, money should not be monopolized through legal tender laws, or through a central money issuing authority that forces society to use its own money as the only medium of exchange in trade transactions to collect taxes on transactions. or be able to borrow. Minarchists (advocates of minimal government intervention) argue that the so-called "enforcement" of taxes is vital to the survival of these markets and that a tax-free market can lead to no market at all. By definition, there is no market without private property, and private property can only exist as long as there is an organization that defines and protects it. Traditionally, the state protects private property and defines it by issuing title deeds, and also appoints a central authority to print or mint money (The Machinery of Freedom, 2022).

Anarcho-capitalists do not agree with the above assessment - they argue that the institution of private property and free markets can be protected through voluntarily funded institutions, following the concepts of individualist anarchism and anarcho-capitalism. A free market can alternatively be defined as a tax-free market, independent of any central authority that uses money as a mode of exchange, even in the absence of a state.

Ethical Justification

The ethical justification for free markets takes two forms. One appeals to the internal moral superiority of autonomy and freedom. The other is a form of consequence theory—the belief that decentralized planning by many individual economic decision-makers produces better outcomes for a more organized, efficient, and productive economy than does a centrally planned economy where a central authority decides what to produce., and distributes goods through non-price mechanisms. An older version of this argument is the Invisible Hand metaphor familiar from the work of Adam Smith.

Modern theories of self-organization say that the internal organization of a system can grow automatically, without guidance or control from an external source. Other teachings, such as some forms of anarcho-individualism (especially those with roots in the 19th century) and mutualism, believe that competition in a free market will cause the price of goods and services to be adjusted to equalize the price of labor invested in these things. This goes against the current mainstream view, which is held by most modern anarchists, which maintains that prices will correspond to the marginal utility of these things, no matter how much labor is put into them.

On Practice

While the free market is an idealized abstraction, it is nonetheless useful in understanding real markets—whether they are artificially created and regulated by governments or non-government agencies. It is also useful in understanding the phenomena of the black market and the shadow economy. Many free-market advocates point to industries such as the drug trade to argue that the phenomenon is spontaneous and can function without government intervention, although some would prefer contracts to be enforceable. In the United States, forced state intervention in the economy during the economic crisis in 2009 was explained as follows:

"If all families and all firms in America simultaneously cut their spending, then no one will spend money, the number of consumers will fall, which in turn will lead to new layoffs and the situation in the economy will worsen even more. That is why the government had to intervene and temporarily increase spending to stimulate demand. That is what we are doing now," the American president said.

- "Obama sees light at the end of the tunnel" (Euronews, 2014).

Index of Economic Freedom

The Heritage Foundation has attempted to identify the key factors that measure the degree of freedom of a country's economy. In 1986, they introduced the Index of Economic Freedom, which is based on almost 50 parameters. This and other similar indicators measure the extent to which the modern economy is free, in most cases, free from government intervention. These variables can be divided into the following main groups:

- Trade policy
- Government financial burden
- Government intervention in the economy
- Monetary policy
- Capital flows and foreign investment
- Banking and finance
- Wages and prices
- Private property rights
- Regulation
- Informal market activity.

Each group is assigned a numerical value from 1 to 5. The index of economic freedom is the arithmetic average of these values, rounded up to hundredths. Initially, countries that were traditionally considered capitalist received high ratings, but the method improved over time. Some laissez-faire economists have argued for a thesis that claims there is a direct link between economic growth and economic freedom, but this claim has not yet been proven, either theoretically or practically. An ongoing debate among scholars on the methodological aspects of empirical research on the relationship between economic freedom and economic growth is still trying to discover what, if any, relationship there is between the two (De Haan, 2007).

In recent years, a significant amount of work has been devoted to exploring the possible relationship between the political system and economic growth. There is no consensus on many of the basic postulates of this relationship, especially concerning causal relationships if any. (AYAL & KARRAS, 1998).

History and Ideology

Some theorists (such as Ludwig von Mises and Friedrich von Hayek) argue that a free market is a natural form of social organization and that the free market will emerge in any society where it is not blocked. The consensus among economic historians is that the free market economy is a specific historical phenomenon and that it arose in the late Middle Ages and at the very beginning of the birth of modern Europe. Other economic historians see elements of the free market in the economic systems of Classical Antiquity and some non-Western societies. By the 19th century, the market certainly had an organized political backing, in the form of laissez-faire liberalism. However, it is unclear whether this support preceded or followed the emergence of this market. Some historians see this as the result of the success of early liberal ideology combined with the specific interests of entrepreneurs.

Marxism

In Marxist theory, the idea of the free market is expressed through a deep and long process of transition from feudalism to capitalism. Views on this issue—emergence or realization—do not necessarily correspond to pro-market or anti-market positions. Libertarians dispute that the market was strengthened by government policy because they believe it is spontaneous. At the same time, Marxists agree with them, since they also believe in its evolutionary nature, although they pursue other goals.

Liberalism

Support for the idea of the free market as the organizing principle of society is highly associated with liberalism, especially during the 19th century. (In Europe, the term "liberalism" includes in its implied sense the ideology of the free market, but when the term is used in the US and Canada, this concept can be associated with government intervention and has acquired a pejorative meaning for free-market apologists.) More recent ideological developments, such as monarchism, libertarianism, and objectivism also support the free market and insist on its purest form. Although the Western world shares largely similar forms of economies, the use of the term in the US and Canada correlates with capitalism, while in Europe "free market" is mostly a neutral term. Contemporary liberalism (of American and Canadian usage), and European social democracy, are making efforts to soften what they see as the problems of an unrestricted free market and accept its existence as such.

Libertarianism

For most libertarians, the free market is still simply non-existent, limited by the degree of government intervention in most of even the most "capitalist" countries in the world. From their point of view, those who say they are promoting a "free market" are speaking in a relative rather than an absolute sense - which means (in libertarian terminology) that they wish enforcement to be kept to a minimum level than is necessary to maximize economic freedom (such necessary enforcement would be, for example, taxation) and market efficiency, by lowering trade barriers, making the tax system neutral in its impact on important decisions such as capital increases, i.e. the elimination of double taxation on dividends from so that financing from own funds is not unprofitable compared to debt financing. However, there are, for example, anarcho-capitalists who do not even entertain the thought of taxation and government intervention, preferring instead to see the defenders of economic freedom in the form of private contracting firms (Jolia, 2015).

Criticism

Critics dispute the claim that, in practice, free markets create perfect competition, or even increase market competition in the long run. The question is also debated whether there should be a free market or whether it is free; many argue that government intervention is mandatory to prevent the so-called market fiasco, which is supposed to be the inevitable result of absolutely strict adherence to free-market principles. These cases range from military service to roads, and some include healthcare. This is the main argument of those who insist on mixed markets, essentially free but with government oversight, to manage and solve social problems.

Laissez-faire critics variously see the "free market" as an impractical ideal, or as a rhetorical device that puts the concepts of freedom and anti-protectionism at the service of the wealthy, allowing them to subvert labor laws and other protections for the working class.

Because no national economy currently in existence proclaims itself fully to be the ideal of the free market, as theorized by economists, some critics of the concept view it as pure fantasy—out of touch with reality in a complex system of opposing interests and various ways of redistributing wealth.

These critics range from those who reject markets outright in favor of planned or collective economies, such as defenders of certain types of socialism, to those who simply wish to see markets regulated to varying degrees.

Externalities

One practical objection is to claim that markets do not take into account externalities (effects of transactions that affect third parties), such as the negative effects of environmental pollution or the positive aspects of education, although this is disputed by those who oppose these manifestations, arguing that pollution can and regularly deals with lawsuits, thanks to the principle of protecting individual freedoms and private property rights. What exactly constitutes externalities can also be contested and be the source of further debate, including the scope of these changes, given the political environment.

Some proponents of market economies (such as John Rawls) believe that governments should not reduce market freedom because they disagree with market manifestation and disagree on the appropriate level of intervention needed to resolve market-created externalities. Others believe that the government should intervene to prevent the market from collapsing while at the same time maintaining the basic nature of the market economy. In the model of the social market economy, the state intervenes where the market does not meet political requirements.

Various Free Market Concepts

Some free marketers have criticized the underlying concepts of the free market, insisting that a truly free market has nothing to do with a capitalist economy. They argue that even limited government pressure, by enacting specific property laws, distorts this market. In a truly free market, these critics insist, the concept of property rights would be different from that currently held by most free-market advocates.

For example, contemporary mutualist Kevin Carson argues for "free-market anti-capitalism." Carson stated that "From Smith to Ricardo and Mill, classical liberalism was a revolutionary doctrine that attacked the privileges of large landowners and their commercial interests. Today we see vulgar libertarians twisting the "free market" theory to defend a modern institution that, on closer inspection, resembles, in terms of power and privilege, the landed oligarchies and merchants of the Old Regime: giant corporations (Carson, 2009).

Carson believes that a true free market society would be "a world in which… land and property are widely dispersed, capital is freely available to workers through joint banks, efficient technology is freely available in every country without patents, and every people is free to develop unhindered." locally without any colonial robbery…"

Martin J. Whitman

Not all defenders of capitalism see free markets as a utilitarian universal. For example, Martin J. Whitman wrote in a discussion with Keynes, Friedman, and Hayek that these "...great economists...have missed a lot of details that are part and parcel of the daily life of every long-term investor." Simultaneously calling Hayek "100% right" in his critique of the command economy, he writes further: "However, it by no means follows, as many of Hayek's students seem sincere to believe, that government is inherently bad and unproductive, while the private sector is inherently good and productive. In well-performing industrial economies, there is a close alliance between the government and the private sector, each of which benefits from such an alliance. As an illustration of this point of view, he points to Japan after World War II, Singapore and other Asian tigers, Sweden and China. A notable exception is the Hong Kong economic zone, which thrives solely on a strictly free market concept" (Whitman, 2004).

He argues, in particular, for the value of public credit and sound tax legislation. In addition, Whitman insists (which is in serious contradiction with Hayek's views) that "the free market situation is also doomed to failure if there are managers who do not respect the external order imposed by various forces above and above the competition." The lack of these ordering forces, says Whitman, leads to:

1. Exorbitant salaries for executives…
2. Poorly funded business with strong prospects of default on loan obligations…
3. Speculative bubbles…
4. The trend towards industrial competition, evolving into monopoly and oligarchy ...
5. Corruption

In doing so, he cites recent examples from the US economy, which he sees as underregulated in some respects, yet overregulated in other respects (he especially opposes the Sarbani-Oxley Act of 2002).

He believes that the seemingly "loose" relationship—between a corporation and its investors and creditors—is, in reality, a mixture of "voluntary exchanges" and "coercion." For example, there is "voluntary activity where each individual makes his or her own decision to buy, sell or refrain from doing so", but there is also what he defines as "coercive activity where each status holder is compelled to comply with the decision majority ... provided that the necessary majority of other holders of status so vote ... ". He cites proxy voting, most mergers and acquisitions, certain cash purchase offers, and bankruptcy reorganizations or liquidations as examples. Whitman also argues that "Corporate America wouldn't work at all if many activities weren't forced."

"I agree with Professor Friedman that, other things being equal, it is far preferable to ensure economic activity through voluntary exchange, relying more on free markets than on coercion. But corporate America wouldn't work at all if many activities weren't coercive" (Whitman, 2005).

CONCLUSION

Free Market - A market system in which the prices of goods and services are the result of an agreement reached freely between sellers and consumers, without the intervention of outside forces. The laws and forces of supply and demand in such a market are free from the influence of government, price-fixing monopolies, or any other power. A free market is a controlled market or a regulated market in which the government intervenes in the regulation of supply and demand through non-market methods, such as laws that prohibit market entry or that directly regulate prices. A free-market economy (market economy) is a market-based economy where the prices of goods and services are freely formed by the forces of supply and demand and they can reach equilibrium without government policy interference. Typically, a free-market economy involves the support of highly competitive markets and the private ownership (or capitalism) of industrial enterprises. Although the free market is largely associated with capitalism in the modern sense of the word (and also in popular culture), anarchists, socialists, etc. often build their theories on free markets.

REFERENCES

Ayal, E. B., & Karras, G. (1998). Components of Economic Freedom and Growth. Western Illinois University.

Ball, P. (2003). *Critical Mass. How One Thing Leads to Another*. Economics.

Barrons. (1995). *Dictionary of Finance and Investment Terms*. Retrieved from: https://www.amazon.com/Dictionary-Finance-Investment-Business-Dictionaries/dp/1438001401

Boettke, P. J. (2015). What Went Wrong with Economics? *Critical Review*, *11*(1).

Carson, K. (2009). *The Iron Fist Behind the Invisible Hand: Corporate Capitalism as a State-Guaranteed System of Privilege*. Wayback Machine.

Cole, J. H., & Lawson, R. A. H. (2007). Economic Freedom in Growth Regressions: Suggestions for Clarification. *Econ Journal Watch*, *4*(1).

Dehaan , & Sturm, . (2007). Handling Economic Freedom in Growth Regressions: A Reply to Cole and Lawson. *Econ Journal Watch*, *4*(1).

Euronews. (2009). *Obama touts Economic Progress*. Retrieved from: https://ru.euronews.com/2009/04/14/obama-touts-economic-progress

Jolia, G. (2015). International Economic Relations. European University. *Journal of Law and Economics*. Retrieved from: https://www.jstor.org/stable/724810

Petsoulas, C. (2001). *Hayek's Liberalism and Its Origins: His Idea of Spontaneous Order and the Scottish Enlightenment*. Routledge.

Popescu, O. (1997). *Studies in the History of Latin American Economic Thought*. Routledge. doi:10.4324/9780203441329

Rotbard, M. (2010). *Power and Market*. Government and the Economy.

Smith, A. (1776). *Wealth of Nations*. Retrieved from: https://books.google.ge/books?id=0lYTWaIAQDYC&pg=PR1&source=kp_read_button&hl=en&redir_esc=y#v=onepage&q&f=false

The Machinery of Freedom. (2022). *Guide to a Radical Capitalism*. Retrieved from: http://www.daviddfriedman.com/Libertarian/Machinery_of_Freedom/MofF_Contents.html

Whitman, M. J. (2005). *Third Avenue Value Fund Letters to our Shareholders. Wayback Machine.*

KEY TERMS AND DEFINITIONS

Absolute Advantage: The liberal economic concept that a state should specialize in the production of goods in which the costs of production are lowest compared with those of other countries.

Classical Liberal Economic Theory: A body of thought based on Adam Smith's ideas about the forces of supply and demand in the marketplace, emphasizing the benefits of minimal government regulation of the economy and trade.

Collective Good: A public good, such as safe drinking water, from which everyone benefits.

Commercial Liberalism: An economic theory advocating free markets and the removal of barriers to the flow of trade and capital as a locomotive for prosperity.

Comparative Advantage: The concept in liberal economics that a state will benefit if it specializes in the production of those goods which it can produce at a lower opportunity cost.

Complex Interdependence: A model of world politics based on the assumptions that states are not the only important actors, security is not the dominant national goal, and military force is not the only significant instrument of foreign policy. This theory stresses cross-cutting ways in which the growing ties among transnational actors make them vulnerable to each other's actions and sensitive to each other's needs.

Developed Countries: A category used by the World Bank (WDI2009) to identify Global North countries, with a GNI per capita of $11,456 or more annually.

Developing Countries: A category used by the World Bank to identify low-income Global South countries with a 2009 GNI per capita below $935 and middle-income countries with a GNI per capita of more than $935 but less than $11,456.

Ecopolitics: How political actors influence perceptions of, and policy responses to changing environmental conditions, such as the impact of carbon dioxide emissions on the temperature of the Earth.

Embedded Liberalism: Dominant economic approach during the Bretton Woods system, which combined open international markets with domestic state intervention to attain such goals as full employment and social welfare.

Exchange Rates: The rate at which one state's currency is exchanged for another state's currency in the global marketplace.

Export Quotas: Barriers to free trade agreed to by two trading states to protect their domestic producers.

Export-Led Industrialization: A growth strategy that concentrates on developing domestic export industries capable of competing in overseas markets.

Fixed Exchange Rates: A system in which a government sets the value of its currency at a fixed rate for exchange about another country's currency so that the exchange value is not free to fluctuate in the global money market.

Floating Exchange Rates: An unmanaged process in which governments neither establish an official rate for their currencies nor intervene to affect the values of their currencies and instead allow market forces and private investors to influence the relative rate of exchange for currencies between countries.

Foreign Aid: Economic assistance in the form of loans and grants provided by a donor country to a recipient country for a variety of purposes.

Foreign Direct Investment (FDI): A cross-border investment through which a person or corporation based in one country purchases or constructs an asset such as a factory or bank in another country so that a long–term relationship and control of an enterprise by nonresidents results.

General Agreement on Tariffs and Trade (GATT): An UN-affiliated IGO designed to promote international trade and tariff reductions, replaced by the World Trade Organization.

Geo-Economics: The relationships between geography and the economic conditions in the behavior of states that define their levels of production, trade, and consumption of goods and services.

Global Commons: The physical and organic characteristics and resources of the entire planet- the air in the atmosphere in conditions on land and sea- on which is the common heritage of all humanity.

Global East: The rapidly growing economies of East and South Asia that have made those countries competitors with the traditionally dominant countries of the Global North.

Global North: A term used to refer to the world`s wealthy, industrialized countries located primarily in the Northern hemisphere.

Global South: A term now often used instead of the Third World to designate the less developed countries located primarily in the Southern Hemisphere.

Global Village: A popular cosmopolitan perspective describing the growth of awareness that all people share a common fate because the world is becoming an integrated and independent whole.

Globalization: The integration of states through increasing contact, communication, and trade as well as increased global awareness of such integration.

Globalization of Finance: The increasing trans nationalization of national international markets through the worldwide integration of capital flows.

Globalization of Labor: Integration of labor markets, predicated by the global nature of production as well as the increased size and mobility of the global labor force.

Globalization of Production: Trans nationalization of the productive process, in which finished goods rely on inputs from multiple countries outside of their final market.

Globally Integrated Enterprises: MNCs organized horizontally with management in production located in plants in numerous states for the same products they market.

Gross National Product (GNP): A measure of the production of goods and services within a given period that is used to delimit the geographic scope of production. GNI measures production by a state's citizens or companies regardless of where the production occurs.

Human Development Index (HDI): An index that uses life expectancy literacy, the average number of years of schooling, and income to assess a country's performance in providing for its people's welfare and security.

Import: Substitution industrialization –a strategy for economic development that centers on providing investors at home incentives to produce goods so that previously imported products from abroad will decline.

Import Quotas: Numerical limit on the number of particular products that can be imported.

Infant Industry: Newly established industries (infants) that are not yet strong enough to compete against mature foreign producers in the global marketplace until in time they develop and can then compete.

International Liquidity: Reserve assets used to settle international accounts.

International Monetary Fund: A financial agency now affiliated with the UN established in 1944 to promote international monetary cooperation, free trade exchange rate stability, and democratic rule by providing financial assistance and loans to countries facing financial crises.

International Monetary System: The financial procedures used to calculate the value of currencies and credits when capital is transferred across borders through trade, investment, foreign aid, and loans.

International Political Economy: The study of the intersection of politics and economics that illuminates why changes occur in the distribution of states' wealth and power.

International Regime: Embodies the norms, principles, and rules. An institution around which global expectations unite regarding a specific international problem.

Liberal International Economic Order (LIEO): The set of regimes created after World War II designed to promote monetary stability and reduce barriers to the free flow of trade and capital.

Liberalism: A paradigm predicated on the hope that the application of reason and universal ethics international relations can lead to a more orderly, just, and cooperative world. liberalism assumes that anarchy and war can be policed by institutional reforms that empower international organizations and law.

Long Cycle Theory: A theory that focuses on the rise and fall of the leading global power as the central political process of the modern world system.

Macroeconomics: The study of aggregate economic indicators such as GDP, the money supply, and the balance of trade that governments monitor to measure changes in national and global economies such as the rates of economic growth and inflation or the level of unemployment.

Marxist-Leninism: Communism theory as derived from the writings of Karl Marx, Vladimir Lenin, and their successors, which criticizes capitalism as a cause of the class struggle, the exploitation of workers, colonialism, and war.

Modernization: A view of development popular in the Global North's liberal democracies that wealth is created through efficient production, free enterprise, and free trade and that countries relative wealth depends on technological innovation and education more than on natural endowments such as climate.

Monetary Policy: The decisions made by state central banks to change the country's money supply to manage the national economy and control inflation using fiscal policies such as changing the money supply and interest rate.

Monetary System: The processes for determining the rate at which each state's currency is valued against every other state, so that purchasers and sellers can calculate the costs of financial transactions across borders such as foreign investments, trade, and cross-border travel.

Money Supply: The total amount of currency in circulation in a state calculated to include demand deposits such as checking accounts in commercial banks, and time deposits such as savings accounts and bonds in savings banks.

Most-Favored-Nation Principle (MFN): the central GATT principle of unconditional nondiscriminatory treatment in trade between contracting parties underscoring the WTO's rule requiring any advantage given by one WTO member to also extend it to all other WTO members.

Multinational Corporations (MNCs): Business enterprises headquartered in one state that invest and operate extensively in many other states,

Neoliberalism: The new liberal theoretical perspective that accounts for the way international institutions promote global change, cooperation, peace, and prosperity through collective programs for reforms.

Neomercantilism: A contemporary version of classical mercantilism that advocates promoting domestic production and a balance of payment surplus by subsidizing exports and using tariffs and non-tariff barriers to reduce imports.

New International Economic Order (NIEO): The 1974 policy resolution in the UN that called for a North-South dialogue to open the way for the less-developed countries of the Global South to participate more fully in the making of international economic policy.

Newly Industrialized Countries (NICs): The most prosperous members of the global South which have become more important exporters of manufactured goods as well as important markets for the major industrialized countries that export capital goods.

Non-Tariff Barriers: Measures other than tariffs that discriminate against imports without direct tax levels and are beyond the scope of international regulations.

North American Free Trade Agreement (NAFTA): An agreement that brings Mexico into the free trade zone linking Canada and the US.

Official Development Assistance: Grants or loans to countries from donor countries are now usually channeled through such as the World Bank for the primary purpose of promoting economic development and welfare.

Opportunity Cost: The sacrifices that sometimes result when the decision to select one option means that the opportunity to realize gains from other options is lost.

Orderly Market Arrangements: Voluntary export restrictions through government-to-government agreements to follow specific trading rules.

Political Economy: A field of study that focuses on the intersection of politics and economics in international relations.

Purchasing Power Parity (PPP): An index that calculates the true rate of exchange among currencies when parity—when what can be purchased is the same—is achieved the index determines what can be thought of with a unit of each currency.

Tariffs: Tax assessed on goods as they are imported into a country.

Third World: A Cold War term to describe the less-developed countries of Africa, Asia, The Caribbean, and Latin America.

Trade Integration: The difference between gross rates in trade and gross domestic product.

Transparency: About the GATT the principle that trade barriers must be visible and thus easy to target.

Virtual Corporations: Agreements between otherwise competitive MNCs are often temporary to join forces and skills to coproduce and export particular products in the borderless global marketplace.

Washington Consensus: The view that Global South countries can best achieve sustained economic growth through democratic governance fiscal discipline free markets a reliance on private enterprise, and trade liberalization.

World-System Theory: A body of theory that treats the capitalistic world economy originating in the sixteenth century as an interconnected unit of analysis encompassing the entire globe.

Compilation of References

Abraham, I., & Rajadhyaksha, A. (2015). State Power and Technological Citizenship in India: From the Postcolonial to the Digital Age. *East Asian Science, Technology and Society*, *9*(1), 65–85. doi:10.1215/18752160-2863200

ACAPS. (2020, November 20). *Azerbaijan and Armenia: Conflict in Nagorno-Karabakh.* Retrieved from reliefweb: https://reliefweb.int/sites/reliefweb.int/files/resources/20201120_acaps_short_note_update_nagorno-karabakh_0.pdf

Ahmad, T., Alvi, A., & Ittefaq, M. (2019). The use of social media on political participation among university students: An analysis of survey results from rural Pakistan. *SAGE Open*, *9*(3), 2158244019864484. doi:10.1177/2158244019864484

Alber, J., & Gilbert, N. (2010). *United in Diversity? Comparing Social Models in Europe and America.* Oxford Scholarship.

Aleksidze, L. (2016). *Dictionary of International Law*. Tbilisi State University. Retrieved from: https://www.britannica.com/topic/hylomorphism

Aleksidze. (2016). *Dictionary of International Law*. Tbilisi State University.

Aleksidze, L. (2016). *International Law. Handbook*. Tbilisi State University.

Alexis de Tocqueville. (1840). *Democracy in America*. Retrieved from: https://www.history.com/topics/france/alexis-de-tocqueville#:~:text=As%20%E2%80%9CDemocracy%20in%20America%E2%80%9D%20revealed,example%20of%20equality%20in%20action

Alexis de Tocqueville. (2017). *The State of Society in France Before the Revolution of 1789.* Retrieved from: https://www.gutenberg.org/ebooks/54187

Alizada, N., Cole, R., Gastaldi, L., Grahn, S., Hellmeier, S., Kolvani, P., Lachapelle, J., Lührmann, A., Maerz, S. F., Pillai, S., & Lindberg, S. I. (2021). *Autocratization Turns Viral: Democracy Report 2021. University of Gothenburg.* V-Dem Institute.

Althusser, L. (2014). Ideology and Ideological State Apparatuses (G. M. Gosgharian, Trans.). Verso Publish.

Anand, P. L. (2017). *International and non-International Armed Conflicts And Application of International Humanitarian Law as Lex Specials.* Academic Press.

Anderson, J., & Rainie, L. (2020). *Broader thoughts from key experts on the future of democracy at a time of digital disruption.* Pew Research Center. https://www.pewresearch.org/internet/2020/02/21/broader-thoughts-from-key-experts-on-the-future-of-democracy-at-a-time-of-digital-disruption/

Annan, K. (2004). *Creation of a common conceptual apparatus in the field of justice for the United Nations. The rule of law and transitional justice in conflict and post-conflict societies.* Report of the Secretary General. United Nations. Retrieved from: https://historyofeconomicthought.mcmaster.ca/aristotle/Politics.pdf

Apata, G. O. (2019). Corruption and the postocolonial state: How the west invented African corruption. *Journal of Contemporary African Studies*, *37*(1), 43–56. doi:10.1080/02589001.2018.1497292

Aquinas, T. (2010). *The Theology Sum. Part II-I. Questions 90-114. K.* Nika-Center.

Aristotle. (2022). *Politics*. Retrieved from: https://iep.utm.edu/aris-pol/

Arklan, Ü. (2016). Sosyal medyanın siyasal amaçlı kullanımı: Ağ kuşağının kullanım alışkanlıkları üzerine bir araştırma. *Gümüşhane Üniversitesi İletişim Fakültesi Elektronik Dergisi, 4*(2).

Army deals blow to Mugabe rival. (2002, January 9) http://news.bbc.co.uk/2/hi/africa/1749933.stm

Arun, teja, polcumpally. (2018). Challenges to Egypt under Al-Sisi Rule. In *India and its Emerging Foreign Policy Challenges*. New Delhi: Vji Publications.

Ayal, E. B., & Karras, G. (1998). Components of Economic Freedom and Growth. Western Illinois University.

Baili. (2020). *England and Wales High Court (King's Bench Division) Decisions*. Retrieved from: http://www.bailii.org/ew/cases/EWHC/KB/1607/J23.html

Bakker, T. P., & De Vreese, C. H. (2011). Good news for the future? Young people, Internet use, and political participation. *Communication Research*, *38*(4), 451–470. doi:10.1177/0093650210381738

Ball, P. (2003). *Critical Mass. How One Thing Leads to Another*. Economics.

Banda, I. (2020). Zimbabwe and US Tensions- DC calls Harare a Foreign Adversary. *Africa Report*.

Barrons. (1995). *Dictionary of Finance and Investment Terms*. Retrieved from: https://www.amazon.com/Dictionary-Finance-Investment-Business-Dictionaries/dp/1438001401

Bartels, R. (2016). Terrorist groups as parties to an armed conflict. In *Terrorism, Counter-Terrorism and International Humanitarian Law* (pp. 56–67). College of Europe.

Barthes, R. (1974). *S/Z: An Essay*. Farrar, Straus and Giroux.

Barthes, R. (1977). *Music Text Image*. Fontana Press.

Baudrillard, J. (1968). *The System of Objects*. Retrieved from: https://arthistoryunstuffed.com/jean-baudrillard-system-of-objects/

Baudrillard, J. (2009). *The Transparency of Evil: Essays on Extreme Phenomena*. Verso Books.

Baumann, Z. (2005). *Liquid Life*. Polity Press.

Becker, K. (2010). *Tactical Reality Dictionary: Cultural Intelligence and Social Control Paperback* (1st ed.). Autonomedia.

Bell, D. (1976). *The Coming of Post-Industrial Society: A Venture in Social Forecasting*. Basic Books. doi:10.1080/00131727609336501

Bellina, S., Darbon, D., Sundstøl, S., & Sending, O. (2009). *The Legitimacy of the State in Fragile Situations*. Norwegian Agency for Development Cooperation.

Belsham, W. (1789). *On Liberty and Necessity. Essays Philosophical and Moral, Historical and Literary, Volume I, Book I, Essay I.* Retrieved from: https://www.informationphilosopher.com/solutions/philosophers/belsham/on_liberty_and_necessity.html

Bennett, W. L. (2012). The personalization of politics: Political identity, social media, and changing patterns of participation. *The Annals of the American Academy of Political and Social Science*, *644*(1), 20–39. doi:10.1177/0002716212451428

Berlin, I. (1969). *Two Concepts of Liberty*. Retrieved from: https://cactus.dixie.edu/green/B_Readings/I_Berlin%20Two%20Concpets%20of%20Liberty.pdf

Bertelsmanstiftung. (2022). *Democracy under pressure worldwide*. https://www.bertelsmann-stiftung.de/de/startseite

Best, S. J., & Krueger, B. S. (2005). Analyzing the representativeness of Internet political participation. *Political Behavior*, *27*(2), 183–216. doi:10.100711109-005-3242-y

Bevir, M. (2014). *The Encyclopedia of Political Theory*. Wayback Machine.

Bieliński, J. (2017). *Political Legitimacy and Normative Disorientation in European Liberal Democracies*. Retrieved from: https://www.jstor.org/stable/26383075

Bilgen, K. (2019). The investigation of the attitudes of preservice teachers regarding the Rights of the Child. *Journal of Education and Training Studies*, *7*(2), 148–156. doi:10.11114/jets.v7i2.3882

Billig, M. (1995). *Banal Nationalism*. Sage Publications.

Boettke, P. J. (2015). What Went Wrong with Economics? *Critical Review*, *11*(1).

Boulianne, S. (2020). Twenty years of digital media effects on civic and political participation. *Communication Research*, *47*(7), 947–966. doi:10.1177/0093650218808186

Boulianne, S., & Theocharis, Y. (2020). Young people, digital media, and engagement: A meta-analysis of research. *Social Science Computer Review*, *38*(2), 111–127. doi:10.1177/0894439318814190

Boutros, A. (2018). The right to rights: Education as the problem and solution to the lack of enforcement of international human rights law. *International Journal of Progressive Education*, *14*(2), 161–175. doi:10.29329/ijpe.2018.139.12

Bracton. (2016). *On the Laws and Customs of England*. Wayback Machine.

Brancati, D. (2019). *Hong Kong protests have taken the globe by storm. Now the world must stand up to China*. https://www.scmp.com/comment/opinion/article/3037678/hong-kong-protests-have-taken-globe-storm-now-world-

Bratton, M. (1999). Political participation in a new democracy: Institutional considerations from Zambia. *Comparative Political Studies*, *32*(5), 549–588. doi:10.1177/0010414099032005002

Bratton, M. (2015). *Power Politics in Zimbabwe*. Lynne Rienner Publishers.

Brinkerhoff, D. W. (2007). *Capacity Development in Fragile States*. ECDPM Discussion Paper 58d.

Britannica. (2022). *Regime. Political Science*. Retrieved from: https://www.britannica.com/topic/regime

Britannica. (2022). *The theory of democracy. Democratic ideas from Pericles to Rawls*. Retrieved from: https://www.britannica.com/topic/democracy/The-theory-of-democracy

Brubaker, R. (1990). Immıgratıon, Cıtızenshıp, and the Natıon-State in France and Germany: A Comparative Historical Analysıs. *International Sociology, 5*.

Budd, J., Miller, B. S., Manning, E. M., Lampos, V., Zhuang, M., Edelstein, M., Rees, G., Emery, V. C., Stevens, M. M., Keegan, N., Short, M. J., Pillay, D., Manley, E., Cox, I. J., Heymann, D., Johnson, A. M., & McKendry, R. A. (2020). Digital technologies in the public-health response to COVID-19. *Nature Medicine*, *26*(8), 1183–1192. doi:10.103841591-020-1011-4 PMID:32770165

Budge, I. (2001). Direct democracy. In P. A. B. Clarke & J. Foweraker (Eds.), *Encyclopedia of Political Thought*. Taylor & Francis.

Caballero, Sierra, & Francisco. (2018). Cyberactivism and social movements. The Oppositional Public Space in contemporary technopolitics. *Revista Latina de Comunicación Social*, *73*, 980–990.

Calzada, I. (2019). Deciphering Smart City Citizenship: The Techno-Politics of Data and Urban Co-operative Platforms. *IEV (Revista Internacional de Estudios Vascos/International Journal on Basque Studies), 63*(1), 42-81.

Calzada, I. (2017). The techno-politics of data and smart devolution in city-regions: Comparing Glasgow, Bristol, Barcelona, and Bilbao. *Systems*, *5*(1), 1–18. doi:10.3390ystems5010018

Caplan, E., Scott, M., Perse, E., & Gennaria, J. (2011). Computer Mediated Technology and Social Interaction. In Communication Technology and Social Change. Routledge.

Carney, T. (2020, January 22). *Applying International Law to the Nagorno-Karabakh Conflict*. Retrieved from OpinioJuris: http://opiniojuris.org/2020/01/22/applying-international-law-to-the-nagorno-karabakh-conflict/

Carson, K. (2009). *The Iron Fist Behind the Invisible Hand: Corporate Capitalism as a State-Guaranteed System of Privilege*. Wayback Machine.

Carter, A. (2012). *People Power and Political Change*. Routledge.

Cassidy, C., Brunner, R., & Webster, E. (2014). Teaching human rights? 'All hell will break loose!'. *Education, Citizenship and Social Justice*, *9*(1), 19–33. doi:10.1177/1746197913475768

Castleberry, A., & Nolen, A. (2018). Thematic analysis of qualitative research data: Is it as easy as it sounds? *Currents in Pharmacy Teaching & Learning*, *10*(6), 807–815. doi:10.1016/j.cptl.2018.03.019 PMID:30025784

Castoriadis, C. (1987). *The Imaginary Institution of Society*. The MIT Press.

Chanturia, G. (2000). *World Geography*. Editing House Meridiani.

Charles Louis de Montesquieu. (1748). *On the Spirit of Laws*. Retrieved from: https://www.goodreads.com/book/show/141958.The_Spirit_of_the_Laws

Cheng, E. W., Chung, H. F., & Cheng, A. (2021). Life satisfaction and the conventionality of political participation: The moderation effect of post-materialist value orientation. *International Political Science Review*, 01925121211006567. doi:10.1177/01925121211006567

Chitadze. (2011). *Geopolitics*. Universali.

Chitadze. (2016). *Political Sciences*. International Black Sea University.

Chitadze. (2017). *World Geography. Political, Economic and Demographic Dimensions*. Scholars Press.

Chitadze. (2021). *European values*. https://eu-gs.ge/wp-content/uploads/2021/12/EU-GS-%E1%83%9E%E1%83%9D%E1%83%9A%E1%83%98%E1%83%A2%E1%83%98%E1%83%99%E1%83%98%E1%83%A1-%E1%83%93%E1%83%9D%E1%83%99%E1%83%A3%E1%83%9B%E1%83%94%E1%83%9C%E1%83%A2%E1%83%98.pdf?fbclid=IwAR0vJVJFskKyWq98LN6JHHDv8OU0L4NZAyEl4qD5FJK6UH-kxkFvymgsfSQ

Chitadze, N. (2016). *Political Science*. International Black Sea University.

Chitadze, N. (2016). *Political Sciences*. International Black Sea University.

Chitadze, N. (2017). *World Geography. Political, Economic, and Social Dimensions*. Scholars Press.

Chochua, D. (2007). *EU Institutes*. GFSIS.

Chomsky, N. (1979). *The Political Economy of Human Rights*. Academic Press.

Chronicle, T. (2022). *President swears in anti-corruption commissioners… 200 cases for Zacc*. The Chronicle. Retrieved 13 January 2022, from https://www.chronicle.co.zw/president-swears-in-anti-corruption-commissioners-200-cases-for-zacc/

Cicero, M. T. (n.d.). *Speech in defense of Aulus Cluentius Gabit*. LIII, 146. Archived July 26, 2014 at the Wayback Machine

Cohen, A., Vigoda, E., & Samorly, A. (2001). Analysis of the mediating effect of personal-psychological variables on the relationship between socioeconomic status and political participation: A structural equations framework. *Political Psychology*, *22*(4), 727–757. doi:10.1111/0162-895X.00260

Cole, J. H., & Lawson, R. A. H. (2007). Economic Freedom in Growth Regressions: Suggestions for Clarification. *Econ Journal Watch*, *4*(1).

Conge, P. J., Barnes, S. H., Kaase, M., Nelson, J. M., Booth, J. H., Seligson, M. A., Seligson, M. A., & Booth, J. H. (1988). The Concept of Political Participation: Toward a Definition. *Comparative Politics*, *20*(2), 241–249. doi:10.2307/421669

Constitutions Rights Foundation. (2010). *Plato and Aristotle on Tyranny and the Rule of Law*. Retrieved from: https://www.crf-usa.org/bill-of-rights-in-action/bria-26-1-plato-and-aristotle-on-tyranny-and-the-rule-of-law.html

Council of Europe, Committee of Ministers. (1977). *A Declaration on territorial asylum in 1977*. Retrieved from: https://www.refworld.org/pdfid/3ae6b3611c.pdf

Council of Europe. (1950). *European Convention for the Protection of Human Rights and Fundamental Freedoms, Article 4*. Retrieved from: https://www.echr.coe.int/documents/convention_eng.pdf

Dahl, R. A. (2010). *On Democracy*. Audibooks.com

Dahl, R. (1989). *Democracy and its Critics*. Yale University Press.

Dahl, R. A. (1998). *On Democracy*. Yale University Press.

Davidson, W. B., & Cotte, P. R. (1989). Sense of community and political participation. *Journal of Community Psychology*, *17*(2), 119–125. doi:10.1002/1520-6629(198904)17:2<119::AID-JCOP2290170203>3.0.CO;2-C

Dawes, C., Cesarini, D., Fowler, J. H., Johannesson, M., Magnusson, P. K., & Oskarsson, S. (2014). The relationship between genes, psychological traits, and political participation. *American Journal of Political Science*, *58*(4), 888–903. doi:10.1111/ajps.12100

De Vos, P., Freedman, W., & Brand, D. (Eds.). (2014). *South African constitutional law in context*. Oxford University Press.

Dehaan , & Sturm, . (2007). Handling Economic Freedom in Growth Regressions: A Reply to Cole and Lawson. *Econ Journal Watch*, *4*(1).

Deibert, R. (2015). The geopolitics of cyberspace after Snowden. *Current History (New York, N.Y.)*, *114*(768), 9–15. doi:10.1525/curh.2015.114.768.9

Deibert, R. (2019). The Road to Digital Unfreedom: Three Painful Truths About Social Media. *Journal of Democracy*, *30*(1), 25–39. doi:10.1353/jod.2019.0002

Delli Carpini, M. X. (2000). Gen. com: Youth, civic engagement, and the new information environment. *Political Communication*, *17*(4), 341–349. doi:10.1080/10584600050178942

Demetrashvili, A. (2010). *Constitutional Law*. Tbilisi State University.

Democracy Barometer. (2020). *The Democracy Barometer is a new instrument to measure the quality of established democracies.* Retrieved from: https://democracybarometer.org/

Denscomben, M. (2003). *The good research guide.* Open University Press.

Diamond, L. (2000). *Developing Democracy.* JHU Press.

Diamond, L. (2020). Breaking Out of the Democratic Slump. *Journal of Democracy, 31*(1), 36–50. doi:10.1353/jod.2020.0003

Doyle, M. (1986). *Empires.* Cornell University Press.

Ekman, J., & Amnå, E. (2012). Political participation and civic engagement: Towards a new typology. *Human Affairs, 22*(3), 283–300. doi:10.247813374-012-0024-1

Essays, U. K. (2015). *Analyzing Charles Taylors Critique Of Negative Freedom Philosophy Essay.* https://www.ukessays.com/essays/philosophy/analysing-charles-taylors-critique-of-negative-freedom-philosophy-essay.php#:~:text=These%20inarticulate%20ideas%20have%20their,resources%2C%20regardless%20of%20the%20time

Etling, B., Robert, F., & John, P. (2010). Political Change in the Digital Age: The Fragility and Promise of Online Organizing. *SAIS Review (Paul H. Nitze School of Advanced International Studies), 30*(2), 37–49. doi:10.1353ais.2010.0016

Etzioni. (2015). *Political Unification Revisited: On Building Supranational Communities.* Retrieved from: https://rowman.com/ISBN/9780739102732/Political-Unification-Revisited-On-Building-Supranational-Communities

EU Publications. (2022). *Maps.* Retrieved from: https://op.europa.eu/en/web/general-publications/maps

Euronews. (2009). *Obama touts Economic Progress.* Retrieved from: https://ru.euronews.com/2009/04/14/obama-touts-economic-progress

European Commission. (2022). *Slavery Convention.* Retrieved from: https://ec.europa.eu/anti-trafficking/1926-slavery-convention_en

European Court of Human Rights. (2022). *General Presentation.* Retrieved from: https://www.echr.coe.int/Pages/home.aspx?p=home

Fejerskov, A. M. (2017). The new technopolitics of development and the global south as a laboratory of technological experimentation. *Science, Technology & Human Values, 42*(5), 947–968. doi:10.1177/0162243917709934

Fisher, J. (2014). When it pays to be a 'fragile state': Uganda's use and abuse of a dubious concept. *Third World Quarterly, 35*(2), 316–332. doi:10.1080/01436597.2014.878493

Flavin, P., & Keane, M. J. (2012). Life satisfaction and political participation: Evidence from the United States. *Journal of Happiness Studies, 13*(1), 63–78. doi:10.100710902-011-9250-1

Flores, B. B., & Smith, H. L. (2009). Teachers' characteristics and attitudinal beliefs about linguistic and cultural diversity. *Bilingual Research Journal, 31*(1), 323–358. doi:10.1080/15235880802640789

Francis, F. (1992). *The End of History and the Last Man.* Retrieved from: https://www.scribd.com/doc/52275991/Book-Summary-Fukuyama-The-End-of-History-or-the-Last-Man?

Frantz, E., Kendall, T. A., Carisa, N., & Joseph, W. (2021). How Personalist Politics Is Changing Democracies. *Journal of Democracy, 32*(3), 94–108. doi:10.1353/jod.2021.0036

Freedom House. (1984). *Freedom in the World. 1983-1984.* Retrieved from: https://freedomhouse.org/sites/default/files/2020-02/Freedom_in_the_World_1983-1984_complete_book.pdf

Freedom House. (2019). *Global Freedom Status*. Retrieved from: https://freedomhouse.org/explore-the-map?type=fiw&year=2020&status[free]=free

Fromm, E. (1994). *Escape from Freedom*. Retrieved from: https://www.amazon.com/Escape-Freedom-Erich-Fromm/dp/0805031499

Fund For Peace. (2019). *Fragile States Index Annual Report*. Author.

Gans, H. (1999). *Popular Culture & High Culture*. Basic Books.

Gao, X., & Jie, T. (2020). From Web to Weber: Understanding the Case of "One-Go at Most" as ICT-Driven Government Reform in Contemporary China. *China Review*, *20*(3), 71–97. https://muse.jhu.edu/article/764071

Gasser, H.-P. (1993). *International Humanitarian Law: an Introduction*. Paul Haupt Publishers.

Geddes, B., Wright, J., & Frantz, E. (2014). Autocratic Breakdown and Regime Transitions: A New Data Set. *Perspectives on Politics*, *12*(2), 313–331. doi:10.1017/S1537592714000851

Geertz, C. (1977). *The Interpretation of Culture*. Basic Books.

Gibson, R., & Cantijoch, M. (2013). Conceptualizing and measuring participation in the age of the internet: Is online political engagement really different to offline? *The Journal of Politics*, *75*(3), 701–716. doi:10.1017/S0022381613000431

Gil de Zúñiga, H., Jung, N., & Valenzuela, S. (2012). Social media use for news and individuals' social capital, civic engagement and political participation. *Journal of Computer-Mediated Communication*, *17*(3), 319–336. doi:10.1111/j.1083-6101.2012.01574.x

Gil de Zúñiga, H., Molyneux, L., & Zheng, P. (2014). Social media, political expression, and political participation: Panel analysis of lagged and concurrent relationships. *Journal of Communication*, *64*(4), 612–634. doi:10.1111/jcom.12103

Goddard, C., & Evans, D. (2018). Primary pre-service teachers' attitudes towards inclusion across the training years. *The Australian Journal of Teacher Education*, *43*(6), 122–142. Advance online publication. doi:10.14221/ajte.2018v43n6.8

Gorbhacev, M. (2007). *Memoirs*. Transworld Publishers Limited.

Gottdiener, M. (1995). *Postmodern Semiotics: Material Culture and the Forms of Postmodern Life*. Blackwell.

Grasso, M. T. (2014). Age, period and cohort analysis in a comparative context: Political generations and political participation repertoires in Western Europe. *Electoral Studies*, *33*, 63–76. doi:10.1016/j.electstud.2013.06.003

Grasso, M. T., Farrall, S., Gray, E., Hay, C., & Jennings, W. (2019). Socialization and generational political trajectories: An age, period and cohort analysis of political participation in Britain. *Journal of Elections, Public Opinion, and Parties*, *29*(2), 199–221. doi:10.1080/17457289.2018.1476359

Grävingholt, J., Ziaja, S., & Kreibaum, M. (2012). State Fragility: Towards a Multi- Dimensional Empirical Typology. SSRN *Electronic Journal*. doi:10.2139/ssrn.2279407

Greer, S. L., Wismar, M., Figueras, J., & European Observatory on Health Systems and Policies. (Eds.). (2016). *Strengthening health system governance: Better policies, stronger performance*. Open University Press.

Grimm, S., Lemay-Hébert, N., & Nay, O. (2014). 'Fragile States': Introducing a political concept. *Third World Quarterly*, *35*(2), 197–209. doi:10.1080/01436597.2013.878127

Grote, R. (1999). Rule of Law, Rechtsstaat and "Etat de droit". In Constitutionalism, Universalism and Democracy: A Comparative Analysis. Nomos Publishers.

GSDRC Applied Knowledge Services. (2011). *The role of communication in governance and development.* GSDRC Applied Knowledge Services. Accessed December 2, 2021. https://gsdrc.org/topic-guides/communication-and-governance/the-role-of-communication/

Guiraud, P. (1975). *Semiology*. Routledge.

Guo, X. (2014). *The Ideal Chinese Political Leader: A Historical and Cultural Perspective*. Wayback Machine.

Gutierrez, M., & Stefania, M. (2017). Technopolitics in the Age of Big Data. In Networks, Movements & Technopolitics in Latin America: Critical Analysis and Current Challenges. Oxford University Press.

Halpern, D., Valenzuela, S., & Katz, J. E. (2017). We face, I tweet: How different social media influence political participation through collective and internal efficacy. *Journal of Computer-Mediated Communication*, *22*(6), 320–336. doi:10.1111/jcc4.12198

Hamilton, A., Madison, J., & Jay, J. (1982). *The Federalist* (J. E. Cooke, Ed.). Wesleyan University Press.

Hamilton, R. E. (2008). *August 2008 and Everything After A Ten-Year Retrospective on the Russia-Georgia War*. Foreign Policy Research Institute.

Harari, Y. N. (2018). Why Technology Favors Tyranny. *The Atlantic.* Accessed November 22, 2021. https://www.theatlantic.com/magazine/archive/2018/10/yuval-noah-harari-technology-tyranny/568330/

Harinen, P., & Halme, J. (2012). *Hyvä, paha koulu. Kouluhyvinvointia hakemassa* [Good, bad school. Seeking school well-being]. Verkkojulkaisuja 56. Helsinki: Suomen UNICEF Nuorisotutkimusverkosto/Nuorisotutkimusseura. Retrieved from https://unicef.studio.crasman.fi/pub/public/pdf/hyva_paha_koulu-1.pdf

Hauer, N. (2021, April 22). *Azerbaijan's 'Ethnic Hatred' Theme Park Draws Ire, Imperils Reconciliation.* Retrieved from RadioFreeEurope | RadioLiberty: https://www.rferl.org/a/azerbaijan-karabakh-theme-park-armenia-ethnic-hatred-aliyev/31217971.html

Hegel, G. (1798). *Social and Political Thought.* Retrieved from: https://iep.utm.edu/hegelsoc/

Heinsch, R. (2015). Conflict Classification in Ukraine: The Return of the "Proxy War"? *International Law Studies*, 324-360.

Held, D. (2000). *Models of Democracy*. Biddles.

Hennink, M. (2014). *Focus group discussions. Understanding qualitative research.* Oxford University Press. doi:10.1093/acprof:osobl/9780199856169.001.0001

Henn, M., & Foard, N. (2014). Social differentiation in young people's political participation: The impact of social and educational factors on youth political engagement in Britain. *Journal of Youth Studies*, *17*(3), 360–380. doi:10.1080/13676261.2013.830704

Herald, T. (2022). *Just In: VP Chiwenga New Minister of Health.* The Herald. Retrieved 13 January 2022, from https://www.herald.co.zw/just-in-vp-chiwenga-new-minister-of-health/

Heritage. (2022). *Origins of Parliament.* Retrieved from: heritage/evolutionofparliament/originsofparliament/birthofparliament/overview/magnacarta/#:~:text=Magna%20Carta%20was%20issued%20in,as%20a%20power%20in%20itself

Hetherington, P., & Noble, B. (2018, March 23). *Russia doesn't just violate international law – it follows and shapes it too.* Retrieved from the conversation: https://theconversation.com/russia-doesnt-just-violate-international-law-it-follows-and-shapes-it-too-92700

Heuschling, L. (2002). *État de droit, Rechtsstaat. Rule of Law*. Dalloz.

Heywood. (2013). *Politics*. Palgrave Foundations.

Heywood. (2021). *Political ideologies. An introduction*. Bloomsbury.

Heywood, A. (2013). *Politics* (4th Revised edition). Red Globe Press. doi:10.1007/978-1-137-27244-7

Heywood, A. (2021). *Political Ideologies* (5th ed.). Retrieved from https://www.pdfdrive.com/andrew-heywood-political-ideologies-5th-edition-pdf-e18896250.html

Heywood, A. (2021). *Political ideologies* (7th ed.). Bloomsbury Publishing.

History. (2009). *Code of Hammurabi*. Retrieved from: https://www.history.com/topics/ancient-history/hammurabi#:~:text=The%20Hammurabi%20code%20of%20laws,and%20finally%20rediscovered%20in%201901

History. (2022). *Pericles*. Retrieved from: https://www.history.com/topics/ancient-history/pericles

History. (2022). *The British Bill of Rights of 1689*. Retrieved from: https://www.history.com/topics/british-history/english-bill-of-rights#:~:text=The%20English%20Bill%20of%20Rights%20was%20an%20act%20signed%20into,Parliament%20power%20over%20the%20monarchy

Hlatywayo, G. K., & Mangongera, C. (2020). *The Challenges for Social Movements in Post-Mugabe Zimbabwe*. https://www.usip.org/publications/2020/01/challenges-social-movements-post-mugabe-zimbabwe

HobbesT. (2002). *Moral and Political Philosophy*. Retrieved: https://plato.stanford.edu/entries/hobbes-moral/

Hoffmann, N., & Hendricks, F. (2018). African perspectives on corruption. *Journal of Contemporary African Studies, 36*(4), 425–432. doi:10.1080/02589001.2018.1584718

Holt, K., Shehata, A., Strömbäck, J., & Ljungberg, E. (2013). Age and the effects of news media attention and social media use on political interest and participation: Do social media function as leveller? *European Journal of Communication, 28*(1), 19–34. doi:10.1177/0267323112465369

Houngnikpo, M. C. (2016). *Guarding the Guardians: Civil-Military Relations and Democratic Governance in Africa*. Routledge. doi:10.4324/9781315586014

Howe, R. B., & Covell, K. (2011). Countering disadvantage, promoting health: The value of children's human rights education. *The Journal of Educational Thought, 45*(1), 59–85.

Hume, D. (2022). *Essays, Moral and Political*. Retrieved from: https://books.google.ge/books?id=IHQPAAAAQAAJ&pg=PR1&redir_esc=y#v=onepage&q&f=false

Hume, D. 1739–1740. A Treatise of Human Nature: Being an Attempt to introduce the experimental Method of Reasoning into Moral Subjects. Floating Press International Churchill Society. (2022). *The worst form of government*. https://winstonchurchill.org/resources/quotes/the-worst-form-of-government/

Huntington. (1991). Democracy`s Third Wave. *Journal of Democracy*.

Huntington. (1993). *The Clash of Civilizations*. Retrieved from: https://www.jstor.org/stable/20045621

Huntington, S. (1993). *The Third Wave: Democratization in the Late Twentieth Century*. Oklohama University Press.

ICRC. (2007). *International humanitarian law and the challenges of contemporary armed conflicts*. ICRC.

ICRC. (2008, August 20). *Georgia/Russian Federation: ICRC arrives in South Ossetia as the humanitarian operation expands*. Retrieved from International Committee of the Red Cross: https://www.icrc.org/en/doc/resources/documents/press-briefing/georgia-briefing-200808.htm

ICRC. (2019). *Implementing International Humanitarian Law: From Law to Action.* International Committee of the Red Cross.

Idzerda, S. (1959). *The Background of the French Revolution.* American Historical Association.

ILO. (2022). *Member States.* Retrieved from: https://www.ilo.org/global/about-the-ilo/how-the-ilo-works/member-states/lang--en/index.htm

Information Commissioners Office. (n.d.). *What is Valid Consent?* Accessed December 7, 2021. https://ico.org.uk/for-organisations/guide-to-data-protection/guide-to-the-general-data-protection-regulation-gdpr/consent/what-is-valid-consent/

Institute of History and International Relations. (2013). *Arab Spring.* Retrieved from: http://history.kemsu.ru/oldversion/ISV/Vasutin/POZD/source/361.htm

Inter-American Commission on Human Rights. (1948). *American Declaration of the Rights and Duties of Man.* Retrieved from: https://www.cidh.oas.org/basicos/english/basic2.american%20declaration.htm

International Labor Organization. (2022). *International Labor Organization Convention No. 29 concerning Forced and Compulsory Labor.* Retrieved from: https://www.ilo.org/dyn/normlex/en/f?p=NORMLEXPUB:12100:0:NO:P12100_ILO_CODE:C029

IPHR. (2021). *When Embers Burst Into Flames: International Humanitarian Law and Human Rights Law Violations During the 2020 Nagorno-Karabakh War.* Global Diligence.

Jalonen, R. (2011). *Lapsen oikeuksien sopimuksen ja sen näkökulmien sisältyminen korkeakouluopintoihin Suomessa.* Sarja B. Projektiraportit ja selvitykset 21, 2011. Humanistinen ammattikorkeakoulu. Retrieved from https://www.theseus.fi/bitstream/handle/10024/34714/978-952-456-113-6.pdf?sequence=1

Jameson, F. (1992). *Postmodernism, or, The Cultural Logic of Late Capitalism.* Duke University Press. doi:10.1215/9780822378419

Jean-Jacques, R. (1762). *Social Contract.* Retrieved from: https://www.britannica.com/topic/The-Social-Contract

Jeffres, W. L. (2011). Media Technology and Civic Life. In Communication Technology and Social Change: Theory and Implications. Routledge.

Jewish Encyclopedia. (n.d.). *Moses.* Retrieved from: https://www.jewishencyclopedia.com/articles/11049-moses

Johnson, G. D., & Wayland, K. (2010). Surveillance and Transparency as Sociotechnical Systems of Accountability. In Surveillance and Democracy. Routledge Cavendish.

Jolia, G. (2015). International Economic Relations. European University. *Journal of Law and Economics.* Retrieved from: https://www.jstor.org/stable/724810

Jones, T. (2019). A global human rights approach to pre-service teacher education on LGBTIs. *Asia-Pacific Journal of Teacher Education, 47*(3), 286–308. doi:10.1080/1359866X.2018.1555793

Joslyn, J. (2019). Bribery in Sub-Saharan Africa: The Mediating Effects of Institutional Development and Trust. *Socius: Sociological Research for a Dynamic World, 5.* doi:10.1177/2378023118824804

Jugert, P., Eckstein, K., Noack, P., Kuhn, A., & Benbow, A. (2013). Offline and online civic engagement among adolescents and young adults from three ethnic groups. *Journal of Youth and Adolescence, 42*(1), 123–135. doi:10.100710964-012-9805-4 PMID:22903193

Jurgens, E. (2013). *The principle of the Rule of Law.* Wayback Machine / Council of Europe Parliamentary Assembly.

Kaasila, R., & Lauriala, A. (2010). Towards a collaborative, interactionist model of teacher change. *Teaching and Teacher Education, 26*(4), 854–862. doi:10.1016/j.tate.2009.10.023

Kahne, J., & Bowyer, B. (2018). The political significance of social media activity and social networks. *Political Communication, 35*(3), 470–493. doi:10.1080/10584609.2018.1426662

Kam, C. D., & Palmer, C. L. (2008). Reconsidering the effects of education on political participation. *The Journal of Politics*, *70*(3), 612–631. doi:10.1017/S0022381608080651

Kamenskaya. (2005). *Politology*. Aspect Press.

Kant, I. (1795). *Perpetual Peace: A Philosophic Essay* (W. Hastie, Trans.). Retrieved from: https://librivox.org/perpetual-peace-by-immanuel-kant/

Kant, I. (1795). *Perpetual Peace: A Philosophical Sketch*. Retrieved from: https://www.mtholyoke.edu/acad/intrel/kant/kant1.htm

Kapanadze, G. (2006). *Policy of the European Union*. GFSIS.

Kaplan, S. (2014). Identifying Truly Fragile States. *The Washington Quarterly*, *37*(1), 49–63. doi:10.1080/0163660X.2014.893173

Karpat, K. (2001). The Rise of Modern Turkey. *The Journal of Military History, 65*(3).

Karumidze. (2004). *International Organization*. Tbilisi State University.

Karumidze, V. (2003). *International Organizations*. Tbilisi State University.

Kassa, S. (2015). Challenges and opportunities of women political participation in Ethiopia. *Journal of Global Economics*, *3*(4), 1–7. doi:10.4172/2375-4389.1000162

Katharine, D., & Verovšek, P. (2021). Promoting Democracy in the Digital Public Sphere: Applying Theoretical Ideals to Online Political Communication. *Javnost - The Public, 28*(4), 358-374. . doi:10.1080/13183222.2021.1955206

Kazakov, M. (2016). *The Christian Church and the Roman Empire in the 4th century*. Wayback Machine.

Keating, A., & Melis, G. (2017). Social media and youth political engagement: Preaching to the converted or providing a new voice for youth? *British Journal of Politics and International Relations*, *19*(4), 877–894. doi:10.1177/1369148117718461

Kertzer, D. (1988). *Ritual Politics and Power*. Yale University Press.

Kessler, C. S. (1978). *Islam and Politics in Malay State*. Cornel University Press.

Khan, M. H. (2006). Determinants of Corruption in Developing Countries: The Limits of Conventional Economic Analysis. In *Chapters*. Edward Elgar Publishing. https://ideas.repec.org/h/elg/eechap/3740_8.html doi:10.4337/9781847203106.00015

Kim, Y., & Chen, H. T. (2016). Social media and online political participation: The mediating role of exposure to cross-cutting and like-minded perspectives. *Telematics and Informatics*, *33*(2), 320–330. doi:10.1016/j.tele.2015.08.008

Kingston, L. N. (2018). *Human rights in higher education: Institutional, classroom, and community approaches to teaching social justice*. Palgrave McMillan. doi:10.1007/978-3-319-91421-3

Kirby, P. (2022, February 3). *Is Russia preparing to invade Ukraine and what does Putin want?* Retrieved from BBC News: https://www.bbc.com/news/world-europe-56720589

Klenner, D. (1999, August 1). *Does international humanitarian law still stand a chance?* Retrieved from International Committee of the Red Cross: https://www.icrc.org/en/doc/resources/documents/misc/57jq6v.htm?fbclid=IwAR0fmqWubtzMBeupK68QVSxO6Rc0ueK7QW8fPifVJblkfOk_IK-Tkx2dels

Körner, K. (2019). *Digital politics AI, big data and the future of democracy.* Deutsche Bank. https://www.dbresearch.com/PROD/RPS_EN-PROD/PROD0000000000497768/Digital_politics%3A_AI%2C_big_data_and_the_future_of_d.pdf?undefined&realload=w0PW0FfqzELp4Jz0nI9xGDZpOR5hNc22qYDSsr/0tY40ogr0mdY9qlOqtoLr2WXo

Krasheninnikova, N.A. (2002). *Magna Carta of 1215 (modern interpretation).* Moscow University.

Krueger, B. S. (2002). Assessing the potential of Internet political participation in the United States: A resource approach. *American Politics Research, 30*(5), 476–498. doi:10.1177/1532673X02030005002

Krueger, R. A. (1988). *Focus groups: A practical guide for applied research.* Sage.

Kruikemeier, S., Van Noort, G., Vliegenthart, R., & de Vreese, C. H. (2014). Unraveling the effects of active and passive forms of political Internet use: Does it affect citizens' political involvement? *New Media & Society, 16*(6), 903–920. doi:10.1177/1461444813495163

Kruk-Larosz. (2007). *La Constitition europeenne et le constitutionnalisme contemporain.* VII-e Congres international de droit constitutionnel.

Kuenzi, M. T. (2006). Nonformal education, political participation, and democracy: Findings from Senegal. *Political Behavior, 28*(1), 1–31. doi:10.100711109-005-9000-3

Kurtzer, J., Lohsen, A., Nzuki, C., & Yayboke, E. (2022). *The Civilian Impacts of a Possible Russian Invasion of Ukraine.* Retrieved from The Center for Strategic and International Studies: https://www.csis.org/analysis/civilian-impacts-possible-russian-invasion-ukraine

Kuusisto, A., & Gearon, L. (2019). Why teach about religions? Perspectives from Finnish professionals. *Religions, 10*(6), 347. doi:10.3390/rel10060347

Kwon, S. (2021). Do Populist Parties Increase Civic Political Participation? Empirical analysis of 30 countries in Europe. *Journal of International and Area Studies, 28*(1), 73–98.

Lacan, J. (2001). *Ecrits: A Selection.* Routledge. doi:10.4324/9780203995839

Lastensuojelun keskusliitto. (2020). *Children's rights.* Helsinki. Retrieved from https://www.lskl.fi/english/childrens-rights/

Lebedeva, M. (2007). *World Politics.* Aspect Press.

Leblebici, H., & Çeliköz, N. (2017). Öğretmen adaylarının çocuk haklarına yönelik tutumları [Prospective teachers' attitudes towards children rights]. *International Journal of Social Sciences and Education Research, 3*(1), 307–318. doi:10.24289/ijsser.270584

Lee, F. L. F., Yuen, S., Tang, G., & Cheng, E. W. (2019). Hong Kong's Summer of Uprising: From Anti-Extradition to Anti-Authoritarian Protests. *China Review, 19*(4), 1–32. https://muse.jhu.edu/article/743118

Levi, M. (1981). The Predatory Theory of Rule. *Politics & Society, 10*(4), 431–465. doi:10.1177/003232928101000403

Levy, B. L., & Akiva, T. (2019). Motivating political participation among youth: An analysis of factors related to adolescents' political engagement. *Political Psychology, 40*(5), 1039–1055. doi:10.1111/pops.12578

Lewin, I. (1985). *The Jewish community in Poland.* Philosophical Library, the University of Michigan.

Lippmann, W. (1998). *Public Opinion: With a New Introduction by Micheal Curtis*. Transaction Publishers. (Orginal work published 1922)

Lipset, M. (1960). *Political Man: The Social Bases of Politics*. The Johns Hopkins University Press.

Loader, B. D., Vromen, A., & Xenos, M. A. (2014). The networked young citizen: Social media, political participation and civic engagement. *Information Communication and Society*, *17*(2), 143–150. doi:10.1080/1369118X.2013.871571

Locke, J. (1690). *Two Treatises on Government*. Retrieved from: https://www.yorku.ca/comninel/courses/3025pdf/Locke.pdf

Locke, J. (2020). *Social Contract*. Retrieved from: https://www.britannica.com/biography/John-Locke

Lowndes, V. (2004). Getting on or getting by? Women, social capital and political participation. *British Journal of Politics and International Relations*, *6*(1), 45–64. doi:10.1111/j.1467-856X.2004.00126.x

Lubell, N. (2016). Limits of the geographical scope of application of IHL in combating terrorism. In Terrorism, Counter-Terrorism and International Humanitarian Law (pp. 67-72). CICR: College of Europe.

Lundy, L., Kilkelly, U., Byrne, B., & Kang, J. (2012). *The UN Convention on the Rights of the Child: A study of legal implementation in 12 countries*. Centre for Children's Rights, Queens University.

Lustig, J. (1982). *Corporate Liberalism: The Origins of Modern American Political Theory, 1890-1920*. University of California Press.

Lyotard, J-F. (1997). *The Postmodern Condition: a Report on Knowledge*. University Press.

Magaisa, A. (2020). *Understanding Judiciary Capture in Zimbabwe*. Big Saturday Read.

Maguchu, P. S., & Maja, I. (2019). The New Zimbabwean Government's War on Corruption: A Lesson for Anti-Corruption and Transitional Justice Scholars and Practitioners? *Journal of Anti-Corruption Law*, *3*, 76.

Mann, C. B., Arceneaux, K., & Nickerson, D. W. (2020). Do negatively framed messages motivate political participation? Evidence from four field experiments. *American Politics Research*, *48*(1), 3–21. doi:10.1177/1532673X19840732

Marx, K. (1992). *Capital Vol. 1: Volume 1: a Critique of Political Economy by Karl Marx*. Retrieved from: https://www.ebay.com/p/38925?mkevt=1&siteid=1&mkcid=2&mkrid=711-153320-877673

Masunungure, E. V. (2011). *Zimbabwe's Militarized, Electoral Authoritarianism*. Columbia University.

Mayring, P. (2014). *Qualitative content analysis: Theoretical foundation, basic procedures and software solution*. GESIS Leibniz Institute for the Social Sciences. Retrieved from http://nbn-resolving.de/urn:nbn:de:0168-ssoar-395173

Mazarr, M. J. (2014, January 15). *The Rise and Fall of the Failed-State Paradigm*. https://www.foreignaffairs.com/articles/2013-12-06/rise-and-fall-failed-state-paradigm

McCray, E. D., & McHatton, P. A. (2011). "Less afraid to have them in my classroom": Understanding pre-service general educators' perceptions about inclusion. *Teacher Education Quarterly*, *38*(4), 135–155.

McKean, E. (2005). *The New Oxford American Dictionary* (2nd ed.). Oxford University Press.

Melo, D. F., & Stockemer, D. (2014). Age and political participation in Germany, France and the UK: A comparative analysis. *Comparative European Politics*, *12*(1), 33–53. doi:10.1057/cep.2012.31

Melzer, N. (2016). *International Humanitarian Law: A Comprehensive Introduction*. ICRC.

Middlekauff, R. (2005). *The Glorious Cause: The American Revolution, 1763—1789, Revised and Expanded Edition*. Oxford University Press.

Milanovic, M. (2007). Lessons for human rights and humanitarian law in the war on terror: Comparing Hamdan and the Israeli Targeted Killings case. *International Review of the Red Cross*, *89*(866), 373–393. doi:10.1017/S181638310700104X

Mill, J. S. (1863). *Utilitarianism*. Retrieved from: https://books.google.ge/books?id=ujgIAAAAQAAJ&dq=editions:OCLC38110333&lr=&source=gbs_summary_s&redir_esc=y

Ministry for Foreign Affairs in Finland. (2011*). Lasten oikeudet paremmin esiin Euroopan unionissa* [Children's rights better highlighted in the European Union]. Eurooppatiedotus. Valtioneuvosto. https://eurooppatiedotus.fi/2011/08/26/lasten-oikeudet-paremmin-esiin-euroopan-unionissa/

Mishra, V., & Arun, T. P. (2021). Understanding Chinese media censorship: From Ming to Jinping. *ORF*. https://www.orfonline.org/expert-speak/understanding-chinese-media-censorship-from-ming-to-jinping/

Mitchell, W. J. (1986). *Iconology: Image, Text, Ideology*. The University of Chicago Press.

Mitrany, D. (1996). A working peace system. Chicago: Quadrangle Books.

Mlambo, C., & Kapingura, F. (2019). Factors influencing women political participation: The case of the SADC region. *Cogent Social Sciences*, *5*(1), 1681048. doi:10.1080/23311886.2019.1681048

Montesquieu, C. (1732). *Spirit of the Laws*. Retrieved from: https://plato.stanford.edu/entries/montesquieu/

Morgan, D. L. (1988). *Focus group as qualitative research*. Sage.

Mubangizi, J. C., & Sewpersadh, P. (2017). A Human Rights-based Approach to Combating Public Procurement Corruption in Africa. *African Journal of Legal Studies*, *10*(1), 66–90. doi:10.1163/17087384-12340015

Müller-Schwefe, M. J. (1961). In Die Religion in Geschichte und Gegenwart, 3. Auflage, Band IV.

Munro, D. (2014). *The Concept of Man in Early China*. Wayback Machine.

Muronzi, C. (2020). *3 years after Mugabe overthrow, many Zimbabweans say life's worse*. Retrieved 13 January 2022, from https://www.aljazeera.com/news/2020/11/14/three-years-since-mugabe-overthrow-zimbabweans-say-life-is-worse

NATO. (2006). *NATO Handbook*. NATO Public Diplomacy Division.

Ndlovu-Gatsheni, S. J., & Ruhanya, P. (2020). *The History and Political Transition of Zimbabwe: From Mugabe to Mnangagwa*. Springer Nature. doi:10.1007/978-3-030-47733-2

Nichols, P. M. (2017). What is Organizational Corruption? In M. S. Aßländer & S. Hudson (Eds.), *The Handbook of Business and Corruption* (pp. 3–23). Emerald Publishing Limited. doi:10.1108/978-1-78635-445-720161001

Njini, F., & Marawanyika, G. (2020). *Zimbabwe Gold Smugglers Shipping over $1.5 billion a year*. Bloomberg.

Noland, A. (2020). Like, share, retweet: Testing competing models of the theory of planned behavior to predict slacktivism engagement. *Journal of Nonprofit & Public Sector Marketing*, *32*(3), 264–285. doi:10.1080/10495142.2019.1589626

Nozick, R. (1975). *Anarchy, State, and Utopia*. Retrieved from: https://www.nationalbook.org/books/anarchy-state-and-utopia/

Nyoni, T. (2017). *The Curse of Corruption in Zimbabwe* (*SSRN* Scholarly Paper ID 3085213). Social Science Research Network. https://papers.ssrn.com/abstract=3085213

Obscura, A. (2017). *The Little-Known Passport That Protected 450,000 Refugees*. Retrieved from: https://www.atlasobscura.com/articles/nansen-passport-refugees

Ødegård, G., & Berglund, F. (2008). Political participation in late modernity among Norwegian youth: An individual choice or a statement of social class? *Journal of Youth Studies*, *11*(6), 593–610. doi:10.1080/13676260802247573

OECD. (2018). *States of Fragility 2018*. OECD. doi:10.1787/9789264302075-

OECD. (2020). *States of Fragility 2020*. OECD. doi:10.1787/ba7c22e7-

Olmstead, C. E. (1960). *History of Religion in the United States*. Retrieved from: https://academic.oup.com/jcs/article-abstract/4/2/222/810658?redirectedFrom=fulltext

Olsson, Å. (2020). Children's rights in Swedish teacher education. *Human Rights Education Review, 3*(2), 49–67. doi:10.7577/hrer.3925

OSCE Office for Democratic Institutions and Human Rights. (2022). *Institutions and Structures*. Retrieved from: https://www.osce.org/odihr

Oser, J., Hooghe, M., & Marien, S. (2013). Is online participation distinct from offline participation? A latent class analysis of participation types and their stratification. *Political Research Quarterly*, *66*(1), 91–101. doi:10.1177/1065912912436695

Otaluka, W. O. (2017). *The cultural roots of corruption: An ethical investigation with particular reference to nepotism* [Thesis]. https://researchspace.ukzn.ac.za/handle/10413/14232

Paine, T. (1791). *The Age of Reason*. Retrieved from: https://www.biography.com/scholar/thomas-paine

Pakhuylu, S. (2013). *Social psychological variables affecting political participation of youth in Turkey* (Master's thesis). Middle East Technical University.

Pamment, J., & Sazonov, V. (2019, June 6). *Hybrid Threats: Humanitarian aid in the Russo-Georgian conflict.* Retrieved from NATO Strategic Communications Center of Excellence: https://stratcomcoe.org/publications/hybrid-threats-humanitarian-aid-in-the-russo-georgian-conflict/83

Parker, A., & Tritter, J. (2007). Focus group method and methodology: Current practice and recent debate. *International Journal of Research & Method in Education*, *29*(1), 23–37. doi:10.1080/01406720500537304

Parry, G., & Anderson, B. (1972). *Participation in politics: By Bryce Anderson and others-edited by Geraint Parry.* Manchester University Press.

Parry, G., Moyser, G., & Day, N. (1992). *Political participation and democracy in Britain.* Cambridge University Press. doi:10.1017/CBO9780511558726

Persson, M. (2015). Education and political participation. *British Journal of Political Science*, *45*(3), 689–703. doi:10.1017/S0007123413000409

Petsoulas, C. (2001). *Hayek's Liberalism and Its Origins: His Idea of Spontaneous Order and the Scottish Enlightenment*. Routledge.

Pew Research. (2012). *Survey questions: Civic engagement tracking survey 2012*. Available at: https://www.pewinternet.org/files/oldmedia/Files/Questionnaire/2012/SurveyQuestions_PoliticalEngagement.pdf

Plutarch. (n.d.). *Complete Works. — Volume 3: Essays and Miscellanies by Plutarch.* Retrieved from: https://www.gutenberg.org/ebooks/3052

Polcumpally, A. T. (2018). Egypt's Uncertain Future under Al-Sisi's Rule. In India and its Foreign Policy Challenges. Vji Publications.

Polcumpally, A. T. (2021). Artificial intelligence and global power structure: Understanding through Luhmann's systems theory. *AI & Society*. Advance online publication. doi:10.100700146-021-01219-8

Pontes, A. I., Henn, M., & Griffiths, M. D. (2019). Youth political (dis) engagement and the need for citizenship education: Encouraging young people's civic and political participation through the curriculum. *Education, Citizenship and Social Justice*, *14*(1), 3–21. doi:10.1177/1746197917734542

Popescu, O. (1997). *Studies in the History of Latin American Economic Thought*. Routledge. doi:10.4324/9780203441329

Poster, M. (1997). Cyberdemocracy: Internet and the Public Sphere. In Internet Culture. Routledge.

Pressreader. (2019). *Public libraries have an important role in sustaining democracy*. Retrieved from: https://blog.pressreader.com/public-libraries-have-an-important-role-in-sustaining-democracy

Przeworski, A. (1991). *Democracy and the Market: Political and Economic Reforms in Eastern Europe and Latin America*. Cambridge University Press. doi:10.1017/CBO9781139172493

Przeworski, A., & Fernando, L. (1997). Modernization: Theories and Facts. *World Politics*, *49*(2), 55–183. doi:10.1353/wp.1997.0004

Qiang, X. (2019). The Road to Digital Unfreedom: President Xi's Surveillance State. *Journal of Democracy*, *30*(1), 53–67. doi:10.1353/jod.2019.0004

Quaranta, M. (2018). Repertoires of political participation: Macroeconomic conditions, socioeconomic resources, and participation gaps in Europe. *International Journal of Comparative Sociology*, *59*(4), 319–342. doi:10.1177/0020715218800526

Quennerstedt, A. (2015). Mänskliga rättigheter som värdefundament, kunskapsobjekt och inflytande: En läroplansanalys [Human rights as value base, object of knowledge and influence: A curriculum analysis]. *Utbildning & Demokrati: Tidskrift för Didaktik och Utbildningspolitik*, *24*(1), 5–27. Retrieved from https://www.oru.se/globalassets/oru-sv/forskning/forskningsmiljoer/hs/humus/utbildning-och-demokrati/2015/nr-1/ann-quennerstedt---manskliga-rattigheter-som-vardefundament-kunskapsobjekt-coh-inflytande--en-laroplansanalys.pdf

Quennerstedt, A. (2010). Children, but not really humans? Critical reflections on the hampering effect of the '3 p's'. *International Journal of Children's Rights*, *18*(4), 619–635. doi:10.1163/157181810X490384

Quintelier, E. (2007). Differences in political participation between young and old people. *Contemporary Politics*, *13*(2), 165–180. doi:10.1080/13569770701562658

Reference, O. (2022). *Democracy*. Retrieved from: https://www.oxfordreference.com/view/10.1093/acref/9780195148909.001.0001/acref-9780195148909-e-241

Regional Refugee Instruments & Related. (2022). *Convention on Asylum. Havana, 1928*. Retrieved from: https://www.refworld.org/docid/3ae6b37923.html

Riddell, R. (1984). *The Economy Four Years after Independence*. doi:10.1093/oxfordjournals.afraf.a097644

Robbers, E. (2006). *Encyclopedia of World Constitutions*. Retrieved from: https://books.google.ge/books?id=M3A-xgf1yM4C&pg=PA626&redir_esc=y

Robinson, C., Phillips, L., & Quennerstedt, A. (2020). Human rights education: Developing a theoretical understanding of teachers' responsibilities. *Educational Review*, *72*(2), 220–241. doi:10.1080/00131911.2018.1495182

Rondeli, A. (2003). *International Relations*. Nekeri.

Rosenberg, A. (1965). *Democracy and Socialism*. Beacon Press.

Roskin, M. (2000). *Countries and Concepts* (7th ed.). Pearson Press.

Rotbard, M. (2010). *Power and Market*. Government and the Economy.

Roth, H. I. (2015). Det sena genombrottet för mänskliga rättighetsutbildningar [The late breakthrough for human rights education]. *Utbildning & Demokrati: Tidskrift för Didaktik och Utbildningspolitik, 24*(1), 29–49. Retrieved from https://www.oru.se/globalassets/orusv/forskning/forskningsmiljoer/hs/humus/utbildning-ochdemokrati/2015/nr-1/hans-ingvar-roth---det-sena-genombrottet-formanskliga-rattighetsutbildningar.pdf

Rothstein, B., & Varraich, A. (2017). *Making Sense of Corruption*. Cambridge University Press. doi:10.1017/9781316681596

Rousseau. (1762). *The Social Contract. Or Principles of Political Right*. Retrieved from: https://www.marxists.org/reference/subject/economics/rousseau/social-contract/

Russet. (1998). *The Third Leg of the Kantian Tripod for Peace: International Organizations and Militarized Disputes, 1950–85*. Cambridge University Press.

Sachariew, K. (1989). States' entitlement to take action to enforce international humanitarian law. *International Review of the Red Cross, N270*(270), 177–195. doi:10.1017/S0020860400073058

Sartori, G. (1987). *Democratic Theory*. Greenwood Press.

Sassen, S. (1996). *Losing control?: sovereignty in the age of globalization*. Columbia University Press.

Schihalejev, O., Kuusisto, A., Vikdahl, L., & Kallioniemi, A. (2019). Religion and children's perceptions of bullying in multicultural schools in Estonia, Finland and Sweden. *Journal of Beliefs & Values*. Advance online publication. doi:10.1080/13617672.2019.1686732

Schmidt, M., & Ritter, G. A. (1990). *The Rise and Fall of a Socialist Welfare State*. Springer.

Schmitter, P., & Karl, T. (1991). *What Democracy Is…and Is Not*. Retrieved from: https://www.journalofdemocracy.org/articles/what-democracy-is-and-is-not/

Schmitter. (2017). *Democratization in the Middle East and North Africa: A More Ambidextrous Process?* Retrieved from: https://www.tandfonline.com/doi/abs/10.1080/13629395.2016.1220109

Schumpeter, J. A. (1908). *Methodological Individualism*. Germany. OCLC 5455469.

Şener, G., Emre, P. Ö., & Akyıldız, F. (2015). Türkiye'de sosyal medyanın siyasi katılıma etkileri. *folklor/edebiyat, 21*(83), 75-98.

Services, O. E. R. (2020). *History of Western civilization*. Retrieved from: https://courses.lumenlearning.com/suny-hccc-worldhistory2/chapter/establishment-of-the-national-assembly/

Shah, A., & Schacter, M. (2004). Combating Corruption: Look Before You Leap: A lack of progress in eradicating corruption could be due to misguided strategies. *Finance & Development, 41*(4). Advance online publication. doi:10.5089/9781451922578.022.A012

Shahbaz, A., & Allie, F. (2021). *The Global Drive to Control Big Tech*. Freedom House. https://freedomhouse.org/sites/default/files/2021-09/FOTN_2021_Complete_Booklet_09162021_FINAL_UPDATED.pdf

Sharma, U., Forlin, C., & Loreman, T. (2008). Impact of training on pre-service teachers' attitudes and concerns about inclusive education and sentiments about persons with disabilities. *Disability & Society*, *23*(7), 773–785. doi:10.1080/09687590802469271

Shubitidze, V. (2009). *Political science*. Georgian Technical University.

Skoric, M. M., & Zhu, Q. (2016). Social media and offline political participation: Uncovering the paths from digital to physical. *International Journal of Public Opinion Research*, *28*(3), 415–427. doi:10.1093/ijpor/edv027

Sloam, J. (2016). Diversity and voice: The political participation of young people in the European Union. *British Journal of Politics and International Relations*, *18*(3), 521–537. doi:10.1177/1369148116647176

Smith, A. (1776). *Wealth of Nations*. Retrieved from: https://books.google.ge/books?id=0lYTWaIAQDYC&pg=PR1&source=kp_read_button&hl=en&redir_esc=y#v=onepage&q&f=false

Smith, B., & Ann, B. C. (2019). *Tools and Weapons: The Promise and the Peril of the Digital Age*. Penguin Press.

Snider, E. A., & Faris, D. (2011). The Arab Spring: U.S. Democracy Promotion in Egypt. *Middle East Policy,* 49-62. https://d1wqtxts1xzle7.cloudfront.net/46753903/j.1475-4967.2011.00497.x20160624-4760-yc6wg7-with-cover-page-v2.pdf?Expires=1637610095&Signature=cmurVotOyOhf--BJVvXDxgyoysIIa5qR8HvlWjUvD7f0bSKVgcc1UuOLaWi6cI9vdsNsHN~34ztNgGYkJ~HJ9y4zQnfoJYBZYZXGNiuIr~R1kS6

Snowden, E. (2019). *The Permanent Record*. Macmillian.

SparkNotes. (2022). *Types of Regimes*. Retrieved from: https://www.sparknotes.com/us-government-and-politics/political-science/politics-and-political-science/section3/

Stahl, H. B. (1957). *Die Religion in Geschichte und Gegenwart* (Vol. I). Auflage.

Staton, H. (2010). *The Statue of Liberty*. Chelsea Clubhouse.

Stevens, H., & Haines, M. B. (2020). TraceTogether: Pandemic Response, Democracy, and Technology. *East Asian Science, Technology and Society*, *14*(3), 523–531. doi:10.1215/18752160-8698301

Stewart, D. W., & Shamdasani, P. N. (1990). *Focus groups: Theory and practices*. Sage Publications, Inc.

Study.Com. (2022). *Political Regimes: Characteristics and Examples*. Retrieved from: https://study.com/learn/lesson/regime-types-characteristics-example.html

Susskind, J. (2018). *Future Politics: Living Together in a world transformed by tech*. Oxford University Press.

Syrjämäki, M., Pihlaja, P., & Sajaniemi, N. K. (2019). Enhancing peer interaction in early childhood special education: Chains of children's initiatives, adults' responses and their consequences in play. *Early Childhood Education Journal*, *47*(5), 559–570. doi:10.100710643-019-00952-6

Tachau & Heper. (1983). The State, Politics, and the Military in Turkey. *Comparative Politics, 16*(1).

Tendi, B.-M. (2013). Ideology, Civilian Authority and the Zimbabwean Military. *Journal of Southern African Studies*, *39*(4), 829–843. doi:10.1080/03057070.2013.858543

Teorell, J. (2006). Political participation and three theories of democracy: A research inventory and agenda. *European Journal of Political Research*, *45*(5), 787–810. doi:10.1111/j.1475-6765.2006.00636.x

The Center for Internet and Society. (n.d.). *Internet Privacy in India*. Accessed December 7, 2021. https://cis-india.org/telecom/knowledge-repository-on-internet-access/internet-privacy-in-india

The Machinery of Freedom. (2022). *Guide to a Radical Capitalism*. Retrieved from: http://www.daviddfriedman.com/Libertarian/Machinery_of_Freedom/MofF_Contents.html

Tibbitts, F. (2009). *Impact assessment of Rights Education Leading to Action Programme (REAP)*. Amnesty International.

Tibbitts, F. (2017). Evolution of human rights education models. In M. Bajaj (Ed.), *Human rights education. Theory, research, praxis* (pp. 69–95). University of Pennsylvania Press. doi:10.9783/9780812293890-005

Tocqueville, A. (2006). *Democracy in America*. Harper Classics. (Orginal work published 1835)

Tola, Ö. (2007). *Türkiye'de üniversite öğrencilerinin siyasal katılım düzeylerinin incelenmesi*. Yayımlanmamış Yüksek Lisans Tezi, Ankara Üniversitesi Sosyal Bilimler Enstitüsü.

Tomsa, D. (2020). Public Opinion Polling and Post-truth Politics in Indonesia. *Contemporary Southeast Asia: A Journal of International and Strategic Affairs, 42*(1), 1-27. https://muse.jhu.edu/article/754333

Torsello, D., & Venard, B. (2016). The Anthropology of Corruption. *Journal of Management Inquiry, 25*(1), 34–54. doi:10.1177/1056492615579081

Tweet, Share, & 11:58, 01 Oct 2020. (2020, October 1). *Zimbabwe to make doctors army employees to stop wage strikes*. Zimbabwe News Now. https://www.zimlive.com/2020/10/01/zimbabwe-to-make-doctors-army-employees-to-stop-wage-strikes/

UK Government. (2022). *Bill of Rights 1688. note X1*. Retrieved from: https://www.legislation.gov.uk/aep/WillandMarSess2/1/2/data.pdf

UK Parliament. (2022). *Bill of rights 1689*. Retrieved from: https://www.parliament.uk/about/living-heritage/evolution-ofparliament/parliamentaryauthority/revolution/collections1/collections-glorious-revolution/billofrights/

UK Parliament. (2022). *English Magna Carta in 1215*. Retrieved from: https://www.parliament.uk/about/living-

UN. (1948). *Universal Declaration on Human Rights*. Retrieved from: https://www.un.org/en/about-us/universal-declaration-of-human-rights

UN. (2005). *Basic Facts about the United Nations*. United Nations Department of Public Information.

UN. (2011). *International Legal Protection of Human Rights in Armed Conflicts*. United Nations Publication.

UN. (2022). *United Nations Treaty Series Online*. Retrieved from: https://treaties.un.org/pages/AdvanceSearch.aspx?tab=UNTS&clang=_en

UN. (2022a). *On December 14, 1967, the UN General Assembly adopted as a recommendation the "Declaration on Territorial Asylum"*. Retrieved from: https://legal.un.org/avl/ha/dta/dta.html

UN. (2022b). *UN General Assembly resolution 1763 A (XVII) of November 7, 1962*. Retrieved from: https://www.refworld.org/docid/456d89064.html

UNHCR. (2022). *The 1951 Refugee Convention*. Retrieved from: https://www.unhcr.org/1951-refugee-convention.html

UNICEF. (2006). *Tutkimus asenteista. Yli puolet yläkoululaisista ei tiedä, että lapsilla on erityisoikeudet* [A study of attitudes. More than half of high school students do not know that children have special rights]. Retrieved from https://www.unicef.fi/unicef/tyomme-suomessa/tutkimukset-suomessa/tutkimus-asenteista/

United Nation Treaty Collection. (2022). *Supplementary Convention for the Abolition of Slavery, the Slave Trade and Institutions and Practices Similar to Slavery. September 7, 1956*. Retrieved from: https://treaties.un.org/pages/ViewDetailsIII.aspx?src=TREATY&mtdsg_no=XVIII-4&chapter=18&Temp=mtdsg3&clang=_en

United Nations Economic Commission for Africa (2016-2003). African Governance Report IV 2016: Measuring Corruption in Africa: The International Dimension Matters. Author.

United Nations General Assembly. (2011). United Nations Declaration on Human Rights Education and Training. GA 66/127, Art.2 paras. 1-2. Geneva: United Nations.

United Nations Human Rights Committee. (2022). *Human Rights Overview*. Retrieved from: https://www.ohchr.org/en/treaty-bodies/ccpr

United Nations Human Rights Office of the High Commissioner. (2022). *International Covenant on Civil and Political Rights*. Retrieved from: https://www.ohchr.org/en/instruments-mechanisms/instruments/international-covenant-civil-and-political-rights

United Nations Human rights Office of the Hugh Commissioner. (2022). *Human rights overview*. Retrieved from: https://www.ohchr.org/en/ohchr_homepage

United Nations. (1948). *Universal Declaration of Human Rights*. Retrieved from: https://www.un.org/en/about-us/universal-declaration-of-human-rights

United Nations. (2005). *Basic facts about the United Nations*. UN Department of Public Information.

United Nations. (2007). *Multilateral treaties deposited with the Secretary-General: Rome Statute of the International Criminal Court*. Retrieved from: https://treaties.un.org/pages/ViewDetails.aspx?src=IND&mtdsg_no=XVIII-10&chapter=18&clang=_en

United Nations. (2022). *Declaration on principles of international law friendly relations and cooperation among states following the charter of the United Nations*. Retrieved from: https://www.un.org/ruleoflaw/files/3dda1f104.pdf

United Nations. (2022). *Universal Declaration of Human Rights*. Retrieved from: https://www.un.org/en/about-us/universal-declaration-of-human-rights

Vagts, A. (1959). *A History of Militarism*. Meridian Books.

Van Deth, J. W. (2001, April). Studying political participation: Towards a theory of everything. Joint Sessions of Workshops of the European Consortium for Political Research, 6-11.

Van Deth, J. W. (2016). What is political participation? In Oxford research encyclopedia of politics. doi:10.1093/acrefore/9780190228637.013.68

Van Deth, J. W. (2014). A conceptual map of political participation. *Acta Politica*, *49*(3), 349–367. doi:10.1057/ap.2014.6

Van, D., & Teun, A. (1998). Ideology. Sage Publications.

Velasquez, A., & LaRose, R. (2015). Youth collective activism through social media: The role of collective efficacy. *New Media & Society*, *17*(6), 899–918. doi:10.1177/1461444813518391

Verba, S., & Nie, N. H. (1972). *Participation in America: Social equality and political democracy*. Academic Press.

Verba, S., Schlozman, K. L., & Brady, H. E. (1995). *Voice and equality: Civic voluntarism in American politics*. Harvard University Press. doi:10.2307/j.ctv1pnc1k7

Vincent, A. (2003). *Modern Political Ideologies*. Blackwell.

Vissers, S., & Stolle, D. (2014). The Internet and new modes of political participation: Online versus offline participation. *Information Communication and Society*, *17*(8), 937–955. doi:10.1080/1369118X.2013.867356

Volosinov, V. (1986). Marxism and the Philosophy of Language (L. Mateska & I. Tutunik, Trans.). Harvard University Press.

Waeterloos, C., Walrave, M., & Ponnet, K. (2021). Designing and validating the Social Media Political Participation Scale: An instrument to measure political participation on social media. *Technology in Society*, *64*, 101493. doi:10.1016/j.techsoc.2020.101493

Wang, S. I. (2007). Political use of the Internet, political attitudes and political participation. *Asian Journal of Communication*, *17*(4), 381–395. doi:10.1080/01292980701636993

Warren, D., & Brandeis, L. D. (1890). *The Right to Private Life*. Retrieved from: https://utrechtjournal.org/articles/10.5334/ujiel.cp/

Wellington Garikai, B., Chiminya, J., & Mudzingiri, C. (2015). *An Explanatory Analysis of the Economic and Social Impact of Corruption in Zimbabwe*. Academic Press.

Whitman, M. J. (2005). *Third Avenue Value Fund Letters to our Shareholders. Wayback Machine.*

Woodcock, S., Hemmings, B., & Kay, R. (2012). Does study of an inclusive education subject influence pre-service teachers' concerns and self-efficacy about inclusion? *The Australian Journal of Teacher Education*, *37*(6), 1–11. doi:10.14221/ajte.2012v37n6.5

Wormuth, F. (1949). *The Origins of Modern Constitutionalism*. Harper & Brothers.

Xiangming, Z. (2017). *On Two Ancient Chinese Administrative Ideas: Rule of Virtue and Rule by Law*. Wayback Machine.

Yamamoto, K. (2014, April 10). Zimbabwe: Mugabe Fighting Corruption? Forget It! *New Zimbabwe*. https://allafrica.com/stories/201404100145.html

Yamamoto, M., Kushin, M. J., & Dalisay, F. (2015). Social media and mobiles as political mobilization forces for young adults: Examining the moderating role of online political expression in political participation. *New Media & Society*, *17*(6), 880–898. doi:10.1177/1461444813518390

Yamniuk, S. (2017). The importance of including human rights education in primary and secondary schools: A focus on empathy and respect. In J. Zajda & S. Ozdowski (Eds.), Globalisation, human rights education and reforms. Globalisation, Comparative Education and Policy Research, vol. 17. Springer. doi:10.1007/978-94-024-0871-3_9

Yoo, S. W., Kim, J. W., & Gil de Zúñiga, H. (2017). Cognitive benefits for senders: Antecedents and effects of political expression on social media. *Journalism & Mass Communication Quarterly*, *94*(1), 17–37. doi:10.1177/1077699016654438

Yoshida, H. (2016). Perceived usefulness of "flipped learning" on instructional design for elementary and secondary education: With focus on pre-service teacher education. *International Journal of Information and Education Technology*, *6*(6), 430–434. doi:10.7763/IJIET.2016.V6.727

Yungweil, H., & Lee, K. S. (2016). Teaching in flipped classrooms: Exploring pre-service-teachers concerns. *Computers in Human Behavior*, *57*, 250–260. doi:10.1016/j.chb.2015.12.022

Zakaria, F. (2003). *The Future of Freedom: Illiberal Democracy at Home and Abroad*. W.W. Norton & Company.

Zambeta, E., Leontsini, M., Askouni, N., Papadakou, Y., & Psochios, N. (2016). *Addressing violence in schools through education for democratic citizenship and human rights education*. Human Rights and Democracy in Action. Pilot Projects on the Council of Europe Charter on Education for Democratic Citizenship and Human Rights Education.

Zembylas, M., Charalambous, C., & Charalambous, P. (2016). Teachers' pedagogical perspectives and teaching practices on human rights in Cyprus: An empirical exploration and implications for human rights education. *Pedagogies*, *11*(3), 197–217. doi:10.1080/1554480X.2016.1182436

Zimbabwe Democratic Institute. (2017). *Zimbabwe Transition in a muddy terrain: Political Economy Under Military Capture*. https://kubatana.net/wp-content/uploads/2017/12/Zimbabwe-Transition-in-A-Muddy-Terrain-Political-Economy-Under-Military-Capture-Terrain.pdf

Zittel, T. (2006). *Participatory democracy and political participation*. Routledge. doi:10.4324/9780203969311

About the Contributors

Nika Chitadze is a specialist in Global and Caucasus geopolitics, World Politics, Human Geography, Democracy/Human Rights, Environmental Security, Combating Terrorism, Energy Security, and strategic affairs. He is currently (from October 2017) the Director of the Center for International Studies and Professor and coordinator of the Doctoral Program at the Faculty of Social Sciences (Direction: International Relations and Politics) at the International Black Sea University (IBSU). He is also President of the George C. Marshall Alumni Union, Georgia – International and Security Research Center. Dr. Chitadze previously served as senior advisor on the National Security Council of Georgia and was Head of the Public Relations Division of the State Agency for Regulation of Oil and Gas Resources of Georgia. He has also held senior positions in the Department of Strategic and Military Policy at the Georgian Ministry of Defense and foreign policy research and analysis center of the Ministry of Foreign Affairs of Georgia. Dr. Chitadze has received his educational credentials in Georgia (Tbilisi State University and Diplomatic Academy of Georgia) as well as several international higher educational institutions, including the University of Oxford in the UK, George C. Marshall European College for Security Studies (Germany), and several other well-known European educational institutions. He is author of more than 310 researches/articles and seven books on Geopolitics, Human Geography and International Relations.

* * *

Natalia Beruashvili has more than 25 years of professional experience in international law, holds Ph.D. in Political Sciences. She also has an LLM in International Tax Law from Edinburgh University, a MA in Commercial Law from Tbilisi State University, and a BA in the English Language from Tbilisi State University. Nato is the author of various publications and articles.

Satu-Maarit Frangou is a university lecturer of media education and researcher at the University of Lapland. Her key research interests are digital pedagogy, technology-mediated creative learning and embodied cognition, neural foundations of learning and memory, life stance and ethics education, arctic and indigenous pedagogical approaches together with social learning.

Valeriya Gonitashvili studied at the Yalta Educational and Auxiliary Complex No. 1 "School-Collegium" of the Yalta City Council of the Autonomous Republic of Crimea, Ukraine. She is graduated from International Black Sea University in Tbilisi, Georgia. Later She continued her study at the University of Lodz, Poland Now she is involved at the MA Program of Eurasian and Caucasus Studies (English-language program) at the Ivane Javakhishvili Tbilisi State University She works at the Ukrainian

Youth Organization of Georgia "Svitanok" - a member of the diaspora of Ukrainians in Tbilisi, regional manager, in charge of the organization of forums Valeria is the author of several articles in the field of political sciences and international relations.

Tanja Joona (Dr.Soc.Sci.) is working as a Senior researcher at the Arctic Centre of the University of Lapland (2000 -) At the moment she is the Finnish Institutional leader of the H2020 project JustNorth (2020-2023): Toward Just, Ethical and Sustainable Arctic Economies, Environments and Societies. www.justnorth.eu Joona's main research interests focus on mainly to the Arctic region, with comparative legal and political aspects of indigenous Sámi society and especially issues dealing with traditional livelihoods, international human rights law and identity questions in the context of justice and equality. She has published numerous amount of scientific peer reviewed articles and has participated international conferences around the world. She has also several positions of trust at the University of Lapland as well as in the society.

Irakli Kervalishvili got his Bachelor's Degree in Economics and Business (Business Administration) at the Ivane Javakhishvili Tbilisi State University (Georgia). Master Degree in the field: Exact and Natural Sciences (Information Technologies) at the Ivane Javakhishvili Tbilisi State University (Georgia) and Master Degree at Computing Engineering (Applied Information Systems) at the University of West Attica (Greece) He is Ph.D. Candidate at Informatics and Control Systems (Control Systems, Automation and Test Engineering) | at the Georgian Technical University.

Pigga Keskitalo works as a Professor in Arctic perspectives at the Faculty of Education in the University of Lapland, Finland. She is a Title of Docent (Adjunct Professor) at the University of Helsinki, Finland and the network researcher at the Migration Institute, Turku, Finland. Formerly, Keskitalo worked for 20 years at the Sámi University of Applied Sciences in the field of Sami teacher education in Norway. At the moment, she is working on an Academy of Finland funded project that aims to develop Sami language distance education. In addition, she is involved in several other research and development projects. Keskitalo's research interests focus broadly on the field of Sami education and its research. For example, she has been involved in developing Indigenous research methods. Keskitalo's PhD dissertation investigated how the Sami curriculum in Norway is conducted at the Sami schools.

Merve Kır is research assistant at Department of Business Administration, Istanbul University. She completed her undergraduate education at Yıldız Technical University, Faculty of Economics and Administrative Sciences, Department of Business Administration in 2019. She is master student at Galatasaray University, Institute of Social Sciences, Department of Business.

Ziya Kıvanç Kıraç, is a lecturer in the Department of Management and Organization at Fırat University, Vocational School of Social Sciences. His PhD is in Political Science. Special areas of study are ideologies, political symbolism and semiotics.

Minna Körkkö works as a university teacher at the University of Jyväskylä, Faculty of Education and Psychology, Department of Education, Finland. Her research interests include teacher professional development, reflection, and supervision.

Süphan Nasir is Professor at Department of Business Administration, İstanbul University. She is chairman of marketing subdicipline and coordinator of business administration e-learning program. She worked as chief editor at International Journal of E-Entrepreneurship and Innovation 2010-2014, and she is also editor of Yükseköğretim Dergisi/Journal of Higher Education (Turkey) since 2010. She also undertaken important roles such as organization committee member and advisory board member of international conferences. Her articles were published in reputable academic journals and she has written chapters for well-known books. Her latest books entitled Modern Entrepreneurship and E-Business Innovations and CRM Strategies in the Digital Era were published in USA in 2013 and 2015, respectively. She has also presented her papers at major international conferences and attended some international conference as keynote speaker. CRM as well as mobile marketing, consumer behavior, innovation management and entrepreneurship are the scope of her interest area.

Merja Paksuniemi, PhD, works as a lecturer at the University of Lapland, Finland. Her research interests are Teacher Training, Culturally Responsive Teaching, Ideologies and Social Contexts of Education. She has published multiple articles and monographs of the research topics and participated in development projects.

Arun Teja Polcumpally is currently a doctoral fellow at Jindal School of International Studies. He is also a Research Associate at Center for Security Studies (CSS). He formerly was an associate at Center of Excellence, AI in Human Security. His area of research is the impact of emerging digital technologies like AI, Block Chain on the global power structure.

Onur Şahin completed his undergraduate education at Yıldız Technical University, Department of Industrial Engineering, his graduate education at Istanbul Technical University, Department of Management Engineering, and his doctoral education at Istanbul University, Faculty of Economics, Department of Business Administration, with his study on Status and Conspicuous Consumption in the marketing department. He started his business life when he was a young undergraduate student, and worked as a business development specialist, production planning officer, supply chain manager, sales planning coordinator in various institutions including Arçelik between 2002-2014 in the sectors of production, textile, trade, energy and tourism. He worked as a faculty member and vice dean at Istinye University in 2018-2019. Since 2014, he has been working as the general manager of Müskebi Turizm A.Ş., which operates in the field of tourism in Bodrum and has 5 different businesses, mainly Club Müskebi Hotel. Dr. Onur Şahin continues his academic studies in the field of strategic marketing management and marketing research together with his professional business life.

Meri Tseruashvili is graduated from International Black Sea University in 2020, and I have a Bachelor's degree in Social Sciences, majoring in International Relations. In 2019, she studied Social Sciences at Vilnius SA University, Lithuania as an Exchange Program student. Currently, she is working as an Invited Specialist at Ilia State University, Foreign Relations Office. In addition, Meri is a research fellow at George C. Marshall Alumni Union, Georgia-International and Security Research Center.

Index

F

G

H

I

K

L

M

N

O

P

R

S

T

U

V

W

www.ingramcontent.com/pod-product-compliance
Lightning Source LLC
LaVergne TN
LVHW060415300926
849162LV00006B/1431